# THE
# NONSUPERPOWERS
# AND SOUTH AFRICA

# THE
# NONSUPERPOWERS
# AND SOUTH AFRICA

## IMPLICATIONS FOR U.S. POLICY

Richard J. Payne

**INDIANA UNIVERSITY PRESS**
Bloomington & Indianapolis

E
183.8
S6
P39
1990

Portions of "Japan: Political Rhetoric and Economic Realities" were originally published in *African Affairs* 86, no. 343 (April 1987). Reprinted with permission.

Written under the auspices of the Center for International Affairs, Harvard University.

The paper used in this publication meets the minimum requirements of American National Standard for Information Sciences—Permanence of Paper for Printed Library Materials, ANSI Z39.48-1984.

∞™

Manufactured in the United States of America

**Library of Congress Cataloging-in-Publication Data**

Payne, Richard J.
    The non-super powers and South Africa : implications for U.S. policy / Richard J. Payne.
        p.    cm.
    Includes bibliographical references.
    ISBN 0-253-34294-5 (alk. paper)
    1. United States—Foreign relations—South Africa.   2. South Africa—Foreign relations—United States.   3. South Africa—Foreign relations—1978–    I. Title.
E183.8.S6P39   1990
327.73068—dc20                                                                89-46340
                                                                                    CIP

1 2 3 4 5   94 93 92 91 90

*In Memory of C. R. G. Carleton*
*and*
*For Jason*

# CONTENTS

## ✳ 9
**Conclusion:** Implications for U.S. Policy

# FOREWORD

Richard Payne's book appears at the beginning of a decade that seems likely to alter fundamentally the distribution of power in the Republic of South Africa. The decade opened dramatically enough, with the release of Nelson Mandela after a quarter-century of prison, the unbanning of the African National Congress, the Pan-African Congress, and the South African Communist Party, and the peaceful accession of South Africa's colony, Namibia, to independence. Whatever reversals, hesitations and, indeed, horrors might lie in the path of South Africa's restructuring, the political and social order based on mandatory racial injustice propped up by police violence at home and the routine projection of military force into the neighboring states at last seems doomed, without appeal, to an early death.

The new atmosphere in South Africa has arisen from the internal contradictions and economic inefficiencies of both apartheid and regional colonialism forced to crisis by the defiant courage and persistence of the black majority and the belated realism of a growing number of white leaders, State President De Klerk in the lead. These changes of 1990 did not occur in a vacuum, however. They took place against a background of fundamental change in the international order, most notably the crumbling of dictatorial rule and socialist economic structures in Eastern Europe, the Soviet Union's abandonment of "adventurist" military positions in the third world, and the rise of Japan and the European Common Market to positions of world economic leadership alongside the United States. Taken together, these changes betokened the end of the East-West conflict as the dominant dimension of international relations and thus altered the role of the superpower protagonists.

The changes in the international environment facilitated the changes in southern Africa. The agreement leading to Namibian independence had been based on diplomatic initiatives originally undertaken under United Nations auspices jointly by the United States, Britain, France, Canada, and West Germany in the 1970s. Putting the agreement into operation, however, required a new environment that permitted an extraordinary degree of cooperation between the United States and the Soviet Union and between the two superpowers and such strategically placed actors as Cuba and the African Front Line States. Had such cooperation been possible a decade earlier, Namibia's independence might not have waited so long, and the destruction and human suffering in Namibia and Angola might have been reduced commensurately.

The changes in the international arena itself had immediate impact within the politics of South Africa itself.[1] The startling rapidity with which the East European dictatorships collapsed has not been lost on South Africa's leaders. At the very least they have been reminded that time is not on the side of those who rule by coercion over a hostile majority. No longer is it possible for the government credibly to claim that South Africa's domestic disturbances result from a "total onslaught" centrally directed from Moscow. The "total strategy" response to that supposed threat provided the P. W. Botha regime with ideal justification for refusal to compromise or negotiate and for the increasing militarization of the South African official decision making. The widely perceived irrelevance of Botha's doctrine has made it easier for his successor, F. W. De Klerk, to restructure the executive and bring decisions under the control of those who have a lesser stake in violent resistance to change. At the same time, the Soviet Union has undercut support for ANC and SACP hard-liners (and for those who have used them as a bugaboo) by leading the flight from scientific socialism, by publicly speculating on the desirability of special guarantees for the white minority in a democratic South Africa, by questioning reliance on the armed struggle, and, through the Namibian settlement, by acquiescing in the dismantling of the ANC's principal guerrilla bases.

Soviet actions have demonstrated that they have neither aspirations nor economic or political interest in attempting to play a dominant role in southern Africa. Rather, the Soviet Union has sought to make it clear that it shares an interest with the Western powers in avoiding the escalation of violent conflict that could disrupt broader interests in international cooperation. That message has been heard in Pretoria. As Foreign Minister Pik Botha told a BBC interviewer in March 1989, the Soviets have a role to play as "part of the solution" in South Africa. It is highly unlikely, however, that any Soviet contribution to a solution will take a direct form or, as in Namibia, that the USSR will join with the United States in brokering a settlement. Rather, the most useful Soviet role would be to continue to stay firmly on the sidelines, thereby creating the conditions for South Africa's principal economic partners (and these include its African neighbors) to encourage fruitful negotiations among the internal parties.

The new openness in Soviet policy has confirmed that all along the stakes of the communist countries in internal South African affairs, and their level of involvement, have been decidedly minor. By contrast, the "nonsuperpowers" that are the subject of Payne's study account for the great majority of economic transactions with South Africa and of the political attention paid to that country's affairs. These middle and lesser powers, most of them closely associated with the United States, form the greatest part of South Africa's relevant external environment and contain the majority of peoples and interests that would be affected by anything that happened in South Africa. Any effective U.S. policy toward South Africa must take these interests and involvements systematically into consideration. The degree of support these varied nations give a policy initiative will greatly affect its likelihood of success.

Such considerations have not often been at the forefront of U.S. discussions of policy toward South Africa, which during the 1970s and 80s opposed "globalist" and "regionalist" perspectives.[2] Despite its name, "globalism" neglected the interests of most of the world; it subordinated policy considerations anywhere to calculations of a supposedly "global" confrontation between the superpowers. The East-West dimension of foreign policy dominated all. However more accurate a view of local realities might be included in a "regionalist" perspective, such a view implicitly assumed the primacy to both sides of America's bilateral relationship with the region in question, an assumption not exempt from its own hubristic errors.

Two eminently respectable reports on U.S. policy toward South Africa reflect how unconsciously pervasive these assumptions have been. *South Africa: Time Running Out* was the influential (and mostly admirable) analysis commissioned by the Rockefeller Foundation in 1978 and published in 1981.[3] In nine pages, this thick volume manages to deal with the South African interests and involvements of all of America's principal allies. The Communist world receives disproportionate prominence, however. East Germany gets twice the space allotted to West Germany; Cuba gets twice the space of Britain and three times that allotted to Japan—implying a wildly distorted view of these nations' relevance to anything happening or likely to happen in South Africa. The 1987 report of the Secretary of State's Advisory Committee on South Africa, by contrast, pays little attention to the concerns of any third parties. The interests and activities of Western Europe, Japan, and Israel do not receive so much as a paragraph in all its forty-nine pages.[4] It is as if U.S. policy could be conceived in a vacuum.

United States diplomacy in the 1990s faces the challenge of being truly global, that is, of understanding the worldwide ramifications of politics directed toward a particular region and of making conscious use of those connections in designing an effective policy. In this increasingly complex international environment, the new globalism means thinking constantly about coordinating policy initiatives with other nations, and this requires sensitivity to their interests and policy traditions, and to the consequences for them of America's international actions, wherever they might occur. This does not mean that the United States will not have interests different in substance or in intensity from those of its allies. The particular domestic resonance of the racial dimension of any South African issue will—and should—continue to be reflected in American policy toward that country in a way that sets some American concerns apart from those of other nations. Nor does it mean that the United States should subordinate its interests to those of others or that it should refuse to take leadership. It requires, however, more complex and wider-ranging calculations of what its interests are, and a new, and perhaps subtler, style of leadership.

Such a shift in U.S. foreign policy will not evolve overnight, nor will the global ramifications of policy toward a region like southern Africa be immediately evident. For those scholars, diplomatists, and serious citizens who want to understand the newly complex international environment as it affects U.S. policies toward South Africa, Richard Payne's book is an essential guide. The individual chapters provide handy reference to the interests and policies of the nations most concerned with South Africa. The book as a whole provides much more: a portrait of South Africa's most relevant external environment, which is also the external environment U.S. policy must take into account if it is to play an effective role in helping shape a new South Africa throughout the 1990s.

William J. Foltz
Yale University
15 April 1990

## NOTES

1. For an early and perceptive South African view of such relationships, see Mark Swilling and F. van Zyl Slabbert, "Waiting for a Negotiated Settlement," *Africa Insight* 19, 3 (1989), pp. 138–46.

2. For a sample of this debate, see relevant chapters in Gerald J. Bender, James S. Coleman, and Richard L. Sklar, eds., *African Crisis Areas and U.S. Foreign Policy* (Berkeley and Los Angeles: University of California Press, 1985).

3. Foreign Policy Study Foundation, Inc., *South Africa: Time Running Out* (Berkeley and Los Angeles: University of California Press, 1981).

4. *A U.S. Policy toward South Africa: The Report of the Secretary of State's Advisory Committee on South Africa* (Washington, D.C.: United States Department of State Publication 9537, January 1987).

# ACKNOWLEDGMENTS

I am indebted to many students, colleagues, friends, anti-apartheid organizations, and various government officials who have made significant contributions to this book. I would like to thank Benjamin White, Ana Maria Downs, Christine Lush, Anneliese Heyl, and Eric Nicoll for assisting me with research, and Kristen Hill and Michele Steinbacher for proofreading the manuscript. I am extremely grateful to Garold Cole and Helga Whitcomb at Illinois State University and Barbara Mitchell at Harvard University for their invaluable assistance in locating library materials. I am deeply indebted to Sherry Stephens for the skill and care with which she typed the manuscript, to Professor Ronald Pope for helping me at the early stages of the project, and to Virginia Owen, Dean of the College of Arts and Sciences, Hibbert Roberts, Chairman of the Political Science Department, and Clayton Thomas, Dean of the Graduate School at Illinois State University for supporting my research efforts.

The Center for International Affairs at Harvard University provided the ideal environment for writing this book. Several colleagues were extremely helpful. I am particularly indebted to Professors Saadia Touval, Samuel Huntington, Jorge Dominguez, Jane Jenson, Susar Pharr, Jennifer Widner, Leroy Vail, Lenore Martin, Louise Richardson, and Dov Ronen for their insights and suggestions. Ambassador Allan Gotlieb of Canada, Christopher Meyer of the Foreign and Commonwealth Office (Britain), Lars-Goran Engfeldt of the Ministry of Foreign Affairs (Sweden), Ambassador Awad Elhassan (Sudan), and Kai Olaf Lie of the Ministry of Foreign Affairs (Norway) were extremely helpful. I would like to thank Professor Roger Fisher of Harvard Law School for his suggestions and generosity, and Janice Rand, Alice Allen, Tom Murphy, Jean Shildneck, and Anne Emerson of the Center for International Affairs for helping to make the year at Harvard enjoyable and productive. Professors Robert Rotberg of Tufts University and William Foltz of Yale read the manuscript. Their interest in my work is greatly appreciated.

Among the numerous individuals and organizations who assisted my research are: Sigvor Thornton, Christopher Kruegler, Sven Hamrell of the Dag Hammarskjold Foundation, Marjorie Ross of the Taskforce on Churches and Corporate Responsibility, Eivor Edvardsson-Kratz of the Swedish Trade Union Confederation, Linda Guebert of the Toronto Committee for the Liberation of Southern Africa, Ole F. Jorgensen of the Royal Danish Embassy in Washington, D.C., Dieter Bielenstein of the Institute for International Relations in Bonn, the German Information Center, the Japan Anti-Apartheid Committee, the Scandinavian Institute of African Studies, Pauline J. Celliers of the South African Consulate of Chicago, the Norwegian Information Service of the United States, U.S. Representative Walter E. Fauntroy, the British Embassy, Aracelly Santana of the UN Centre Against Apartheid, Stuart Bell of the Anti-Apartheid Movement in London, David Ben-Rafael of the Consulate General of Israel, Anita Jansson of the Africa Groups of Sweden, John Groves of the Department of External Affairs (Canada), and Richard Knight of the American Committee on Africa.

I wish to acknowledge the financial support I received from the Ford Foundation/National Research Council and Illinois State University which enabled me to spend the year at Harvard University to complete the manuscript. I am grateful for the support of many friends, especially Carol and Richard Miller, Bill and Maria Brisk, Sharon O'Connor, Kathleen Richardson, Joyce Hope Scott, Jane Guyer, Jo Sullivan, and Beverly Dale. Above all, I would like to thank my son Jason for his insights and for assisting my research efforts while in Cambridge.

# INTRODUCTION

For much of the Cold War period American policy toward South Africa was influenced by its global rivalry with the Soviet Union. This led to an exaggerated emphasis on the strategic importance of South Africa's minerals as well as the Cape sea route to the United States and its West European allies. It also influenced the formulation and implementation of policies that made little sense on the ground, and led to a unilateralist bias (the superpower's burden) that reduced the effectiveness of those policies, no matter how genuine American leaders were about promoting change in South Africa. Given the revolutionary changes in Europe, the decreasing relevance of the Soviet dimension in southern Africa, and significant changes within South Africa itself, the United States has an opportunity to concentrate on assisting the transition to democracy in South Africa without having to focus on Cold War considerations. To accomplish this, American policymakers will have to cooperate with the nonsuperpowers. This requires an understanding of their viewpoints, traditions, interests, and policy constraints. This book, by focusing on the nonsuperpowers' policies toward South Africa primarily from 1984 to 1990, provides information essential to the formulation of an effective American policy in a new strategic environment.

South Africa's system of apartheid or forced racial separation has been discussed, condemned, and declared to be only a few years from being abolished since its inception in 1948 when the Afrikaner National Party gained political control of the country. However, President F. W. de Klerk's decision in 1990 to release Nelson Mandela, to unban the ANC and other opposition groups, and to negotiate the country's future with ANC representatives was a significant departure from previous policy. Few issues have received so much international attention, and few countries, despite their widespread abuses of human rights and destruction of human life, have been so consistently singled out for isolation from the international community. Idi Amin's Uganda, Pol Pot's Cambodia, and Mengistu's Ethiopia all escaped sustained international pressure. Why not South Africa? South Africa is the only society which regards itself as part of Western civilization that has enshrined racial domination in its constitution. For more than three centuries, whites, who constitute approximately 15 percent of the population, have deprived the black majority of basic human rights; for over three hundred years blacks have denied the white minority's claim of legitimacy and have continued to find ways to empower themselves. The struggle against apartheid is essentially a continuation of the great crusades against slavery and racial discrimination in the Western world. Furthermore, apartheid must be analyzed in the context of colonialism. European subjugation of Africans was accompanied by the concepts of the racial superiority of whites over blacks and the inherent right of the former to dominate the latter. Consequently, race became the major issue of the 20th century, and South Africa represents the last vestige of legal racial domination. With the emergence of the United States as the leading world power after 1945, domestic racial problems soon became entangled in the web of international politics. Furthermore, as colonies gained their independence, the idea of racial superiority was directly challenged as being unacceptable. In a nutshell, apartheid is an anachronism which deeply offends both blacks and whites and which goes against universal principles of human rights that arose after World War II, partly in response to the Nazi extermination of six million Jews. For these reasons, apartheid is an emotional issue and is strongly condemned by all the countries examined in this book, despite their adoption of different strategies for influencing change in South Africa.

Unlike Europeans who lived in African countries such as Kenya and Zimbabwe but viewed Europe as their home, Afrikaners severed ties with that continent more than three centuries ago and regarded themselves as Africans. Their primary objective, like that of the Pilgrims who came to Massachusetts, was to find an alternative to the persecution and religious intolerance so prevalent in Holland, Germany, and France during the 17th century. Although affluent whites today do leave South Africa for Australia, the United States, and elsewhere, one can safely assume that the vast majority of white South Africans will remain and continue to play a role in their country's future. In light of this reality, blacks and whites will have to face the future together and develop broader concepts of nationalism that will include the various racial groups. The South Africans themselves will have to resolve their conflicts and deal constructively with their differences, but this will be possible only when blacks have succeeded in gaining sufficient power to persuade whites that apartheid no longer serves white interests. International actors can help create conditions that will weaken Afrikaner control while strengthening the black majority.

A central assumption of this book is that it is still possible for South Africans to transform their country into a relatively egalitarian society without experiencing widespread violence and bloodshed. Indeed, the major challenge for countries concerned about abolishing apartheid is to find non-violent strategies for effecting change in a country where violence is already endemic. None of the countries examined supports violent revolutionary confrontation in South Africa, and even the African National Congress (ANC) seems to have shifted away from violence as a strategy to more politically oriented measures for bringing about change. Moreover, the Soviet Union, the major supporter of the ANC's armed struggle, has demonstrated greater interest in diplomatic initiatives in southern Africa, is less enthusiastic about Third World conflicts in general, and has been more willing to engage in discussions with representatives of the South African government. While this does not mean that violence will not continue, it suggests that there are new opportunities for a relatively peaceful transition to a non-racial South Africa, provided that greater attention is given to non-violent strategies for a change. Although such an approach could be criticized on the grounds that it would take too long to dismantle the apartheid system, there is no evidence to support speculations that a violent confrontation would lead to a quicker demise of apartheid or create a post-apartheid society that is more respectful of human rights than the current minority regime. Unfortunately, the prevailing view in the world today, despite rhetoric to the contrary, is that force as a method of resolving conflicts among nations is efficacious and that non-violent strategies are ineffective, a view that persists despite widespread evidence that wars and revolutions are extremely costly in economic terms as well as in the tragic loss of lives. All too often, after long expensive campaigns on the battlefields and in the jungles, many wars end without a decisive victor and the process of negotiation, which should have been given serious consideration prior to war, is seen as the logical approach to resolving the conflicts.

The complex realities of southern Africa suggest that only a non-violent strategy will reduce the intensification of racial conflict and create an atmosphere conducive to inter-group as well as intra-group negotiations. It is clear that future race relations in South Africa will be determined to a large extent by the process by which racial domination is terminated. Sanctions, generally viewed as an alternative to military force, can be used in conjunction with other actions to convince white South Africans that abolishing apartheid is in their interest. The effectiveness of sanctions depends on the measures selected, how they are implemented, and the circumstances under which they are removed. Passage of the Comprehensive Anti-Apartheid Act in 1986 over President Reagan's veto not only marked the first major defeat for a popular president but also heightened expectations of the impact sanctions would have on the South African government's apartheid policy. The general assumption was that American business connections with the white minority regime were of such significance as to give the U. S. government extraordinary leverage vis-à-vis Pretoria. While disinvestment and other economic sanctions were viewed as key instruments for U. S. policymakers to utilize in their efforts to dismantle apartheid, it may be argued that the overwhelming support for sanctions was not so much an indication of their expected effectiveness but rather an expression of America's abhorrence of racial stratification in South Africa and a reaffirmation of its commitment to racial equality at home. The moral component of American foreign policy was clearly on the ascendancy for primarily domestic reasons. Nevertheless, the general perception was that sanctions would have an immediate impact on South Africa due principally to the tremendous pressure generated by widespread anti-apartheid activities, a factor influencing the Reverend

Leon Sullivan, author of the Sullivan Principles, to set June 1987 as the date by which apartheid would have to be abolished in order for him to support continued involvement of American companies in South Africa, despite their adherence to the Principles he articulated.

Although significant changes have occurred in South Africa, apartheid as a system of racial domination is strongly supported by the South African government. Obviously, the white minority has no intention of relinquishing power to the black majority, despite visible cracks in the foundation of apartheid and the proliferation of anti-apartheid groups throughout the South African society. However, while the State of Emergency has enabled the government to reestablish control through ever-increasing coercive power, the main political challenges remain, and a return to the status quo is highly unlikely. Furthermore, contrary to Pretoria's claim that sanctions are ineffective, evidence clearly shows that the economy is facing a recession and that there is a substantial drop in income for whites in general and for black workers in particular. By focusing primarily on American actions, one risks underestimating the durability of white rule and exaggerating American influence. A more accurate analysis of the impact of external influences on apartheid must take into consideration the declaratory statements and actual South Africa policies of other international political actors. If American policy toward Pretoria is to be more effective, greater attention must be given to how other countries perceive apartheid and to their underlying interests in South Africa.

Thus, this book examines the South African policies of the nonsuperpowers, i.e., those states lacking the military power of the United States and the Soviet Union. While countries such as Japan and West Germany are unquestionably strong economically, their impact on international politics at present is limited—for reasons which will be discussed in chapters three and four—consequently, they are regarded as nonsuperpowers. Unlike the United States, they lack large internal markets or natural resources, a factor which influences their economic and political relations with Pretoria. Some countries, such as Brazil, Canada, and Australia, compete directly with South Africa for markets. What is clearly demonstrated in all the chapters is that domestic interests, perceptions of national security interests, and cultural links combine to shape the various countries' policies toward South Africa. States such as Japan, Britain, and West Germany, with major economic stakes involved, place a higher priority on trade and financial considerations than on questions of morality, despite frequent condemnations of the evils of apartheid in U.N. speeches and press releases. This is not to dismiss morality as a factor in their foreign policies. Moral considerations, however, do not supersede realpolitik assessments of national interests, even in countries such as Canada, Denmark, Norway, and Sweden that strongly oppose apartheid and are actively involved in attempts to abolish it.

The complexity of the ties between the nonsuperpowers and South Africa is demonstrated by the relationship between the white minority government and the black-ruled neighboring Frontline States which are inextricably linked to South Africa. For example, while Robert Mugabe, Zimbabwe's leader, vociferously condemns apartheid and castigates Margaret Thatcher at Commonwealth meetings for not agreeing to impose tougher sanctions against Pretoria, trade between Zimbabwe and South Africa continues. Similarly, Zambia's deteriorating economy forces Kenneth Kaunda to rely on South Africa despite rhetoric to the contrary. And as the South African-supported guerrilla movement in Mozambique, Renamo, continues to kill innocent civilians and destroy Mozambique's infrastructure, South African authorities have negotiated an agreement with that country to train and equip as many as three battalions of the government's troops—to protect mutually beneficial projects from attacks by Renamo. Many of these contradictions reflect the historical interdependence of southern Africa; others emanate from competing economic and military interests within the ruling elite in South Africa itself. These factors help to complicate the formulation of the nonsuperpowers' South Africa policies. By analyzing what the nonsuperpowers are doing about apartheid, this book covers a seriously neglected aspect of the debate on the effectiveness of sanctions as instruments of change and challenges assumptions about the ability of the United States to unilaterally influence change in South Africa. On the other hand, it suggests that through developing a unified domestic stance on South Africa, relating strategies to objectives, and coordinating its efforts with those of the nonsuperpowers, the United States can assist in convincing white South Africans to dismantle apartheid and work constructively with black South Africans to protect their long-term interests. However, given the complex realities of international politics in southern Africa, the growing unification of Western Europe, the myriad of interests of the nonsuperpowers, and competition among them for markets and access to raw materials, the probability of achieving workable comprehensive international sanctions seems relatively low. Furthermore, in light of other competing American foreign policy interests, a desire to ease tensions in the Western alliance, economic and political developments in Eastern Europe, an escalating trade deficit, and a huge national debt, U.S. influence on its allies regarding the apartheid issue is likely to be reduced. Although international actors can help to empower blacks and to establish a relatively egalitarian society in South Africa, only South Africans themselves can dismantle apartheid and create a non-racial society. Once they have resolved their differences, it is very likely that they will play a significant role not only in southern Africa but also throughout the African continent.

# THE NONSUPERPOWERS'
# SOUTH AFRICA POLICIES

*Interests and Strategies*

Analysis of the nonsuperpowers' policies toward South Africa is complicated by several factors, the most outstanding of which is the contradiction
between declaratory policies strongly condemning apartheid and advocating its abolition on the one hand and an unwillingness or inability to
sacrifice national interests and a general realization that external influences
on South Africa may be limited on the other. This inconsistency springs
from divergent group goals within particular societies as well as deliberate
attempts by governments to mislead domestic and international observers
through obfuscating facts. Linguistic problems only exacerbate this situation. Furthermore, the conflicting interests of different agencies (the Foreign Ministry and the Ministry of International Trade and Industry in
Japan) or different individuals (Helmut Kohl, Hans-Dietrich Genscher,
and recently deceased Franz Josef Strauss of West Germany) influence
governments to pursue a two-track policy and to issue pronouncements
which belie reality. However, such confusion often serves the goals of
foreign policymakers, as will be shown throughout this book. Another
factor to be taken into consideration is the significant role played by
non-state actors such as multinational corporations and anti-apartheid
movements in the formulation of the nonsuperpowers' foreign policies
as well as the tendency of these global actors to pursue objectives which
may directly conflict with those of nation-states. A third factor is the
difficulty inherent in ascertaining which audience a particular government
is addressing. For example, Brazil's anti-apartheid policy could be construed as being aimed primarily at its domestic multi-racial audience,

whereas Scandinavia's policy could be viewed as being geared to international audiences and institutions such as the Third World and the United Nations. A fourth factor relates to intended targets. Policymakers, Britain's Prime Minister Margaret Thatcher for example, have argued that their objective is to assist in black empowerment, but their critics charge them with supporting the apartheid regime by not imposing more stringent sanctions against the white minority government. Given the interdependence of racial groups in South Africa as well as that country's economic ties with neighboring Frontline States, it is not always easy to distinguish one target from another. While this dilemma is used by some states to protect their economic and political stakes in South Africa, it also demonstrates that there can be honest disagreements among countries with good intentions over appropriate strategies for ending apartheid.

Equally important is the role of the United States. Although clearly a superpower, America cannot be excluded from any analysis of nonsuperpower relations with Pretoria because of its direct involvement with and influence on so many nonsuperpowers. This does not mean that U. S. policy simplifies the analysis of these countries' foreign policies. On the contrary, the complex nature of American policy toward southern Africa helps to complicate efforts to understand why other countries adopt certain positions. On the one hand, American policy is driven by a moral component which is expressed in terms of strong anti-apartheid sentiments and a belief in the dignity of the individual; on the other, it is influenced by a preoccupation with anti-communism and Soviet expansion.[1] Thus, when South Africa is seen in the East-West context, anti-apartheid sentiments often recede. Under these circumstances countries such as Japan and Israel can hide behind Washington's policy and continue their economic and military ties with Pretoria.

A sixth factor relevant to an analysis of the nonsuperpowers' relations with South Africa is the emotional nature of apartheid, especially in countries with (a) multi-racial populations (such as Brazil, Australia, and Canada); (b) negative experiences with discrimination (Israel); and (c) historical association with implementing racial policies (West Germany). This factor affects analysis directly because it influences the availability and quality of information on countries' ties to Pretoria. The final factor to be considered is directly related to conflicting interests among the nonsuperpowers. As will be shown, their policies converge or diverge depending on developments within South Africa or within the countries themselves, on the intensity of international public opinion, and on the countries' vulnerability to South African or American pressure. These seven factors are closely intertwined with the nonsuperpowers' perception of their national interests and thus with their South Africa policies. As T. B. Millar put it, all foreign policy is an expression of the national interest.[2]

## FOREIGN POLICY AND NATIONAL INTERESTS

Defining national interests, however, is not always straightforward. For the most part, national interests are vaguely defined by governments and are based on deeply held values within a given society. But not all decisions in the name of national interests correspond with these values or achieve what is best for the people's welfare, in part due to policymakers' predilection for invoking the term national interests to disguise ill-conceived foreign policies or to avoid serious discussion of an issue. More precisely, national interests may be defined as a finite set of intrinsically important goals either essential or beneficial to a country's survival, its prosperity, the psychological well-being of its population, or any combination of these.[3] Efficient foreign policies are usually based on an objective analysis of a hierarchy of interests. Donald Nuechterlein has developed a four-tiered scale of priorities as the cornerstone for more accurately defining the value a country attaches to specific policy issues.[4] In order of importance, this scale includes: (1) survival interests, where a state's existence is at stake; (2) vital interests, where serious harm to a country could occur if strong actions were not taken relatively soon; (3) major interests, where a nation could suffer if it does nothing to counteract a foreign threat; and (4) peripheral or minor interests, where little damage would result if a "wait and see" policy were adopted.[5]

But foreign policy decisions are responses to more than international stimuli; they are influenced by a myriad of complex and often nebulous domestic factors which are extremely difficult to quantify or logically organize. In other words, forces at work within a society may also contribute to the quality and content of its external behavior.[6] As an analysis of the nonsuperpowers' relations with South Africa demonstrates, the various countries' foreign policies are strongly influenced by internal conditions and the personalities and perceptions of those responsible for formulating and implementing them. Thus, the international relations of any state are shaped in part by domestic needs and political demands articulated from within the political system, by the processes through which policy is formulated, and by those who aspire to manage them.[7]

Factors which combine to influence the nonsuperpowers' relations toward South Africa include: the various countries' economic interests; ideological and geopolitical considerations; cultural and family ties to South Africa; domestic racial problems or sensitivity to racial issues; perceptions of the Soviet threat in southern Africa; concerns about international public opinion; a country's self-perception; military interests; the importance of international and regional organizations to particular countries; a country's relative isolation from the world community; relations with Africa and the Third World in general; and developments within South Africa itself. Given the number and diversity of countries included in this book, it is reasonable to expect that the prominence of apartheid as a foreign policy issue will differ significantly from one nation to another depending on the particular country's reliance on trade with South Africa, its access to alternative markets and suppliers, its racial and ethnic composition, its economic ties with the rest of Africa, and so on.

## ECONOMIC INTERESTS

Economic relations between the nonsuperpowers and South Africa predominate foreign policy considerations and assist in complicating strategies designed to induce Pretoria to abolish apartheid. South Africa itself has pursued a policy of closer integration into the Western political economy, with its primary objective being to inhibit Western policymakers from applying severe economic sanctions against it as a means of promoting meaningful political change and diminishing white control.[8] Pretoria's principal argument in relation to Western economic interests in South Africa has always been that Western access to its raw materials depends upon the preservation of the present political structure.[9] However, analysis of recent developments throughout post-colonial Africa indicates that political independence has not radically altered traditional economic arrangements with the colonial powers. Current trends are toward closer economic ties not only between Africa and the West but also between communist states and capitalist societies. Indeed, despite strident anti-apartheid rhetoric in the Frontline States, Zimbabwe and Zambia in particular, black majority rule there has left virtually all economic transactions with South Africa unchanged. Apart from the fact that countries must deal with the reality of economic interdependence and global markets, serious attention must be given to multinational corporations (MNCs) whose interests transcend what are increasingly becoming artificial national boundaries. Despite the general assumption that MNCs are extensions of particular nation-states, reality is far more complex. Few countries, including the United States, have complete control or exclusive jurisdiction over MNC's activities, a factor which exacerbates problems of enforcement in relation to economic sanctions. This is demonstrated in discussions of the nonsuperpowers' South Africa policies.

Considering the tremendous international pressure for sanctions against the white minority regime, an analysis of trade between the nonsuperpowers and South Africa must begin with the caveat that it is extremely difficult to get accurate data on actual trade. Another factor to be considered is the complex set of interests involved. As tables 1 and 2 clearly indicate, countries such as Japan, West Germany, Britain, and the United States have much greater economic interests in South Africa than Canada or Scandinavia (Denmark, Norway, and Sweden). Consequently, the former group of states is more reluctant than the latter to sever economic

TABLE 1: **Imports From South Africa, by Country 1986–87**

| Country | 1986 US$mn | 1987 US$mn | 1986 % CHANGE on 1983–85 | 1987 % CHANGE on 1983–85 | 1987 % CHANGE on 1986 |
|---|---|---|---|---|---|
| Japan | 2,248 | 2,455 | 32% | 44% | 9% |
| Italy | 1,914 | 1,786 | 18 | 10 | −7 |
| U.S.A. | 2,476 | 1,320 | 8 | −42 | −47 |
| West Germany | 1,255 | 1,248 | 31 | 30 | −1 |
| Britain | 1,226 | 1,088 | 2 | −9 | −11 |
| France | 488 | 581 | −23 | −9 | −11 |
| Taiwan | 236 | 510 | 57 | 146 | 57 |
| Belgium-Luxembourg | 361 | 384 | 14 | 21 | 7 |
| Hong Kong | 348 | 425 | 31 | 22 | −7 |
| Spain | 290 | 318 | 68 | 84 | 10 |
| Switzerland | 87 | 266 | 4 | 218 | 206 |
| Zimbabwe | 250 | | 5 | | |
| Israel | 203 | 212 | 18 | 23 | 5 |
| Netherlands | 191 | 188 | 38 | 36 | −2 |
| Zambia | 142 est. | 128 est. | 19 | 10 | −11 |
| Australia | 107 | 105 | −7 | −9 | −2 |
| Malawi | 116 | | 2 | | |
| Austria | 95 | 107 | 17 | 31 | 13 |
| Canada | 256 | 106 | 69 | −30 | −59 |
| Denmark | 103 | 6 | −27 | −96 | −94 |
| Mauritius | 68 | 75 | 67 | 86 | 11 |
| Portugal | 61 | 73 | 59 | 91 | 20 |
| Brazil | 60 | 71 | 86 | 119 | 18 |
| Argentina | 31 | 55 | 71 | 203 | 77 |
| Mozambique | 56 | | −5 | | |

*Source:* Commonwealth Experts Group, *Statistics on Trade with South Africa* (1988).

TABLE 2: Exports to South Africa, by Country 1986–87

| Country | 1986 US$mn | 1987 US$mn | 1986 % CHANGE on 1983–85 | 1987 % CHANGE on 1983–85 | 1987 % CHANGE on 1986 |
|---|---|---|---|---|---|
| West Germany | 1,940 | 2,545 | –3% | +28% | +31% |
| Japan | 1,357 | 1,882 | –17 | +23 | +39 |
| Britain | 1,250 | 1,556 | –19 | +1 | 25 |
| U.S.A. | 1,144 | 1,253 | –38 | –33 | 10 |
| France | 404 | 466 | –13 | 0 | 13 |
| Italy | 352 | 455 | –20 | 3 | 30 |
| Taiwan | 222 | 430 | +3 | 99 | 94 |
| Netherlands | 254 | 288 | 6 | 20 | 13 |
| Switzerland | 243 | 272 | 9 | 22 | 12 |
| Belgium-Luxembourg | 210 | 272 | –3 | 26 | 30 |
| Singapore | 144 | 213 | | | 48 |
| S. Korea | 100 est. | | –11 | | |
| Hong Kong | 75 | 123 | –25 | 24 | 64 |
| Sweden | 112 | 113 | –24 | –23 | 1 |
| Spain | 85 | 98 | –15 | –2 | 15 |
| Canada | 137 | 88 | 2 | –35 | –35 |
| Austria | 76 | 75 | 8 | 7 | –1 |
| Israel | 65 | | –23 | | |
| Brazil | 60 | | –46 | | |
| Ireland | 41 | 61 | 7 | 61 | 49 |
| Australia | 53 | 58 | –35 | –30 | +9 |
| Argentina | 49 | | –61 | | |

Note the very large drop in South African imports in 1985 and 1986, caused by financial sanctions, but followed by an increase in 1987. For that reason, it is useful to measure against the 1983–85 average.

*Source:* Commonwealth Experts Group, *Statistics on Trade with South Africa* (1988).

ties with Pretoria. Furthermore, some countries such as Canada, Australia, and Brazil have positive economic interests in restricting South Africa's access to world markets because they have similar economies, essentially the same exports, and a great demand for foreign capital.

Severe economic problems within Israel and the Frontline States (Zambia, Zimbabwe, Mozambique, Lesotho, and to a lesser extent Botswana) reduce options available to them. As chapter eight shows, the frontline countries and South Africa are mutual hostages. A combination of historical, military, and economic factors similarly influences Britain, Japan, and West Germany to emphasize trade with South Africa. Britain's economic links with that country began in the early 1800s and are well-established. Both Japan and Germany were imperialist powers defeated in World War II and were prevented from playing a major role in international politics. However, both were encouraged to focus on economic revitalization and, lacking raw materials and large internal markets comparable to those in the United States, they concentrated on trade. Because both rely heavily on imports to maintain their postwar economic machines, access to raw materials and markets has become a major foreign policy objective for them, one which usually overrides moral considerations.

South Africa's minerals comprise the overwhelming proportion of its trade with the nonsuperpowers and have been widely regarded as its most important source of leverage vis-à-vis the West.[10] As Table 3 illustrates, South Africa and the Soviet Union are the main suppliers of platinum, chromium, manganese, and vanadium, minerals essential for industrial economies and advanced military weapons. Platinum is used in the automotive, electrical, electronic, medical, dental, chemical, and petroleum industries as well as in jewelry making. Chromium is used for producing stainless steel, alloy steels, metal for tanks, ships, military vehicles, industrial equipment, military aircraft, and naval propulsion systems.[11] Manganese is utilized in the production of steel, dry cell batteries, and pig iron. Vanadium is used in machinery, low alloy steels, titanium alloys, and as a catalyst in chemical processes.[12] Because South Africa controls the lion's share of these minerals, its leaders have threatened to deny industrial societies access to them if they imposed sanctions against the apartheid regime. It has been argued that South Africa's position is rendered doubly important because of competition between the United States and the Soviet Union.[13] Access to strategic minerals has been an underlying argument for not seriously offending Pretoria. There are several problems with this analysis, however. First, it assumes perpetual hostility between the Soviet Union and the West, an assumption which is increasingly invalid. Second, it overlooks material as well as ideological gains that would accrue to Moscow if it became an alternate supplier of the various minerals. As Joseph Hanlon and Roger Omond observed, the U.S.S.R. would enhance both its image in the Third World and its profits by trading with the West.[14] Third, importing countries have had

TABLE 3
**World Reserve Base for Selected Nonfuel Minerals**

| Mineral | Units | Amount | Percent of Total Reserve |
|---|---|---|---|
| PLATINUM | millions of troy ounces | | |
| South Africa | | 970 | 80.8 |
| U.S.S.R. | | 200 | 16.7 |
| United States | | 16 | 1.3 |
| Canada | | 9 | 0.8 |
| Other | | 5 | 0.4 |
| World Total | | 1200 | 100.0 |
| CHROMIUM | millions of metric tons | | |
| South Africa | | 5715 | 83.6 |
| Zimbabwe | | 753 | 11.0 |
| U.S.S.R. | | 129 | 1.9 |
| Turkey | | 73 | 1.1 |
| United States | | 0 | 0.0 |
| Other | | 164 | 2.4 |
| World Total | | 6834 | 100.0 |
| MANGANESE | millions of metric tons | | |
| South Africa | | 7711 | 70.8 |
| U.S.S.R. | | 2268 | 20.8 |
| Australia | | 490 | 4.5 |
| Gabon | | 399 | 3.7 |
| United States | | 0 | 0.0 |
| Other | | 18 | 0.2 |
| World Total | | 10,886 | 100.0 |
| VANADIUM | thousands of metric tons | | |
| South Africa | | 7802 | 47.1 |
| U.S.S.R. | | 4082 | 24.7 |
| United States | | 2177 | 13.2 |
| China | | 1633 | 9.9 |
| Other | | 862 | 5.1 |
| World Total | | 16,556 | 100.0 |

Source: U.S. Department of Commerce, *Office of Strategic Resources*, (June 11, 1985).

enough warning to stockpile various minerals and to develop substitutes for some of them. Japan, the U.S., and France have substantial stockpiles,[15] but West Germany and Britain seem to be more vulnerable because they have either refused to stockpile (in the case of West Germany) or have sold accumulated stocks due to budgetary considerations (in the case of Britain).[16] Finally, South Africa itself is extremely vulnerable to any disruption in exports because of its weak economic condition and its need to maintain a certain level of black as well as white employment in order to continue to enjoy black acquiescence and white support, both essential for maintaining apartheid.

## GENERAL INTERESTS OF THE NONSUPERPOWERS

Directly related to trade with South Africa are the nonsuperpowers' economic interests in countries of black Africa for whom apartheid is an assault on their dignity as human beings. Competition among Western European countries for markets in the Third World in general and in Africa in particular highlights the political and economic risks engendered through association with Pretoria. As Robert Price put it, concern with black Africa's reaction probably is partly responsible for the international failure of separate development.[17] This observation is supported by Pretoria's concerted efforts to develop relations with African states and thereby achieve a measure of legitimacy. South Africa's participation in negotiations on Cuban troop withdrawal from Angola in exchange for Namibia's independence was in part calculated to gain black African acceptance. Few Western countries are likely to openly embrace Pretoria as long as it remains isolated on the continent. Indeed, Prime Minister Margaret Thatcher justified her 1984 meeting with President P. W. Botha on the grounds that some African leaders had met with him.

Nigeria's linkage of trade with black Africa and the economic and diplomatic isolation of South Africa is the most obvious example of how the nonsuperpowers' relations with South Africa are affected by their interests in black Africa. However, this leverage is mitigated by deteriorating economic conditions throughout Africa. Nigeria, for example, experienced a precipitous drop in oil revenues from $25 billion in 1980 to approximately $6 billion in 1987. From 1985 to 1987, per capita income plunged from $800 to $380, and Nigeria earned the dubious distinction of being reclassified by the World Bank from a middle-income to a low-income country.[18] Africa as a whole is suffering from declining economic growth, overpopulation, and massive external debt.[19]

Despite these problems, the nonsuperpowers cannot risk their interests by recklessly trading with South Africa. Israel is perhaps the only country that has paid relatively little attention to African states, partly because of its general isolation from them. But this is changing for reasons that will be explained in chapter five. Other states such as Japan, Britain, and West Germany have used transfusions of financial assistance as one method of reducing Africa's criticism of their relations with Pretoria.

Cultural and family ties constitute another interest of nonsuperpowers such as Britain, Israel, and West Germany. Approximately one million South Africans hold British passports and are eligible for consideration to settle in Britain.[20] Israel is concerned about the welfare of about 125,000 South African Jews, probably its most generous supporters per capita. Similarly, West Germany's links with approximately 25,000 persons of German background in Namibia and South Africa influence its policy toward Pretoria.

An additional general interest of some nonsuperpowers grows out of domestic racial considerations. By strongly opposing apartheid, countries such as Britain and Canada reassure the world and their increasingly multi-racial societies that they are genuinely interested in racial harmony and equality. Racially homogeneous states—West Germany, Japan, and Scandinavia, for example—would not be expected to link international public relations with domestic politics. What, then, explains Scandinavia's consistent opposition to apartheid?

Widespread domestic condemnations of apartheid in Denmark, Norway, and Sweden can only be understood within a cultural, political, and historical context. Chapter six examines this in great detail. As small states, the Scandinavian countries have always expressed great interest in protecting human rights and in international institutions such as the League of Nations and the United Nations.[21] Canada has likewise regarded the United Nations as a forum in which it can project its foreign policy concerns and gain Third World support. However, membership in institutions like the Commonwealth and the European Community directly infringes on various countries' South Africa policies. Britain's entry into the European Community has contributed to the diminution of the Commonwealth's importance in its overall foreign policy objectives. Consequently, the Commonwealth's demands for wider and tighter sanctions against South Africa are studiously ignored by Britain. Canada, on the other hand, having smaller stakes in South Africa and a greater need for the Commonwealth to safeguard its national goals, elevates it above relations with Pretoria and has been a leading advocate of stiffer sanctions.[22]

Another general interest of the nonsuperpowers in South Africa until 1989 was the prevention of communist, primarily Soviet-Cuban, expansion in the region. The prevailing view was that the Soviet Union sought to undermine Western economic and security interests and would gain from a violent resolution of racial conflict in South Africa.[23] Others argue that the hatred of capitalism by young black South Africans, who equate white business with apartheid, is the most serious threat to the West.[24]

Consequently, the nonsuperpowers adopted divergent and sometimes conflicting policies to achieve their shared objective of eliminating Soviet involvement in southern Africa. South Africa effectively exploited these anti-communist sentiments in order to maintain white domination.

Unique among the nonsuperpowers is Israel's interest in cultivating close economic, political, and military ties with South Africa.[25] This is perhaps the most controversial, confusing, contradictory, and shortsighted strategy for protecting Israel's national interests. To a large extent, this problem springs from Israel's history, anti-Semitism in South Africa and elsewhere, an overriding concern with national security, its policies toward Palestinians, and the Holocaust syndrome which leads to a degree of moral parochialism. Egypt's concerted campaign to deny Israel's right to exist and to isolate it internationally began as soon as Israel was created in 1948. As chapter five explains, the isolation of Israel occurred in stages and was due in part to the effectiveness of the Arabs' strategy, to African economic vulnerabilities which provided OPEC with tremendous political leverage after the oil embargo in 1973, and to serious miscalculations by Israeli leaders. Israel's military establishment in particular displayed enthusiasm for developing stronger links with Pretoria, a development that inadvertently assisted the Arab strategy of further isolating Israel. Hence, the basis of Israel's alliance with South Africa was their shared status as pariah states; both perceived their very existence to be at stake.[26] Unlike the small Scandinavian countries, which value international organizations as instruments of foreign policy, outcast states, though small, regard international practices and resolutions as less binding,[27] thus further contributing to their isolation in the international community.

Finally, nonsuperpowers, particularly the Western countries, want to promote democratic values and embrace countries practicing them. Western states have come to expect, and practice, a high degree of sensitivity toward each other's needs and interests and are conscious of their common values, objectives, and vulnerability.[28] Many of them share an interest in including South Africa in this network but are ambivalent about relations with that country because of its system of apartheid. Further complicating this interest of the nonsuperpowers is the realization that while South African leaders rarely operate within the same set of ideas, assumptions, and processes as the West, they still emphasize the existence of strategic, economic, and technical links which constitute a community of interest.[29] In light of this, it is imperative to understand white South Africans' perception of reality before assessing strategies employed by the nonsuperpowers to effectuate change and protect their interests in South Africa. Attempting to understand their perception of reality must not be construed as agreeing with it. By putting themselves in South Africa's shoes, as it were, policymakers in the various countries might be better positioned to formulate more workable policies toward Pretoria.

## UNDERSTANDING THE AFRIKANERS' REALITY

A state's reality, like an individual's, is constructed from the sum total of its selectively remembered experiences. Essentially, reality is strongly influenced by perceptions, or misperceptions. Perceptions relate primarily to the process of stereotyping: those viewed as the outgroup are perceived as possessing undesirable attributes, without regard to any realistic basis.[30] Perceptions are transmitted to future generations through the process of socialization, which is carried out by the media, schools, churches, parents, peer groups, and authority figures in a society.[31]

Membership in the community further reinforces and stabilizes beliefs. As social animals, most individuals want to belong to a group, are extremely aware of group expectations of what is appropriate behavior, and tend to view events through the group's perspective rather than as objective observers. Since changing one's views of reality as perceived by the group would result in one's emotional isolation from it, one is under tremendous pressure to anchor one's beliefs in what the group perceives as real.[32] Moreover, the fact that these perceptions and assumptions are usually unreflective, visceral, and deterministic mitigates the possibility of one taking actions based on critical thinking;[33] to scrutinize is tantamount to heresy.

Perceptions comprise the cornerstones of ideology, and apartheid is an ideology. Ideology encourages polarization of thinking; the world is viewed in terms of good versus evil and communists versus anti-communists; one side is seen as pure and virtuous while the opponents are perceived as evil and vicious. To assume the worst about the other side's intentions and to adopt a worst case scenario are regarded as only prudent.[34] As Arthur Schlesinger contends, ideology undermines reality by isolating problems from the turbulent stream of change and treating them in splendid abstraction from the whirl and contingency of life.[35] Ideology also leads to hypocrisy and contradictions. Nowhere is this more evident than in South Africa. Robert Rotberg views South Africa as a complex of contradictions, noting that even though South Africa has "divided itself along lines of color, it cannot escape the interdependence of all strands of a single people bound together by geography, history, economic realities, and the cement of circumstance." But apartheid could not survive if it accepted this reality and abandoned polarized thinking and the threatening enemy.[36]

Afrikaner nationalism is a direct outgrowth of historical experiences which were perceived as threats to the survival of the Afrikaner people. When the British occupied the Cape and outlawed the slave trade in 1807, this humanitarian action was taken to be a threat to the Afrikaners. The abolition of slavery in 1833 and the imposition of British law, language, and customs on Afrikaners in Cape Province ultimately motivated more than 12,000 of them to participate in the Great Trek inland between 1836 and 1843.[37] Military clashes between Afrikaners and Zulus in the interior, especially at Blood River in 1838, and several attempts by Britain to control territory occupied by Afrikaners served to augment the Afrikaner perception of both blacks and British as enemies.

Subsequent to Blood River, major conflicts were between the Afrikaners and British; blacks no longer presented an immediate threat.[38] In fact, the decisive event that crystallized Afrikaner nationalism was the Anglo-Boer War of 1899–1902 during which British military forces waged a brutal campaign against the Afrikaners in the Transvaal and elsewhere.[39] Of all their remembered experiences, Blood River and the Boer War predominate in shaping contemporary Afrikaner perceptions of reality. The fact that Afrikaners comprise only 9% of the population of South Africa serves to perpetuate the racist theme in Afrikaner mythology and the threat perception.[40]

Since apartheid is equated with Afrikaner survival, any threats against this system of enforced racial separation are taken very seriously. The higher the perceived threat, the greater the probability of group solidarity. Conversely, the smaller the perceived threat, the greater the likelihood that group fragmentation will occur.[41] External pressures against apartheid and various activities of the African National Congress (ANC) were frequently exploited by Afrikaner leaders to preserve group cohesion. Addressing the annual congress of the National Party in Durban on August 15, 1985, former President Botha declared that "our enemies, both within and without, seek to divide our peoples. They seek to create unbridgeable differences between us so as to prevent us from negotiating peaceful solutions to our problems."[42] What Botha was saying, given the Afrikaner perception of reality, was that apartheid would be threatened by divisions in the white community in general and more specifically among Afrikaners, who are viewed as "the people."

ANC political and military activities and Soviet support of them constituted one of the gravest threats to apartheid, at least from Pretoria's perspective. Although the government now refers less frequently to the communist-inspired total onslaught, the general perception among white South Africans is that the communist threat is real, that the ANC and the United Democratic Front collaborate to discredit and undermine the government, and that communists control the ANC.[43] National liberation movements are viewed as integral components of communist revolutions. From the South African government's perspective, liberals, churchmen, students, and workers who oppose apartheid comprise a broad national front under the "vanguard party," the ANC.[44]

Inadvertently, the failure of democracy in the vast majority of African countries provides Pretoria with a poignant argument against majority rule in South Africa, despite significant differences between the newly independent states and South Africa. Many white South Africans regard "majority rule" in Africa as essentially synonymous with despotic one-party governments that are acceptable to the communists.[45] Whatever the reasons for the failure of democracy in Africa, there is abundant evidence of the demise of constitutional democracy, the pervasive use of coercive power, and the personalization of power. Larry Diamond, an astute observer of African politics, states that "Africa's experience with liberal democracy has not been a happy one. In a relatively short period of time, virtually all of the formally democratic systems left behind by the departing colonial rulers gave way to authoritarian regimes of one kind or another."[46] This development reinforces the Afrikaners' perception of reality by perpetuating their image of Africans as incapable of governing a pluralistic society in a manner that would protect the interests of all groups. In addition, religious beliefs and cheap African labor undergird the Afrikaners' perceptions of reality.

Religion's ubiquitous influence on the Afrikaners' political thought, social stratification, education, and culture cannot be overlooked. Religious values are inseparable from apartheid and current political thinking in South Africa. In any society, behavioral patterns that unite a religious group are represented by explicit symbols. These symbols represent truth in concentrated form and provide an interpretative and evaluative framework as well as a motivation for corresponding action.[47] This is especially applicable to the ruling Afrikaner group which has combined religion and ethnicity to create an extreme form of nationalism in a country where they are a distinct minority. Religion is a determining influence on the personal beliefs, corporate behavior, and the self-justification of Afrikaners at all levels of government, including the white parliament, the police force, and the military.[48] All prominent Afrikaners are likely to be members of the Dutch Reformed Church, the citadel of apartheid and an expression of Afrikaner nationalism.

From the Afrikaners' perspective, God is an activist who calls the elect (the Afrikaners), who promises and punishes, and who brings forth life from death in the course of history. God imbues all history with meaning and works His will through Afrikanerdom.[49] The Afrikaners' distinct language, Afrikaans, and culture as well as their isolation from the outside world strengthens their belief that they were specifically chosen. This perception colors their interpretation of their historical experiences.

British imperialist expansion and the Zulu army were perceived in dualistic and contradictory terms; on the one hand they were seen as incarnations of evil and as a threat to the Afrikaners' racial purity, and on the other, as God's agents for uniting the Afrikaner people and as a foil against which God revealed His greatness and glory to His people, the Afrikaners.[50] Suffering, such as that endured by Job of the Bible, is perceived as God's way of testing the Afrikaners' commitment. This "righteous suffering" can be viewed as an assurance of God's favor.[51] The

Predikants (clergy) became instrumental in fostering and propagating these myths, particularly the myth of the Covenant. By the second half of the twentieth century Predikants had construed the myth of the Covenant, which grew out of the conflict between Afrikaners and Zulus at Blood River in 1838, as meaning that Afrikaners were a chosen people with a God-given mission to rule South Africa[52] and to dominate black Africans who were regarded as sub-human.

Feelings of racial superiority were buttressed by abundant cheap black labor. Unlike in the United States where whites comprised the majority of the population, blacks were the majority in South Africa, with implications far more profound and obdurate. As George Fredrickson notes, in contrast to South Africa, there were not enough blacks in America to do all the menial low-status work and too many whites to give all of them a protected or privileged economic status within a capitalist economy.[53] Besides, Afrikaners never adopted the strong laissez faire practice which emerged as the dominant economic philosophy in the West in general. The capitalist class in South Africa had no incentive to interrupt the flow of cheap labor. Instead, it developed an active partnership with the government and assisted in maintaining white domination in the realm of work as well as in politics by denying blacks equality under the law.[54]

By effectively preventing blacks from engaging in skilled jobs, and thereby frustrating their aspirations of upward economic mobility, Afrikaners were able to justify apartheid by alluding to the technological and educational inferiority of blacks.[55] The consequence of political power or the lack of it became extremely clear; economic and political structures were essentially inseparable. Economic and political power was restricted to the dominant group by its policy of depriving blacks of land, thereby destroying their economic independence; by reserving certain jobs for whites only; by limiting educational opportunities for blacks (or by miseducating them); and by prohibiting the formation of black labor unions.[56]

Attempts to modify this rigid system have been strenuously resisted by white middle- and lower-class workers whose jobs depend to a large extent on prohibiting black competition. Although some whites approve of removing some restrictions on black labor, an overwhelming majority support continued white control because it guarantees them a privileged lifestyle. Apartheid allows almost all whites to enjoy a standard of living equivalent to that of upper-middle class groups in Western Europe and North America, but without them having to protect the privileges with price barriers.[57] Paradoxically, white reliance on cheap labor and the inherent contradictions and inequalities of apartheid have contributed to the emergence of new forces within South Africa that are not only seriously challenging Afrikaners' perception of reality but also are creating irreparable fissures in apartheid's ideological, economic, and political foundation.

## Emerging New Realities

Political mythology is common to people everywhere and changes as circumstances are altered. White South Africans are not significantly different from people elsewhere; their perception of reality, as we have seen, is determined to a large extent by their economic, political, social, and psychological interests and needs. But perceptions generally linger long after objective realities have changed. For example, as Robert Rotberg observes, it is generally argued that Afrikaners are psychologically unique, that compromise is foreign to their nature, that they would rather fight than trade, that the lessons of the frontier have not, in the face of adversity, taught adaptation and resourcefulness.[58] Undoubtedly, this may be an accurate description of many Afrikaners. However, as Rotberg contends, analysis of current developments in South Africa suggests that it is inapplicable to a significant number of Afrikaners. While romantic notions of an Afrikaner *Laager* or fortress are reassuring to many ambivalent about the future, the reality is that the *Laager* is crumbling from within and is increasingly susceptible to external pressures.

When Afrikaners were primarily impoverished farmers, miners, and laborers with little interest in formal education and the urban lifestyle, their behavior was relatively consistent with the visceral aspects of apartheid. However, industrialization in South Africa brought about significant economic and social modifications that have had direct consequences for apartheid. As Afrikaners left the countryside to work in the bureaucracy, factories, and industrial plants, and as more of them became urbanized technocrats, business executives, and entrepreneurs, their political outlook was sufficiently transformed to create an irreversible process of fragmentation within the Afrikaner community.[59] Ironically, the success of the Afrikaner mobilization engineered by apartheid has been accompanied by intensifying social stratification within Afrikanerdom and by the emergence of conflicting class interests and diverging needs for different economic and political arrangements.[60]

Economic expansion and labor practices which protected whites from black competition contributed to growing financial prosperity for whites. Rising incomes allowed them to engage in more leisure activities and reduced their desire for having larger families, thus further exacerbating the demographics of South Africa. The growth of rural Afrikaner families gave them a numerical advantage over English-speaking South Africans, a fact that permitted them to gain political control of the country even though they had lost the Anglo-Boer War. However, as their numbers declined relative to the general population, there were not enough whites to do the jobs generated by industrial expansion and white affluence. The level of economic development required to maintain the high living standards whites had come to expect from apartheid could not be realized without undermining apartheid's restrictions on black technical advancement. The new reality was that the economy was too complex to be managed by whites alone.[61]

Not surprisingly, the business community became one of the most outspoken critics of apartheid's economic restrictions because it now perceived them as expensive liabilities. There are several explanations for this shift. First, Afrikaner business people successfully challenged the commercial dominance of the white English-speaking community to such an extent that by the early 1980s both groups shared many common interests. Furthermore, young successful urban Afrikaners became increasingly alienated from the rural roots of apartheid, were more committed to free enterprise and less dependent on political patronage controlled by proponents of a rigid racial ideology.[62] Second, business people were more vulnerable to international economic sanctions. Third, black activists' association of capitalism with apartheid proved worrisome to business groups. Fourth, business became deeply concerned that increasingly violent conflict between blacks and whites in South Africa would become institutionalized if apartheid were not modified.[63] As in any society, conflict is usually bad for business. Indeed, South Africa's attractiveness to foreign capital was its "stability" and very high profits. Fifth, apartheid was restricting economic growth by artificially dampening black consumer demands. Finally, rigid apartheid was incompatible with the reality of global markets. For business, the costs of apartheid were intolerably high.[64]

Responding to these realities, six South African employer organizations, representing approximately eighty percent of the employment strength of the country, issued a public statement in January 1985 that called for the following reforms: (1) full participation by all South Africans in a private enterprise economy and in the political structure of the country; (2) citizenship for all South Africans; (3) termination of forced removal of blacks; (4) the administration of justice to be safeguarded by the courts; and (5) free trade unions.[65] This last point reflects heightened awareness of black trade union political and economic power in an industrialized economy.

Apartheid's architects did not envision black trade unions and generally believed that whites could effectively suppress violent challenges to minority domination. By the mid-1970s both assumptions had been called into question by black trade unions which were gaining increased recognition, and by young blacks, radicalized by their experiences in the Soweto uprising of 1976 and imbued with the new black consciousness articulated by Stephen Biko.[66] These developments fundamentally challenged apartheid by weakening the myth of black powerlessness and dependence on an oppressive system.

As an examination of the South Africa policies of the nonsuperpowers shows, international pressures combined with domestic developments to help bring about a new reality in South Africa. International hostility, particularly from Western countries once considered allies, put additional strain on the apartheid regime's resources. ANC guerrillas, supported militarily by the Soviet Union and joined by a growing number of whites, were becoming more of a threat, especially to farmers on the border with black African states.[67] And the government's response to these problems actually triggered new fissures in apartheid's structure.

The major schism was in the National Party, the guardian of apartheid. While some Afrikaner members of the all white parliament called for negotiations with black leaders, others demonstrated their opposition to reforms instituted by former President Botha by joining the ranks of the right-wing Conservative Party. By 1988 the National Party had lost a significant number of Afrikaner votes but had gained more votes among English-speaking whites, who traditionally had supported the anti-apartheid Progressive Federal Party.[68] Major support for the Conservative Party came from Afrikaner farmers who were badly hurt by drought, high interest rates, government pricing decisions, and by the Ministry of Agriculture's decision not to grant an increase in the maize producer price after decades of regular yearly raises.[69] The government was clearly preoccupied with urban unrest and maintaining apartheid by enhancing the military's fighting capabilities. Another source of Conservative Party strength came from unemployed white workers, those fearing unemployment in a stagnant economy,[70] and new white immigrants from Angola, Mozambique, and Zimbabwe.

For the first time since the formal implementation of apartheid in 1948, the National Party was confronted with escalating violence from white extremist groups that advocated strict racial segregation. The Afrikaner Resistance Movement, led by Eugene Terre Blanche, and the Whites' Freedom Movement, led by Carel Boshoff, are the best known radical groups. Both are pro-Nazi and anti-Semitic organizations,[71] a factor influencing Israel's policy toward South Africa. From the local South African Jewish perspective, Botha was far more reasonable than ultraright conservatives who traditionally have been anti-Jewish.

Beleaguered on the Right, the National Party must deal with a new reality on the Left, namely, limited but growing white resistance to military service, primarily among more affluent families in the English-speaking community. Approximately three-fourths of all resisters come from this group.[72] Yet, apartheid's existence depends more and more on military might. Fighting in distant places like Angola, where South African whites have suffered heavy casualties for the first time, was not part of apartheid's plan; it did not anticipate being defeated by a non-white military force. Younger urban whites do not consider that apartheid's survival should send them as soldiers into black townships where they might have to fight people they know either as servants, laborers, or friends. While some whites such as Ivan Toms, a physician, have gone to jail instead of joining the military, others have simply evaded the draft by leaving the country. The tragedy of this new reality has been manifested by several suicide attempts (and successes) among conscripts.[73]

A final new reality that challenges the generally accepted assumptions of apartheid comes from academic circles, principally from Afrikaner professors at Stellenbosh University. Historically, Stellenbosh has been synonymous with Afrikanerdom and was the intellectual stronghold of apartheid philosophy. Six of South Africa's eight Prime Ministers were graduates. However, while Botha was Chancellor of the university in 1987, approximately 360 academics signed a petition of no confidence in the National Party.[74] Intellectuals are deeply divided on questions pertaining to South Africa's political and economic reform. Many continue to subscribe to old perceptions of reality; others are ambivalent. Although few whites advocate complete political equality for blacks in a unitary system,[75] it is obvious that the Afrikaners' motto, "Unity Makes Strength," no longer commands great attention in a society at the crossroads of change.

These developments provide opportunities for the nonsuperpowers to improve their ability to influence Pretoria. However, a comprehensive approach to apartheid would have to take into consideration the nonsuperpowers' varying perceptions of their national interests, their perceptions of their ability to effectuate change, the costs that would accrue to different countries, and the present conflicting strategies for helping to abolish apartheid.

## THE NONSUPERPOWERS' STRATEGIES FOR CHANGE

In the process of resolving conflicts, the general tendency on the part of governments is to focus on what they should do rather than on what they want done, who is best suited to do it, and what price they are willing to pay. Specifying the objective must be the beginning of analysis.[76] The starting point should be the other government's problem. The key question to answer is what decision we want them to make or refrain from making. Once this is identified, the immediate task is to develop various strategies for influencing events in the direction favorable to us.[77]

Several constraints prevent policymakers from selecting certain courses of action. Constraints range from very weak to very strong compulsions. The strongest constraints prohibit a state from moving in a particular field of action, while others provide motives for avoiding particular steps. In the final analysis, policymakers tend to balance the cost or risk the constraint imposes against probable benefits of the measures under consideration.[78] Few policymakers can escape restraints in an interdependent international economic and political system. Since interdependence is essentially mutual dependence, interdependent relationships will involve costs as well as benefits because, by definition, interdependence limits autonomy.[79] Therefore, any strategy implemented by the nonsuperpowers vis-à-vis South Africa will inevitably result in some losses or gains. Given the complexity of the problem and multiplicity of actors involved, some countries could profit at the expense of others by adopting varying strategies. Such risks are generally associated with the use of economic sanctions as a political strategy.

## ECONOMIC SANCTIONS

Although economic sanctions are usually associated with the governments of various states, some of the most effective and direct sanctions are applied by nonstate actors such as multinational corporations whose investments and other business interests are negatively affected by political instability within a country. Evaluation of political risks is an integral component of any international business planning activity. Companies disinvest because a number of factors contribute to low profits over an extended period of time. Disinvestment is a reaction to existing problems as well as potential difficulties and occurs when the discrepancy between organizational goals and the situation confronting the company becomes intolerable.[80] Therefore, unless conditions in South Africa change dramatically, both foreign and domestic sources of investment will shrink. Compared to transnational business enterprises, governments base their decision to impose sanctions on far more imprecise considerations. Consequently, the wisdom of their actions is vulnerable to attacks.

International sanctions are often debated without much attention given to the prevailing realities which persuade governments to utilize them. After World War I, the League of Nations was formed to encourage nations to settle disputes peacefully. Despite the League's failure to prevent a devastating second World War, or perhaps because of it, countries tried to resolve their differences through discussions in international forums, principally the United Nations, rather than on battlefields. International sanctions were part of this design for a new world order.[81] Given Pretoria's direct challenge to the fundamental principles of equality and human rights upon which this new order was established, it became the most obvious target of international sanctions. Scandinavian countries, for example, strongly supported the United Nations and its efforts to maintain international peace and also became leading proponents of sanctions against South Africa. Two additional developments which prompted greater reliance on sanctions were the Cold War and growing international economic interdependence.[82]

Technological advancements in nuclear weapons accompanied the emergence of the Cold War between two of World War II's allies: the United States and the Soviet Union. Since a nuclear holocaust was now a reality nobody wanted, the superpower confrontation assumed the more indirect forms of military conflict in newly developing countries of the Third World and of economic coercion. The United States and the Soviet Union continued to augment their nuclear arsenals with ever more dangerous weapons in the hope that neither side would be tempted to use them. Essentially then, the relative disutility of military power elevated economic coercion as an important instrument of foreign policy.

Revolutions in communications and transportation further enhanced economic instruments of foreign policy by helping to create a global economy in which economic isolation was a serious disadvantage. No major country, not even the United States, could realize economic development if isolated from world markets and international financial transactions. This reality, no matter how vigorously denied by nations, has generated economic vulnerabilities, especially for countries like South Africa which depend heavily on exports of primary materials. In South Africa's case, the objective of sanctions is to persuade Pretoria's minority government to negotiate majority rule. However, there are other factors that shape a nation's decision to implement sanctions, only some of which are directly related to imposing hardships on a target country in order to influence it to alter its policies.[83] The objectives of sanctions may be divided into two interrelated categories: symbolic and instrumental. While regarded principally as expressive, symbolic actions may be undertaken for instrumental purposes as well.[84] A state's international image is inseparable from its ability to project its power. As Harold Lasswell and Abraham Kaplan contend, political symbols function directly in the power process, serving to set up, alter, or maintain power practices.[85] To a large degree, foreign policy is symbolic. But foreign policy decisions are in many cases inextricably linked to domestic realities. Sanctions against South Africa are adopted to express disapproval of apartheid as well as to reassure domestic groups that the country is fully committed to racial equality. Among the nonsuperpowers, Canada, Australia, and Brazil are the best examples of countries linking domestic concerns about race to their South Africa policies.

Foreign policy objectives usually associated with the instrumental purposes of sanctions are summarized by Lawrence Brady. They include the following:

> (1) to bring about a diplomatic loss of face; (2) to signal to the target country that the resolve to resist its aggression is not lacking; (3) to raise the possibility that others will condemn its behavior; (4) to lessen the possibility of military conflict; (5) to alter the status of the target country as the dominant supplier of critical resources to allies; and (6) to reduce other forms of economic leverage that may be used by a potential adversary to harm the national interests of the initiator.[86]

Many of these goals are pursued by several of the nonsuperpowers. South

Africa's diplomatic isolation is demonstrated by its concerted efforts to find friends in Africa, Asia, and Latin America. Further, strong positions taken by Canada, Scandinavia, Australia, and the United States have influenced reluctant Western European states such as Britain and West Germany to implement sanctions against Pretoria. Finally, other countries are becoming alternative suppliers of embargoed products from South Africa. In the process of implementing sanctions, whether symbolic or instrumental, states generally assess costs and benefits that might accrue to them as a result of their decisions. However, given the fact that countries adopt sanctions for a variety of reasons, attempts at precise measurements of costs and benefits are not always useful.

If sanctions are taken for solely symbolic purposes, the question of whether they are more costly to the target than to the sender becomes largely irrelevant. As David Baldwin astutely observed, for the rational statesman the cost comparison is not between his country and the target but rather between his costs and his benefits with respect to his alternatives.[87] International and domestic realities permit very few countries to be neutral on apartheid. On the other hand, military action against South Africa is not a viable option. Under these conditions, sanctions are the more attractive alternative.

Analysis of sanctions as an instrument of foreign policy generally fails to compare the costs of sanctions to the costs of military involvement. Interestingly enough, governments usually are willing to sacrifice their young men and women, impose severe economic burdens on their citizens, and risk losing equipment worth billions of dollars to fight for certain values. Perhaps Britain's policy in the Falklands (where about 1800 people live) is the best example of this reactive nationalism. However, Britain fervently opposes economic sanctions as instruments of foreign policy in relation to South Africa.

Although history is replete with examples of the tragic costs of war, the common assumption that military force is more effective than economic measures is rarely challenged. Part of the problem is caused by the tendency to expect economic sanctions to work immediately. But as William Minter put it, measured by such standards, almost any kind of political action—war, diplomacy, foreign aid, propaganda—can be labeled a failure.[88] Yet the effectiveness of sanctions is fraught with several difficulties. First, the capability of governments to enforce compliance with sanctions may be seriously limited. The global nature of the economy and the complexity of transnational business operations make it relatively easy for companies to violate sanctions legislation. Second, not all governments are equally committed to making sanctions effective. Third, countries may be unwilling to absorb costs associated with sanctions because of domestic pressures. Finally, the unevenness of their implementation encourages other governments to adopt a more liberal interpretation to avoid forgoing commercial opportunities.[89] Nevertheless, sanctions can have an impact on the target country even though there are violations. Sanction-busters will demand higher compensation for their work, thus imposing substantial costs on the target government. In the case of South Africa, sanctions have undoubtedly deprived that government of some needed resources to fight the war in Angola, compensate farmers, and fund white luxury consumption.[90] It is now clear that sanctions are motivating many white South Africans to examine the assumptions of apartheid. But sanctions are also viewed as encouraging as well as hindering another strategy, namely, black empowerment.

## BLACK EMPOWERMENT

Black empowerment is far more nebulous and contradictory than economic sanctions as an approach to abolishing apartheid. Some nonsuperpowers, such as Britain and West Germany, have genuine misgivings about the efficacy of sanctions and fear that black South Africans will suffer more severe damage than the white minority government if comprehensive economic sanctions are imposed. These countries argue that economic sanctions might destroy opportunities for black economic advancement, thus guaranteeing the status quo or promoting an extremely violent revolution which would result in a Pyrrhic victory at best. However, countries such as Canada and Scandinavia believe that sanctions against South Africa, combined with economic and technical assistance to the Frontline States in order to reduce their dependence on Pretoria, can contribute to black empowerment by simultaneously weakening white power and enhancing black influence, principally through affecting their psychology of power. Perhaps the most crucial ingredient of black empowerment, only peripherally associated with the policies of the nonsuperpowers, is the realization by blacks that their acquiescence is essential to the perpetuation of a system that is oppressing them.[91] This aspect of black empowerment appears inconsistent with strategies that focus on changing the behavior of the white minority through dialogue or constructive engagement with government officials in Pretoria. The multiplicity of views on how to achieve black empowerment through nonviolent methods suggests a degree of interdependence between international and internal action as well as among all the strategies discussed.[92]

Black empowerment is primarily concerned with the psychological dimension of power. To a large extent, all power is based on the psychology of oppressors and victims alike. Domination, racial or any other kind, is maintained by structural and psychological means which evolve slowly over time.[93] Victims inadvertently participate in their own repression by accepting the perceptions and values of the dominant group. Eventually, their sense of powerlessness and incompetence is so deeply entrenched that there is little motivation to effectuate change. Domination will continue until victims develop increased self-respect, self-awareness, self-affirmation, and self-assertion.[94]

Tangible aspects of power, such as military force and police brutality, are rendered increasingly ineffective in a society where people have the will to resist, and to accept casualties—as they would in war—as the price of freedom. Only when an individual's self-perception is transformed can change be realized. Equally important, the individual's belief in his or her ability to accomplish change and to prevent others from controlling his or her actions is crucial to maintaining freedom in future. If individuals are not empowered, then any post-apartheid government, no matter what its color, will be at least as tyrannical as the current minority regime.[95]

At the root of the concept of black empowerment is the often overlooked reality that white South Africans will not relinquish power unless they perceive it to be in their interests to do so. Until there is a decisive shift in the balance of power in South Africa there is little prospect that whites will agree to meaningful negotiations with the black majority.[96] Many nonviolent organizations in South Africa, especially church-related groups, are in the forefront of black empowerment. While several nonsuperpowers are assisting these developments, their main approach to black empowerment is centered around economic advancement and trade union activity.

The major assumption of proponents of economic advancement as an instrument of black empowerment is that economic growth will eventually lead to greater prosperity for all South Africans and a concomitant change in the values and conditions undergirding apartheid. The main argument is that the way to break down inequalities is to open up the economy to everybody.[97] However, economic growth has not transformed South Africa into a more egalitarian society. Indeed, careful analysis of the relationship between economic growth and political change in South Africa between 1917 and 1970 reveals that the African population received about 18 percent of total income in 1917; by 1970 its share had risen to only twenty percent of the total, despite considerable urbanization and industrialization.[98] Although economic growth is an important stimulus for change in many societies, there is no apparent connection in South Africa because apartheid's elaborate bureaucratic, military, and political structures militate against any dilution of white control. Nevertheless, middle-class individuals are more likely than poverty-stricken masses to mobilize black South Africans against apartheid. Economic growth is a component of black empowerment not only because it helps to change values but also because it strengthens trade unions. Apartheid's Achilles' heel is its dependence on black labor in virtually all sectors of the economy and in white homes. A strictly segregated South African society would cease to function. Black workers, particularly those in trade unions, have tremendous potential power. High growth rates augment the unions' ability to play a greater role in the economy and to use this position to gain political leverage.

Not surprisingly, labor unions are the most powerful black political organizations in South Africa despite continued repression and the imprisonment of many respectable black leaders in the country. Through striking, trade unions foster great self-awareness and assertiveness among blacks and demonstrate the economy's vulnerability to internal pressures. As Christopher Coker put it, strikes are even more likely to inflict sustained damage to South Africa than sanctions imposed by its principal trading partners.[99] In the process of bargaining with companies and government officials, black labor union leaders develop negotiating skills essential in the political struggle for a non-racial South Africa. Both sanctions and black empowerment can contribute to change. But nonsuperpowers' policies must also take into account the white minority government's perception of its choices.

## THINKING ABOUT THEIR PERCEPTIONS OF CHOICES

White and black South African leaders are responding to their currently perceived choices. Although both sides have legitimate interests, they may also have unrealistic expectations because of their inability or unwillingness to examine the other side's reality. While anti-apartheid groups have succeeded in mobilizing widespread support among all racial groups and cannot be ignored by the government, the state security apparatus has become more oppressive and pervasive. Anti-apartheid movements cannot seize power; at the same time, the government cannot restore its credibility and legitimacy either internally or internationally.[100] The old assumptions which supported apartheid are no longer unquestioned, and the contradictions, interdependence, and cooperation inherent in a relationship characterized by domination and victimization are now paradoxically, clearly working to undermine apartheid.

White South African leaders must make some hard choices. Apartheid has created an artificially high standard of living for whites at the expense of blacks. Those dependent on the government for their power and position in society will resent modifications of apartheid and violently oppose dismantling it. However, maintaining apartheid in the same old way is too expensive, and Pretoria's efforts to modernize apartheid through selective reforms are not acceptable to blacks.

The international community must also be satisfied, a fact evidently understood by Botha and his successor F. W. de Klerk. In a 1985 speech Botha noted:

> In taking decisions in the interest of our country the government must have regard to the fact that circumstances and events in the rest of the world have a definite influence on our country and our subcontinent. It is our responsibility to take cognizance of the implications of the views of both

TABLE 4

**The White Government's Currently Perceived Choice**

QUESTION: Shall we openly negotiate with the African National Congress?

| *If We say "Yes"* | *If We do NOT say "Yes"* |
|---|---|
| —We undercut the legitimacy of the government. | +We retain the authority of the government. |
| —We confer legitimacy on the ANC. | +We continue to weaken the legitimacy of the ANC. |
| —We give the communist-influenced ANC a big role in South Africa's future. | +We keep communist influence out of the government. |
| —More right-wing constituents will desert us. | +We maintain our constituent support. |
| —Negotiating with the ANC will not solve any significant problem. | +We maintain control of the process of change. |
| —We will be on a slippery slope. | +We can buy time. |
| —We will be in a weaker position. | +We keep our options open. |
| *But:* | *But:* |
| +We appear reasonable. | —We appear uncompromising. |
| +We reduce acts of violence. | —We further divide the country. |
| +We ward off additional sanctions. | —We invite more sanctions. |
| +We enhance our international status. | —We risk increased isolation. |
| +We win support from African states. | —We incur substantial costs for maintaining the status quo. |
| +We cut our losses by facing reality. | |

*Source:* The author is indebted to Roger Fisher, Williston Professor of Law at Harvard Law School and Director of Harvard's Program on Negotiation, for this idea.

friendly and hostile countries, and to take into account the effect of our decisions on the Republic of South Africa's foreign relations. Our goal is to extend these relations; the interests of South Africa demand no less.[101]

Even Botha regarded the idea of retreating into a *laager* as a myth. South African leaders are evidently more sensitive to external opinion than is commonly assumed. In November 1988 Botha warned white extremists that reimposition of rigid segregation in towns under their control would militate against his efforts at ending South Africa's isolation and warding off additional economic sanctions which, in his view, were hurting South African living standards.[102] President F. W. de Klerk, by releasing Walter Sisulu and seven other ANC members and by desegregating South Africa's beaches in late 1989, and by freeing Nelson Mandela, unbanning the ANC and other opposition groups, and by negotiating with ANC repre-sentatives in early 1990, also demonstrated sensitivity to international pressures. Table 4 gives an example of the minority government's dilem-mas.

Afrikaners have real as well as imagined fears. Examining them does not imply agreement. However, any attempt to negotiate a peaceful resolu-tion of South Africa's racial problems must take these fears into considera-tion. The challenge for policymakers in the countries included in this book (and for those not covered) is to contribute to changing the currently perceived choices of both blacks and whites and to provide better alterna-tives.

# 2

# BRITAIN

## The Imperative of Economic Growth

Although Britain's status as a superpower was terminated by the devastation it experienced during World War II, the humiliation it suffered in the Suez crisis, and the subsequent loss of its colonial empire, it remains an important international actor, especially in relation to South Africa. Among the factors accounting for Britain's continued influence are: (1) its historical association with southern Africa; (2) its role as the colonial power in South Africa itself; (3) its membership in the Commonwealth; (4) extremely close ties between Britain and the United States; (5) its significant investments in and trade with South Africa; (6) its participation in the industrial countries' Group of Seven; (7) its membership in the European Community; and (8) its position as a permanent member of the Security Council. These connections place Britain in a unique position to influence international responses to apartheid. But they also render British policymakers vulnerable to international pressure from a myriad of sources.[1] Consequently, apartheid has received continuous attention in Britain, and successive British governments, both Labour and Conservative, have displayed a marked degree of concern for the future of South Africans throughout the post-war period, even though the white minority regime's reputation has meant that such a posture involved serious diplomatic costs for Britain,[2] particularly within the Commonwealth. Nevertheless, economic ties with Pretoria have outweighed all other considerations.

While economic interests have strongly influenced Britain's policy toward apartheid, historical and moral factors have also helped to shape policy. These different interests combine to make Britain's policy toward South Africa consistently ambiguous. On the one hand, strong anti-apartheid sentiments in Britain and that country's extensive knowledge of Africa in general lead policymakers to condemn apartheid on moral grounds and to support the U.N. arms embargo and the sports boycott against South Africa. On the other hand, British attitudes toward business and economic realities in Britain dissuade the government from imposing meaningful economic sanctions against apartheid.[3] Pointing out that, unlike many proponents of sanctions, Britain has large economic interests in South Africa, Sir Geoffrey Howe, former Secretary of State for Foreign and Commonwealth Affairs, bluntly stated that "punitive sanctions would damage those interests. Of course we do not want to sacrifice them in pursuit of a policy which we believe to be profoundly mistaken."[4]

Britain's South Africa policy emphasizes a peaceful negotiated end to apartheid through dialogue and contact with the white minority government. An underlying assumption is that blacks are largely irrelevant to the process of change primarily because the ruling Afrikaners control economic, military, and political power in the country. Therefore, positive sanctions or rewards for progress rather than negative sanctions or punishment for failure are preferred, and economic expansion is regarded as the main instrument for undermining apartheid. As James Barber noted, "British businessmen and financiers, armed with the seductive thesis that morality and profit go hand in hand, are unlikely to abandon it."[5] Furthermore, economic conditions in Britain augment this approach, as is evidenced by Prime Minister Margaret Thatcher's refusal to support sanctions against South Africa during the 1989 Commonwealth meeting and her eagerness to lift those in place following Mandela's release in 1990.

Similar to Japan's strategy of hiding behind the United States in international affairs, Britain tends to involve others in an effort to downplay its extensive ties with South Africa. This strategy has been so successful that the United States instead of Britain, despite the latter's extensive trade, investments, and historic ties with South Africa, has been the principal target of anti-apartheid activities and is widely perceived as having the major responsibility for helping to abolish apartheid,[6] a perception influenced by domestic factors and the United States' status as a superpower. Spreading responsibility for the West's relations with South Africa is pursued by Britain through the European Community, and Britain is instrumental in shaping the Community's response to South Africa,[7] with West Germany and Portugal in supporting roles. Within the E.C., Britain has focused on promoting the growth of European Political Cooperation, the process by which members of the Community attempt to harmonize their foreign policies and try to formulate a joint foreign policy.[8] By working through the European Community, Britain's strong stance against sanctions is hidden, to some extent, by the actions of countries such as Holland and Denmark. Although there have been some compromises, British policy has not changed dramatically.

## How British Foreign Policy is Made

The process by which foreign policy is formulated and implemented in Britain directly determines the amount of influence that anti-apartheid groups can exercise over that country's policy toward South Africa. Unlike in the United States, where power is decentralized among fifty different states and their local jurisdictions, and where there theoretically is an equal partnership between the legislative and executive branches in foreign affairs, in Britain the prime minister and her cabinet do not share power over international affairs with Parliament. Consequently, Parliament does not have the equivalent role of Congress in setting the country's foreign policy, and anti-apartheid groups cannot influence British policy by lobbying Parliament as they can influence U.S. policy through their access to members of Congress. Failure to understand this can only lead to unrealistic expectations by anti-apartheid groups in America which believe that other countries' policies toward South Africa can be changed by public opinion as easily as America's.

In Britain the leaders in Parliament are members of the prime minister's cabinet and are responsible for sponsoring bills which Parliament can debate. The legislative process in the United States is quite different. Only members of Congress can introduce legislation and the President usually does not have control over both the House and the Senate. Even if his party holds large majorities in both houses, this does not guarantee that the President will successfully implement his programs because power is clearly diffused in the United States, by intention. In Britain, the cabinet—the prime minister and her ministers—controls various roles that are divided between the legislative and executive branches in the United States. Cabinet members are simultaneously the symbolic heads of government, leaders of the majority party in Parliament, managers of the business of Parliament, and the heads of major administrative departments. It is from these multiple roles that the cabinet derives its power.[9] Parliament's involvement in the foreign policy process is relatively insignificant, especially when compared to its American counterpart, and members of Parliament, who generally lack detailed knowledge of foreign affairs, perceive their responsibility in terms of publicizing and alerting cabinet ministers' attention to particular aspects of policy. As Barber observes, Parliament influences foreign policymaking only in the negative sense that ministers are aware that some of their actions may be publicly debated.[10] Only in policy areas requiring money can Parliament exert considerable influence because of its constitutional power over financial matters.

The prime minister and her cabinet have clearly inherited the power in foreign affairs traditionally associated with the monarch. Through the professional foreign policy bureaucracy and various cabinet committees, the prime minister controls Britain's relations with other countries. Prior to Margaret Thatcher's appointment as prime minister, the professional diplomatic service and the foreign policy bureaucracy were more powerful. Basically, members of these groups, recruited primarily from Oxford and Cambridge universities, shared common assumptions about Britain's international relations. As Wolfram Hanrieder and Graeme Auton put it, it is a self-selecting, self-perpetuating elite, peculiarly cohesive and—when it chooses—remarkably impervious to external pressure.[11] Although this elite's power has diminished under Thatcher, British foreign policy remains consistently conservative, largely because Prime Minister Thatcher's own conservative philosophies augment rather than undermine approaches favored by the foreign policy elite. The major change has been greater personalization of power by Prime Minister Thatcher, her reliance on a close group of advisers who share her values and whose intellect and opinions she can respect, and her general lack of tolerance for opinions with which she fundamentally disagrees.[12] Generally speaking, however, the British seem to have shared views of their country's international role and the importance of economic issues in foreign policy.

## ECONOMIC INTERESTS AND FOREIGN POLICY

Britain's decline following the Second World War focused its attention away from military power to economic growth and reconstruction, an objective shared by Japan and West Germany. All three countries suffered severely during the war; all lacked sufficient domestic natural resources to sustain their economic growth; and they relied on the United States to protect their security interests, although Britain to a much lesser degree than Japan and West Germany. For all of them economic goals became synonymous with foreign policy objectives. While Britain clearly recognized that it needed a strong economy, its position as a major world trader and a banking and financial center also made it cognizant of the interrelationship between successful diplomacy and domestic economic growth.[13] Unlike Japan and West Germany, which enjoyed extraordinary economic expansion, Britain experienced a precipitous fall from being Europe's leading economic power to a position slightly ahead of Italy by 1981.[14]

For a country which had previously enjoyed unsurpassed political power, its new economic status had profound psychological and political implications. Perceptions of Britain as a great power remained among many of its citizens as well as among citizens of its former colonies, which were now part of the Commonwealth, long after Britain's postwar decline. Labour and Conservative governments alike recognized the pivotal position of economic interests in the country's foreign policy. As in the cases of Japan and West Germany, private business became so directly involved in foreign policy formulation that one British scholar concluded that "to a considerable extent, the national interests which the British government is promoting and defending abroad are those of British finance and industry."[15] Protecting these interests became inextricably linked to Britain's desire to regain some of its former diplomatic stature.

Issues such as apartheid could not interfere with economic transactions essential for Britain's domestic economic health and its global diplomacy and, despite rhetorical differences between the Labour and Conservative parties, neither party while in power reduced Britain's economic ties with South Africa.[16] Conservatives especially wholeheartedly endorsed the British ideology of laissez-faire, which meant that political considerations had to be separated from trade matters. Conservative governments, especially under Thatcher, "deferred to the Bank of England and regarded the standing of the Sterling and the level of reserves as the sole test of internal as well as external economic policy."[17] These attitudes and realities militate against the imposition of major sanctions as key instruments of Britain's South Africa policy. Britain remains extremely reluctant to advocate sanctions in areas where its economic interests would be adversely affected, although Thatcher's call for sanctions against Argentina for its invasion of the Falklands/Malvinas is a major exception. Britain's refusal to support American sanctions against the Soviet Union reflects its general opposition to using economic instruments for political purposes. When President Carter restricted American technology and grain exports to the Soviet Union in 1979 following its invasion of Afghanistan, Thatcher refused to reduce trade with the U.S.S.R. In fact, in 1980 when total U.S. exports to the Soviet Union fell by 54 percent compared to 1979, British exports climbed by 67 percent.[18] Similarly, Thatcher, despite her close friendship with President Reagan and their shared ideological views toward Moscow, disagreed with Reagan's decision to apply sanctions against the Soviet natural gas pipeline. Other Western European governments rallied behind Britain, primarily because they were principal consumers of Soviet natural gas. While Reagan tried to prevent foreign subsidiaries of American companies and foreign enterprises holding U.S. licenses from having to honor contracts to build the pipeline, Thatcher directed British companies to comply with British law and continue working, and Britain's trade secretary, Lord Cockfield, went as far as invoking the Protection of Trading Interests Act of 1980, arguing that America was threatening British trading interests.[19]

Given the deteriorating economic conditions in Britain, especially in areas outside London and southeast England, it is highly unlikely that the British public would support sanctions that would result in the loss of an estimated 120,000 jobs. Despite criticisms of Thatcher's social policies, there was widespread agreement in Britain that her policies helped the country pull itself out of economic stagnation. Under her leadership Britain experienced a strong economic growth of around 3 to 4 percent for the period from 1980 to 1988, the government balanced its budget for the first time in about three decades in 1988,[20] and British investors changed their country's status from a net debtor to a net creditor of more than \$114 billion, second only to Japan.[21] However, Britain's trade deficit continues to be a serious problem, another reason for the government's reluctance to impose economic sanctions against South Africa. Available evidence indicates that economic interests continue to predominate as the major factor shaping British South Africa policy.

## PUBLIC OPINION AND FOREIGN POLICY

Public opinion on apartheid seems to exert little influence on the actual policies of many Western European governments, Britain and West Germany in particular. Although Britain's long history of involvement in South Africa and its close cultural and economic ties with that country would suggest greater awareness of apartheid by the average British citizen, peculiar characteristics of policymaking in Britain render public opinion on foreign affairs virtually ineffective and largely irrelevant. Unlike Washington, London seems impervious to public opinion.

There are several reasons for this difference. First, foreign policy issues are viewed as being beyond the concern of ordinary citizens, even though many of them are cognizant of developments in world affairs. In a society still dominated by a class system, most people are prepared to leave foreign policymaking to government experts.[22] Second, international relations matters in Britain generally do not require legislation, thus preventing detailed discussion of proposals in Parliament and denying anti-apartheid interest groups an opportunity to influence foreign policy legislation. Furthermore, international issues are not paramount in British politics, an indication of Britain's decline from a world power to more of a regional actor with limited global responsibilities.[23] Third, economic problems after World War II in a growing welfare state demanded more attention from politicians and the general public alike. Finally, because British foreign policy is shielded in secrecy, many issues are not clearly articulated and vital information is usually classified for several years. As William Wallace put it, while there is sufficient nonconfidential information available to support intelligent discussions among experts, wider public interest is discouraged by the poverty of explanation and justification characteristic of British foreign policy.[24]

However, members of Parliament, especially those from opposite parties, can ask questions on behalf of their constituents and, unlike the American President's practice of refusing to answer questions directly, the government in Britain is required by tradition to give specific answers to specific questions. But in terms of actual influence on foreign policy and access to information, the American system provides numerous opportunities for the public to be well-informed and to shape policy, even against the wishes of the Executive. The effectiveness of anti-apartheid groups in the United States, compared to their ineffectual European counterparts, sometimes obscures the fact that anti-apartheid activity is widespread in Britain.

In contrast to economic pressure groups that have direct access to policymakers and that have been organized to influence Britain's foreign commercial and economic policies for at least two hundred years,[25] anti-apartheid organizations have been less influential. In many cases these two groups express political views which are in direct conflict. Given the primacy of commerce in British foreign relations, business groups have consistently enjoyed a privileged position in politics, and their objectives usually prevail over those of marginal groups. But anti-apartheid movements are deeply rooted in Britain, many of them outgrowths of the anti-slavery campaigns which were extended to South Africa in the early 19th century.

Due to Britain's involvement in South Africa, London has always been a major base for South African exiles, and similar to anti-colonial movements which fought for independence from Britain by mobilizing support in London, many South African nationalists, including members of the African National Congress, locate in London to continue their struggle against apartheid. Several black and white South African exiles in London have devoted their lives to anti-apartheid activities not only in Britain but also throughout Europe and North America. Their commitment to racial equality in South Africa contributes to keeping apartheid in the forefront of British politics, and this is reinforced by the media's focus on South Africa.[26] Anti-apartheid groups are visible throughout London, especially outside South Africa House where many individuals were arrested for demonstrating in 1987 and 1988. When Tony Banks, a member of Parliament, asked the Secretary of State for the Home Department, Douglas Hogg, why peaceful demonstrators were detained, Hogg replied that they had attacked the South African embassy and assaulted police officers.[27] Such activities keep apartheid in British news.

Major anti-apartheid groups in Britain include the Defense and Aid Fund, the South African Non-Racial Olympic Committee, and various church, labor, and university groups. Among the political parties, Labour and the Liberals have been most vocal in their opposition to apartheid. The Labour Party traditionally has supported issues associated with working classes, ethnic minorities, and the underprivileged.[28] However, the actual policies of Labour governments toward South Africa cannot be sharply distinguished from those of the Conservative Party. Because the Liberal Party has not recently controlled the government, evaluating what its actual policy would be is more difficult. Nevertheless, its activities indicate genuine concern about racial discrimination in South Africa and Liberals consistently have voted for sanctions and have pressured the government to oppose apartheid. Furthermore, two Liberal Party leaders,

Jeremy Thorpe and David Steel, actively participated in the Anti-Apartheid Movement.[29]

Labor unions, traditionally major supporters of the Labour Party, also attempted to shape Britain's policy on apartheid, but under Thatcher their influence has precipitously declined, beginning with her successful confrontation with Arthur Scargill, the mineworkers' leader, in 1979. Significant restructuring of the British economy further weakened trade unions' power. With privatization of industry, more workers are now stockholders in the companies that employ them, thus changing their relationship with management from one of confrontation to one of cooperation. Simultaneously, more workers are unemployed, especially in areas such as Birmingham, Manchester, Liverpool, and other industrial centers in the north of England. The trade unions' relative weakness was clearly demonstrated by the expulsion of the 330,000-member electricians' union from the Trades Union Congress in early September 1988.[30] Anti-apartheid groups are not alone in their effort to influence Britain's South Africa policy.

South African government officials' active recruitment of supporters in Parliament and elsewhere in British society is demonstrated by the establishment by South Africa's Department of Information of front organizations to place advertisements in European and American newspapers; to finance visits by members of Parliament to South Africa (Operation Bowler Hat); and to pay Labour Party members of Parliament to lobby for South Africa and spy on anti-apartheid groups in Britain.[31] Britain's central role in various international organizations as well as its economic stakes in South Africa make it a target for both sides in the struggle for political power in South Africa.

## ETHNICITY AND FOREIGN POLICY

British foreign policymakers, while not pressured by powerful ethnic groups, are keenly aware of race as a factor in Britain's South Africa policy. Members of Parliament often compare racial stratification in South Africa with the fight against slavery and the atrocities of Nazi Germany but come to divergent conclusions about appropriate strategies for eliminating apartheid. Minority political parties generally favor decisive steps, whereas the majority Conservative Party takes a more cautious approach. In his speech to Parliament, the former Foreign Secretary Sir Geoffrey Howe stated that:

> We in Europe should approach the subject carefully because European history is not free of racial conflict. We have no right to strike a self-righteous pose on the subject. European history has taught the world tragic lessons about the evil of discrimination against human beings on grounds of creed or race.[32]

This statement reflects the relative inability of racial minorities in Britain to influence their government to take a stronger stance against South Africa.

There are several reasons for the lack of political power among minority groups. First, the vast majority of them are immigrants from Asia, Africa, and the Commonwealth Caribbean who are preoccupied with adjusting to their new country. Immigrants in Canada and Australia seem to exhibit similar behavior. Second, racial polarization in Britain is not as severe as it was in the United States with its long history of slavery. Relatively few whites in Britain favor the kind of racial separation that existed in America, although they anticipate problems if blacks, Asians, and whites live in an integrated area.[33] Third, like the general British public, minorities have little access to information or believe that they should focus on foreign policy. Fourth, blacks and Asians play an insignificant role in the leadership of major political parties, although this is likely to change with the election of two blacks to Parliament in 1987. Fifth, there is no common group identity or ideology that has been forged in a struggle with white society and that has found expression in organized political activity.[34] Finally, there are too few minorities and they are too dispersed to have a decisive impact on foreign policy issues, which are debated at the national political party level.[35] Ethnicity has entered discussions of Britain's South Africa policies not so much from domestic sources but rather from the Commonwealth, especially from African members. Unlike most of the nonsuperpowers, Britain's historical ties with South Africa and the Frontline States, many of which are Commonwealth members, profoundly influence its relations with Pretoria.

## BRITAIN'S HISTORICAL TIES TO SOUTH AFRICA

South Africa, seemingly peripheral to events in Europe, usually found itself entangled in the intricate webs of European power politics. Dutch, French, and German Huguenots and settlers, who later became known as Afrikaners, were only remotely connected to Holland through the Dutch East India Company, which established a refueling station at Cape Town. Nevertheless, European military conflicts, which often spilled over into distant areas as the balance of power was readjusted in Europe, had a direct impact on South Africa. Holland's decline and French victories in the Napoleonic wars culminated in the expulsion of the Dutch government from Holland by French occupation forces and Britain's establishment of a caretaker government in South Africa in 1795 at Holland's request. Although Dutch control was restored in 1803 when Britain voluntarily left South Africa, shifting alliances—Holland having joined France against Britain—resulted in the end of Dutch rule in South Africa and the ascendancy of British imperial might in 1806 when Britain seized the Cape to prevent Napoleon from cutting the route to India.[36] British rule also marked the end of isolation for Afrikaners (also known as Boers) and the introduction of British values which clashed sharply with beliefs held by many Afrikaners.

Humanitarianism in Britain, which was directly related to the aggressive anti-slavery campaigns of William Wilberforce and Thomas Clarkson, was transferred to South Africa, where the principal objective was to end slavery and establish a free society in Cape Colony. The slave trade was abolished in South Africa in 1807, as it was throughout the British Empire. Similar to its efforts in West Africa to stop the slave trade, Britain focused on cutting off sources of slaves in South Africa and compiled in 1816 a registry of blacks already enslaved in an attempt to diminish violations of the anti-slave trade law.[37] Registered slaves were guaranteed certain basic rights by British authorities. For example, Afrikaners were prevented from arbitrarily punishing or mistreating slaves, and those found guilty forfeited control of the abused slave. Field work could not be done on Sundays and working hours during the week were set at ten in the winter and twelve in the summer, and slaves who worked additional hours were entitled to compensation. Furthermore, children between the ages of three and ten got three days of schooling, and those under the age of eight could not be separated from their parents. Perhaps most challenging to Afrikaners' perception of Africans as nonpersons was the Nineteenth Ordinance, passed in 1826, which provided for a guardian of slaves and permitted slaves to testify against slaveholders in criminal court.[38] Finally, in 1833 about 39,000 slaves in South Africa were freed when Britain abolished slavery throughout its empire.

Confronted with radically different values as well as the imposition of British law, language, and administration, many Afrikaners left Cape Colony around 1835 to develop a society in the interior where their own values could be protected. Major military conflicts with the Zulus during their trek, especially at Blood River where the idea of the Covenant originated, contributed to the Afrikaners' belief that they were God's chosen people with a right to subjugate Africans. Constant conflict between whites and blacks bred a legacy of hatred, mistrust, and racial domination of blacks by whites. While British authorities and missionaries were concerned about the inhumane treatment of the Africans, other interests prompted them to invade the newly established Natal Boer Republic in 1842. Apart from worries about loss of control over Afrikaners in the interior, British commercial interests wanted to eliminate competition from Port Natal where many Dutch ships stopped as they bypassed Cape Town.[39] Britain's response to Natal's challenge of the Cape's domination of overseas trade was to annex Natal in 1845 as a British colony. Eventually, the Afrikaners managed to settle two new Republics, Orange Free State and the Transvaal.

Two radically different traditions existed in South Africa: one of racial stratification and exclusion in Orange Free State and the Transvaal and another of relatively good race relations in Cape Town and Natal. Whereas in the British controlled areas Africans comprised about five percent of the electorate and were recognized as having a legitimate political role to play in South Africa, Afrikaners saw Africans as subhuman, as an abundant source of cheap labor, and as subject to the demands of whites.[40] There was no intention of including blacks in political life, and there would be absolutely no social equality between Afrikaners and Africans. The latter tradition prevailed, partly due to faulty assumptions made by the British when the Union of South Africa was formed in 1910, and is now the ruling philosophy of South Africa. Ironically, Afrikaner political ascendancy sprang from their military defeat by the British in the Boer War of 1899–1902.

War between the British and Afrikaners was triggered by a combination of nationalism, British imperial designs, German commercial interests in the Transvaal, and, above all, diamond and gold discoveries in the Transvaal. When diamonds were discovered in 1867, Britain annexed the Transvaal but decided to restore independence to this Boer Republic in 1881 following a successful revolt by the Afrikaners. However, the discovery of gold in the Transvaal in 1885 marked the end of its independence, heightened Anglo-German rivalries, and sharpened British-Boer antagonisms. Gold attracted to the Transvaal large numbers of English-speaking settlers or Uitlanders (outlanders) who outnumbered the Afrikaners by 1895.[41] German immigration also increased, along with huge infusions of German capital. Unlike previous German settlers who identified with Anglicized Dutch and British settlers on the Cape, the new immigrants identified with Germany at a time when Cecil Rhodes, Britain's foremost imperialist in southern Africa, was concerned about Afrikaner and German efforts to frustrate his goal of purchasing Delagoa Bay in Mozambique from Portugal. Portugal's control of Delagoa Bay allowed Paul Kruger, President of the Transvaal, to be independent of British shipping routes for trade and deprived Rhodes of a British trade monopoly.[42] Germany's interest in the Transvaal (discussed in chapter three) and its overt support of Kruger's decision to exclude Uitlanders from political participation in the Transvaal stirred British nationalism and partly influenced Rhodes to engage in the fateful Jameson Raid in December 1895.

The Jameson Raid, poorly planned and executed, was justified on the grounds that conflicts between Uitlanders and Afrikaners endangered security and lives in the Transvaal.[43] Rhodes's objective was far more ambitious than restoring order; he wanted to overthrow Kruger's government and reduce the Afrikaner Republic to a British protectorate so that he could control trade routes as well as gold mining. Since Kruger was clearly cognizant of Rhodes's plans, it was relatively easy for the Afrikaners to capture the leaders of the insurrection. Rhodes, who accepted responsibility for the raid, resigned as Prime Minister of Cape Colony, and Jameson, who organized it, was sent to Britain to be tried, only to serve less than five months in prison after a guilty verdict. The other leaders, including Frank Rhodes, Cecil's brother, were sentenced to death, but Kruger commuted the sentences into fines of £25,000 each.[44] Despite Kruger's leniency and Britain's denial of complicity in the raid, this event was the direct precursor of the Anglo-Boer War.

Immediately after the raid, Orange Free State and the Transvaal concluded a military treaty for mutual protection, Germany falsely raised Afrikaners' expectations of significant German support in the event of Anglo-Boer hostilities, and British nationalism was vigorously resurrected. The Transvaal proceeded to build its military defenses and British troops gathered on the borders of the Afrikaner Republic, even as the two sides negotiated. When Britain refused to withdraw its forces from the border, negotiations were terminated, and war erupted on October 11, 1899.[45] Greatly outnumbered by the British, Afrikaners turned to guerrilla warfare and engaged in a widespread sabotage campaign. Britain responded by burning Afrikaner farms and putting Afrikaner women and children into deplorable concentration camps where as many as 20,000 died. Defeated on the battlefields, the Afrikaners eventually were able to gain political power because of their growing nationalism and serious miscalculations by British authorities when the Union of South Africa was formed. Ironically, it was the defeated Boers who won British compassion, not the Africans.

Election politics in Britain in 1906, shortly after the war, focused attention on South Africa and the inefficient British military campaign. The Liberal Party, which was sympathetic to the Afrikaners, won the election and proceeded to unite the two British colonies and the two Boer Republics to form the Union of South Africa in 1910. Two conflicting organizing principles, one based on racial hatred and denial of equality for Africans, and the other based on partial political rights and greater social equality, were permitted to coexist in the Union of South Africa. British leaders erroneously assumed that superior British values would prevail and that Afrikaners would gradually accept the idea of racial equality.[46] Overlooked was the fact that in the process of making compromises to consolidate the Union, the overwhelming white electorate would ignore black aspirations. Britain also postponed the resolution of conflicting franchise assumptions in the British colonies and the Boer Republics. Finally, Britain underestimated the Afrikaners' nationalism, their contempt for outsiders, their population growth rates,[47] and their deep racial hatred, which was supported by their religious convictions. By 1948 when the National Party gained political control of South Africa, the British were relatively powerless to prevent the Afrikaners from imposing hideous race laws at a time when concepts of human rights and racial equality were gaining worldwide support.[48] But if Britain was unable to prevent apartheid from becoming the constitutional framework of South Africa, Britain's leadership position in the Commonwealth prevented it from escaping responsibility for its serious errors which contributed to the rise of Afrikanerdom; its close ties with the apartheid regime also became a source of friction within the Commonwealth.

## THE COMMONWEALTH'S INFLUENCE ON BRITISH POLICY

As Britain's colonies gained their independence and became members of the Commonwealth, the issue of race predominated. Since colonialism was based in part on the assumption that racial characteristics determined one's status, it was inevitable that racial issues would be emotive. The Commonwealth, inadvertently, reminded citizens of newly independent African, Asian, and Caribbean states that they had once been in a position of social and political subservience.[49] Apartheid became an extremely sensitive issue within the Commonwealth because of that organization's principles against racial discrimination and because the worst aspects of apartheid were being implemented as many African and Asian countries were becoming more assertive about racial equality. South Africa's membership in the Commonwealth focused attention on the issue, especially following the Sharpeville massacre in March 1960.

Prior to Sharpeville, South Africa's Prime Minister Hendrik Verwoerd had announced that a referendum on the question of changing his country's status to a republic would be held. A vote in favor of a republic would require South Africa to apply for continued membership in the Commonwealth, thereby creating an opportunity for the Commonwealth's Afro-Asian members, who were now in the majority, to vote against the apartheid regime.[50] Britain's Harold Macmillan, on the other hand, opposed efforts to expel South Africa. British policy was that neither the United Nations nor the Commonwealth could legitimately intervene in the internal affairs of a member state. Despite widespread opposition to apartheid, Britain, partly out of concern for English-speaking South Africans and its commercial interests, refused to make more than token adjustments in its friendship with South Africa, supported South Africa's retention in the Commonwealth until the last moment, and subsequently ensured that its departure would not significantly alter their relationship.[51]

After its expulsion, South Africa enjoyed strong support from Britain's Conservative government until 1964, when Labour, under Harold Wilson's leadership, came to power. South Africa continued to benefit from Commonwealth preferences and from membership in the Sterling Zone, both based upon bilateral agreements with Britain.[52] Although the Afro-Asian bloc had succeeded in getting rid of South Africa, they lacked the economic power to pressure the U.K. to make more than incremental policy changes. While Wilson clearly recognized the importance of racial issues and their negative effects on Commonwealth unity, no dramatic steps were taken.

African and Asian states seemed to be constantly checked by their depend-ence on the Commonwealth and their realization that open confrontation with Britain on apartheid could irreparably damage the organization, to their detriment more than Britain's. In light of this perception, they usually couched their appeal to Britain in pragmatic terms, arguing, for example, that British arms sales to Pretoria could further Soviet interests in southern Africa.[53]

Britain also clearly benefits from its membership in the Commonwealth. As a major trading nation, access to overseas markets is of vital importance to Britain. Commonwealth countries take approximately thirteen percent of British exports, and this market is likely to grow. Nigeria alone buys almost $2 billion worth of British exports, and approximately a third of British income from overseas investments, excluding petroleum, comes from Commonwealth countries.[54] But the Commonwealth is no longer central to Britain's foreign policy in general and her foreign economic policy in particular. The vast majority of Commonwealth members are mini-states, which would be even less politically significant without their ties to this international organization. The Commonwealth is often their most important link with the rest of the world and the best qualified advocate for their special needs and problems.[55] Many larger states such as Nigeria, Zambia, and Zimbabwe are too preoccupied with internal political and economic problems to significantly influence British foreign policy toward South Africa, despite their strong opposition to apartheid.

Britain's own economic difficulties forced it to shift its focus away from the Commonwealth and toward the European Community (EC). By 1981 nearly fifty percent of Britain's total trade was with the EEC specifically, and around sixty percent was with the EC and European states linked to it.[56] This trend is continuing as Western Europeans move toward greater European unity in 1992. Britain's leverage vis-à-vis the Commonwealth is further enhanced by the fact that the member countries must rely on Britain to gain access to the EC, the world's largest trading unit. Consequently, it is in their interest to have a stronger Britain that can be influential in the EC and simultaneously increase its aid to poorer Commonwealth members. Few countries are willing to risk these tangible economic benefits by pushing Britain too hard on apartheid. Furthermore, many of the governments have lost the moral high ground in their struggle against racial discrimination in South Africa because of their own serious internal ethnic and racial problems. These factors combine to propel Can-ada and Australia into leadership positions in the Commonwealth and into the position of the most prominent Commonwealth opponents of apartheid, while Britain has become increasingly disengaged from Com-monwealth actions against South Africa.

Prime Minister Thatcher reluctantly agreed to minimal measures against apartheid after the Commonwealth meeting at Lyford Cay in the Bahamas in 1985 during which conflicts within the Commonwealth were brought into the open as Zambia and others threatened to leave or to vote Britain out if it did not take stronger actions against South Africa. Their general assumption was that only stronger pressures would bring about fundamental political change in South Africa,[57] and their frustration was vented at Britain because all the other members are relatively powerless; they need Britain to exert influence on Pretoria. By 1987, when the Commonwealth meeting was held in Vancouver, confrontation over South Africa had somewhat subsided, and the Commonwealth's Okanagan Statement on Southern Africa was replete with "with the exception of Britain." The other Commonwealth leaders could not persuade Thatcher to implement "wider, tighter, and more intensified" sanctions against South Africa,[58] partly because the most vocal African advocates of sanctions, Zambia and Zimbabwe, failed to implement the measures they strongly supported in 1985. Instead their interdependence with South Africa moderates their actual policies. The 1989 Commonwealth Summit Conference in Kuala Lumpur, Malaysia did not alter this reality.

## BRITAIN'S ECONOMIC INTERESTS IN SOUTH AFRICA

Britain's economic interests in South Africa have always been of paramount importance in its policy toward the apartheid regime, and neither Labour nor Conservative governments have taken substantive measures to reduce British trade with and investments in South Africa. The Conservatives in particular have clearly articulated a policy of removing government interference with business at home as well as overseas.[59] Many leaders of the Conservative party have had personal business interests in South Africa, and the Monday Club, an influential right-wing group of the Conservative Party, firmly has rejected even the token criticism of apartheid that Prime Minister Macmillan had conceded at the height of the Commonwealth debate on South Africa's participation in that organization.[60] The South African Foundation, a lobbying group, has found it relatively easy to build impressive connections with business leaders in Britain, partly because of Britain's extensive commercial activities in South Africa. For most of modern South African history, English-speaking whites have dominated the economic sector, a factor facilitating contemporary commercial relations between the two countries.

The British government actively promotes international trade because of Britain's weak economy and its dependence on foreign markets for its exports. Similar to Japan, Britain must trade to survive and is therefore extremely sensitive to possible barriers to commercial transactions. Like the Japanese, the British endeavor to separate economic matters from political and other considerations. However, due to international pressures against apartheid and continuing instability within South Africa, it is very difficult to dichotomize politics and economics. Therefore, the British government promotes trade while contending that economic growth is the most pragmatic approach to ending apartheid. Consistent with this view, the government established an Export Credit Guarantee Scheme for British exporters who deal with South Africa.[61] Various government advisory organizations are also utilized. For example, Lord Jellicoe, Chairman of the British Overseas Trade Board, a government body, visited South Africa in 1984 to promote economic relations.[62] The South Africa Trade Association also augments government efforts to promote trade. This association, composed of leading British and South African businessmen, provides its members with relevant economic data about trade and investment opportunities in South Africa and tries to facilitate commerce between the two countries.[63] Britain's aggressive trade policies and its unwillingness to use economic sanctions to achieve its declared goal of helping to end apartheid have inadvertently enhanced Pretoria's leverage.

High unemployment in Britain, estimated at twelve percent in 1988, militates against the utilization of coercive economic instruments to achieve foreign policy objectives and bolsters Thatcher's claim that trade with South Africa protects jobs in Britain as well as jobs in South Africa for blacks. Approximately three million people were unemployed in Britain in 1988, despite greater prosperity in London and the southern part of England. This reality made Thatcher's views attractive to the electorate. However, given the complexity of interests involved, especially those of transnational corporations, it can also be argued that business practices, which are obviously designed to maximize profits for companies and their stockholders, contribute to unemployment. For example, many multinational firms purchase South African fruit, especially apples, at lower prices than what they pay European and British growers in order to increase their profits. Companies such as S and W Berisford, Alex Clark, Lockwoods Foods, Peabody Foods, and Stephens of Brotherton dominate the market in Britain and purchase from both British and South African farmers.[64] Similarly, preferential agreements covering South African coal, iron, and steel also result in job losses as British employees in these industries are negatively affected by new industrial politics in Europe aimed at closing unprofitable coal mines and inefficient iron and steel plants. Lower priced South African products are imported.[65]

Britain's main imports from South Africa are minerals, industrial raw materials, fruit, paper, pulp, and wool. Strategic minerals such as platinum, chromium, and vanadium are regarded to be of critical importance to Britain's economy and defense industries. Japan, the United States, West Germany, and Britain remain the major importers of South African products. In 1987 the value of Britain's imports stood at $1,088 million, down from $1,226 million in 1986, or eleven percent, compared to $1,320 million for the United States which was down by forty-seven percent from $2,476 million in 1986. Japan's imports rose from $2,248 million in 1986 to $2,455 million in 1987, or nine percent.[66] Major British exports to South Africa included a range of manufactured goods, automobiles, machinery, and various financial services. According to the Anti-Apartheid Movement and the Shipping Research Bureau, Britain also exports oil. Britain has always voted against resolutions in the U.N.'s Security Council calling for an oil embargo against South Africa, even though since 1979 British petroleum exports have been covered by guidelines that theoretically ensure that oil goes only to members of the European Community and the International Energy Agency.[67] Major loopholes in these guidelines allow British North Sea oil to be sold to South Africa through third countries, and companies such as Royal Dutch Shell, Crawford and Russel, Brown and Root, Northsea Engineering Industry, the Howden Group, and Humphries and Glasgow allegedly sell oil and petroleum products to South Africa.[68] In 1987 the value of British exports to South Africa were valued at $1,156 million, up from $1,250 million in 1986, an increase of twenty-five percent. U.S. exports climbed from $1,144 million in 1986 to $1,253 million in 1987, or ten percent. Japan's trade expanded more dramatically, from $1,357 million in 1986 to $1,882 million in 1987, an increase of thirty-nine percent.[69] In addition to trade, British companies have large investments in South Africa.

Britain historically has been the largest source of foreign investments in South Africa, and English-speaking white South Africans have remained the major entrepreneurial class in their country. In 1961, for example, British investment represented fifty-nine percent of South Africa's foreign liabilities and more than seventy percent of all direct foreign investment there. By 1970, due to competition from other countries, British holdings decreased to about fifty-five percent of all foreign assets, more than the combined shares of all other countries.[70] By 1988 the British share was roughly forty percent and the total value was about $9.1 billion.

Due principally to deteriorating political and economic conditions in South Africa and strong pressures from anti-apartheid groups in the United States for companies to disinvest, British companies such as Barclays Bank found it more profitable to withdraw from South Africa than to remain. Britain, however, does not legally prohibit companies from making new investments; the government, while asking companies to voluntarily comply with the ban on new investments, has interpreted the ban in such a way as to exclude from its provisions financial transactions and bank loans in support of normal trading activities, portfolio investment, or increased investment from funds earned inside South Africa.[71] Following Mandela's release, Britain unilaterally decided to lift the ban on new investments.

Many British corporations have joint ventures with South African firms and are often run by locally recruited managers, making them virtually indistinguishable from indigenous South African companies.[72] Although such ventures are formed to lessen pressure from anti-apartheid groups and shareholders in Britain, many are the result of South Africa's stringent import policies. Pretoria, threatened with sanctions for over forty years, has responded by trying to become more self-sufficient by passing local content legislation to encourage foreign companies to invest directly in manufacturing subsidiaries in South Africa.[73]

One of the most controversial issues involving British investments, prior to Namibia's independence in 1990, was uranium mining by Rio Tinto Zinc Corporation in Namibia's Rossing mine. The first major contract between Rio Tinto and the British government, signed in 1968, provided for the delivery of 7,500 tons of uranium from Namibia to Britain's Atomic Energy Authority. This occurred while the Labour Party was in power. When Margaret Thatcher became Prime Minister, she appointed the former Rio Tinto Zinc's director, Lord Carrington, as her Foreign Secretary.[74] According to the Anti-Apartheid Movement in London, Britain undermines the ban on uranium imports into the United States under the Comprehensive Anti-Apartheid Act of 1986 by processing uranium into uranium-hexafloruide in Britain and exporting it to the United States as a British manufactured product.[75]

Compared to American firms, British companies face less public pressure and are generally less interested in engaging in political actions widely perceived in the United States as contributing to the end of apartheid. When the American Chamber of Commerce in South Africa suggested that foreign business associations cooperate to exert pressure on Pretoria, British firms argued that such activities would be inappropriate for them. Similarly, the British Industry Council in South Africa, which coordinates British companies' responses to questions concerning apartheid, unanimously rejected the idea of lobbying the South African government.[76] Both the British government and the companies tend to focus instead on the Code of Conduct for Companies from the European Community as the standard by which their behavior should be appraised.

The EC Code, based on the British Code of Practice and similar to the Sullivan Principles, is designed to nullify major apartheid laws which deal with employment and race relations in the workplace. It calls for companies to (1) allow their employees to join trade unions; (2) give equal pay for equal work and provide equal opportunities for all employees; (3) develop occupational training programs; (4) improve living conditions for their employees; (5) abolish segregation in the work place; and (6) encourage black businesses by subcontracting.[77] These provisions are voluntary, and many firms hide behind the Code instead of taking aggressive measures against racial discrimination in South Africa. But the actual purpose of the Code was to justify British investments in South Africa and to deflect international pressures for economic sanctions and corporate disinvestment.[78] The British government's policies toward business and economic problems in Britain seem to preclude any radical changes in its commercial links with South Africa. Furthermore, Britain's economic interests in black African states do not provide the various governments with sufficient leverage to counteract the conservative tendencies of British business in South Africa.

During the mid-1970s and early 1980s the possibility of countervailing measures by African states, particularly Nigeria, against British companies' extensive trade links with South Africa was taken seriously. Nigeria, a leading oil producer, was widely perceived as Africa's new economic power that could seriously challenge South Africa's dominant position on the continent. A major objective of Nigeria's foreign policy was to isolate South Africa economically, politically, militarily, and culturally by forcing companies to choose between the two countries, and by enlisting widespread international support against Pretoria.[79] From Britain's perspective, Nigeria posed a credible threat because it could (1) galvanize African states against Britain; (2) influence other Western states which depended on Nigeria's petroleum and markets to exert pressure on Britain; and (3) take direct action against British interests in Nigeria itself.[80] Nigeria implemented its threat against Barclays Bank in 1976 following reports that Barclays' South African subsidiary had purchased approximately $13 million worth of South African defense bonds that were used to help fight the war against black nationalist guerrillas, many of whom were supported by Nigeria.[81] In early 1978 the Nigerian government ordered the removal of all public money from Barclays of Nigeria and demanded that the bank reduce its foreign employees by a third. In 1979 Nigeria nationalized British Petroleum (BP), claiming that a tanker chartered by BP, and which called at a Nigerian port, was owned by South Africans.[82] However, Nigeria took no further actions against British companies after 1979, even though many of them operated in both South Africa and Nigeria. By the mid-1980s Nigeria no longer seemed to pose a credible threat to Britain, largely because its political affairs were in chaos and its economy was bankrupt. Overly ambitious schemes, widespread corruption, agricultural decline, and plummeting petroleum prices severely weakened Nigeria's bargaining power.

## FAMILY AND CULTURAL TIES

British economic interests in South Africa are strengthened by social relationships and individual bonds between British citizens and English-speaking white South Africans. Historical antagonism between the Afrikaners and the British continues to complicate Britain's policy toward Pretoria. While Margaret Thatcher may view the Boers in terms of their heroic resistance to British domination and sympathize with their dilemma of wanting to retain white control under difficult circumstances, there is a noticeable division between English-speaking South Africans and the Afrikaners. Until quite recently, the National Party depended almost totally on Afrikaner support, and the opposition Progressive Federal Party represented English-speaking whites, many of whom deplored the harsh racial domination legislated in 1948 when the Nationalists gained political power. Historically more outward-looking and sensitive to world opinion, English-speaking whites wanted South Africa to remain within the Commonwealth. Afrikaners, however, resented external interference and viewed links with Britain as being inconsistent with their growing nationalism.[83]

Approximately forty percent of the five million white South Africans are of British birth and descent. Of these two million persons, at least half of them may be entitled to claim the right to immigrate to Britain. Many of them have British passports and dual British and South African citizenship. Like Israel, which is concerned about South African Jews, British politicians cannot ignore British citizens abroad or their relatives throughout England, Scotland, Northern Ireland, and Wales. While many Afrikaners severed their links with the Netherlands more than three hundred years ago, English-speaking South Africans have cultivated relations with Britain for almost two hundred years.

Historical ties have been strengthened by immigration. British settlers flocked to South Africa in the early 1800s and actually outnumbered the original European settlers, the Afrikaners, by the early 20th century. Since 1945 Britain has been the source of more than fifty percent of white immigrants to South Africa, with the exception of the mid-1970s and early 1980s when large numbers of Portuguese citizens fled Angola and Mozambique and white Rhodesians left Zimbabwe. About half the whites leaving South Africa usually go to Britain, a migration which fluctuates according to economic developments in Britain and political instability or increased repression in South Africa.[84] As conditions deteriorated in South Africa in 1961 and again from 1976 to the present, many English-speaking whites decided to leave South Africa. In addition, improved economic opportunities in Britain reduced the flow of immigrants from that country, creating a serious shortage of skilled labor in South Africa.

This movement of people has created two contradictory reactions in Britain to apartheid. On the one hand it fosters emotional ties between relatives and broader "kith and kin" feelings among Britons. British sympathy for white South Africans in general is also based on a general belief that white rule is preferable to black rule in South Africa, although racial discrimination is tolerated less by the English-speaking community. Those who actively promote better relations with Pretoria, many of them members of Parliament, have family, friends, and business contacts and interests in South Africa.[85] On the other hand, personal bonds have also engendered very strong anti-apartheid commitments among South African exiles living in Britain. A significant number of them have influential positions in the Anti-Apartheid Movement in London and access to the Labour and Liberal parties. Exiles are generally extremely politicized South Africans who, for a variety of reasons, could no longer fight apartheid inside their country. Since both kith and kin sentiments and anti-apartheid feelings resonate in British politics and society, it is not surprising that British citizens are aware of developments in South Africa. The British media carries more news and analysis on South Africa than the media of any other country in the world, and the largest foreign press bureau in London is that of the South African Argus newspaper chain.[86]

The promotion of tourism between Britain and South Africa continues, and cultural ties are both encouraged and challenged. When the United States banned direct flights to and from South Africa, British Airways, which is very profitable to South Africa, made a determined effort to attract South African-U.S. air traffic through a wide range of promotional advertisements.[87] While many Europeans and Japanese subscribe to the view that one nation's sanctions are another's opportunity, there are additional considerations in relation to continuing direct flights between Britain and South Africa, the most obvious of which is family ties. South Africans with British passports are not as committed as the Afrikaners to staying in South Africa and have more interaction with the outside world. Many British citizens visit their relatives in South Africa and would like to maintain continued direct access to them in case of emergencies. Although David Owen and other members of Parliament argue that contacts with relatives would continue if flights were diverted to neighboring Frontline States,[88] British citizens seem unconvinced that African states would be as reliable as South Africa.

## MILITARY AND STRATEGIC INTERESTS

Britain's historical relationship with South Africa, its extensive economic interests, the intensification of Cold War ideologies, and the generally accepted assumption that the security of Western countries depended in part on the Cape route being under the control of an ally contributed to military cooperation between the two countries. Implementation of legislation to strengthen racial discrimination against black South Africans seemed irrelevant to Britain's security interests, and in 1955 the Simonstown Agreement with South Africa was signed. It provided for joint naval exercises, arms sales, and general collaboration on intelligence and defense matters.

When white and black police officers fired indiscriminately at black protesters at Sharpeville in 1960, Western countries reassessed their policies toward the apartheid regime. The United States in particular was experiencing its own racial conflicts which were meticulously exploited by the Soviet Union as the two superpowers struggled for the hearts and minds of citizens of newly independent Third World countries. Pretoria's success at brutally crushing the civil disobedience movement in the 1950s—at the time Britain supplied weapons probably used to suppress dissent—clearly worried many in Britain, Western Europe, North America, and Commonwealth countries. It also provoked the United Nations into action.[89]

The U.N. Security Council voted in 1963 for a nonmandantory arms embargo against South Africa. International action against Pretoria created serious dilemmas for Britain, especially for Harold Macmillan's Conservative Party then in power. Several Conservatives in Parliament expressed reservations about what they perceived as Britain's abandonment of the white Commonwealth when South Africa was expelled and were reluctant to enforce an arms embargo against Pretoria. But to escape embarrassment, naval visits to Simonstown were drastically curtailed. Between 1961 and 1965 only five frigates and four submarines visited the base for maintenance and repairs.[90] The Conservatives, however, continued arms sales to South Africa, and although the new Labour government under Harold Wilson agreed to observe the boycott when it came to power in 1964, numerous loopholes existed. Since the arms embargo to which Britain subscribed clearly frustrated the objectives of the Simonstown agreement, British businessmen and politicians opted for a liberal interpretation of the former and argued for honoring existing contracts under the latter. For example, the British believed that some military equipment could not be used by South African authorities to suppress blacks, and that weapons essential for ensuring security interests around the Cape were exempt from the embargo. Spare parts and replacement systems needed by South Africa were also excluded. More important, no action was taken against subsidiaries of British firms located in South Africa which manufactured military equipment.[91] However, in order not to be totally inconsistent with the U.N. embargo, and in response to anti-apartheid pressures within the Labour Party, Wilson decided to terminate supplies of new armaments in 1966 once most outstanding contracts had been fulfilled.[92]

By 1967 Britain had concluded that the Simonstown agreement should be renegotiated in light of changed circumstances. South Africa's contribution to Western security interests was perceived as being less crucial, and perhaps a political liability. Britain's reassessment had a severe psychological impact on the white minority regime. An important component of South Africa's leverage vis-à-vis the West, often used to justify apartheid, was removed. Assumptions about the strategic significance of the Cape route were no longer blindly accepted.[93] But political, strategic, and economic interests are not constant, and Britain's Conservative Party did not wholeheartedly subscribe to Labour's South Africa policies.

European countries, principally France, Italy, and West Germany, took advantage of Britain's high visibility and quietly sold arms to South Africa. While Britain's military cooperation with Pretoria diminished, France's expanded to such a large degree that by the late 1960s it had displaced Britain as South Africa's primary supplier of military weapons. Given the pivotal role of business in Britain's foreign relations and the Conservatives' belief in separating economic interests from political considerations, France, Italy, and West Germany had to be challenged. Another factor influencing British policy was the Soviet navy's increased involvement in the Indian Ocean amidst growing instability in Rhodesia, Mozambique, and Angola. Egypt's decision to close the Suez Canal during the Six-Day War with Israel in 1967 revitalized the view that the Cape was of strategic interest. Soviet naval exercises in the area underscored this argument. Finally, many Conservatives expressed strong support for the white minority in both South Africa and Rhodesia.[94]

When the Conservatives under Prime Minister Edward Heath returned to power in 1970, Labour's policies were reversed. Two days after the election, Hilgard Muller, South Africa's foreign minister, visited Edward Heath and Foreign Secretary Sir Alec Douglas-Home in London, and approximately one month after their meeting, the Conservative government made public its decision to resume arms sales to South Africa, thereby altering the previous policy of more or less adhering to the U.N. arms embargo.[95] Concerted efforts were made to strengthen South Africa's navy and to increase the frequency and size of joint naval exercises. The largest exercise involved a flotilla of eleven British warships and lasted fourteen days. However, this total disregard for African, international, and domestic opposition to apartheid backfired. When Labour defeated the Conservatives in 1974, the arms embargo was reimposed, contracts for military weapons were abrogated, and the Simonstown Agreement was cancelled on June 15, 1975.[96] Cooperation on military intelligence, however, continued through South African military attachés in London.

Members of Parliament persistently questioned Thatcher's Conservative government on the relationship between military attachés from the South African Embassy and personnel from defense forces and the Defense Department. In response to questions from Tony Banks, Secretary of State for Defense Stanley stated that from 1983 to 1986 South African attachés, as part of organized groups of attachés from other foreign and Commonwealth countries, made about thirty visits to defense installations and attended six defense-related social and ceremonial functions in Britain. He also indicated that in November 1983 the South African air attaché visited search and rescue establishments at Pitreavie and Bulmer, and in May 1984 the military attaché visited the army school of physical education.[97] International pressure following South Africa's declaration of a State of Emergency in 1986 forced Western European countries not to grant accreditation to South African military attachés and to withdraw theirs from South Africa in protest. Lynda Chalker, Minister of State at the Foreign and Commonwealth Office, informed the South African government in July 1986 that Britain would not grant accreditation to the current military attaché, Colonel Crowder.[98] Two British military attachés in South

Africa were withdrawn in September 1986 as part of the package of EC sanctions, a decision reluctantly taken by Margaret Thatcher who bemoaned the loss, noting that "it means we don't get as much information as we should otherwise."[99]

Britain's sympathy toward the white minority regime indirectly motivates private citizens to violate the arms embargo and to collaborate militarily with South Africa. Companies such as British Petroleum, Imperial Chemical, and Plessey contribute to South Africa's defense. BP, which owns several hundred gasoline stations and half of the largest oil refinery in South Africa, sells oil to the police. Imperial Chemical controls about forty percent of AECI, its South African affiliate, which makes explosives for the mining industry as well as tear gas for the police and army. Plessey, an electronics manufacturer, allegedly supplied South Africa with high technology communications and radar equipment in 1987 in violation of the arms embargo.[100] In 1985 British courts found four British citizens guilty of conspiring to smuggle high technology parts for guided missiles as well as aircraft spares and artillery gun sight gears to South Africa. Michael Gardiner, the leader, was sentenced to fifteen months in prison and fined approximately $170,000.[101] In February 1986 British customs officials discovered that cargoes aboard the ship St. Maguire at Felixstowe, described as agricultural machinery bound for South Africa, were actually components of one hundred and forty mm howitzers being exported in violation of the U.N. arms embargo.[102] Indeed, it may be argued that Britain's strategies for eliminating apartheid inadvertently encourage such violations.

## STRATEGIES

British policymakers have stated their unequivocal opposition to comprehensive economic sanctions as an instrument of foreign policy, although this is not consistently practiced. In South Africa's case, it is unlikely that Britain will adopt severe measures. With the Commonwealth's importance diminished, the African states reversing into greater economic decline, and an unstated but widespread recognition of human rights abuses throughout Africa, Britain is under less pressure from these sources to change its policies. Unlike the situation in Rhodesia, Britain has no constitutional responsibility for South Africa, and African states have clearly lost the moral authority to appeal to Britain's morality because of their own disregard for the individual's freedoms. Furthermore, Britain's economic progress and growing competition for international markets have made its economic interests in South Africa even more important.[103] Thus, only limited sanctions have been supported by Britain. Its basic strategies are to oppose economic sanctions, to encourage economic growth and black empowerment without jeopardizing its own relationship with the white minority regime, and to provide economic, technical, and military assistance to the Frontline States.


## SANCTIONS

Britain's position on economic sanctions reflects serious confusion, whether deliberate or unintentional, in its overall South Africa policy. Statements from the Foreign and Commonwealth Office indicate that while the Conservatives are opposed to sanctions as an instrument of foreign policy, they present no credible alternatives for bringing about peaceful change in South Africa. Contradictory demands within the black South African community in relation to sanctions contribute to Britain's muddled policy. Archbishop Desmond Tutu's argument that punitive sanctions would assist in forcing the white minority regime to seriously consider abandoning apartheid and creating a non-racial society is countered by Chief Gatsha Buthelezi, who advocates economic growth as the more constructive approach to ending white domination. Britain's interests play a role in influencing policymakers in London to accept the latter strategy.

Britain's view, articulated by Prime Minister Thatcher and her former Foreign Minister Geoffrey Howe, is that economic sanctions are counterproductive and will actually force the white community to retreat further into the *laager*. Instead of encouraging peaceful change, punitive actions are seen as hardening white attitudes, strengthening the right wing, compelling Pretoria to develop a siege economy, and undermining black employment.[104] But Britain's opposition to punitive sanctions appears to be based less on a careful analysis of how such measures would erode apartheid and more on the fact that significant alterations of the status quo could create severe economic problems for Britian. Many British citizens residing in South Africa are likely to leave in the event of dramatic changes, and almost 120,000 British workers could be unemployed as a consequence of comprehensive sanctions against South Africa. As Howe put it, "One is entitled to ask: What guarantee is there that, if those jobs were destroyed in Britain, they would not be recreated elsewhere in the world?"[105] However, if sacrificing these jobs would help end racial oppression and advance individual freedoms in South Africa, would Britain change its view? When confronted with Argentina's aggression in the Falklands/Malvinas, Thatcher not only called for international sanctions but also dispatched the Royal Navy and marines to restore freedom for 1,800 British subjects almost 8,000 miles from Britain. While this action demonstrates the widely held view among nations that achieving freedom sometimes requires individual sacrifices, including a willingess to sacrifice one's life, Britain's policy toward South Africa involves no meaningful sacrifices. In short,

Britain is skillfully evading the challenge to bring about peaceful change in South Africa, despite its declaratory policies.

British policymakers generally refer to Rhodesia as an example of the failure of economic sanctions to effectuate political and social transformation. David Owen, leader of the Social Democratic Party in 1986, noted that in addition to an extremely porous border between Rhodesia and South Africa, sanctions were not carefully and determinedly applied and that successive British governments connived in breaking sanctions.[106] Former Prime Minister Edward Heath also contends that a myth has developed about Rhodesian sanctions: "It is not time to say that sanctions had no effect on Rhodesia. They did take a long time, but they had the effect of inducing Mr. Smith to negotiate with Lord Home, when he was Foreign Secretary, something which Mr. Smith had previously refused to do."[107] The Rhodesian case presents serious analytical problems as well as practical dilemmas for British policymakers; those who regard sanctions as ineffective in the Rhodesian case unintentionally argue for the efficacy of military force. If sanctions did not bring Ian Smith to the negotiating table, then the logical assumption is that guerrilla activities induced him to perceive his interests in a different light.

Since 1960 the Labour Party has endorsed limited economic sanctions. Following the Sharpeville massacre, it joined the Liberal Party and the Trade Union Congress in boycotting selected South African products for a month. Labour M.P.s are the most articulate advocates of economic measures against Pretoria and constantly criticize the Conservatives for assisting Pretoria by their reluctance to enforce sanctions and by acting as a brake on pressure against the white minority regime in the EC and the Commonwealth.[108] But, as indicated earlier, Labour in power does not behave radically differently from Conservatives in power. Neither party has been willing to drastically alter British policy toward South Africa, with the exception of arms sales under Labour. Consistent pressure against apartheid comes from the Anti-Apartheid Movement, the Church of England, the Roman Catholic church, the National Union of Students, and labor unions. For example, Barclays Bank decided to withdraw from South Africa, partly because of intensive campaigns against it by these groups.

British public opinion is generally supportive of the Conservatives' policy against economic sanctions, contrary to claims by the opposition. A Harris Research Centre poll in 1986 showed that only half of the British public believed that the government should impose economic sanctions, and most opposed specific sanctions. For example, sixty-four percent rejected a ban on direct flights between Britain and South Africa; sixty-eight percent did not favor a ban on all sporting contracts, and fifty-nine percent opposed a trade embargo. Only a moratorium on new investments received a slim forty-six to forty-three percent majority.[109] The British public remains largely indifferent to debates on South Africa, despite widespread awareness of apartheid. Britain's decision to adopt primarily symbolic measures against Pretoria was influenced by growing international pressures against apartheid.

Denmark's ban on all trade with South Africa in May 1986, in an effort to push the EC toward economic sanctions against Pretoria, was opposed by Britain, West Germany, and Portugal. Similarly, a Dutch proposal calling for a boycott of imports of South African fruit, vegetables, coal, iron, steel, and wine was vetoed by Howe and West German Foreign Minister Hans-Dietrich Genscher. Britain, which consumes almost half of South Africa's fruit and vegetable exports to the EC, advocated positive measures such as scholarships, legal assistance for detainees under the state of emergency, and pooling European humanitarian aid to promote peaceful political change.[110] Prime Minister Thatcher continued to rely on constructive engagement and negotiations, despite recommendations by the Eminent Persons Group for more stringent measures against apartheid.

In 1986, Britain successfully persuaded EC leaders to postpone a decision on additional sanctions until Foreign Secretary Howe had an opportunity to meet with President Botha to discuss (1) the release of Nelson Mandela and other political prisoners; (2) lifting the ban on the ANC and other political organizations; and (3) starting a national dialogue with "authentic leaders" of the black community. Failure of Howe's mission would result in consideration of a ban on new investments in South Africa, and on imports of coal, iron, steel, and Krugerrands.[111] From Thatcher's perspective, Howe was continuing the Eminent Persons Group mission that was suddenly abandoned when South Africa launched military raids against Zimbabwe, Zambia, and Botswana. Not surprisingly, Howe failed to convince Botha to begin serious negotiations with the black majority.

On September 25, 1986, Britain reversed its policy on sanctions and agreed to join other EC countries in a sanctions package that included a ban on (1) nuclear cooperation with South Africa; (2) new investments; (3) arms sales; (4) oil exports; (5) investment credits; (6) Krugerrands; (7) export of computers; and (8) export credits insurance.[112] Britain did not fully endorse the entire package, and compliance with several measures it supported was voluntary. By late 1987 it was clear that British and West German reluctance to fully endorse sanctions had rendered the EC package virtually meaningless. A web of legitimate loopholes through which trade and continued links with South Africa could be maintained was created by qualified definitions and exception clauses.[113]

## ECONOMIC GROWTH AND BLACK EMPOWERMENT

In the United States the demise of constructive engagement has led to greater emphasis on black empowerment as a strategy for ending apartheid. The basic assumption is that economic growth will eventually help to eliminate racial barriers and to undermine structural aspects of apartheid. However, careful analysis suggests that focusing on economic growth alone can only perpetuate the status quo as far as political power is concerned. Britain's preference for black empowerment as an instrument of change is predicated on the belief that any hostile action would force whites into the *laager* of self-reliance. But this view disregards the current trend of economically isolated societies to open up. Iran, the U.S.S.R., Vietnam, and China are examples of countries which have discovered that economic isolation in an interdependent world is suicidal. While it is clear that reduced economic growth would have an adverse effect on the future prosperity of all races in South Africa and on South Africa's neighbors,[114] economic growth alone is unlikely to alter fundamental political structures and result in power sharing. Apart from the fact that there is no direct correlation between black economic prosperity and whites' willingness to include blacks in the governing of South Africa, if white South African leaders wanted to encourage black political participation they could talk with black leaders and allow non-violent opposition parties to operate freely, a step taken by de Klerk in early 1990.

But economic growth can contribute to change. From Britain's perspective, economic prosperity has led to an increase in black economic power, the emergence of black trade unions, and improved facilities for black education and training. Industrialization is viewed as a major spur to dismantling apartheid as the needs of a modern society override political dogma and racial barriers are broken down.[115] British policymakers also argue that a high rate of economic growth is needed just to keep up with the annual growth in the black work force, and that without it there would be severe social and economic consequences for blacks.[116] Although blacks would undoubtedly suffer from a serious economic decline, one can argue that apartheid could also face a severe setback because the strategy of white domination includes some employment opportunities for blacks. Since the existence of apartheid depends to a large extent on black cooperation and acquiescence, to be effective, black empowerment as a strategy would have to focus on education as well as communication with black political organizations.

British assistance to black South Africans is an integral component of its strategy of black empowerment. However, if this approach is the moral equivalent of war on apartheid, it is likely to fail because of the relatively small sums of money allocated. Britain gives about $4.89 million each year to European Community projects designed to assist those who confront apartheid and are suffering from it. Another $34.23 million was allocated for the 1987–1992 period to help promote black South African economic advancement and training. Furthermore, approximately five hundred black South African students were in Britain on scholarships in 1988.[117] At best, these figures represents an incremental approach to what is generally perceived as a crisis situation in South Africa. Relations with the ANC seem to support this view.

In 1985 Britain established secret contacts with the ANC and openly received Oliver Tambo, the ANC's leader, on June 24, 1986, in an apparent reversal of its policy of not talking with "terrorists" who do not renounce violence. While the meeting with Lynda Chalker was not an indication that Britain officially recognized the ANC, it marked a shift in the government's policy, a development denounced by Pretoria as being a capitulation to terrorism as a political weapon.[118] According to Chalker, the central objective of contacts between British officials and the ANC was to bring home the importance of a suspension of violence on all sides in South Africa in order to promote a constructive dialogue. Another concern was the role of communists within the ANC. In Chalker's view, "if the Communists take over, Nationalists will be denied the means of political expression. That is why we have called for an end to apartheid."[119] She seemed oblivious to the fact that black South Africans are presently denied basic human rights in a non-communist South Africa.

## BRITAIN'S POLICY TOWARD THE FRONTLINE STATES

Many of the Frontline States (Botswana, Lesotho, Swaziland, Zambia, Malawi, and Zimbabwe) are members of the Commonwealth and have significant historical, economic, and political ties to Britain. As discussed in chapter eight, these states are economically and strategically interdependent with South Africa, due in part to Britain's colonial rule of much of the area. In an attempt to diminish their dependence on South Africa, the various countries decided to form the Southern Africa Development Coordination Conference (SADCC) in 1980, which emphasized economic development and the construction of alternative transportation routes for member states. Mozambique and Zimbabwe are generally regarded as the major states by British policymakers. Mozambique is important because of its transport routes to the Indian Ocean, and Zimbabwe is viewed as the political key to the region because of its relatively strong economy, excellent infrastructure, and its military strength.

Britain provides financial and technical assistance to SADCC. In addition to $1,335 million in bilateral aid to individual countries in the region betwen 1980 and 1986, Britain allocated about $73.35 million to SADCC's projects, which included the rehabilitation of the Limpopo railway from Chicualacuala to Maputo in cooperation with both Zimbabwe and Mozambique.[120] While these actions may strengthen the economies of the Frontline States and reduce their dependence on transportation routes through South Africa, they also allow South Africa to continue to play a significant role in the region. South African authorities, concerned about both their international image and economic interests in the region, encouraged Western countries to help Mozambique with investments routed through South Africa. Prime Minister Thatcher, a friend of Samora Machel, leader of Mozambique until his death in an airplane crash in 1987, indicated that British investment in the Frontline States should go through South Africa. In light of Britain's huge economic stakes in southern Africa, this decision undoubtedly benefits British businesses based there. Perhaps more important, financial transactions through South Africa would not only reinforce that country's position as the center of the region, but would also provide it with scarce capital and assist in its export-led recovery.[121] Britain's interests would not adversely affect South Africa.

When David Owen and other opposition members of Parliament advocated a ban on direct intercontinental air travel into South Africa, Thatcher argued against this move, pointing out that such flights are conducted under legal contract, and that specific obligations in those contracts could not be suddenly abrogated.[122] Moreover, the approximately one million South Africans with British passports and relatives in Britain could not be overlooked. The basic idea behind banning direct flights was that if planes had to land at airports in neighboring black states, the balance of power in the region would be slightly shifted in their favor, and if Pretoria launched military attacks against its neighbors, direct flights between them and South Africa would be terminated. The psychological impact on apartheid could be profound, even if South African aviation technicians assisted the Frontline States. Another way of empowering the Frontline States is to provide military assistance.

South Africa's destabilization of the neighboring countries is widely viewed as part of its general strategy of weakening them and ensuring their continued reliance on South African markets, transportation, and investments. Equally important, destabilization also enhances Pretoria's military and political power vis-à-vis states that offer assistance to the ANC. But South Africa's defense establishment's objectives have not necessarily been in harmony with the interests of South Africa's business community. While the military has supported the Mozambican National Resistance Movement, or Renamo, businessmen have been concerned about the adverse economic effects of Renamo's ruthless activities in Mozambique. As mentioned earlier, English-speaking South Africans have traditionally been business-oriented. Britain's decision in 1985 to provide limited military training for Mozambique's army at Zimbabwe's army base in the Inyanga Mountains close to Mozambique's border, and to supply radios and uniforms could be construed as an attempt to protect business interests jeopardized by Renamo's destruction of Mozambique's infrastructure,[123] especially the Cabora Bassa dam. It can also be seen as a low-cost political move by Thatcher to deflect criticism of her strong opposition to economic sanctions against Pretoria. British advisors freely admit that a program designed to train about three hundred troops a year cannot have a great impact on Mozambique's army or prevent Renamo from widespread sabotage.[124] South Africa is neither threatened nor deterred by such a small program.

It seems clear that Britain's policy toward South Africa is not seriously aimed at influencing the white minority regime to share power with South Africa's black majority. Negotiations with Pretoria are calculated to preserve the political status quo while hoping for a reduction in racial oppression. Whatever British leaders may think of the status quo in South Africa, it is clear that they have no inclination or incentive to disturb a profitable relationship.

# 3

# WEST GERMANY

*Comprehensive Evolutionary Change*

West Germany's foreign policy is inextricably linked to the emergence of human rights as a pivotal issue in the internal politics of many countries and as a broadly shared objective of the international political system. More than any other factor, Nazism directly influenced Western countries to reevaluate their commitment to widely accepted concepts of legal positivism which emphasized subordination of individual freedoms to dictates of the state or community. Even the liberals of nineteenth century Germany, who embraced natural law and natural rights, viewed rights as belonging to communities rather than to individuals. By 1918 proponents of legal positivism argued that justice was essentially the correct enforcement of the law, and law was the command of the sovereign. Rights were what the courts allowed one to do.[1] The tragic consequences of legal positivism were manifested when Hitler came to power and made the courts subservient to him, forcing them to deprive Jews of their rights. His hatred of Jews and other groups he regarded as subhuman culminated in an abhorrent systematic program of genocide against them that shocked the conscience of mankind and mobilized world opinion against the concept and practice of racial superiority and discrimination. Under these circumstances, South Africa's system of apartheid, implemented in 1948, became an anomaly and anathema in the postwar international society.

While there is a strong desire in West Germany to pursue a foreign policy that has a clear moral basis, there is no evidence to suggest that this concern with moralism extends to black South Africans. Apart from the fact that Germany seems to subscribe to a Eurocentric view of human rights that generally exempts African leaders from responsibility for their abuse of individuals' freedoms and usually disregards the suffering of

Africans, the historic guilt that motivates Germany's moral concerns is specifically related to Jews. As Lily Feldman stated, Germans were desperate to put their recent past far behind them, and Jews settling in Israel were fleeing a Europe defined for more than a decade by Germany. Germany wanted to forget a past that Jews refused to forget.[2] What is called "the special relationship" between Israel and West Germany is built primarily on a persistent appreciation of morality and guilt. But Israel and West Germany have failed to adopt a more inclusive view of and respect for human rights. Both countries seem to suffer from a moral parochialism that views rights as exclusively belonging to one group and not the other. As is discussed in chapter five, Israel's demands for preferential treatment from West Germany, based on moral grounds, do not influence it to extend the same consideration to West Bank Palestinians or South African blacks. Similarly, West Germany is far more concerned with protecting its economic interests and the welfare of the white minority regime than it is with aggressively implementing a policy that would contribute to greater freedoms for the black majority.

West Germany's South Africa policy is closely akin to Britain's in that both countries advocate peaceful change but fail to provide the necessary resources to assist the transition from white domination to a multi-racial South African society. Despite the overwhelming military, economic, and political power at the disposal of the white minority government, both Britain and West Germany are apparently preoccupied with the possibility of black racism replacing white racism.[3] Consequently, both favor a policy of constructive engagement which presupposes respect for the sovereignty and territorial integrity of states. Thus the West German government refrains from interfering in South Africa's internal affairs, while continuing to safeguard its economic interests and declaring its support for peaceful change. Like Britain, it opposes meaningful sanctions against Pretoria and takes advantage of European Political Cooperation and the prominence of the United States in world affairs in order to dilute any actions that might significantly affect its interests in South Africa and simultaneously to avoid negative international public opinion. Bonn's approach to the South African problem is clearly influenced by the broader setting in which its foreign policy is made and by the historical circumstances that shaped the newly created state of West Germany in 1949.

## FOREIGN POLICYMAKING IN WEST GERMANY

Defeated in World War II, Germany was divided by the Soviet Union and the Western allies to create East Germany under communist domination and West Germany under allied occupation. The Occupation Statute, which established West Germany, granted the new political entity limited sovereignty. The Allied High Commission, which succeeded the military governors of the occupation regime, controlled West Germany's diplomatic and commercial relations with other countries and was granted authority to supervise internal political and economic developments.[4] Germany was deprived of moral credibility, military and political power, economic strength, and sovereignty, the key characteristics of an independent country. Its national security interests were largely determined by the power and rivalry of the United States and the Soviet Union. In fact, had it not been for Cold War polarization between East and West, the Western powers would have had little interest in removing economic and political restrictions imposed on West Germany and restoring its military capability. Without the need to contain the spread of communism by rearming West Germany, there would have been little incentive to assist Bonn in achieving its objectives of political and economic recovery.[5]

The strategic and political interests of the Western allies in the wake of the Korean war influenced them to terminate their regulations of major industries and recognize West Germany's sovereignty over its domestic and international affairs. The gradual removal of economic controls resulted in the opening of production bottlenecks that had retarded economic recovery since the late 1940s.[6] However, even after West Germany acquired the right to conduct its own foreign policy, its international relations were strongly influenced by other countries' interests. Instead of Bonn's own foreign relations affecting its international milieu, West Germany's policy and interests were determined by the bipolar structures of postwar Europe.[7] Its major foreign policy goals of reintegration into the world community, loyalty to the Western alliance, reunification of a divided Germany, and economic and political recovery reflected this new reality.

## BONN'S POLICY IN WASHINGTON'S SHADOW

West Germany's realization of its foreign policy objectives depended to a large extent on its relationship with the Western alliance in general and with the United States in particular. Containment of communist expansion, which emerged as Washington's primary concern, established an interlocking diplomatic, military, and economic structure that set the framework for West Germany's foreign policy agenda.[8] Like Tokyo, Bonn, especially under Chancellor Konrad Adenaur (1949–1963), found hiding behind Washington to be an attractive strategy, despite severe limitations in its choices. In light of West Germany's recent past, Adenaur elevated its reintegration into Western Europe to a principal foreign policy goal. Reconciliation with France and organizational links with NATO (The North Atlantic Treaty Organization) and the European Economic Community (EEC) were extremely important to Adenaur's overall objective. Active participation in and consultation with these organizations continue to be crucial to West Germany's foreign policy toward a changing Europe as well as toward South Africa. Germany, like Britain, views European political cooperation as preferable to countries following their own policies. With the demise of Portuguese rule in Mozambique and Angola in the mid-1970s, European Political Cooperation in relation to southern Africa intensified.[9] But as chapter two points out, such cooperation has generated discussions of measures that would accelerate racial equality in South Africa without much concrete action being taken to prompt change and has allowed Britain and West Germany to moderate demands for economic sanctions and other punitive measures against Pretoria. By advancing European economic integration and playing an active role in NATO, Bonn has succeeded in establishing itself as a legitimate Western ally and simultaneously has diminished its dependence on Washington.

West Germany's growing economic power, a reduction in ideological hostility between the United States and the Soviet Union, and significant political changes in Eastern Europe combined to contribute to a changing foreign policy in Bonn. By the 1970s West Germany began to conduct what could be regarded as a more normal foreign policy, one that reflected greater self-assertion and decreased sensitivity to the claims of others.[10] In 1963, for example, Chancellor Adenaur prevented the shipment of large-diameter steel pipes to the Soviet Union under pressure from Washington, the latter regarding them to be of strategic significance. However, when President Carter imposed sanctions against Moscow for invading Afghanistan, Bonn was not entirely cooperative. Its interest in restoring relations with East Germany and expanding trade with the Soviet Union and its allies took precedence over American concerns. Similarly, in 1982 Chancellor Helmut Schmidt refused to comply with U.S. sanctions against the Soviet pipeline that was being constructed to bring Siberian natural gas to Western Europe. Lack of European cooperation forced President Reagan to lift sanctions against the U.S.S.R. at the end of 1982.[11]

Although Chancellor Helmut Kohl's ruling coalition attempted to restore closer ties with Washington in 1983, the shift toward an independent foreign policy was clear. Like Japan, West Germany was cautiously searching for a world role commiserate with its economic power, and reflecting the general European movement away from America and toward a united Europe, West Germany was less responsive to U.S. demands. While older Germans remember both the sufferings of World War II and American generosity during the Berlin airlift and the implementation of the Marshall Plan, succeeding generations' views of the United States are influenced more by Vietnam, Watergate, and the proliferation of nuclear weapons on German soil.[12] Bonn's desire to maintain good relations with Washington and Western Europe does not preclude its search for a new foreign policy.

Both Japan and West Germany challenge postwar assumptions about their role in the international economic and political system. Their economic prosperity and the declining utility of military force in the nuclear age influence them to emerge from behind Washington's shadow on the one hand and to remain relatively detached from international conflicts on the other. In West Germany there is tension between the tendency of Germans to remain inward-looking and preoccupied with domestic problems and the attempts by Bonn's Western partners to involve it in more international problems.[13] But Washington has not articulated an unambiguous policy on what Germany's new role should be, partly because American policymakers seem to have difficulty dealing with the changing economic and political realities that have altered the preeminent role of the United States in world affairs. The tension between these two perspectives of Germany's role in the world is reflected in its foreign policy process as well as in its actual relations with South Africa.

## INFLUENCES ON THE FOREIGN POLICY PROCESS

If American foreign policy has suffered from the lack of long-range planning, West Germany's emphasis on clear theoretical constructs as a rationale for its foreign policy decisions also prevents it from responding to crises that do not fit neatly into an overall analytical model.[14] This is particularly pertinent to South Africa's system of apartheid which itself is an anomaly. The problem is compounded by the European parliamentary tradition that essentially insulates foreign policy from domestic pressures and by traditional European realpolitik that de-emphasizes the right of governments to involve themselves in the internal affairs of other countries.

The dominant role of the chancellor in Bonn's foreign policy process, akin to that of the British prime minister, prevents emotive interest group politics from helping to shape the country's international relations. The architects of the West German Basic Law of 1949 intentionally created a strong parliamentary executive. In addition to being chiefly responsible for establishing broad foreign policy guidelines, the chancellor retains authority to appoint cabinet ministers, hold them accountable to him, and to replace them if necessary. Furthermore, the constitution's framers rendered it difficult for the Bundestag (parliament) to remove the chancellor by requiring that body to elect a successor before it can vote him out of office.[15] West Germany's first leader, Konrad Adenauer, set the precedent of a strong chancellor by initially serving as his own foreign minister. However, in light of Germany's restricted role in foreign affairs at the time, Adenauer could only have had a marginal impact. Nevertheless, he managed to define the office for his successors. In addition to the chancellor's preeminent position, coalition politics within the government significantly influence the foreign policy process.

## COALITION POLITICS

In 1983 a center-right coalition composed of Chancellor Helmut Kohl's Christian Democratic Union, Foreign Minister Hans-Dietrich Genscher's Free Democratic Party, and the late Bavarian leader Franz-Josef Strauss's Conservative Christian Social Union came to power in West Germany. Given the diversity and conflict inherent in such a coalition, consensus can be achieved only by finding the lowest common denominator acceptable to proponents of contending viewpoints. Bold policy initiatives are extremely rare and the status quo is far more attractive than a policy designed to engender political change. This is especially true of West Germany's South Africa policy. Conflict between coalition members results in an ambiguous and muddled foreign policy. Although this can be viewed as a serious drawback, in relation to Bonn's policy toward Pretoria, it is an asset from Kohl's perspective. Disagreements between the Conservative Christian Social Union and the Free Democratic Party allow Kohl to pursue a two-track South Africa policy and to issue pronouncements which do not accurately reflect reality, making West Germany's policy not radically different from Japan's. However, there is far more debate about, and much greater familiarity with, South Africa in West Germany than in Japan. Nevertheless, the emphasis on consensus in both societies and their immense economic stakes in South Africa influence government officials to pursue a deliberately vague foreign policy vis-à-vis the apartheid regime.

Conflicting and divergent positions on South Africa within the conservative-liberal governing coalition reflect the interplay of domestic and international politics as well as different perceptions of the South African problem and how it should be resolved. Until his death in late 1988, Strauss played a pivotal role in Bonn's relations with Pretoria. His conservative constituency in Bavaria undoubtedly supported his individual foreign policy initiatives. But the South African issue was only a manifestation of a deeper long-standing rivalry between Strauss and Genscher over the former's ambitions to participate more directly in the formulation of West Germany's foreign affairs and his efforts to undermine Genscher's position as a guarantor of foreign policy continuity.[16] Open disagreements between Strauss and Genscher forced Chancellor Kohl to adopt a conciliatory approach toward the former in order to avoid direct challenges to his leadership of the coalition. The net result has been a paradoxical South Africa policy, characterized by much debate and few operational policy changes.

Strauss generally regarded South Africa as a staunch Western ally against Soviet expansion in southern Africa and initially supported efforts to overthrow Marxist regimes in Mozambique and Angola. Genscher, on the other hand, endorsed the concept of regional détente and called for independence for Namibia.[17] From Strauss's viewpoint such demands were unrealistic. To prevent communist influence in southern Africa, Strauss was prepared to allow South Africa's minority government a certain amount of leeway, and unlike Genscher, who views the ANC and Nelson Mandela as legitimate contenders for power, he saw the ANC as a terrorist organization and Nelson Mandela as a leader of this terrorist movement.[18]

The influence of domestic considerations on foreign policy issues is clearly demonstrated by the positions taken by Strauss and Genscher in international forums dealing with South Africa. While Strauss was primarily concerned about his conservative constituents who were motivated by strong nationalistic feelings, Genscher's foreign policy reflects relatively liberal West German ideas on apartheid.[19] Genscher is also more sensitive to international public opinion and is reluctant to make Bonn conspicuous by adopting positions that are contrary to those of its Western allies and Third World countries. But Genscher is also limited by his constituents who do not favor any radical departures from mainstream German views on how to deal with apartheid. Consequently, he strongly condemns Pretoria's policies and advocates political change but, at the same time, is extremely cautious in order to avoid antagonizing the white minority government and endangering West Germany's extensive economic interests in South Africa.[20]

Strauss, on the other hand, generally disregarded international opinion, rejected concrete pressures against South Africa, and strongly disagreed with some conservative and liberal politicians who endorsed Genscher's view that apartheid cannot be reformed and must therefore be abolished. Strauss, and a significant segment of the Christian Democratic Union and the Christian Social Union, embraced Botha's reform programs, which did not include political equality for black South Africans.[21] In a nutshell, Strauss called for modifications that would not radically alter the status quo. Yet, despite Genscher's vociferous condemnation of apartheid, his opposition to economic sanctions and other punitive actions that might influence change in South Africa also strengthens the status quo. Thus, despite divergent opinions within the Bonn government, actual policies remain essentially unaltered.

Chancellor Kohl's strategy of letting his coalition partners pursue different policies is demonstrated by Strauss's visit to southern Africa in early 1988. By appointing Strauss as Bonn's envoy to Mozambique and South Africa in an effort to resolve conflicts between Renamo, backed by Pretoria, and the Mozambican government, Kohl apparently heightened the ideological rivalry between Genscher and Strauss. While in southern Africa, Strauss went to Namibia and the South African homeland of Bophuthatswana and talked with Jonas Savimbi who leads Unita (Union for the Total Independence of Angola), the major guerrilla group fighting the Angolan government. Chancellor Kohl, responding to criticism from

Genscher and opposition members of the Bundestag, contended that these activities were carried out by Strauss as a private citizen, and not as part of Bonn's South Africa policy.[22] However, these divergent approaches and opinions within the coalition government do not interfere with West Germany's policy of protecting its economic interests in South Africa.

## ECONOMIC INTERESTS AND FOREIGN POLICY

Germany's defeat in World War I led to the dismantling of its colonial empire in Africa and its removal from great power status in world politics, and attempts to regain territory by conquest in World War II also proved futile. Unlike Britain, which emerged from both conflicts with most of its colonies directly under its control and later as independent states of the Commonwealth, West Germany could entertain no illusions of playing a major international political role. Defeated, discredited, and deprived of national sovereignty, West Germany, like Japan, concentrated on economic and monetary power in the context of European and transatlantic integration as soon as economic controls imposed by the Western allies were removed.[23]

Similar to Japan and Britain, West Germany is extremely dependent on foreign sources of raw materials for its industries and on international markets for its finished products. These countries' perceptions of reality are bound to conflict with the United States' because of the latter's abundant natural resources and huge internal markets. In light of Germany's peculiar historical circumstances, its interest in international issues is primarily motivated by economic concerns, a factor which precludes engaging in political controversies that would have detrimental economic consequences. West Germany's vulnerability to external political and economic developments galvanized its consensus on the need for policies that would provide ready access to foreign customers and suppliers. Therefore, all West German governments, whatever their partisan complexion, have endeavored to eradicate impediments to trade expansion.[24] The prevailing view is that the government's responsibility is to provide the right "framework conditions," that is, a climate conducive to technological innovation and investment by business enterprises that is accomplished through tax relief, eliminating fiscal obstacles, and reforming corporate legislation.[25]

Foreign economic policy, which is essentially tantamount to foreign policy in general, emanates from the interaction of business interest groups, various institutions, and global developments. The remarkable stability and consistency of West Germany's foreign economic policy may be due to social and structural factors rather than the relative power of individual pressure groups.[26] But such a distinction is basically meaningless because there is no clear division between business and government. From its immediate postwar position of economic backwardness and extreme poverty, West Germany developed particular institutional and political arrangements that encouraged rapid economic reconstruction at home and expansion abroad soon thereafter.[27] As is the case in Japan, economic groups exercise a pervasive influence on West Germany's foreign policy because of their pivotal role in society. Although business groups, especially banks and large multinational corporations, carefully avoid usurping the government's nominal role of defining West Germany's national interests in relation to other countries, they are vigilant and, if necessary, they directly intervene in foreign affairs when they perceive that their interests are threatened by the government's different interpretation of the national interest. They do not wait to respond to proposals advanced by bureaucratic agencies and legislative bodies. As Ulrich Albrecht notes, the bureaucracies make every effort to ascertain the views of the most influential speakers of the business community on German foreign economic policies.[28]

Among the reasons for the influence exercised by economic interests are: (1) the almost symbiotic relationship between private enterprise and the foreign policy bureaucracy; (2) the prevalence of government by committee which allows industry to become an instrument of foreign policy; (3) the widely accepted practice of allowing associations of German banks and industry to receive foreign delegations and to conduct their own international diplomacy, often in cooperation with official representatives of the Federal government; (4) the close interaction and mutual dependence between foreign economic interests and the Ministry of Economics; and (5) the connection between the government's legitimacy and economic prosperity in a society that has come to expect its political leaders to effectively manage the economy.[29] Even though West Germany had Western Europe's largest economy and a trade surplus of over $73 billion in 1987, there was still cause for concern as unemployment hovered around 2.5 million and showed little promise of improving. In 1987 the economy slowed down, growing by roughly 1.7 percent, compared to 2.5 percent in 1986.[30] In addition, the influx of East German refugees in late 1989 only exacerbated this problem. Under these circumstances, and with increasing competition from other Western European countries, Japan, and the newly industrialized countries of Asia, it is unlikely that the influence of economic interests will be noticeably diminished in relation to Bonn's South Africa policy. And despite widespread debate in West Germany on apartheid, chances are not very high that public opinion will persuade the government to radically alter its course.

## PUBLIC OPINION AND FOREIGN POLICY

Public opinion in West Germany is shaped to a large degree by historical factors as well as by the general population's current perceptions of its role in international affairs. Foreign policy has traditionally been regarded to be beyond the concerns of ordinary citizens and more within the province of government authorities, especially the chief executive. The revolutionary spirit, which imbued American foreign policy with a sense of morality and the average citizen with the belief that he or she could have opinions on external relations, was essentially missing in Western Europe in general and in Germany in particular. In many of these countries parliamentary control over foreign policy was unacceptable, and the average person expected such matters to be decided by their leaders and their professional staffs.[31] Although there is widespread political participation in West Germany, traditional perceptions continue to prompt West Germans to embrace a more authoritarian view of the state.

More than Americans, West Germans are more dependent on the state and view themselves as being essentially subservient to it. Their concept of the state differs from that of most Americans. As Lewis Edinger observed, what the state does is vaguely perceived by many West Germans not so much as an expression of the people's will but as an action of an abstract organizational entity.[32] This impersonal bureaucratic organization is not the object of intense feelings of loyalty or alienation but is seen in structural-functional terms. The average citizen is like a poorly informed shareholder in a giant corporation who votes for the directors and gets a return on his/her investments. Basically, the citizen is a passive actor who regards policymaking elites as powerful leaders who can handle problems by themselves. As Edinger pointed out, policy processes are evaluated in primarily economic terms: the state distributes goods and services in exchange for payments rendered such as taxes and other citizenship duties.[33]

Prior to the independence of Angola and Mozambique, the Soweto uprising in South Africa in 1976, and Stephen Biko's death in 1977 while detained by South African police, West Germans outside academic, business, and church circles showed little interest in apartheid. Although there is currently much public debate on South Africa, apartheid remains a less emotive issue in Germany than it is in the United States or Britain and is not a major foreign policy preoccupation, despite the existence of a sizeable body of informed public opinion. According to Deon Geldenhuys, public discussions of apartheid conducted with so much expertise, passion, and frankness have never been taken into account in policy specifically pursued by Bonn. They are simply ignored.[34] Even if the government paid attention to these debates, there would be only incremental changes because mainstream public opinion is generally supportive of gradual modifications of the status quo in Pretoria. However, numerous anti-apartheid groups are expanding their efforts to educate the public about the nature of apartheid and are attempting to find effective ways of pressuring Bonn into taking concrete measures that would effectuate meaningful changes in South Africa. Anti-apartheid groups' ability to induce change in Bonn's South Africa policy is limited by societal values which equate criticism of business activities with communism. This is especially true of the ruling elite whose perceptions are partly shaped by their experiences in a divided Germany, with Soviet troops on the borders. The Anti-Apartheid Movement's alleged communist connections further erode its credibility in a society that is generally disinclined to question government authorities about West German foreign policy. Moreover, given the central role of business in Germany's postwar reconstruction and its emergence as a leading world economic power, business activities are viewed as being almost sacrosanct by the general public and policymakers. In attacking capitalism for its support of South African racism, anti-apartheid groups strike at the heart of West German identity, and in portraying businessmen as racists they touch a nerve that is still raw.[35]

Churches are among the most visible and outspoken groups in West Germany, and have consistently encouraged Bonn to adopt a more humanitarian approach vis-à-vis South Africa. The long involvement of German missionaries in South West Africa (Namibia) has strengthened their bonds with Africans and sharpened their awareness of apartheid's harshness. Their efforts to assist the transition to a non-racial society in South Africa have been criticized by conservative media and politicians who contend that churches are supporting terrorist activities.[36]

In a society where one becomes a Catholic or Protestant at birth unless demands are made to be exempt, churches find that critical detachment toward Bonn's foreign policy can result in a conflict between ecumenical objectives and national loyalty. When the World Council of Churches adopted the Program to Combat Racism in 1971, for example, churches came under direct pressure from the government and their members. Their investigation of the role of German banks and companies in supporting South African products was regarded as illegitimate interference in politics.[37] Anti-apartheid activities are discouraged even more directly. The close relationship between church and state in West Germany is a double-edged sword. While churches are guaranteed regular income from registered members, every public act of ecumenical solidarity that is perceived as national disloyalty is paid for by a secession of registered members of the church. This amounts to a loss of the tax legally imposed on these members, which is used to finance various church-related functions—including anti-apartheid demonstrations.[38] Budgetary constraints inevitably affect the churches' willingness to confront policymakers.

West Germany's parliamentary system and its domination by the chancellor combine to further frustrate attempts by anti-apartheid groups to induce Bonn to change its South Africa policies. Even opposition political parties are ineffective. The spokesman for the SPD (Social Democratic Party) Parliamentary Group for South African Affairs, Gunter Verheugen, regularly criticized the ruling coalition's failure to implement specific policies against apartheid. However, despite the SPD's propensity to articulate the concerns of students and Third World specialists who advocate a more liberal policy, its ability to shape the foreign policy process remained extremely limited.[39] Opposition parliamentary groups are confronted with widespread support for the current South African regime by leaders in Bonn and with an effective public relations campaign conducted by the South African Embassy. However, several members of parliament who have extensive links with German business oppose what they regard as the government's appeasement policy in South Africa and berate it for its friendly relations with oppressive and dictatorial regimes throughout Africa.[40]

Other anti-apartheid groups include labor unions and academics. The position of trade unions in West Germany in relation to apartheid is analogous to that of trade unions in Japan. To advocate economic sanctions would repudiate fundamental German values as well as jeopardize their own economic security. Academics, on the other hand, are relatively unrestricted in their evaluations of foreign policy options. In fact, special institutes provide government officials with valuable information, and there is extensive scholarly debate on South Africa. The Institute of International Relations in Bonn, headed by Dieter Bielenstein, publishes an extremely valuable newsletter on African affairs and works closely with the Friedrich Ebert Foundation. Because professors are highly respected and are seen as objective experts, they can indirectly influence foreign policy.[41] Yet, countervailing interests preclude radical departures from the status quo.

## ETHNICITY AND FOREIGN POLICY

Although West Germany is racially and ethnically homogeneous, Germany's experience with racial hatred and the Holocaust continues to have an impact on its foreign policy. However, racial considerations do not override business interests in South Africa, partly because Germany, unlike Britain, lost its African colonies shortly after it acquired them, and arrived in Africa only in 1885 after the slave trade was abolished. Nonetheless, West Germans are generally very sensitive to racism within the European context and especially in relation to Jewish communities worldwide. Not surprisingly, many West Germans throughout society and at all levels of government make every effort to avoid what could be construed as neo-racism in their country.[42] Perhaps the Jenninger case best demonstrates West Germany's dilemma.

Philipp Jenninger, president of the Bundestag (parliament) until November 1988, delivered a speech at a special parliamentary session marking the fiftieth anniversary of Kristallnacht, the precursor of the Holocaust, in which he attempted to remind his colleagues about Hitler's rise to power and his general acceptance by the German people. Jenninger recalled how the Nazis had restored Germany's economic health by eradicating mass unemployment and had renewed a feeling of optimism and self-confidence in German citizens. Referring specifically to Jews, Jenninger asked rhetorically, "hadn't they in the past perhaps assumed a role they had no right to assume. . . ? Didn't they even deserve to be put in their place?"[43] Jenninger's courageous attempt to remind his colleagues how their country became firmly ensnared in the grip of totalitarianism resulted in his resignation because he inadvertently appeared to justify Hitler's slaughter of the Jews. This case shows West German sensitivity to racial issues as well as their unwillingness to be openly confronted with their painful past.

Like most European countries, Germany does not have large racial minorities. Consequently, politicians do not have to justify their positions on South Africa to their constituents the way many members of the U.S. Congress are inclined to do. Furthermore, the general public is less aware of black South Africans' grievances and appears to sympathize with the white minority.[44] But evidence indicates that more than 600,000 racially mixed Germans, children of black American occupational personnel and German mothers, are fully accepted by their communities and have not been subject to group discrimination or racial prejudice. It is important to note, however, that contact with their American fathers was severed in the vast majority of these cases.[45] The primary concern with race in West Germany centers around large numbers of South European guest workers, especially the Turks.

West Germans tend to view migrant laborers as temporary residents, even though many of them have lived in the country since the early 1960s. Strained relations between the Turkish communities and the larger society are due in part to cultural differences and fear of foreign competition. Appearances, language barriers, and differences in religious beliefs and general attitudes all contribute to mistrust of and overt hostility toward Southern Europeans. Many European societies find assimilation undesirable principally because ethnicity and nation tend to be synonymous. In contrast to the melting pot concept and ethnic pluralism in the United States, German society is more homogeneous and inward looking. One can be either German or Turkish, not both. In a tight job market, fierce competition for work exacerbates the problems of alienation and intolerance.[46] It can be assumed that West Germans' experiences with guest workers have an indirect influence on their perceptions of racial politics in South Africa.

## HISTORICAL LINKS WITH SOUTH AFRICA

Germany's economic problems, political divisions, and lack of a strong navy prevented its participation in the scramble for overseas territories until 1885, when the Berlin Conference was held to systematically divide the African continent among various European countries. Germany's interest in South Africa remained negligible until around 1890 when gold mining in the Transvaal attracted German capital and settlers to the area. German expansion in southern Africa occurred within the context of great power rivalry in Europe, particularly in competition with Britain which had used its naval supremacy to control the Cape.

German missionaries entered the Boer Republic of the Transvaal in the 1840s but operated independently. The discovery of diamonds in Kimberly in 1867 lured German entrepreneurs and capital to the Transvaal where they played a significant part in the development of the diamond fields. These self-made businessmen's connections with the German government were tenuous, and most of them formed close relationships with the British and Anglophile Dutch settlers in Cape Colony, thereby further diminishing their specifically German characteristics and loyalties.[47] When British efforts to frustrate the Afrikaners' objectives in the Transvaal and Orange Free State influenced Boer leaders to seek assistance from Britain's rivals, Prussia initially and Germany later, Germany's preoccupation with its own internal problems and a general lack of serious interest in the Transvaal made it unwilling or unable to render diplomatic or military aid, thereby facilitating Britain's annexation of the Transvaal in 1877. Only Afrikaner determination to resist British expansionism allowed the Transvaal to regain a relative degree of autonomy. But Germany's interest in the region was gradually emerging. In 1886 the Society for the Promotion of German Interests in South Africa was established, in 1888 a German consul was sent to Pretoria, and later that year a German Society was established in the Transvaal.[48]

German economic interests in the Transvaal escalated with the discovery of gold on the Witwatersrand in 1886, and German immigration increased. The new German settlers, part of the growing *uitlander* (foreign) community in the Transvaal, were more directly linked to Germany than their predecessors and increasingly hostile toward the British. The approximately five thousand German residents strongly supported Paul Kruger's government and its desire for a military alliance with Germany. They invested roughly three hundred million marks in gold mining and related industries and became some of the most important stockholders, in direct competition with British interests and the British imperialist Cecil Rhodes. Germans supplied materials for the railroads and managed to gain a monopoly on dynamite sales to the Boer Republic, and German heavy industry became more dependent on exports of weapons, ammunition, and mining equipment to the Transvaal.[49] Simultaneously, concerted efforts were made by Kruger to exclude British economic interests and deny English-speaking miners equal political rights in the Afrikaner Republic, and when the German government decided to intervene in 1894 to support Kruger's policy vis-à-vis British subjects, Britain took the threat seriously.[50]

Rhodes's dream of a united South Africa under British control clashed with Kruger's strong belief that Afrikaners should be left alone to govern themselves in their own republics. The economic component of Boer independence centered around access to ports not under British jurisdiction for the Transvaal's trade, particularly access to Delagoa Bay, which was part of Mozambique, then Portugal's colony. While Rhodes tried to purchase Delagoa Bay from a declining Portugal, the German government encouraged the Portuguese to retain control and admonished British authorities that any alteration of the status quo would be unacceptable.[51] German financial ties with the Transvaal would obviously be jeopardized if British imperialists were able to impose a British protectorate over the Boer Republics and enjoy a trade monopoly. An independent Transvaal was obviously in Germany's interest.

Economic considerations and European diplomacy induced Germany to offer support to the Afrikaners, despite its inability to actually implement such a promise. But neither Kruger nor Rhodes could fully understand Germany's unreliability. In addition to safeguarding its interests in the Transvaal, the German government was apparently exploiting the South African situation in order to coerce Britain into joining the Triple Alliance, composed of Germany, Austria, and Italy.[52] When the Jameson Raid was launched against the Transvaal, Germans in the Republic offered Kruger their assistance and called for German intervention, which proved unnecessary because the Boers were aware of the plot and had captured the major participants without great difficulty.

Following the Raid, Germany once again raised the Boers' expectations of external help. In January 1896 the German government sent Kruger a telegram congratulating him on his successful handling of the Jameson Raid, and the German War Ministry offered military assistance to the Transvaal which was rapidly building its military power.[53] The Germans were quick to point out to the Boers the advantages of buying German Mauser rifles, the same weapons as those used in German South West Africa (Namibia). However, in 1898, on the eve of the Second Anglo-Boer War, Germany concluded an agreement with Britain that provided for the partition of Angola and Mozambique between them if Portugal were unable to retain them due to financial exigencies.[54] Britain would finally get Delagoa Bay, something Germany had previously tried to prevent. Abandoned by Germany, the Afrikaners fought courageously but hopelessly against the military might of the British Empire. At the same time, Germany was ruthlessly consolidating its control over neighboring Namibia.

Germany's claim to Namibia, established in 1884, was recognized by the British following the Berlin Conference largely because Britain was confident that Germany's fascination with what was essentially a desert would reduce its ability to mount a serious challenge to British objectives in South Africa. But Germany's brutality in Namibia was of great concern to the British who regarded themselves as more humanitarian in their dealings with Africans. Namibia's population, numbering only about a half-million, was divided into three main groups: the Herero, the Nama, and the Ovambos. In 1897 a rinderpest epidemic destroyed virtually all the Herero's cattle, causing not only economic disaster but also undermining the group's social and political stability.[55] These problems were exacerbated by the gradual encroachment of German settlers on Herero lands and the oppressive policies of the colonial administration. When the German military responded to a minor disturbance among the Bondelswartz people in 1904 with great cruelty, the Herero, under Samuel Maherero's leadership, revolted, killing approximately one hundred German settlers. Berlin's retaliation was swift and barbaric. Germany launched a full-scale war under the command of General von Trotha whose final objective was the extermination of the Herero. With fourteen thousand troops von Trotha massacred more than seventy percent of the Herero people and the same proportion of the Nama who later joined the uprising under the 80-year-old Hendrik Witbooi. Two thousand Germans were killed before a horrified government in Berlin recalled General von Trotha.[56] Germany's defeat in the First World War terminated its rule in Africa and severely reduced its role in South Africa.

By 1934 relations between Germany and the Union of South Africa were gradually being restored, although English-speaking white South Africans and many Afrikaners who fought Germany were unable to forget the pro-German sentiment among leading Afrikaners. The first major postwar agreement between the two countries provided for an exchange of German manufactured goods for South African wool and other raw materials. By 1938 Germany was buying twenty-five percent of South Africa's wool exports, making it that country's principal foreign wool customer.[57] German manufactured exports included locomotives, automobiles, and Junker aircraft. German and South African airlines worked out special transfer flights: South African planes flew passengers as far as Athens, where they were transferred to Lufthansa and taken to destinations throughout central Europe.[58] The outbreak of the Second World War once again resulted in diminished trade between Germany and South Africa. However, South Africa's implementation of apartheid, a philosophy frightfully reminiscent of Nazism, would make future relations between Pretoria and Bonn an extremely sensitive issue among many West Germans.

## WEST GERMANY'S ECONOMIC INTERESTS IN SOUTH AFRICA

West Germany's economic interests remain paramount in its relations with South Africa. Germany's heavy dependence on foreign markets for about a third of its manufactured products, its vulnerability to raw materials shortages, its growing integration within the European Community, and the general interdependence of national economies combine to propel economic welfare ahead of general political issues. Foreign policy and domestic economic and social issues are intricately fused leading to changes in how foreign policy issues are viewed and evaluated on the domestic political scene.[59] Like Japan, West Germany clearly separates economic matters from political considerations and tries to avoid regulating their international trade. Free trade is a deeply rooted societal value that has important ramifications for Bonn's South Africa policy.

Anti-apartheid groups in West Germany and elsewhere are generally critical of Germany's extensive economic interests in South Africa. But the government argues that activities of private enterprise and private citizens are beyond its purview. There is widespread support for this approach to economic issues, and even Social Democratic leaders who are generally critical of Bonn's South Africa policy do not advocate utilizing economic ties for political purposes. Similar to Japan, Britain, and France, West Germany approaches southern Africa from a business viewpoint.[60] Racial and moral issues are not central concerns, despite verbal disapproval of apartheid. Developments within South Africa, however, are forcing Bonn to reconsider its policy of separating business from politics.

Although restrictions imposed by the Western Allies on West German economic activities immediately after the Second World War virtually eliminated trade between South Africa and West Germany, by the mid-1950s, when cold war politics and military considerations influenced the allies to encourage economic growth in West Germany, Bonn quickly recovered its prewar share of the South African market, estimated at eight percent. Between 1958 and the early 1970s West Germany proceeded to capture about one-fifth of the market,[61] and by 1983 it had replaced Britain as South Africa's most important European partner. In 1986 it supplied forty-two percent of European Community exports to South Africa and took sixteen percent of that country's exports to the E.C.[62] Data for 1986 and 1987 show that West Germany, Japan, Britain, and the United States accounted for two-thirds of all sales to South Africa. In 1987 the value of Germany's imports from South Africa stood at $1,248 million, down from $1,255 in 1986. Exports rose from $1,940 million in 1986 to $2,545 million in 1987, an increase of thirty-one percent.[63]

Major German imports from South Africa included strategic raw materials such as chromium, copper, platinum, coal, iron and steel, nickel, uranium, and ferro-alloys; animal feed, wool, fresh and canned fruit; inorganic chemicals and manufactured goods; and gold. By the late 1970s West Germany became one of the main customers of South African uranium, and South Africa continued to be its principal supplier until 1987. Reductions in exports of South African uranium would undoubtedly benefit Canada and Australia. Despite arguments in Bonn about the strategic importance of South Africa's resources, the government officially decided against stockpiling in 1981, leaving this to the discretion of industrial companies and market forces.[64]

Although only less than one percent of West Germany's exports goes to South Africa, a wide range of manufactured products are sold to that country. These include basic metals, mechanical and electrical engineering products, and transport equipment. Given the nature of apartheid and the international condemnation of it, much trade is conducted in secrecy. For example, in 1985 the Japanese firm Hitachi sold computers to Persetel, one of several computer companies within the giant South African Barlow Rand group, in cooperation with the West German multinational enterprise, BASF.[65] The porousness of international markets makes it extremely difficult to ascertain the extent to which multinational firms conduct secret transactions with South Africa. Oil is another example. West Germany, like Britain, Saudi Arabia, Oman, the United Arab Emirates, and Brunei, disregards violations of the oil boycott against Pretoria, has no mechanisms for implementing the EC oil embargo, and has generally voted against U.N. efforts in this area. It is alleged that West German companies such as Lungi, Arge, Hoechst, Linde, Preussag, and Howaldswerke/Deutsche Werft, and the oil trading company Marimpex routinely export oil to South Africa.[66] Because Bonn does not prohibit petroleum exports to South Africa, these companies are not violating the law.

Overall, West Germany is not as dependent on trade with South Africa as Bonn claims. According to the 1987 U.S. Department of State Report to Congress on industrial democracies' relations with South Africa, cessation of commercial ties between the two countries would not cripple West Germany's economy, but its impact would be felt and certain firms would be seriously affected.[67] However, Germany's heavy reliance on international trade reduces the likelihood that it will sever ties with South Africa. In addition to trade, West German investments in South Africa are extensive.

Approximately three hundred West German companies have investments in South Africa, including nearly all major German industrial corporations. The largest investments are in the motor vehicle, machinery, and chemical sectors. In 1986 South African investments accounted for about two percent of total German direct investments abroad, up sharply from the relative stagnation of the early 1980s.[68] While many American firms disinvested in 1986, German companies such as Daimler-Benz AG and Bayerische Motoren Werke AG (BMW) continued their expansion programs begun in 1982 and 1983. Daimler-Benz completed retooling its East London factory and announced plans for additional investments. BMW opened an $18 million headquarters building in Johannesburg.[69] West German enterprises employ roughly forty-five thousand workers, half of whom are black. This has been used to justify Bonn's protection of German firms' investments in South Africa through credits granted by the government-controlled Hermes insurance corporation. In 1986 the level of Hermes export guarantees was lowered, and in 1987, in line with the E.C.'s requirement of guidance, Bonn recommended that German companies stop investing in South Africa.[70] As in the case of Britain, the E.C. Code has been generally ineffective in controlling the behavior of German companies operating in South Africa.

Although companies receiving Hermes credits are required to sign a statement indicating their willingness to implement the provisions of the Code, widespread skepticism in Bonn concerning the ability of companies to effect political change and the appropriateness of such a role render the Code virtually meaningless. Furthermore, West Germany's aggressive business practices with the former communist countries in Eastern Europe seem to render moral arguments against business-as-usual with South Africa indefensible. Widespread abuse of human rights in many African countries and these states' excruciating economic difficulties reduce their leverage vis-à-vis German firms operating in South Africa, and their influence on Bonn's Pretoria policy seems negligible.

African leaders usually evaluate West Germany's policy toward the continent within the context of Bonn's relationship with South Africa. While West Germany is unlikely to alter its position on South Africa in response to African criticisms in international forums, it nonetheless attempts to minimize damage to what is otherwise an important economic relationship with the continent by assuring African leaders of its opposition to apartheid. For example, during a luncheon for African ambassadors in Bonn in February 1988, Minister of State for Foreign Affairs Helmut Schaffer condemned apartheid and pledged the continuation of West Germany's policy in Africa. Similarly, Foreign Minister Hans-Dietrich Genscher emphasized that Africa would remain an important area in West Germany's foreign policy, noting that over forty percent of Bonn's development aid went to African countries in 1987.[71] From Germany's viewpoint, Africa's economic problems surpassed political considerations such as apartheid.

Trade between West Germany and black Africa has remained fairly constant between 1982 and 1989. Imports from Africa in 1982 represented 6.7 percent of all German imports, and exports to Africa averaged 4.4 percent of the German export market. Although the volume of trade continued to expand in 1985, with Africa registering a surplus of $3.5 billion with West Germany, Africa's inability to pay German firms for various goods and services discouraged German businessmen from increasing their investments, especially in Nigeria.[72] By 1987 Nigeria, which was West Germany's second largest source of imports in 1986, fell to fourth place after South Africa, Libya, and Algeria, due primarily to a drop in oil exports as well as plummeting oil prices. Nigerian oil shipments plummeted from 14.5 million tons to 4.7 million tons between 1980 and 1988, partly because the nickel content of its petroleum was significantly higher than the statutory ceiling imposed by Bonn, making it less competitive than Brent crude from the North Sea.[73] Furthermore, extremely serious foreign debt problems prompted many African countries to impose restrictions on German imports, although some of these restraints were later removed due to increased and facilitated access to credits. West Germany was a chief advocate of debt rescheduling and reductions in interest rates charged to African states. In addition to economic factors, Bonn's Pretoria policy is influenced by cultural and family links to South Africa.

## WEST GERMANY'S CULTURAL AND FAMILY TIES WITH SOUTH AFRICA

West Germany and South Africa have strong historical ties, beginning with settlement of the area by Huguenots of Dutch, French, and German backgrounds. As discussed earlier in this chapter, Afrikaners repeatedly sought to enlist German support in their struggle against British encroachments on the Boer Republics, and many Germans migrated to South Africa and Namibia in the late 19th and early 20th centuries. There are approximately twenty-five thousand ethnic Germans in Namibia and roughly seventy thousand South Africans with ancestral ties to Germany. There has always been a more favorable image of South Africa in West Germany than elsewhere in Europe, including The Netherlands and Britain.

While business interests and members of the Bundestag have promoted good relations between Bonn and Pretoria, the fate of ethnic Germans in Namibia seems to have shaped West Germany's policy on that country. Prior to 1980 West Germany relied on South Africa, which controlled Namibia in violation of U.N. resolutions and rulings issued by the International Court of Justice, to protect people of German ancestry in the territory. Cultural agreements with Namibia were promoted and close diplomatic contacts regarding Namibia were maintained with South Africa, even though many Western nations refused to recognize South Africa's jurisdiction over the former German colony and League of Nations Mandate. Under pressure from German missionaries and churches in Namibia, many of which supported Swapo (the South West Africa Peoples Organization) through the World Council of Churches and the Lutheran World Federation, Bonn began a more flexible policy on Namibia. Germany became an active member of the Contact group, along with France, Britain, Canada, and the United States, and tried to persuade South Africa to leave. West German officials developed extensive contacts with Swapo and encouraged ethnic Germans in Namibia to do likewise.[74] Close links continue between churches in Namibia and their parent churches in Germany.

German-South African cultural ties were formalized by an agreement in 1962 designed to cultivate friendly relations and collaboration in cultural fields and to promote better understanding between citizens of the two countries. The agreement provided scholarships for South Africans (primarily whites) to study in West Germany and fostered the exchange of scientists, journalists, and artists.[75] West Germany was the only country within the European Community to maintain a formal cultural agreement and came under increasing pressure from anti-apartheid groups as well as its European partners to terminate it. In response to this pressure, German officials decided not to end the agreement, but to modify it instead, placing greater emphasis on educational programs for black South Africans. Conservatives within Bonn's ruling coalition strongly objected to any amendments in the agreements, claiming that such a move was an unnecessary and punitive action against South Africa.[76] For his work in promoting South African-German relations and strenuously opposing attempts to adopt punitive measures against Pretoria in West Germany, the late Franz-Josef Strauss received South Africa's highest award for foreigners in 1984.[77]

Tourism between the two countries also helps to create cultural and social bonds. By 1987 Pretoria had managed to cut off the outside world from reports of political unrest in the townships, thereby creating a feeling of normalcy among many Western Europeans. With a relatively strong deutsche mark and a rand that had declined to half its value between 1985 and 1989, West German tourists regarded travel to South Africa as an incredible bargain. Furthermore, since Bonn and most European governments allowed airlines to fly directly to South Africa, tourists had easy access to the country. Thus, West German airlines benefited from decisions by the United States, Scandinavia, and others not to permit direct flights to South Africa.

## MILITARY AND STRATEGIC LINKS

The primacy of trade in West Germany's foreign policy influences the government to implement export laws that are weak enough for companies to circumvent them. Compared with the United States, there is a general lack of administrative regulations and not enough personnel to enforce them. Consequently, West German companies are relatively free to export almost anything, including military weapons and technology, to South Africa. Ideological competition between East and West Germany and Bonn's concerns about Soviet expansion in southern Africa have further contributed to the growth of military links between West Germany and Pretoria. Following the familiar pattern of behavior many countries have adopted toward South Africa, the West German government condemns arms sales and reiterates its support of the arms embargo, even as German companies violate U.N. restrictions against arms sales to South Africa. Bonn defends itself against allegations of military cooperation with Pretoria by claiming that it has observed the arms embargo since 1963, fourteen years prior to the mandatory U.N. arms embargo, that its export legislation requires an arms export permit for all military weapons trade, irrespective of destination, and that it does not approve exports of arms to South Africa, licensing agreements, or the assembly of weapons in South Africa by German companies.[78] But anti-apartheid groups and opposition political parties in West Germany contend that the government is aware of widespread violations of the embargo. Stung by such criticism, the German Federal Press and Information Office issued a document which accused anti-apartheid groups of deliberately attempting to undermine the country's international status and credibility, thereby striking at the West as a whole and strengthening the Soviet Union's position in international affairs.[79]

However, available evidence suggests that West German companies are violating the arms embargo against South Africa, and that sometimes the government is aware of breaches of its own legislation against such practices. For example, in 1980, the Public Prosecutor in Düsseldorf corroborated press reports that there had been a secret investigation of the activities of Rheinmetall AG. This company allegedly delivered an ammunition filling plant to South Africa, in violation of West Germany's export laws. Rheinmetall argued that special export permits were granted by government authorities, but the Federal Ministry of Economic Affairs claimed that an export permit for the ammunition filling plant had only been issued for Paraguay.[80] When Rheinmetall was found guilty in 1986 of shipping arms to South Africa between 1977 and 1980, company managers were given light fines and probationary sentences of up to two years.[81]

West German weapons sales to South Africa since 1963 have included military trucks; an assembly plant, Atlantis Diesel Engineering, for engines used in military vehicles; two mine sweepers, which Bonn claimed were approved for civilian research; navigation systems for torpedo boats and helicopters; and anti-tank missiles, jointly produced by West German and French companies. Equally important, West Germany and its firms allegedly gave the NATO codification system to South Africa's military forces and designed and furnished the subterranean command center near the Simonstown naval base, which collects and analyzes data about activities in the southern Atlantic and Indian oceans. Furthermore, government-financed research institutes and companies involved in manufacturing military weapons in West Germany share information with South African firms that make military equipment.[82]

West Germany's collaboration with South Africa on submarines and in the nuclear field continued to be debated in 1989, especially after the

West German company Imhausen-Chemie was accused by the outgoing Reagan administration of playing a central role in the design and construction of the Libyan chemical plant, which Washington contended was designed to make poison gas. Although Reagan left office without carrying out his threat to bomb the Libyan plant, he succeeded in forcing Bonn to finally admit that its companies were involved in the Libyan project. Chancellor Kohl was openly attacked by the Social Democrats and others for his clumsy attempts to deny knowledge of German ties to the plant which was partially destroyed by fire in March 1990. Norbert Gansel, a Social Democrat and member of the Bundestag, accused Kohl of being personally responsible for the world's perception of Germany as pursuing a contradictory policy of publicly calling for a global ban on chemical weapons while secretly tolerating their production in crisis areas.[83]

Anti-apartheid groups in Germany and elsewhere have consistently alleged that Bonn and Pretoria cooperate in the nuclear field, and that such collaboration contributed to South Africa's ability to produce nuclear weapons. One of the earliest contacts between the two countries was in 1963 when West German banker Herman Abs offered to cooperate with South Africa in nuclear research. The outcome was the establishment of a rocket research center and an ionosphere station in Namibia.[84] West German companies' exports of low-enriched uranium to South Africa accelerated its ability to produce high-enriched uranium for bombs. Bonn's tendency to look the other way, despite its support of the Nuclear Nonproliferation Treaty, prompted Washington in 1981 to ask German officials to stop the Hempel Group in Düsseldorf from sending enriched uranium to South Africa and heavy water to Argentina.[85] Similarly, West Germany was severely criticized for its disregard of the arms embargo when it assisted South Africa with the construction of submarines.

In 1986, Howaldswerke Deutsche Werft AG, a government-owned shipbuilding company, and Ingenieurkontor Lubeck, an engineering firm, were accused of delivering microfilms of blueprints of the U-209 submarine to the South African Embassy in Bonn from 1984 to 1985. The new submarines, designed to launch short-range missiles and sabotage missions, would replace older models that South Africa has used in military actions against neighboring states. In December 1986, the U.N. Special Committee Against Apartheid sent a letter to Bonn's Permanent Representative to that organization, informing him of these allegations. On July 15, 1987, the Chairman of the Special Committee received a letter from West Germany's Deputy Permanent Representative stating that investigations into the alleged infringements of the U.N. arms embargo were incomplete.[86] Although Bonn denied being involved, opposition Social Democrats discovered a copy of a letter Franz-Josef Strauss had sent to Chancellor Kohl in July 1984 which indicated that Kohl had agreed to allow the contract, worth approximately $285 million, between the German firms and South Africa to proceed without the government's written approval.

Faced with increasing international opposition, Bonn shifted all the responsibility to Strauss and contended that the government did not approve selling the plans to South Africa. When pressed on why the companies were not prosecuted, the government defended its inaction by arguing that prosecutions were not started because the quality of the plans was below legal standards.[87] Opposition members of the Bundestag, led by Norbert Gansel, rejected this explanation and continued their investigation.

## IDEOLOGICAL COMPETITION WITH EAST GERMANY

Ideological differences between West Germany and the German Democratic Republic as well as fluctuations in their relationship affected the former's South Africa policy. While reunification of the two Germanies remained an important West German foreign policy objective, Bonn's ability to maneuver was determined to a large extent by relations between Washington and Moscow. Both Germanies were constrained by their relative dependence on their respective political and economic associations, and Bonn's willingness to hide behind Washington to protect its own interests was matched by East Berlin's desire to demonstrate its importance to the Soviet Union, in an effort to enhance its leverage vis-à-vis Moscow.[88] West Germany's emerging policy toward South Africa was shaped to some degree by East Germany's more aggressive approach to military conflicts in southern Africa.

East Germany decided to support African resistance against the Portuguese in Mozambique in the early 1960s and by 1969 extended military assistance to the Mozambique Liberation Front (Frelimo), its main liberation movement. The Popular Movement for the Liberation of Angola was the other major recipient of East German military equipment, medical supplies, logistical support, military advisers, and medical treatment for wounded combatants. In addition to its interests in raw materials and other products from Africa, East Germany's policies had been motivated by its desire to forge strong links with existing and potential black governments throughout sub-Saharan Africa to further distinguish itself from West Germany.[89] East Germany was one of the first countries to criticize South Africa's attempts to deprive blacks of South African citizenship through the creation of so-called independent homelands. West Germany's contacts with South African leaders such as Buthelezi were viewed by East Germany as evidence of Bonn's interest in investing in the homelands while officially disassociating itself from the homeland policy.[90] While East Germany focused on providing military assistance to southern African liberation groups, including the ANC and Swapo, West Germany concentrated on giving economic aid for development projects and trade. But West Germany's ambiguous policy toward South Africa and its tendency to view apartheid from an East-West perspective allowed the East

Germans to enhance their political credibility among African states. When leaders such as Strauss equated anti-apartheid groups with communists, called the ANC and Swapo terrorist groups, and developed close personal ties to key figures in Pretoria, East Germans emphasized that their hands were clean because of their unequivocal opposition to apartheid.[91]

Ideological competition between the two Germanies, which had subsided during the late 1970s and the early 1980s, was reactivated to some extent by the election of the more conservative political coalition led by Chancellor Kohl. The East-West perception of southern African conflicts gradually came to dominate discussions in Bonn. Furthermore, compared to the previous SPD government led by Chancellor Helmut Schmidt, when the CDU/CSU coalition returned to power in late 1982, Bonn's foreign policy became more consistent with Washington's.[92] However, the shifts in relations with East Germany were only incremental. In 1983 Strauss, formerly one of the most outspoken critics of détente with the East and an advocate of non-recognition of East Germany, called for closer ties between the two Germanies and approved a West German loan of a billion marks to an East German government desperate for hard currency.[93] By late 1989 dramatic political developments in East Germany, particularly the free movement of people to West Germany and Bonn's promise of substantial economic assistance to East Berlin, led to fundamental changes in relations between the two countries. Nevertheless, ideological considerations continued to be a factor in Bonn's Pretoria policy and its strategies for encouraging change in South Africa.

## STRATEGIES

West Germany's strategies for peaceful political change in South Africa have mirrored Britain's as well as Japan's. These countries strongly oppose economic sanctions as primary instruments of foreign policy, and despite their rhetoric condemning apartheid, their policies are essentially supportive of the status quo. Only the SPD and the Greens favor strong sanctions against Pretoria. Leaders in Bonn advocate increased dialogue between all groups but do not suggest how to bring them together or how a government which does not intend to relinquish power can be persuaded to do so under normal conditions.[94]

## SANCTIONS

While there are some influential politicians within the CDU/CSU coalition who regard sanctions against Pretoria as an effective strategy, the main proponents of punitive measures are anti-apartheid groups, whose access to the policymaking process is severely limited, and members of opposition political parties. Although the Greens have continuously called for comprehensive sanctions as a means of applying sufficient international pressure to influence Pretoria to dismantle apartheid, their strong association with anti-nuclear protests in West Germany diminished their ability to persuade more conservative policymakers to view apartheid as a moral issue rather than as an extension of the East-West conflict. The SPD remained the major opposition party with enough credibility to have an impact on Bonn's South Africa policy in regard to sanctions.

Coercive economic measures as instruments of political change received more attention from the SPD after 1982. Similar to their Labour counterpart in Britain, the SPD took a strong moral stance against apartheid and advocated sanctions after its term in office ended. During Chancellor Helmut Schmidt's administration, calls for any type of coercive economic actions were categorically rejected, partly because of the SPD's heterogeneous social base and the need to consider possible unemployment resulting from a trade embargo among its traditional working-class membership.[95] However, with deteriorating conditions within South Africa and growing international pressures for sanctions, SPD leaders became ardent supporters of punitive measures. Between 1986 and 1989 the SPD argued that Bonn demonstrated its insincerity about fighting apartheid by its sustained efforts to prevent convincing steps from being taken and by its deliberate lack of an unambiguous South Africa policy.[96] In April 1988 during a debate on South Africa in the Bundestag, Gunter Verheugen, deputy of the SPD in the Bundestag, called for Bonn to use its leadership position within the European Community to encourage the immediate adoption of the following sanctions: (1) the prohibition of credits and loans; (2) the recall of the ambassadors of the EC member states in South Africa; (3) the reduction of diplomatic personnel of South African embassies in EC member states; (4) the introduction of the obligation of a visa for South African travelers; (5) the termination of air traffic to and from South Africa; and (6) the strict observance of the U.N. arms embargo against South Africa.[97] But these suggestions were largely ignored by a government that has consistently stated its opposition to restrictive measures against Pretoria. Chancellor Kohl, like Prime Minister Thatcher, contended that imposing economic sanctions would neither be effective nor moral. In its reply to questions from the SPD Parliamentary Group, the government rejected what it termed a "policy of pin-pricks," pointing out that apart from West Germany's interest in unimpeded commerce, the suitability of sanctions for promoting peaceful change and their impact on black South Africans and the neighboring countries would have to be considered.[98]

Bonn advanced a number of arguments to buttress its position. First, punitive economic actions by destroying productivity would make South Africa the largest recipient of economic aid on the continent. The demands by neighboring states for both sanctions against Pretoria and economic compensation for themselves were viewed as illusory. Second, there was conflicting advice from Africans on economic sanctions. For example, Buthelezi favors more economic growth as a solution while Desmond Tutu favors economic restrictions. Third, sanctions might cause a breakdown of the South African economy and fuel open violence. Fourth, sanctions would trigger conflicts between violent extremist groups on both sides. Fifth, the introduction of compulsory visas for South Africans entering West Germany would be counterproductive. The government believed that more contacts between South Africans and the outside world would help end apartheid. Sixth, a discontinuation of Hermes export guarantees would subject German companies to severe disadvantages in competition with other firms and exacerbate the unemployment situation in Germany without ending apartheid. Finally, denying South African airlines landing rights in Germany would jeopardize the government's policy of dialogue with Pretoria. Furthermore, because numerous airports in Western and Central Europe impose no restrictions on South African airlines, South African traffic to Europe would be virtually unaffected.[99]

International pressures, however, induced Bonn to reconsider its rigid opposition to sanctions. In 1985, following South Africa's declaration of a State of Emergency, West Germany withdrew its Hermes credit guarantees for German exports to South Africa. Furthermore, Bonn's strategy of using European Political Cooperation to delay or avoid imposing sanctions backfired when the European Community spelled out specific measures to be taken by all member states to clearly demonstrate their opposition to apartheid.[100] However, Britain, Germany, and Portugal prevented major actions from being adopted, and their South Africa policies seem to encourage companies to routinely violate E.C. sanctions.

## ECONOMIC GROWTH AND BLACK EMPOWERMENT

Like Britain, both the West German government and the SPD believe that empowering black South Africans will contribute to political change, although the latter has regarded sanctions as an integral part of any empowerment strategy and has more enthusiastically embraced the idea of political cooperation with the ANC. Obviously concerned about Africa's worsening economic conditions, as well as its own business interests in South Africa, Bonn has emphasized that conflicts must be resolved by negotiation. As Genscher argued, hunger and need, disease and misery cannot be combatted by military means. Instead, schools, hospitals, new industries, jobs, and productive agriculture are needed.[101] Germany favors an end to apartheid through an evolutionary non-violent process and views economic restrictions as detrimental to the achievement of its policy objectives. Instead, it focuses on education as the principal way of empowering blacks.

German educational programs include instruction for blacks in German-language schools in South Africa that are subsidized by the West German government. Despite some white parental opposition to racially integrated schools, the German government has continued its policy of opening the schools to all races.[102] Bonn also cooperates with South African educational authorities in an effort to promote additional education at the Science Education Center for about half the five hundred secondary school teachers of scientific subjects in Soweto. West Germany sends two teachers and the projects director, the German-South Africa Chamber of Trade and Industry in Johannesburg and the German Embassy are represented on the governing board, and numerous members of the German business community financed construction of the building, completed in 1983. An additional educational initiative is a scholarship program for about a hundred black students at open white universities. This program is administered by the German Academic Exchange Service (DAAD) in collaboration with the multi-racial South African Institute of Race Relations. Another program provides scholarships through DAAD for black South Africans to study in West Germany. And the government channels about $1 million through various church organizations to provide legal assistance and further educational opportunities. It is estimated that total direct aid to education, excluding that given to churches, amounted to $2 million in 1987.[103] Somewhat more controversial and tentative are Bonn's relations with black political groups and their leaders.

Unlike the Scandinavian countries and Canada, West Germany does not provide aid to the ANC as an organization, but individual members can qualify for scholarships in Germany. Bonn also supports aid programs for nongovernmental organizations designed to benefit members of liberation groups, "as long as they contributed to an improvement of the educational, social, and economic status of population groups that became distressed."[104] Furthermore, West Germany showed greater readiness to meet with Buthelezi than with Oliver Tambo, leader of the ANC.

Given Bonn's position on sanctions, and Buthelezi's opposition to external pressures that would have a negative impact on economic growth in South Africa, West German leaders have made a concerted effort to encourage his strategies for black empowerment. Furthermore, Buthelezi is perceived as a moderate with whom the white minority government could negotiate South Africa's future. In early 1986 he was invited by the CDU-affiliated Konrad Adenauer Foundation to visit Germany and met with Chancellor Kohl and Foreign Minister Genscher.[105] Oliver Tambo, a more controversial figure in both West Germany and South Africa, was invited by Willy Brandt of the Social Democratic Party to visit Germany later the same year. Tambo, whose visit was widely covered by the press, met with various elected officials, Ernst Breit (president of the German Trade Union Federation), representatives of the Evangelical Church in Germany, and Genscher. In June 1988 Tambo returned to Germany and issued a joint statement with Willy Brandt calling for stronger European sanctions against Pretoria.[106] But compared with its relatively insignificant commitment of financial resources for programs that could contribute to black empowerment in South Africa, Bonn allocated a substantial amount of money to the Frontline States.

## West Germany's Policy Toward the Frontline States

Assisting the Frontline States was not only consistent with West German economic interests in southern Africa as a whole, but was also compatible with Pretoria's emphasis on increased economic development and with Bonn's political objectives. In addition, the activities of the Soviet Union and East Germany in the region could not go unchallenged. Thus, Bonn's response was to use economic assistance to achieve its foreign policy goals. But West Germany also regarded South Africa's destabilization policy as a threat to Bonn's economic interests and urged Pretoria to cease its aggression against its neighbors. Foreign Minister Genscher linked many of the problems in southern Africa to South African support for Renamo, the Mozambican Resistance Movement.[107] However, unlike Britain, West Germany refused to provide the victims of South African military raids with military assistance. Instead, it focused on giving economic development aid to individual members of the Southern African Development Coordination Conference (SADCC).

Zimbabwe, SADCC's strongest member politically and economically, received DM 56.6 million in 1986 from West Germany. Most of this money was allocated for road construction, supplying power to the rural areas, vocational training, the development of mineral and raw material resources, and health care and family planning. As early as 1980, Genscher had promised Zimbabwe DM 7 million in technical assistance when he attended independence ceremonies in April of that year. A few months later Bonn's Development Minister, Rainer Offergeld, signed a DM 50 million credit agreement in Harare for rebuilding roads, bridges, and wells destroyed during the struggle for independence.[108]

Mozambique, Zambia, Botswana, and Lesotho also received significant financial assistance from West Germany. Perhaps in an effort to improve its image throughout Africa, West Germany emerged as Lesotho's principal donor in the early 1980s. In addition to funding projects such as rural development, Bonn sent technical advisers to the Central Planning and Development Office and provided training and equipment for Lesotho's Mounted Police and paramilitary force.[109] Approximately DM 29 million in grants was given in 1986 for sewage systems in rural villages, agriculture, the establishment of small- and medium-sized companies, and vocational training in trade and industry. Similarly, Zambia received

DM 50 million in 1986, partly to help deal with its foreign exchange problems. Rural development, water supply, and vocational training projects were also funded.[110]

In the case of Mozambique, West Germany's policy was influenced to a large extent by political considerations such as Mozambique's socialist policies and its relations with East Germany. Before leaving office in 1982, the SPD signed an agreement with Mozambique that provided financial aid, previously withheld because of President Samora Machel's refusal to sign the Berlin Clause, which stipulated that a party to a treaty with West Germany implicitly recognized the State of Berlin as part of the Federal Republic.[111] Despite initial opposition from Strauss and other officials in the new governing CDU/CSU coalition, by 1984 most West Germans' perceptions of Mozambique had changed, due in part to Strauss's own détente with East Germany. Furthermore, South Africa's decision to conclude the Nkomati Accord with socialist Mozambique disarmed the more conservative German groups who had opposed Bonn's relations with Machel.[112] Severe economic problems and violence in Mozambique rendered West Germany's financial assistance crucial.

Bonn's relations with the Frontline States have been essentially consistent with its policy of promoting gradual alterations in the status quo in South Africa. Like Britain, West Germany considers its economic interests in South Africa to be paramount and remains unconvinced that economic sanctions would help to accomplish the overall objective of bringing about a non-racial South African society.

# 4

# JAPAN

## Political Rhetoric and Economic Realities

Despite the fact that Japan is South Africa's largest trading partner and its biggest customer for strategic raw materials, particularly chromium and platinum, anti-apartheid activity in Japan is essentially nonexistent and there is little international condemnation of Japan's policies towards the white minority regime. Japan's policy of *seikei bunri*, separating politics from business, and its reluctance to include human rights considerations in its trade policies are accepted by the Japanese public. The public also appears to agree with the government's conservative economic policy which emphasizes efficiency to the exclusion of concern about equity. Furthermore, this approach is supported by the ruling conservative Liberal Democratic Party, the national bureaucracy, and big business and financial institutions, a coalition which has traditionally dominated that country's foreign economic policy-making process.[1] Official policy statements, which are ambiguous and do not reflect the reality of Japan's relationship with South Africa, usually escape close domestic and international scrutiny. This chapter examines the incongruity between Japan's political rhetoric condemning apartheid and its strong economic ties with the white minority regime.

Japan's argument that as long as other industrial countries engage in business and trade with South Africa it will have to do likewise is no longer credible, especially in light of the fact that since the Commonwealth meeting in Nassau in 1985 and the passage of the Comprehensive Anti-Apartheid Act in the United States in 1986, many West European countries, Canada, Australia, the United States, and Scandinavia have imposed a variety of sanctions against South Africa. However, it is unlikely that Japan will rush in to fill a vacuum resulting from European and American withdrawal, despite its increased trade with South Africa. In addition to South Africa's deteriorating economic environment, Japan has to consider the global implications of close ties with the apartheid regime. Developments in South Africa have contributed to the merging of pragmatism and morality. Opposing apartheid now makes business sense and, given Japan's heavy dependence on trade for its survival, it can hardly risk receiving negative international attention. To safeguard its long-term interests, Japan is establishing trade links with and investing in many black African states, as well as taking a strong political stand against apartheid, even as its trade with South Africa grows.

Japan's South Africa policy demonstrates, to a large extent, its emphasis on economic nationalism as opposed to political ideology and military power. Although clearly an economic giant, Japan has not emerged as a military superpower because of conditions enforced by the United States and its allies after Japan's defeat in the Second World War. Furthermore, Japan has not articulated a foreign policy commensurate with its new position in the international economic and political system, partly because it can hide behind the United States. Although maintaining a low profile in international politics is no longer possible due in part to America's relative economic decline and Japan's clear ascendancy, Japan cannot be classified as a superpower in the traditional sense; it lacks the military might and nuclear arsenals generally associated with the superpowers, the United States and the Soviet Union. Even though Japan is regarded as a nonsuperpower in this book, the fact that power in an interdependent world with nuclear missiles is increasingly based on economic considerations cannot be overlooked. Indeed, both the Soviet Union and the United States will have to grapple with this reality in the foreseeable future; both superpowers will be forced to pay greater attention to internal economic conditions, and this will be reflected in their foreign policies.

## JAPAN'S SEARCH FOR ITS ROLE IN THE WORLD

Ideological rivalries between the United States and the Soviet Union during the postwar period failed to draw Japan into the political arena. According to Donald Hellman, the major factor in keeping Japan outside international politics was U.S. policy and the extraordinary international conditions that prevailed for more than thirty years after World War II.[2] Similar to West Germany, Japan was prevented from playing a major political role in world politics but was encouraged to focus on its economic recovery in an open international economic system that the United States had helped to shape.[3] Japan's foreign policy was basically nonexistent, as was West Germany's for many years subsequent to its creation in 1945; both countries assumed the role of passive actors that reacted flexibly to developments initiated by others, while avoiding taking their own initiatives and concentrating instead on economic expansion.[4] As in the case of West Germany, there was a general consensus within Japanese society that economic growth was the country's first priority. While the Soviet Union and the United States became entangled in Third World conflicts, Japan used its relative political isolation to concentrate on economic prosperity. Difficult foreign policy decisions that could have divided the nation and diverted attention from economic goals were avoided. In this climate, the Japanese government could maintain a domestic consensus focused on trade and improving its citizens' standard of living, making the country more of a "trading company" than a nation-state, a nation without a foreign policy in the usual sense of the word.[5]

Economic success, however, is altering this reality and forcing Japan to assume greater international responsibilities commensurate with its status as an economic superpower. While the United States experienced unprecedented trade deficits and indebtedness to foreigners in the 1980s, Japan enjoyed an ever expanding trade surplus and accumulated enough capital to become a major investor in the United States and elsewhere. It was already evident by the mid-1970s that Japan had grown too large economically to hide behind the United States,[6] especially when American foreign policy seemed to flounder. Japan, however reluctantly, is having to assume a more active role in international affairs to protect its economic interests and access to raw materials not only in South Africa but throughout the Third World. Increasingly, Japanese political leaders are recognizing that in an interdependent world politics and economics cannot be neatly separated.[7] Economic might and political influence are inextricably linked. Given Japan's reliance on an international system relatively free of major military conflicts, it is in Japan's interest to maintain that system. Consequently, Japan is now expected to give additional attention to preventing disputes that emanate from growing interdependence and to assist in the peaceful resolution of regional conflicts in the areas such as southern Africa.[8] But Japan's changing circumstances will end its isolation from international politics—an isolation which helped it to emerge as a great economic power—and subject it to greater international scrutiny and pressure on issues such as apartheid.

Japan's emerging position in the international political system is complicated by misgivings in Western nations about that country as a dominant power, and by domestic opposition to its entanglement in military conflicts abroad. Furthermore, in trying to define its new role in world politics, Japan is confronted by insufficient military power, the absence of a clear ideological mission,[9] the dual diplomacy practiced by Tokyo, and outsiders' inability or unwillingness to understand it. Among the many reasons for foreigners' relative lack of understanding of Japan are: the Japanese reluctance to allow outsiders sufficient contact for comprehension of their society; a long history of isolation; language barriers; and deliberate attempts by Japanese authorities to obfuscate facts in sensitive cases such as South Africa. Perhaps the most important problem is related to outsiders' perception of Japan. The general view of Japan is that it is a typical sovereign nation-state with a central government and one leader who takes ultimate responsibility for national decision making. But according to Karel Van Wolferen, this fiction prevents foreigners from understanding Japan.[10] As will be discussed, policymaking in Japan is less centralized than elsewhere in the industrial world, with greater emphasis placed on consensus than on conflict among groups. A major concern of Japanese officials is to maintain a careful balance among semi-autonomous groups that share power, particularly the bureaucrats, some political organizations, businessmen, and industrialists.[11]

Decentralization of decision making and factional politics in Japan deprive the prime minister of a clear leadership position in domestic policy. To compensate for this relative lack of dominance in internal affairs, the prime minister tends to emphasize foreign policy because of its relative unimportance to many Japanese citizens. As F. Quei Quo put it, Japanese prime ministers use international affairs for publicity purposes to enhance their personal reputation.[12] However, since they generally fail to gain full support from the various groups that comprise the power structure of the country, their statements are not always meaningful. In the final analysis, current political realities in Japan prevent political leaders from playing an important role in foreign affairs[13] and diminish their credibility simultaneously. It is not uncommon for members of the U.S. Congress to get frustrated with Japanese leaders for not keeping their promises on trade issues, a frustration also experienced by anti-apartheid groups who see Japan's trade with South Africa expand even as it expresses its strong opposition to apartheid. South Africa's Foreign Minister Pik Botha's visit provides an excellent example of what occurs in Japan. When Botha arrived in Japan in September 1986, he received a cool reception from his Japanese counterpart, Tadashi Kuranari, who emphasized that new sanctions against apartheid would be implemented. Japanese businessmen, however, met with Botha individually and welcomed him cordially at a luncheon in his honor.[14] This dual diplomacy allows Japan to appear diplomatically cool in its relations with South Africa without jeopardizing its economic interests. The gap between rhetoric and reality is better understood by examining how foreign policy is made in Japan.

## FOREIGN POLICY IN JAPAN

Foreign policymaking in Japan is closely related to what are perceived as the nation's security interests. As indicated earlier, national security, defined in military terms, was not Japan's principal priority because it was guaranteed by the United States. Instead, the highest priority was placed on economic growth and development, and foreign policy became indistinguishable from economic policy. Even Japan's relations with its Asian neighbors ultimately depended on economic considerations. Japan's role in the world and the mix of economic, political, and military commitments it should make received much less attention,[15] at least until recently. If Japan's economic expansion heightened its awareness of its dependence on imported raw materials from Third World countries and its need for access to markets in the United States, Western Europe, and elsewhere, the oil crisis of 1973 further underscored its vulnerability. Unlike the United States, which has abundant natural resources, Japan is forced to make foreign policy decisions based foremost on its economic interests.[16] Confronted with what they perceive to be "Japan bashing" in the United States and Western Europe and mounting competition from the newly industrialized countries of Asia, Japanese leaders are increasingly sensitive to political issues that might interfere with free access to markets and sources of raw materials. It is in this context that Tokyo's South Africa policy must be analyzed.

Several factors that combine to influence Japan's policy toward South Africa in particular and its foreign policy in general include: cultural characteristics, the relationship between the business community and the government, the influence of the bureaucracy, and the role of public opinion. These are directly related to Japan's perception of its interests and affect how it responds to developments in its external environment.[17]

## CULTURAL FACTORS

Maintaining good relations and offending no one are hallmarks of Japanese society and foreign relations, a direct outgrowth of its strong emphasis on consensus and its tightly-knit groups. Unlike the United States where individualism is considered a virtue, cooperation is stressed and rewarded in Japan, and there is no moral basis for resisting the group.[18] Ultimately, the individual in the larger society is part of a group, and group membership is cemented by a complex set of reciprocal obligations, thus the need for consensus.[19] Because consensus requires compromise and widespread agreement on key objectives, before proposals are presented to the larger group, informal negotiations occur, and there are prior consultations with members who are reluctant to support a particular policy or who are opposed to it.[20] Obviously, this approach is feasible in societies where citizens have common perceptions of national interests and are relatively isolated from the outside world. In this regard, Japan is quite similar to the Scandinavian countries discussed in chapter six. However, unlike Japan, the Scandinavians view international organizations and their active participation in them as essential to the protection of their national interests.

Japan's isolation and deeply rooted sense of cultural identity and homogeneity combine to reinforce its feeling of separateness from other cultures, especially those beyond the traditional Confucian circle. Qualities of xenophobia and exclusiveness were natural outgrowths of isolation[21] and have become factors which directly influence Tokyo's relations with South Africa. Isolation tends to foster the belief that one's culture is unique and superior, a view that can have negative implications for a country which must deal with the outside world. While Japan has been extremely successful in business matters, it is likely to suffer from that same amorality that has guided its business practices when it confronts issues such as apartheid. Japan's expanding trade with South Africa and its racial attitudes are in part due to this myopic view of the world. As Clyde Haberman observes, what really ruffles Japanese officials is not so much trade with South Africa itself as the awkwardness of being that country's major trading partner; the Japanese, in general, do not really care at all about apartheid.[22]

Another aspect of Japanese culture which contributes to its indifference to apartheid is the Japanese attitude toward suffering. Although they have a strong sense of human compassion, their relative isolation prevents them from extending this to South Africans. Moreover, it seems that the idea of suffering to achieve particular objectives is of great importance, and endurance is viewed as a virtue.[23] Reinforcing these attitudes is the relative lack of equality or commitment to equality in Japanese society, which is characterized by a hierarchical social structure, despite challenges to such social stratification. Superior-inferior and inferior-superior patterns are seen by Robert Scalapino as creating the key reference points for all relations and for providing the basis on which individuals establish their identity.[24] Derogatory comments made by Japanese officials about racial minorities in the United States reflect their inability or unwillingness to come to grips with the concept of equality among individuals. Discrimination in Japan itself seems to underscore difficulties that country will encounter as it projects its new foreign policy into areas such as southern Africa.

Countries with multi-racial populations and a commitment to racial equality take a much stronger stance against apartheid. Their challenge is to find ways of including citizens from diverse racial and ethnic backgrounds in the economic, political and social mainstream. The United States has achieved this objective to a much greater extent than any other major industrial society, with the possible exception of Canada. Japanese traditions and cultural values have resulted in an entirely different approach to racial issues, even though many Japanese abroad have been victims of discrimination. However, as is often the case, former victims usually conclude, erroneously, that undesirable behavior can continue as long as they are not the victims. Although the Japanese are taking measures to eliminate racial discrimination, their sense of racial difference, a sort of racist caste system, remains embedded in their society.[25] While Americans emphasize their country's diversity, Japanese pride themselves on their uniqueness, resist assimilating ethnic minorities, and are so concerned with being an ethnically homogeneous society that their concept of citizenship remains almost identical with a concept of racial purity.[26]

Koreans living in Japan are the principal victims of discrimination despite racial and cultural similarities between Koreans and Japanese. It is generally believed that what came to be the Japanese population was actually a blended population drawn from the Korean peninsula and from agricultural communities already present in the Japanese islands.[27] Even though Koreans and other minorities comprise only five percent of the Japanese population, they are systematically excluded from being fully integrated into that society as equal citizens. So strong is the emphasis on conformity that Japanese children who are educated abroad are severely handicapped when they return because the society refuses to accept them into the mainstream educational system.[28] Far more prevalent and severe is the discrimination against children of Japanese and non-Asian parents, especially against children with a black parent. The latter have been stereotyped in the media, and public opinion surveys done before 1983 showed that Japanese tend to rate blacks on the bottom of the list of their racial favorites, immediately below Koreans.[29] These attitudes inevitably influence Japan's policy toward the white minority regime in South Africa, a government which is based on the concept of racial superiority, and which regards Japanese who conduct business in the country as "honorary whites." Cultural factors also affect the attitudes of the businessmen who help to shape Japanese foreign policy.

## BUSINESS GROUPS AND FOREIGN POLICY

The primacy of economic growth and reconstruction in Japan's foreign policy elevated business groups to the pinnacle of power in the decision making process. In fact, Japan's extraordinary industrial transformation over such a short period of time would have been extremely difficult without close cooperation and consensus between big business and various government agencies.[30] Since foreign policy is essentially economic policy, business interest groups have tremendous power over its formulation and implementation. Indeed, business and government are not clearly separated as businessmen are directly involved in diplomacy in a manner similar to their German counterparts. Since the mid-1960s, participation by businessmen in Japanese diplomacy has been considered a constant rather than an intermittent phenomenon.[31] They represent the government in many different official capacities, ranging from roving ambassadors appointed by the Foreign Ministry to representatives at international conferences on trade.

To a much greater extent than in the United States, the Japanese business community exercises significant financial control over the country's ruling conservative Liberal Democratic Party. Not only are they the main financial supporters, but they also have very close connections with leading politicians. While the Foreign Ministry can also influence business through its specialized knowledge of foreign affairs and access to information, business can influence appointments to the Foreign Ministry through its close ties with the Liberal Democratic Party.[32] All three groups are clearly interdependent and must rely on consensus to achieve their own particular objectives. Businessmen may also influence foreign policy decisions by their participation in various clubs established by Japan's political leaders to provide contacts with business leaders, through their representation on government deliberative councils and advisory commissions, and through personal contacts with powerful bureaucrats.[33]

## BUREAUCRATS AND PUBLIC OPINION

Bureaucrats are far more crucial than public opinion is to the foreign policy process. They have enjoyed unchallenged authority for much of Japan's postwar history because of their close association with business groups and government officials. As Scalapino observed, Japanese democracy, while bolstered by widespread political freedom, competitive elections, and the legal supremacy of the Diet (Japan's parliament), in the final analysis, coexists with a powerful bureaucratic state.[34] Under these circumstances, the role of public opinion in influencing foreign policy decisions is limited. Generally, public opinion, when it is expressed, seems to be largely ignored by the ruling elites who have been the key architects of Japan's policy. Government leaders tend to respond only to the most extreme demands of public opinion, especially regarding major foreign affairs issues.[35] Since few Japanese citizens are aware of apartheid, and anti-apartheid activity is relatively rare, public opinion is likely to remain an unimportant factor in Japan's South Africa policy, and trade considerations will continue to predominate.

## JAPAN'S TRADE WITH SOUTH AFRICA

The dominance of trade in Tokyo's relationship with South Africa was evident from the beginning of the twentieth century. Both Egypt and South Africa were viewed by Japan as gateways to Europe as well as potential trading partners. Although commercial links were established with Kenya and other countries along Africa's east coast, Japan clearly focused on South Africa, especially during World War I when Germany lost its position as South Africa's second largest trading partner after

Great Britain. Japan's exports to South Africa, valued at 454,000 yen in 1912, increased to 18,343,000 yen in 1918, while its imports, which were practically nonexistent in 1912, jumped to 29,449,000 yen by 1918. In 1920 South Africa's exports to Japan declined to 8,206,000 yen and imports climbed to 73,895,000 yen.[36] As Britain, France, and Germany resumed their economic activities at the end of the war, trade between South Africa and Japan declined, with the trade imbalance in Japan's favor.[37]

This trade surplus triggered strong anti-Japanese feelings among white South Africans, especially the Afrikaners who were determined to rid the country of all Asians, including Japanese. The Immigration Act of 1913 was utilized to exclude Asian immigrants as well as to prevent Japanese from expanding trade and commerce. Japan's efforts to obtain preferential treatment for its citizens, however, were aided by South Africa's economic difficulties, particularly in the wool industry. The Great Depression closed many overseas wool markets at a time when South Africa was overproducing wool and facing serious competition from Australia. Japan, a major consumer of wool—mostly from Australia—decided to import South African wool in exchange for equal treatment for Japanese in South Africa. The prohibition against Japanese immigrants was removed, and all Japanese citizens in South Africa were given the same treatment as whites.[38] Economic considerations forced the Afrikaners to modify further discriminatory policies against the Japanese following the flight of foreign capital in response to the Sharpeville Massacre in 1961. South Africa's isolation pushed it to make new friends among pariah states in Latin America and elsewhere and to encourage more Japanese investments. Between 1962 and 1968, the value of Japanese-South African trade rose from about $178,974,000 to $551,591,000, and by 1980 the figure stood at $3,593,738,000, twenty times what it was in 1960. Indeed, South Africa's extensive economic ties with Japan influenced it to grant Japanese the status of "honorary whites" in the Republic in 1961,[39] a designation which permitted them access to all white areas, housing, and cultural activities and allowed them to engage freely in business.

There are several reasons for Japan's decision to develop strong economic links with South Africa. First, Japan's growing economy depends on imports of essential minerals such as platinum, chromium, manganese, cobalt, and vanadium which are abundant in South Africa and not readily available elsewhere. Chromium is used to produce stainless steel and electrolytic chromium metal for ships, industrial equipment, and naval propulsion systems; manganese is used to make steel, pig iron, and dry cell batteries; and cobalt is essential for the manufacture of superalloys for industrial and aircraft gas turbine engines, magnetic materials for various electric applications, catalysts, and for metal cutting and mining tool bits. Second, South Africa represents an expanding market for Japanese products. Third, South Africa's reputation for being a reliable trading partner is well established; its export bodies maintain tight quality control and honor contracts. As Martin Spring has observed, reliability of supply is extremely important for resource-poor Japan, where space and financial considerations preclude massive stockpiles of materials at factories.[40] Japan's desire for continued access to mineral resources has ensured that trade between the two countries is extensive. So crucial are these resources to Japan's global exports (computers, precision instruments, cars, steel, etc.) that the Japanese have committed themselves to long-term contracts to buy coal, chromium, platinum, uranium, manganese, and iron ore from South Africa while making token gestures to placate critics of apartheid.

The arrangement to obtain uranium following the oil crisis is a good example of Japan's policy. During the 1973 crisis Japan's almost total dependence on foreign petroleum supplies forced it to increase its uranium imports dramatically. Its power companies signed contracts as early as December 1973 to cover an estimated eighty percent of import needs for a ten-year period. Kansai Electric Power Company and Mitsubishi Corporation of Japan, the Rossing mining group of South Africa, as well as the Japanese and South African governments were parties to the agreement that provided for sale to Japan of 8,200 short tons of uranium from the Rossing mine in Namibia. Mitsubishi, in cooperation with the Japanese government, exchanged nuclear technology for a guaranteed supply of uranium, despite U.N. resolutions prohibiting trade with Namibia.[41] Similarly, Japan imported high-grade Rhodesian chrome through South Africa, although it claimed to support the U.N. embargo against Rhodesia. Discrepancies between Japanese figures, which showed that it imported 719,469 metric tons of chromium in 1971 and 445,263 metric tons in 1972, and South African statistics, showing that only 353,375 tons and 253,083 tons respectively were exported to Japan during those two years, ignited African criticisms of Japan's role in strengthening minority rule in Rhodesia.[42] Tokyo responded to pressure from African states by placing restrictions on South African high-grade chrome in 1974. However, its dependence on chromium for manufacturing various kinds of steel and for transportation and power-generating industries influenced it to largely ignore international sanctions.

Political instability in Namibia and South Africa, growing international pressure for sanctions against apartheid, and passage of the Comprehensive Anti-Apartheid Act in the United States in 1986 combined to persuade Japanese businessmen to reduce their reliance on South Africa's uranium. By 1988, Japan's huge electric power companies decided to announce plans to terminate such purchases for their nuclear plants.[43] Given Japan's vulnerability to interruptions in the flow of raw materials, industry and government leaders did this only after finalizing plans to mine Chinese uranium. Since Japan's other major suppliers, Canada and Australia, supported strong sanctions against South Africa, Japan's decision to stop buying South African uranium could be viewed as beneficial to these countries. Canada, for example, supplies Japan with approximately forty percent of its uranium, and Japanese, French, and Canadian companies have significant investments in the uranium mines.[44]

In addition to minerals, Japan's imports from South Africa include citrus fruit, wool, and eggs. Japan, with Canada, has also been a major market for South African sugar; indeed, the Japanese market is so important that South Africans have geared sugar processing to the requirements of Japan's mills, standards other customers must accept.[45] By 1986 Japanese companies were also importing large amounts of corn from South Africa. Approximately 1.2 million tons were shipped to Japan between January and November, 1986, compared to only 21,514 tons in 1985 and none in 1984, when South Africa suffered from severe drought. This market is important to both countries. South Africans wish to remain competitive in world markets and to dilute trade sanctions; Japan profits from the lower prices offered by South Africa as part of its effort to reduce its isolation. Furthermore, Japanese cornstarch manufacturers prefer South Africa's white corn which is harvested, washed, and dried by hand over America's yellow corn which is picked, washed, and dried by machine.[46]

Japanese exports to South Africa include motor vehicles, car parts, electrical and mechanical equipment, steel, textiles, chinaware, toys, sewing machines, television sets, cameras, watches, radios, tape recorders, electrical appliances, and computers. Japan continues to sell computers directly to South Africa as well as through European dealers and under the names of European computer firms such as Siemens and BASF, which trade directly with South Africa. Direct sales alone amounted to $40 million in 1985.[47] It also supplies South Africa with advanced technology through licenses from Japanese corporations and direct sales which are often facilitated by government-subsidized trade credits from Japan's Export-Import Bank.[48] Japanese firms, for example, provided much of the technology for South Africa's oil-from-coal project, as well as offshore drilling rigs which are utilized in an attempt to reduce that country's vulnerability stemming from its lack of domestic oil production. Trade between the two countries remains strong (see tables 5 and 6). Even as Japan's External Trade Organization is actually promoting commerce with South Africa, the government is encouraging Japanese companies to invest in black Africa and expand trade partly in order to lessen opposition to its ties with Pretoria as well as to reduce its dependence on South Africa.

## JAPAN'S ECONOMIC TIES WITH BLACK AFRICA

Japanese investments in black Africa are concentrated in shipping-related activities in Liberia, a country selected by major shipping states because of its flags of convenience policy. Liberia received over eighty percent of all Japanese investments in Africa in 1981 and sixty-two percent in

TABLE 5
**Japan's Trade with South Africa**
**(In current US $mn)**

|      | Imports  | Exports  |
| ---- | -------- | -------- |
| 1976 | 938.50   | 883.35   |
| 1977 | 1,014.77 | 853.57   |
| 1978 | 921.50   | 868.29   |
| 1981 | 1,556.20 | 1,991.06 |
| 1982 | 1,860.28 | 1,667.27 |
| 1983 | 1,584.00 | 1,736.50 |
| 1984 | 1,603.40 | 1,825.36 |
| 1986 | 2,248.00 | 1,357.00 |
| 1987 | 2,455.00 | 1,882.00 |

*Sources: Africa Contemporary Record, 1979–1980;* Customs Bureau, Ministry of Finance, Tokyo; Japan Tariff Association; *Africa,* No. 147 (November 1983); *Statistics on Trade with South Africa,* compiled by the Commonwealth Experts Group (1988).

TABLE 6
**Main Items of Trade in 1985**
**(In current US $mn)**

| Japan's Exports to South Africa |     | Japan's Imports from South Africa |     |
| ------------------------------- | --- | --------------------------------- | --- |
| Cars                            | 369 | Coal                              | 378 |
| Car Parts                       | 206 | Metallic-minerals                 | 289 |
| VTR tape                        | 91  | Platinum                          | 246 |
| Radio, T.V.                     | 51  | Ferrous alloy                     | 160 |
| Generator, motor                | 44  | Gold                              | 52  |

*Source:* The Japanese Embassy (Washington, D.C.).

1983.[49] Since 1973, however, greater emphasis has been placed on finding critical mineral resources, especially uranium, iron ore, chromium, and oil. One of the most active firms involved in uranium exploration and mining is the Power Reactor and Nuclear Fuel Development Corporation which has operations in Mali, Niger, Guinea, Gabon, and Zambia. Niger, regarded as the most promising source of uranium, is already a producer. Overseas Uranium Resources Development Company (a Japanese consortium), the Niger government, Cogema of France, and Spain's Enusa are mining uranium at Akouta, and Tokyo Uranium is searching for deposits in Mauritania.[50] The Japanese government's Metal Mining Agency is supporting chromium exploration efforts in Sudan's Ingesana Hills, and Japanese firms are exploiting iron ore deposits in Liberia, Senegal, and Mauritania, and manganese in Gabon. Mitsubishi Petroleum Development

Company and C. Itoh are working with Elf-Gabon of France to increase oil production levels.[51]

Manufacturing investments are mainly in motor vehicles, textiles, consumer electronics, fishing nets, batteries, and motor bikes. In 1984 Africa took one-fifth of all Japanese knockdown vehicles for assembly in local plants. In Nigeria, the main country involved, Mitsubishi assembles two-ton trucks and Honda puts together motor bikes.[52] Overall, Japanese investments remain relatively modest, especially when compared with Japanese exports to Africa. Faced with African criticism of its trade with South Africa and rising protectionist policies in Western markets, Japan views Africa as a potentially significant market, especially for automobiles. Its vehicle exports to Africa have increased to such a large extent that over sixty percent of all cars sold in Africa are Japanese, and Nigeria alone surpassed South Africa as Japan's largest customer on the continent in 1981.[53] In addition to automobiles, Japan's exports to Africa include tape recorders, television sets, radios, and video tape recorders. As Table 7 indicates, Japan enjoys a favorable trade surplus with black Africa.

In addition to trade and investments, Japan is also providing foreign aid. However, this assistance remains below that of most industrialized countries, despite Japan's record $60 billion trade surplus in 1985. Prior to 1985, Japan's official development assistance was only 0.23 percent of its Gross National Product, compared with an average of 0.35 percent of OECD countries.[54] Furthermore, aid is heavily concentrated on about seven countries which act as suppliers of essential raw materials and with which Japan has strong economic ties. Reacting to criticism of its policies, the Japanese government donated $20 million in 1981 and $165

TABLE 7
Japan's Trade with Africa
(Excluding South Africa)
(In current US $mn)

|  | Imports | Exports |
|---|---|---|
| 1976 | 1649.6 | 6447.88 |
| 1977 | 1403.7 | 6659.50 |
| 1978 | 1029.17 | 4789.57 |
| 1980 | 2672.68 | 5944.24 |
| 1981 | 3022.80 | 7595.32 |
| 1982 | 1914.54 | 5312.81 |
| 1983 | 1683.51 | 4264.47 |
| 1984 | 1491.85 | 4504.12 |

Sources: *Africa Contemporary Record, 1979–1980;* Customs Bureau, Ministry of Finance, Tokyo; Japan Tariff Association; *Africa,* No. 147 (November 1983).

million in 1984 to famine victims, and in 1985 Prime Minister Nakasone promised to double Japan's development assistance over a seven-year period starting in 1986.[55]

In 1987 the Japanese government's aid policy toward southern Africa closely resembled that of Canada, Britain, West Germany, and the Scandinavian countries. Like Britain and West Germany, Japan's relations with the Frontline States seem to be partly designed to deflect criticism of its expanding trade with South Africa. Japan's decision to send an economic survey mission to Tanzania, Zambia, Zimbabwe, and Mozambique in March 1987 reflected Japan's interest in building better relations with the countries' leaders as well as securing an economic position in an area increasingly viewed as one of Africa's most promising regions for economic development. Like many other nonsuperpowers, Japan is trying to help the Frontline States reduce their dependence on South Africa by contributing aid to the transportation and agricultural sectors of the economy.[56]

Diplomatic relations with black Africa are also instrumental in strengthening ties. Several African governments, despite serious economic difficulties and reductions in diplomatic staffs around the world, have reinforced their representation in Japan, and many leaders, including Presidents Moi, Mugabe, Nyerere, and Kaunda, have visited Japan. In November 1984, Japan's Foreign Minister Shintaro Abe, the Japanese Crown Prince, and some members of parliament toured ten African states and reiterated their government's official policy on apartheid.[57]

## OFFICIAL SANCTIONS AND ECONOMIC REALITIES

Japan was the first major industrialized country to prohibit its citizens from directly investing in South Africa. As early as 1974 the London-based Japan International Bank Ltd. announced that it would immediately halt loans to the South African government as well as to private individuals.[58] However, restrictions against investments are extremely porous and serve to obfuscate the economic realities. Some companies circumvent the ban by investing through their overseas subsidiaries. The most common practice by far, permitted by the Japanese government, is for firms to build factories in South Africa using local capital. Japanese companies transfer patents, technology, management and engineering skills to their locally franchised partners without making any direct investments. The automobile industry especially has benefited from this practice.

Toyota established its first assembly plant in South Africa in 1962 and was joined later by other Japanese car manufacturers such as Nissan, Mitsubishi, Isuzu, and Mazda. Toyota SA is the company's largest plant outside Japan and the major producer of motor vehicles in South Africa. Altogether, Japanese model cars assembled in South Africa under licensing agreements have accounted for at least thirty-five percent of that country's car sales since 1981.[59] By 1987 Toyota and Nissan had acquired about 40 percent of the South African car market and, based on preliminary figures for 1988, sales were likely to continue to grow. Toyota's exports to South Africa increased by approximately thirty-six percent in January and February 1988, compared to the same period in 1987. Furthermore, representatives from Toyota and Nissan indicated that because their government was too vague on sanctions against Pretoria they would not attempt to reduce their sales to Africa.[60] In theory, Toyota's operations in South Africa are not directly controlled by the home company, and Japan does not have the equivalent of the Sullivan Principles or the EC Code for black employees, many of whom are employed in low-level jobs and receive substandard wages. The same applies to other Japanese companies such as Bridgestone, Yokohama, Toyo Rubber (tire companies); Hitachi, Sanyo, Sony, Sharp, Pioneer, Sansui, Fuji, Akai Cannon, and Matsushiti (manufacturers of electronic and electrical appliances); and Honda, Yamaha, and Suzuki (motorcycle firms).

Theoretically, Japan cannot demand that companies in South Africa comply with the equivalent of the Sullivan Principles because there is, according to the government, no Japanese investment in South Africa. Interestingly enough, in October 1985 Japanese officials announced "action standards" by which Japanese firms in South Africa would abide. These guidelines, which are voluntary, are similar to those in the EC Code discussed in chapter two. But since there is no direct Japanese investment in South Africa, at least in theory, these standards could only be applicable to representative offices that Japanese firms have there, which do not employ many blacks. South African companies that are licensed to manufacture Japanese products are not under Japan's jurisdiction and therefore would not have to comply with directives from Tokyo. Furthermore, companies were simply asked to cooperate in the program announced by Japan.[61] Essentially, nothing changed. Some Japanese firms technically comply with the ban against investing in South Africa by locating their operations in nominally independent homelands, a practice Japan has not prevented.[62] Indeed, by extending official trade credits to South Africa through its Export-Import Bank and by purchasing raw materials on long-term contracts, the Japanese government indirectly invests in South Africa. Such purchases provided the financial foundation for investments in the ports of Saldanha and Richards Bay, developed primarily to supply Japan with iron ore and coking coal, respectively.[63]

Another factor undermining the policy against direct investments is the absence of legal restrictions against Japanese foreign exchange banks and securities companies financing South African residents. Japanese officials, while regarding such loans as legal, have called the practice undesirable and have urged banks to make cautious considerations.[64] Similarly, the Japanese government has only requested all those concerned to cooperate in the voluntary halting of imports of Krugerrands and all other South African gold coins,[65] thus allowing the yearly $50 million dollar trade to continue. Most anti-apartheid activists regard the purchase of Krugerrands and South African gold as direct support of apartheid, a view endorsed by the United States. But Japan, like many European countries, continues to import gold.

Japan also points to the fact that diplomatic relations with South Africa have been downgraded to the consular level as evidence to support its claim that it has taken more severe measures against Pretoria than those taken by other countries. In reality, diplomatic relations do exist, and in terms of personnel and activities, the two consular offices in South Africa are much more important and influential than Japanese embassies in Nigeria and Kenya, two major markets for Japanese products.[66] Conducting relations at a lower level seems calculated to reduce black African antagonism, discourage close international scrutiny, and protect Japan's interests in Africa and elsewhere. After agreeing in 1961 to establish diplomatic relations, Tokyo decided in 1964 to maintain consular representation following growing international opposition to Pretoria's inhumane treatment of the black majority. Similarly, Japan's decision to suspend sporting, cultural, and educational exchanges with South Africa was taken shortly after the oil crisis of 1973–74. This crisis underscored Japan's vulnerability due to its heavy dependence on imported raw materials and influenced it to reexamine its policy of benign neglect toward Africa on the one hand and excessive entanglement with South Africa's white minority regime on the other. In an apparent effort to demonstrate its commitment to black Africa, Japan sent Foreign Minister Kiumra in 1974 on a ten-day tour of Ghana, Zaire, Nigeria, Egypt, and Tanzania.

Following South Africa's 1985 declaration of a state of emergency and the violence which accompanied it, Japan took measures to curtail the export of computers to apartheid-enforcing agencies such as the Ministry of Defense, the Defense Force, the Ministry of Law and Order, the police, the Armaments Development and Production Corporation, the National Institute for Defense Research, and the Ministry of Justice.[67] It also reiterated its long-standing ban on arms exports and imports from South Africa and reaffirmed its restrictions on cultural, sporting, and educational exchanges with South Africa, and in September 1986 steel and iron imports were banned. Although Japan has refused to issue visas to South Africans representing the minority regime since 1974, it does not prevent its citizens from traveling to South Africa to attend conferences or participate in sporting events.[68]

At the United Nations in 1986 Japan was obviously more vocal in its opposition to apartheid than it was earlier when it abstained on controversial issues, knowing that the United States or Britain would probably veto any serious actions against Pretoria. In December 1985 Japan called for courageous steps toward the abolition of apartheid, the release of

Nelson Mandela and all other political prisoners, and urged Pretoria to negotiate with representative black leaders, including those of the African National Congress. Tokyo contended that institutionalized racial discrimination in South Africa was the most serious and systematic denial of freedom and equality anywhere in the world.[69] Japanese delegates to the U.N. usually stress their country's advocacy of racial equality, as Japanese representatives have done since 1919 when Japan was virtually alone in the struggle against discrimination. However, until relatively recently Japan was primarily concerned about the treatment of its own citizens abroad, not black South Africans. Japan itself was a colonial power that discriminated against inhabitants of its colonies (Korea, Taiwan, and parts of the South Pacific).

However, international pressures and Japan's growing realization of its new role in world politics seem to have influenced its leaders to take concrete steps toward eliminating apartheid by assisting the process of black empowerment. Between 1986 and 1988 the Japanese government increased financial assistance to black South Africans to study in South Africa as well as in Japan. Twenty-two scholarships were provided through the Japan-Africa Friendship Society in Tokyo for blacks to study in South Africa and about $100,000 was allocated in 1987 for blacks to study in Japan for one year. In addition to educational grants, Tokyo contributed approximately $400,000 to nongovernmental organizations to assist victims of apartheid within South Africa.[70] These actions represent a major departure from its policy of separating economics from politics and mark a heightened Japanese sensitivity to being South Africa's major trading partner at a time when anti-apartheid sentiment is widespread.

Compared to the United States or Britain, Japan does not have to pay much attention to public opinion on the issue of minority rule in South Africa largely because the vast majority of Japanese citizens are indifferent to, and uninformed about, apartheid. Consequently, it does not have to clarify its policies toward South Africa or implement stronger sanctions to meet the demands of interest groups. Nevertheless, in 1988 preview screenings of the movie "Cry Freedom" were held in the National Diet building at the Foreign Ministry, the first time the government had made a major effort to inform its citizens about apartheid. Most Japanese subscribe to the myth that racial discrimination is nonexistent in Japan, despite obvious problems with Koreans and the Ainu, Japan's aboriginals. Afraid to acknowledge their own racial problems at home, few Japanese are interested in racial discrimination elsewhere.

Labor unions, one of the groups most likely to oppose apartheid, are virtually nonpolitical and are not very concerned about South Africa, compared to their counterparts in Western Europe, Scandinavia, and North America. Apart from issues relating to working conditions and pay, Japanese unions do not generally criticize management's policies nor do they combine their resources to influence government policies.

But there is evidence of growing political awareness about apartheid by Japan's trade unions. In March 1986 about 220 trade union officials and other concerned Japanese citizens participated in a meeting held in observance of the Week of Solidarity with Peoples Struggling against Racism and Racial Discrimination. Among the trade unions involved were the General Council of Trade Unions of Japan (SOHYO), the Japanese Confederation of Labor (DOMEI), the Federation of Industrial Organizations (SHIN-SANBETSU), and the Japanese Private Sector Trade Union Council. Together these organizations represent about ten million workers.[71] They urged the Japanese government to impose more stringent sanctions against South Africa and to issue a public report on Japan's business ties to South Africa.[72] Given the relative lack of influence of public opinion on foreign policymaking in Japan, such a report was unlikely to materialize.

The Japan Anti-Apartheid Committee (JAAC), formed in 1964, is the only significant group that attempts to mobilize public opinion and openly criticizes Japan's relations with South Africa. Its small size, about 100 active members, makes it relatively impotent. JAAC protests against banks, such as Daiwa and Sumitomo, which allegedly invested in South Africa indirectly through European financial companies, and tries to pressure Japan's External Trade Organization to terminate activities designed to promote trade between the two countries and to close its office in South Africa. JAAC also demonstrated daily in front of the South African consulate in Tokyo in 1985, invited ANC representatives to Japan to participate in seminars, and raised approximately $10,000 to support the ANC's freedom school.[73] JAAC's efforts to influence the government to distance itself from Pretoria are opposed by powerful groups such as the Japan-South Africa Parliamentarians Friendship League, the Nippon Club of South Africa, and the Springbok Club in Tokyo.

The Friendship League, founded in 1984 and composed of approximately forty members of parliament from the conservative ruling Liberal Democratic Party, advocates establishing full diplomatic relations with South Africa, strengthening economic ties, and promoting greater friendship between Japan and the Republic. They contend that greater economic interaction and technological exchanges with South Africa are likely to contribute to the elimination of apartheid because white South Africans would have to recognize the technological ability of non-white races. Furthermore, from their perspective, Japanese participation in South Africa's economy helps improve conditions for black South Africans.[74] Likewise, the Nippon club, based in Johannesburg, endeavors to cultivate close ties between Japan and South Africa, encourages friendship among Japanese in South Africa, promotes trade, and organizes cultural and athletic activities. It also sponsors the Japanese School of Johannesburg, which is designed to advance commerce by permitting businessmen to bring their families with them. The South African government provided the land and the Japanese government subsidizes the school by sending teachers from Japan and paying approximately sixty percent of the school's total operating costs.[75] While the school interacts with the white community through cultural, educational, and sporting exchanges, there is no evidence to indicate any ties with blacks. Finally, the Springbok Club in Japan is an organization of Japanese businessmen and government officials who have been stationed in South Africa and South Africans engaged in commerce or associated with consular and other official activities in Japan. One of its major contributions is the development of extensive political, diplomatic, economic, and cultural networks between and within the two countries.[76]

Despite strong official Japanese statements condemning apartheid and various sanctions which on the surface lend credibility to the generally accepted view that Japan has distanced itself from the white minority regime, available evidence suggests that these actions actually serve to deflect international criticism of the extensive economic ties between the two countries. Similarly, by encouraging Japanese companies to invest in and trade with black Africa and by providing financial assistance to selected African countries, Japan has succeeded in reducing opposition to its relationship with South Africa from the rest of the continent. Furthermore, the relative lack of international pressure on Japan can also be attributed to the absence of a highly organized, broadly based anti-apartheid movement in Japan, a general lack of awareness or concern about apartheid among the Japanese public, and the control of the country by a coalition of the ruling conservative Liberal Democratic Party, the national bureaucracy, and big business and financial institutions which emphasize efficiency to the exclusion of concerns about equity.

Success, however, has created unexpected problems for Japan. By 1987 it emerged as South Africa's most important trading partner, with a combined total of $4.33 billion for imports and exports.[77] Its new status drew unprecedented attention to its relations with South Africa, with the United Nations, the United States, and many Third World states applying pressure on Japan to reduce its trade with Pretoria. Concerned with this new image, the Foreign Ministry, without much success, urged companies to diminish their commercial transactions with South Africa. Japan's exports to South Africa increased more than forty-five percent in the first half of 1988, to $1.14 billion, compared with the same period in 1987.[78]

A major reason for this gap between rhetoric and reality is Japan's practice of dual diplomacy and the dominant role of business in the country's foreign economic policy process. The Ministry of International Trade and Industry (MITI) has been extremely effective in keeping the guidelines issued by the Foreign Ministry vague and basically meaningless. Essentially, the diplomats have been prevented from clearly articulating Japan's policy toward South Africa. Conflict between the two Ministries could, however, be construed as being deliberate and consistent with

Japan's practice of dual diplomacy. In other words, Japan could be seen as using the Foreign Ministry to voice the government's opposition to apartheid, while MITI supports businessmen who take advantage of the opportunities created by sanctions imposed by other industrialized countries.[79]

Although the Japanese have succeeded in projecting an anti-apartheid image while continuing to do business through locally owned subsidiaries (a practice which some Western firms adopted as divestment pressures increased), widespread political violence in South Africa and mounting pressure on the United States and Western Europe to pursue policies designed to assist in the abolition of apartheid will render it increasingly difficult for Japan to hide behind the United States and continue its present practice of separating politics from business in South Africa. Recent steps taken by the Japanese government clearly indicate that there is a new reality emerging in Tokyo that will be more consistent with the political rhetoric of the Foreign Ministry.

# 5

# ISRAEL

## The Politics and Economics of National Security

National security has dominated Israel's domestic and foreign policy concerns since its inception in 1948 and plays a pivotal role in its relations with South Africa. Unlike Japan and West Germany, which were denied full sovereignty and the right to rebuild their military might subsequent to their defeat in World War II and were forced to rely on the United States and its Western European allies for protection, Israel was responsible for guaranteeing its own security, albeit with substantial American assistance. While West Germany, Japan, and, to a lesser extent, Britain could concentrate on economic reconstruction under Washington's hegemony, obvious and persistent threats to Israel's existence from neighboring Arab states focused that country's attention on building military power sufficient to ensure self-preservation. But as all other considerations—economic, social, and political—became subservient to the military aspects of national defense, issues of morality were increasingly relegated to the back burner, and violations of human rights by the Israeli government were often justified in terms of national security.

This almost Hobbesian approach to international relations, combined with and influenced by the internal dynamics of Israeli society, the Arabs' success in isolating Israel in the world community, and Palestinian resistance in the Occupied Territories, prompted closer Israeli-South African collaboration and, paradoxically, ultimately eroded the moral and economic foundations of Israel's security and contributed to the emergence of widespread international sympathy for Palestinians in the West Bank and Gaza. Israel's unnecessarily brutal response to the Palestinian Intifada or uprising stood in marked contrast to its image as the victim of Arab aggression and influenced news reporters to compare the situation in the Occupied Territories to that in South Africa, despite official Israeli protests against such analogies. These problems were exacerbated by Israel's continued emphasis on the Holocaust as the crucial remembered experience shaping its domestic and foreign policies and from which it derives a large measure of its moral authority.

Nazi Germany's decision to exterminate approximately six million Jews was the most important factor leading to the creation of Israel and remains the critical event that continues to shape its character. Kristallnacht, or the night of broken glass, was the harbinger of the unprecedented geno- cide that occurred later. On November 9, 1938, anti-Jewish riots, led by the Nazis, erupted throughout Germany. Jewish homes and businesses were destroyed and looted, approximately one thousand Jews were killed, and about thirty thousand were arrested and sent to concentration camps. Although the destruction was triggered when a young Jew living in France allegedly shot a minor German official in Paris, Germany's adherence to legal positivism, combined with Hitler's hatred of Jews, set the stage for Kristallnacht and the Holocaust that followed.[1] Nazi Germany used the legislature to formulate and implement laws designed to enshrine the racial superiority of one group of people over another. The Nuremberg race laws deprived Jews of their German citizenship, outlawed marriages and sexual relations between Jews and Germans, and dismissed all Jewish officials, among other things. What was clearly legal was also obviously a violation of the fundamental rights of the individual, a fact largely ignored by the rest of the world. That widespread indifference to the extermination of Jews is deeply buried within Israel's national conscious- ness, and the Holocaust itself has obsessively preoccupied leaders such as Menachem Begin.

Israel's conflicts with the Arabs as well as its relations with other coun- tries were perceived by Begin in the context of the Holocaust. All his life, especially during his prime ministership, he used a language that repeatedly stressed that the Arab struggle against Israel was another mani- festation of anti-Semitism.[2] That both Arabs and Jews are Semites was conveniently ignored by Begin in his attempts to mobilize Israeli and world opinion against the Palestinians. Despite the fact that the Israeli- Palestinian conflict is primarily related to nationalism, Begin and many Israelis construed every act of Palestinian violence as evidence of "anti- Semitism." This tendency was most pronounced during the 1982 invasion of Lebanon when Begin explicitly invoked the memory of World War II.[3] Yasser Arafat was clearly viewed as Hitler reincarnated, and Israel's Pyrrhic victory was compared to Germany's defeat by the Allies. Referring to Israel's siege of Beirut, Begin stated that he felt like "a Prime Minister empowered to instruct a valiant army facing Berlin where, among innocent civilians, Hitler and his henchmen hide in a bunker deep beneath the surface."[4] This distortion of reality combined with real threats to Israel's security and collective memories of the Holocaust significantly affect its foreign policies.

Whereas West Germany's external relations were circumscribed partly because of the Holocaust, Israel's acceptance into the world community was facilitated by that horrifying experience, despite the efforts of Arab states to isolate it. If burying the recent past was in West Germany's interest, constantly reminding the world of the evils of anti-Semitism and ensuring that the Holocaust would not be repeated became the hallmarks of Israel's policies. It is on this contradiction that the special relationship between those two countries is based, the perpetuation of which depends on the persistent appreciation of morality.[5] But a degree of moral parochialism marked Jewish responses to the Holocaust; the emphasis on the uniqueness of this experience influenced many Israelis to deny wrongs suffered by other groups, including Palestinians and black South Africans.

Israelis' belief in the exceptional nature of their treatment by Nazi Germany led to the development of a psychology of entitlement—a common reaction among most victims—which prompted them to demand things that ordinary people are seen as not having the right to demand. Furthermore, Israeli leaders not only demanded reparation for the Holocaust but were unwilling to accept that such suffering could ever be fully compensated. Gradually the Israeli public has come to share the policymakers' view that Israel has a moral right to exact preference from Germany.[6] However, beyond this specific relationship, Israel behaves like an ordinary state in international politics. Contradictions and complexities inherent in this dual approach are demonstrated by analysis of Israel's South Africa policy. As Israel became more isolated in world affairs and its concerns with security grew, fundamentalist religious groups and the Likud Party influenced the adoption of policies toward South Africa that were significantly different from those prior to 1977 and clearly contrary to the principles of Judaism.

Similar to Britain, West Germany, and Japan, domestic factors and the imperative of international trade for national security lead Israel to strongly condemn apartheid even as it collaborates with the white minority regime, especially in military matters. But Israel's emphasis on morality as a cornerstone of other countries' policies vis-à-vis the Jewish state makes its relationship with South Africa a very sensitive issue. Furthermore, because Judaism condemns the immorality of racism, and Jewish history is replete with instances of anti-Semitism and racial persecution, as Naomi Chazan observed, it has become increasingly difficult for Israelis to reconcile their antipathy to any overt manifestation of racism with their cooperation with South Africa.[7] But until 1987, when Congress was scheduled to review U.S. military assistance to countries supplying military equipment to South Africa, Israel's foreign policymakers, like their Japanese counterparts, did not appear to be seriously concerned about the enormous gap between their anti-apartheid rhetoric and their economic and security connections with the white minority regime.

Confronted with growing criticism of its close ties with Pretoria, Israel adopted a strategy of more forcefully disapproving South Africa's actions and justifying relations between the two countries. Israel's Ministry of Foreign Affairs released several statements in 1986 and 1987 to demonstrate its strong anti-apartheid position. According to these documents, the government's position is that apartheid must be abolished because it is not reformable, and that Israel will join the international community and the parliamentary democracies in any concerted action aimed at the elimination of apartheid.[8] However, adopting policies similar to those of other industrial countries would have little effect on Israel's relationship with Pretoria especially in light of the fact that Japan, West Germany, and Britain hide behind the United States or rely on European Political Cooperation in order to avoid taking measures that would weaken the white minority regime and seriously threaten their substantial economic interests in South Africa.

Both former Prime Minister Shimon Peres and former Vice-Premier Yitzhak Shamir supported their government's view of apartheid as a "despicable regime which has no place in our world." Speaking in Cameroon, a country with which Israel has reestablished diplomatic links, Peres asserted that apartheid is the ultimate abomination and an expression of the cruelest inhumanity and committed Israel to "do everything possible to eliminate this odious system," without specifying steps to be taken.[9] Similarly, Shamir noted that Israel could not remain silent in the face of racial discrimination, wherever it may be, adding that "we reject and condemn apartheid as a political, social, and economic system."[10] Yet Israel attempted to justify its ties with Pretoria by implicating the Arab states in violations of the oil embargo against South Africa. More important, Israeli foreign policymakers defended their South African policies on the basis of national security.

According to the Foreign Ministry, what should be kept in mind when considering the country's position on the issue of apartheid "is that Israel is still in a state of war with a number of Arab countries—a situation not of its own choosing. This state of war at times compels Israel to take steps and undertake measures, when its very existence may be at stake, that it would much rather refrain from having to undertake."[11] Perceptions of Israel as a weak embattled state, despite its awesome military might, elevated security and the alliance with South Africa above moral concerns, much to the dismay of the American Jewish community. Israel's South Africa policy, as Chazan put it, mirrors in a nutshell the contradictions between Israeli society's egalitarianism and its discrimination, its tolerance and its exclusivity, its militarism and its deep-seated commitment to peace, its ideals and its realities.[12]

Given the politics of the Middle East, Israel's brutal treatment of Palestinians in the Occupied Territories, Arab efforts to exploit the close relationship between Israel and South Africa, the infamous 1975 U.N. resolution equating Zionism with racism, and Israel's unwillingness to be more sensitive to anti-apartheid sentiments in the United States and Western Europe, comparisons between Israel and South Africa became widespread. The Israeli Foreign Ministry expressed concern about the "odious comparisons overseas" between the two states and instructed Israeli representatives abroad how to respond. The following distinctions were stressed: (1) in Israel the principle of equality governs the status of Arabs within the Green Line; (2) Israel has no intention of ruling over the inhabitants of the territories and wants to negotiate a political solution; (3) the conflict with the Palestinians, as opposed to the white-black confrontation in South Africa, it is not an internal problem but connected to the Arab-Israeli conflict as a whole; and (4) unlike South Africa, Israel does not deny basic human rights to the Palestinians.[13] Although many of these points are partially valid, the reality is far more complex than they seem to suggest. For example, Israel's reluctance to support the U.S. decision to talk with the Palestinian Liberation Organization in 1988 in order to find a political solution stood in direct contradiction to the second point, and the U.S. State Department Report on human rights in Israel, issued in 1989, clearly invalidated the last point.[14] Thus, despite fundamental differences between Israel and South Africa, comparisons between the two countries have continued as Israel has adopted a hardline approach to the Intifada. It is the fusion of domestic politics and strong military ties between Pretoria and Israel that has helped to distinguish the latter from the other nonsuperpowers.

## FOREIGN POLICYMAKING IN ISRAEL

While the overall objectives of Israel's foreign policy have remained constant since 1948, internal as well as external developments have caused priorities to be rearranged and reevaluated, and strategies adopted for achieving various goals have also been altered as perceptions of threats to national security changed. Indeed, as the pre-1967 geographical definition of Israel was expanded by government officials and a plethora of fundamentalist religious groups, primarily as a consequence of war, some of the major Israeli foreign policy objectives became relatively unimportant. The turbulent Middle East environment, escalating violence, and the Arabs' refusal to expressly recognize Israel's right to exist influenced that country to elevate national defense above all other foreign policy concerns. Additional national goals include: (1) resolving the Arab-Israeli conflict; (2) securing widespread diplomatic recognition; (3) counteracting Arab efforts to isolate the country by creating a worldwide network of mutually beneficial economic, military, and cultural links; (4) serving as a home for Jewish immigrants; (5) strengthening emotional, cultural, religious, and historical bonds between Israel and world Jewry; and (6) promoting human rights, civil liberties, and democratic values.[15] Israel's ability or willingness to achieve these objectives was affected by the emergence of the right-wing political factions of the Likud Party, led by Menachem Begin. For example, while Israel, unlike West Germany, encouraged immigration, albeit primarily of Jews, efforts by extremist religious groups to redefine who is a Jew seriously threatened emotional bonds between American Jews and Israel. Nevertheless, the vast majority of Israelis continued to subscribe to the above objectives, to a greater or lesser extent. But the Israeli electoral system, which guarantees that small political groups can have a major impact on the country's foreign policy aims, complicates the formulation and implementation of strategies for the achievement of both domestic and external policies.

Israel's political system contains many features of European parliamentary democracies. Like Britain, Israel has no written constitution, and the one hundred and twenty member Knesset (parliament) is legally supreme. This body's decisions cannot be overridden by the courts or the executive. Similar to Britain, the Prime Minister, a member of the Knesset, is the head of his or her party as well as the head of government. However, because no political party has ever managed to win a majority of votes in national elections, all of Israel's Prime Ministers have been forced to form coalition governments.[16] Furthermore, due to Israel's electoral system of proportional representation in which a political group that receives about one percent of the votes cast is entitled to a seat in the Knesset, coalition politics becomes a herculean task and diminishes the ability of policymakers to use specific strategies to achieve broadly supported foreign policy objectives. To a much greater extent than in Britain, the Israeli Prime Minister's power depends on his or her personal characteristics, especially in the absence of a clear and immediate threat to the country's security.

As in the case of Konrad Adenaur of West Germany (1949–1963), David Ben-Gurion, Israel's first Prime Minister (1948–1963), dominated his country's defense, security, and foreign policymaking. Faced with military threats from neighboring Arab states immediately after Israel was created, the founders of the new state allowed Ben-Gurion to be both Prime Minister and Minister of Defense, and the Cabinet and the public generally acquiesced to Ben-Gurion's decisions.[17] Although the Cabinet became more influential during Ben-Gurion's "semi-retirement" from 1954 to 1956, it was not until after his resignation in 1963 that the Cabinet was able to play a significant role in shaping Israel's foreign policy. Ben-Gurion's successor, Prime Minister Levi Eshkol, created the Ministerial Committee on Security and Defense (MCDS) within the Cabinet to assume major responsibility for making Israel's foreign policy. This group's decisions were brought to the full Cabinet for ratification or rejection. However, when Foreign Minister Golda Meir became Prime Minister in 1967, she relegated the MCDS to a much less prominent role while simultaneously increasing the power of the full Cabinet over international affairs. But Meir was undoubtedly in charge of foreign policy and relied heavily on a small group of colleagues,[18] a practice effectively used by Margaret Thatcher of Britain a decade later. However, regardless of who ruled or how they governed, national security remained the paramount foreign policy concern.

## NATIONAL SECURITY AND FOREIGN POLICY

Israel's foreign policy, like that of any other state, is influenced by its remembered experiences as well as its current self-perception, its perception of its adversaries and their perception of Israel, and tangible military threats to its security. However, unlike most countries, Israel's legitimacy and its right to exist have been foremost in the minds of its citizens from its inception. In light of its relatively small population of approximately four million, its geographic proximity to its adversaries, a history of conflict with them, and conscription of both men and women, national security predominates over all other considerations. Despite the peace agreement with Egypt in 1979 and a cessation of military aggression from Arab states since 1973—excluding the Palestinian Liberation Organization (PLO)—Israel perceives itself to be in a permanent state of war, a view that pervades all aspects of the Israeli society.[19] This perception is reinforced as the Arab states respond to what they regard as Israel's aggression by acquiring more military weapons. Thus the Jewish state's conduct, like that of its adversaries, remains motivated chiefly by the potently anarchic nature of the regional and wider international environment.[20]

Israel's fears are magnified by the suffering endured by Jews for centuries and the horrors of the Holocaust, which facilitated the creation of the country. The first Arab-Israeli war in 1948, in which Israel lost about one percent of its population so soon after Germany's systematic efforts to exterminate all Jews, strengthened its determination never to become a victim. As Gideon Rafael, the former Director General of Israel's Foreign Ministry and its ambassador to several countries, stated, "this first Arab-Israeli war threatened the national and physical survival of the people of Israel at a time when it had begun to shake off the ashes of the Holocaust and had undertaken the most solemn and challenging task of the new Jewish state—the rehabilitation of the remnants of European Jewry."[21] While these experiences ensured that national security would always be regarded as essential for the protection of the state's survival interests, emphasis on the military component of security contained the inherent risk of negating other vital national interests, a development that could ultimately undermine national security. As will be discussed, security considerations influenced Israel's leaders to develop close military ties with the white minority regime in South Africa. Emphasis on the military aspect of security jeopardized Israel's objectives of gaining international legitimacy and reducing its isolation in the world community. Israel's invasion of Lebanon in 1982 seriously fractured national consensus on strategies relating to national security and changed international perceptions of the Jewish state from victim to aggressor, even among its closest allies in Western Europe and North America. News of Israel's implication in the massacres of several hundred Palestinians in the Sabra and Shatilla refugee camps by Phalangist troops raised a storm of protests within Israel and focused attention on rising criticism of the war in Lebanon that had been brewing within the government and among the public.[22] By 1989 it was clear that the foundations of Israel's regime and the country's institutional structures had become incapable of supporting its politics, and that minor adjustments were no longer adequate to the challenge of facing some of the basic tenets of the Ziònist ethos.[23] Israel's relations with South Africa exacerbated these problems, and its handling of the Intifada contributed to its total isolation on the issue of Palestinian rights in the Occupied Territories. Comparisons between Israel and South Africa became increasingly common on the evening news, and it was apparent that the issue of preserving the former's democratic foundation and its Jewish character could not be neatly divorced from the question of the occupation.[24] Excessive reliance on military force created serious problems for Israel.

Palestinian protests in the West Bank and Gaza effectively changed international public opinion on the Palestinian-Israeli conflict, and the government's policy of beating Palestinians triggered protests within Israel in early 1988 by mainly leftist groups of individuals, whose numbers were estimated at between thirty thousand and fifty thousand.[25] Defense Minister Yitzhak Rabin's policy of allowing the army to use "might, power, and beatings" resulted in barbaric scenes of soldiers crushing the limbs of Palestinians with rocks and other instruments. These developments shocked the world, damaged Israel's image as an enlightened country, and led Rabbi Alexander Schindler, president of the Union of American Hebrew Congregations, to urge Israeli leaders to end a policy that many American Jews regarded as "an offense to the Jewish spirit and a betrayal of the Zionist dream."[26] As Palestinians continued to throw stones and block roads with burning tires, their casualties mounted and images of Israel as the victim were no longer credible even to its most ardent supporters in the United States and elsewhere. President Reagan's decision to reverse American policy of not talking with the PLO, after Arafat unequivocally declared that Israel has the right to exist and renounced terrorism, infuriated many Israeli officials and prompted columnists such as George F. Will, Norman Podhoretz, and William Safire to describe this development as a serious threat to Israel's survival.[27] But as Abba Eban, Israel's Foreign Minister from 1966 to 1974, pointed out, "the Israeli defense system is one of the wonders of the world. Never in history has so small a community been able and ready to wield such a vast capacity of defense, deterrence, and reprisal."[28] Despite efforts to portray Israel as vulnerable, it was now seen as the aggressor and a major violator of human rights.

According to the U.S. State Department report on the Israeli-occupied West Bank and Gaza Strip, Israeli defense forces responded to the Palestinian uprising "in a manner which led to a substantial increase in human rights violations." The report also noted that there was widespread beating of unarmed Palestinians and of persons not participating in violent activities, and that more than twenty thousand Palestinians were wounded and over three hundred and fifty seven killed, and that more than one hundred and fifty seven Palestinian homes were blown up because someone in the family participated or was suspected of participating in the uprising.[29] Israel defended its policy of using force, rebutted every point in the report, and accused the State Department of "not giving full consideration to the actions of local extremist elements and the major dilemmas which these cause for Israel."[30] But as an Israeli soldier told Prime Minister Shamir when he visited troops in the West Bank in early 1989, to achieve order soldiers have to "act brutally toward a people free of crime. I feel humiliated by this behavior. The situation has become a catastrophe. It is breaking us and strengthening the Arabs."[31] Furthermore, members of Congress—including Representative David R. Obey and Senator Patrick Leahy, who chair Congressional panels that appropriate foreign aid— viewed Israel's treatment of the Palestinians as unacceptable and pointed out that human rights violations could weaken Congressional support for American aid to Israel.[32] By failing to pursue political solutions to the Intifada, Israel lost the moral high ground vis-à-vis apartheid and weakened both internal and external support for its national security.

## ECONOMIC INTERESTS AND FOREIGN POLICY

National security considerations and economic interests are closely linked in Israel's South Africa policy. Unlike Japan and West Germany where economic growth is paramount, Israel's involvement in several military conflicts shifts its attention away from focusing primarily on economic development. More specifically, military operations have prevented Israel from fully utilizing its resources for economic expansion and domestic social programs. Furthermore, its goal of remaining a refuge for Jews throughout the world and maintaining socialist institutions associated with the Histradrut labor union federation and the kibbutz collective movement have rendered market forces secondary. Israel's small size and its lack of significant mineral, energy, and water resources only exacerbate problems emanating from its large military expenditures.

By the early 1980s internal and external debts which had grown through continuous budget deficits since 1973 seriously affected Israel's economic growth and fueled inflation,[33] and the Palestinian uprising in 1987 led to a further deterioration of the economy. Arab boycotts and strikes caused a decline in the purchase of goods by at least one-third, entailed huge military expenditures and decreased production by forcing more Israeli workers to do additional reserve duty as cheap Arab labor became erratic, crippled the country's vital tourist industry, and contributed to rising unemployment. Economic growth declined from 5.2 percent in 1987 to one percent in 1988, unemployment rose from six percent in 1986 to seven percent in 1988, and the trade deficit which stood at $1.9 billion in 1985 had escalated to roughly $3.5 billion in 1988.[34] In 1989 Finance Minister Shimon Peres proposed austerity measures that included layoffs of approximately 4,000 government employees; devaluation of the shekel (the national currency); reductions in subsidies for food and gasoline; the imposition of user fees for education and health services; and increased profits for industrialists and exporters.[35] Under these circumstances, it is unlikely that Israel will sharply curtail its economic relations with South Africa, and, given the country's overriding concern with national security, arms sales are likely to play an important role in economic revitalization efforts. However, burgeoning defense needs in a declining economy may impede economic transformation which, in turn, could threaten the economy's ability to provide resources essential for national security.[36]

Israel's industrialization reflects its emphasis on ensuring its survival through military power as well as the realization that international trade would significantly contribute to the viability of its economy. Consequently, military related industries were established for the dual purpose of meeting the country's defense needs and manufacturing products for domestic civilian consumption and international trade. Not surprisingly, metals, electronics, aerospace equipment, and defense-related items dominate Israel's industrial exports, and weapons sales are critical to the economy as a whole. Anywhere from fifty-eight thousand to one hundred and twenty thousand people are employed in the defense industry,[37] and the spinoff effects on the civilian sector are not inconsequential.

Following the Yom Kippur War in 1973, arms sales began to assume a greater role in Israel's quest for military superiority in the Middle East. Several factors account for this development. First, Israel's negative experience with its Western European allies during the war reinforced its tendency toward self-reliance. Self-sufficiency in military equipment was viewed as a means of achieving greater political independence.[38] Second, the need to counteract the newly acquired Arab power, based on the Organization of Petroleum Exporting Countries' (OPEC) ability to determine oil prices, influenced Israel to promote arms sales. Third, the rapid growth of global arms sales in the mid-1970s, especially to Egypt, Syria, Jordan, and Saudi Arabia, increased competition for overseas markets. Finally, the relative success of the U.N. arms embargo against South Africa forced that country to find suppliers willing to ignore arms sanctions, and Israel's growing international isolation facilitated Israeli arms sales to Pretoria.[39] Economic realities and national security concerns weigh against the implementation of anti-apartheid measures that would seriously affect Israel's economic and, hence, defense interests.

## INTERNAL DIVISIONS, THE NEW ZIONISM, AND FOREIGN POLICY

As a country of immigration for Jews dispersed around the world, it is almost inevitable that Israel will continue to be confronted with problems springing from the diverse cultural, religious, and political attitudes found among various groups within society. Therefore, despite attempts to project an image of unity internationally, Israel has been more sharply divided on non-defense issues than most Western democracies. Ethnic cleavages, particularly between European Jews (Ashkenazi) and Oriental and North African Jews (Sephardi), are the most important. Compared to the Ashkenazi who faced persistent discrimination and annihilation in Nazi Germany, Sephardic Jews were relatively free to practice their religion and were subject to far less persecution, especially in Morocco and Egypt.[40] European Jews, more highly educated and technically trained than immigrants from elsewhere, dominated Israel's political, economic, and social system from the country's inception. Despite the recent upward economic and political mobility experienced by many Sephardi, the Ashkenazic establishment continues to attempt to accommodate non-European Jews, who comprise the majority of Israel's population, by measures such as compensatory education, social integration of intermediate schools, and ethnic patronage appointments.[41] Sephardic Jews' influence in the Likud and their growing economic and political power enhance their ability to shift Israel's South Africa policy away from anti-apartheid positions adopted by the Labor party until its defeat in 1977.

In addition to cleavages between Ashkenazic and Sephardic Jews, Israel's internal cohesion is weakened by religious rivalries along an orthodox-secular continuum; ideological factions; the impact of the war in Lebanon; geographical distinctions; and national groups dividing the majority of Jews from the approximately 700,000 Arab Israeli citizens,[42] who remain targets of discrimination in a country that views Arabs in general as threats to its survival. Divisions in Israel were sharpened when the Likud government coalition came to power in 1977 under Menachem Begin, who advocated the annexation of historical Palestine in its entirety not only for national security but also in the name of religious messianism.[43]

The idea of partitioning Palestine in order to provide homelands for both Jews and Palestinians was clearly unacceptable to Begin. The belief that the new Zion could only be created through military might was an integral part of the philosophy of the Irgun Zvai Leumi, the group affiliated with the Revisionist camp and led by Begin after its founder, Vladimir Jabotinsky, died.[44] The New Zionism, based largely on Begin's ideas and on the neo-Revisionist and religious strands of Zionism, profoundly affected Israel's foreign policy in general and its South African policy in particular after 1977. Several factors contributed to the emergence and perpetuation of the New Zionism. These include: demographic changes through which Sephardic Jews became the country's majority; the decreasing probability of a major military confrontation with the Arab states after the peace agreement with Egypt in 1979, thus eroding the internal consensus that was based on a serious external threat; the intensification and proliferation of religious cleavages and conflicts; the emergence of Gush Emunim, or Bloc of the Faithful, as an institutional force in Israeli society and politics; and the failure of Israel's major political parties to win enough votes to enable them to reduce the influence of minor fundamentalist religious groups.[45]

Begin's efforts to redefine Israel to include all of Palestine and his refusal to compromise with the Palestinians on the issue of a homeland galvanized Sephardic support for the Likud, contributed to the demise of the old Labor-National Religious Party coalition, and solidified Likud's electoral strength among the religious parties.[46] Since 1977 the vast majority of Sephardic Jews have voted for the Likud and parties to its right and have consistently advocated a hard-line foreign policy and expressed opposition to any political and humanitarian concessions to Palestinians.[47] In addition to strong negative sentiments against Arabs, the Sephardic Jews' reluctance to compromise is partly influenced by economic and social factors. Prior to Israel's occupation of the West Bank and Gaza in 1967, Sephardim did the work now done by the Arabs and were economically, socially, and educationally disadvantaged. As in any society, competition between groups and attempts to create social distance between them in a stagnant economy often culminate in fear and hatred, as is the case in relation to the Sephardim and the Arabs.

A major characteristic of the religious groups was their unwillingness to negotiate. This tendency was augmented by Likud's appointment of Benjamin Netanyahu as Israel's deputy foreign minister. When the United States decided to communicate with the PLO, Netanyahu, who has taken hard-line positions on most foreign policy issues, spearheaded the government's diplomatic fight against the PLO, as well as against Abba Eban and other Israelis who met with the PLO, "with a zeal bordering on the obsessive."[48] Under these circumstances it seems unlikely that Israel's policy toward South Africa will emphasize negotiation and compromise between blacks and whites, or that Pretoria would take such suggestions from Israel seriously. Indeed, many Israelis tend to view the opposition to apartheid in essentially the same way as they see the PLO. Israel's international isolation and what appears to be the Likud's indifference to world opinion also affects that country's relations with South Africa.

## INTERNATIONAL ISOLATION AND FOREIGN POLICY

Israel's foreign policy is shaped by the concerted efforts of Arab states to isolate it in international politics, by miscalculations on the part of Israeli foreign policymakers, and, to some extent, by the proponents of New Zionism who view isolation in religious terms. Although the international community strongly supported the creation of a state for Jews so recently threatened with extermination, Egypt, Syria, and other Arab states viewed the settlement of Palestine by Jews and the displacement of the Palestinians in terms of Arab nationalism. Consequently, the Arab League organized a boycott against trade and communications with the new state.[49] Though inconsistently applied, these sanctions not only made commercial relations difficult for Israel but also contributed to its reluctance to impose sanctions against other countries. As will be discussed in greater detail, the Arabs' success in helping to isolate Israel, especially in black Africa where Israelis had endeavored to build close relations, prompted the Jewish state to develop stronger ties with Pretoria, a decision which contributed to further isolating Israel.

The complacent view, shared by many Israelis, that whatever Israel does is irrelevant to the decisions of "hostile forces" also diminished its international contacts.[50] Frustrated by a United Nations increasingly dominated by the Afro-Asian countries, Israeli foreign policymakers adopted a "Fortress Israel mentality" and relied almost totally on the United States and Western Europe instead of countering Arab moves to isolate it with adroit diplomacy. Indeed, Ben-Gurion dismissed the United Nations as "Oum Shmoum"—or "nothing United Nations"—despite that organization's pivotal role in Israel's creation.[51] As the country's ostracism became more widespread, it took on many of the characteristics of a pariah state. Pariah or outcast states are generally small and are involved in regional conflicts in which their very existence is at stake. Israel, South Africa, Taiwan, and, to a lesser extent, South Korea are generally regarded as international pariahs. According to Efraim Inbar, outcast states usually view international practices and resolutions as less binding on their behavior than on that of other countries.[52] Respect for international law is further eroded by the ideologies which accompany the siege mentality experienced by pariahs. In Israel's case, the New Zionism intensifies both the perception and reality of international isolation.

The ideological zealousness of the Likud's key supporters and their overwhelming reliance on military might to accomplish their objectives reinforce Israel's isolation. Ideology tends to obscure reality, magnifies perceived threats, divides the world into good versus evil, and dehumanizes the other side. Thus, when national security becomes intertwined with religious ideology, perceptions of reality are further distorted. Isolation is not only viewed in religious terms but also can become a self-fulfilling prophecy. Those on the right of the political spectrum in Israel who argued that the country could not depend on the international community justified their position by pointing to Israel's international problems and to traditional Jewish isolationism, while those who advocated political flexibility based their views on the link between Israel's improved foreign standing and the amelioration in its security situation.[53] From 1977 to 1989 beliefs associated with the New Zionism dominated the political debate and shaped Israel's policy toward South Africa. In their Hobbesian view of international relations, security overrode concerns with other countries' affairs or any preoccupation with justice and morality.[54] The extent to which public opinion could influence the policymakers who subscribed to this new ideology to significantly alter the country's South Africa policy was limited.

## Public Opinion and Foreign Policy

National security considerations, with all their implications, appear to be the predominant factor responsible for the relative absence of opposition to and debate on apartheid among the Israeli public. Unlike in Britain or West Germany, where there is considerable discussion of the South African issue in parliament and by numerous anti-apartheid groups and exiled South Africans of all races, the great majority of the Israeli public has shown no measurable concern or opposition, and discussion in the Knesset has been limited, especially prior to 1987. As Benjamin Joseph observed, "looking at the Knesset record in the 1970s and early to mid-1980s, one finds that the legislative body has had very little to say about Israel's second most important ally after the United States. The topic came up for debate perhaps once or twice in all those years,"[55] despite rapidly expanding economic and military relations between the two countries.

Apart from the practice of interest groups in Israel expressing their views primarily through political parties, Israel's ties to South Africa, like many other controversial issues, are deemed to be national security matters. There is a general consensus throughout the government that security issues should not be openly questioned, and that debate on apartheid should not be encouraged. The Israeli press has been urged by the government to "stay away from this sensitive matter of national interest," and the Central Bureau of Statistics does not publish full details of commerce between Israel and South Africa.[56] Deprived of reliable information in a society that perceives its very existence to be constantly threatened, few Israelis are engaged in anti-apartheid activities. Other than a small number of individuals such as Shlomo Avineri and Yosef Beilin and groups such as Israelis Against Apartheid, there is no record of demonstrations or sit-ins demanding that ties between the two countries be severed.[57] In contrast to Britain, West Germany, Canada, and Scandinavia, Israel's unwillingness to criticize apartheid is influenced by the fact that it shares with the apartheid regime similar threat perceptions.

Both Israel and South Africa are regarded as international pariahs and perceive themselves as being surrounded by hostile states which are determined to destroy them and their democratic traditions. While Pretoria equated ANC activities with the communist threat, Israel's fundamentalists in the Likud view the PLO as the embodiment of Nazism. Consequently, they perceive their survival as contingent upon their overwhelming military superiority vis-à-vis their neighbors and their willingness to use force against actual or potential adversaries.[58] Although Israelis object to comparisons between the two societies, the state-run television network often views developments in South Africa within the context of events in Israel or in the occupied territories. For example, resistance in Soweto was explained as criminal violence perpetrated by communist elements and outside agitators, and the ANC and other anti-apartheid groups are referred to as terrorists.[59] Yet Israel's policy, to a much greater degree than those of the other nonsuperpowers, can be influenced by Jewish communities in South Africa and the United States.

Diaspora Jewry, consistent with the view that Israel should be a place of refuge for all Jews, articulates its opinions on Israel's foreign as well as domestic policy through the World Zionist Organization and the Jewish Agency. Although major political parties in Israel have always obtained support from external Jewish organizations, it was Menachem Begin who accelerated the process of integrating foreign elements into domestic politics by mobilizing Jewish communities, especially those in the United States, to back peace negotiations with Egypt and to support a series of policy measures. Groups such as Peace Now, the Civil Rights Movement, Gush Emunim, and Kach also turned to the outside for financial assistance.[60] The barrier against external intervention in domestic affairs was further weakened between 1986 and 1989 when Shimon Peres and others attempted to sway domestic attitudes in an international peace conference and dialogue with the PLO by lobbying Jewish organizations and foreign governments to put pressure on Israeli policymakers.[61] Such efforts allow South African and American Jews to have an impact on Israeli public opinion about apartheid.

South African Jews, although a separate group, are officially part of the white community and enjoy various benefits that accompany that designation. As Neville Rubin observed, "it is ironic that South Africa is one of the few countries in which Jews, by virtue of race, are legally placed in a position of privilege."[62] But anti-Semitic attitudes among right-wing Afrikaners make the Jewish position in South Africa precarious. This insecurity has influenced the Board of Deputies, which acts as the Jewish community's representative, to silence individual Jews who openly criticize apartheid. The Board's policy of not taking a position on apartheid and of cultivating friendly relations with the Afrikaner rulers was strongly repudiated by Leslie Rubin, one of the founders of the Liberal Party (1953) and the first liberal elected to represent blacks in the South African Senate in Cape Town, and by other liberal Jews. Contrasting the Board's silence following the Sharpeville massacre in 1960 and the glowing eulogies by two chief Rabbis for Prime Minister Verwoerd, Rubin concluded that the Jews had moved from initial revulsion against apartheid, through tolerance, to support.[63] Similarly, Helen Suzman, until recently the leader of South Africa's main opposition party, the Progressive Federal Party, has devoted her life to fighting apartheid. And Jews for Social Justice in Johannesburg and Jews for Justice in Cape Town as well as Jewish students are known for their anti-apartheid activities.[64] However, many Jews subscribe to the views of the white minority and oppose black majority rule. Unlike American Jews who are further removed from the situation and are leaders in the struggle for equality in their own country, South African Jews are generally more supportive of Israel's policies.

Although American Jewish leaders emphasize the primacy of Israel's security and its right to conduct international commercial transactions, many are uncomfortable with Israel's close relationship with Pretoria, especially its military trade.[65] In addition to their history of liberalism and active participation in the American Civil Rights Movement, many U.S. Jews are leading exponents of sanctions against apartheid and, with black Americans, have spearheaded anti-apartheid legislation in Congress. Their efforts to maintain and ameliorate relations with black Americans as well as their concerns about increasing anti-Semitic acts by neo-Nazi groups in the United States influence them to try to persuade Israel to reduce its involvement in South Africa.[66] However, strong sentiments on ethnic relations in Israel itself also have had an impact on its South Africa policy.

## ETHNICITY AND FOREIGN POLICY

Compared to Japan and West Germany, which are largely racially homogeneous, Israel's ethnic diversity is complicated by the Arab-Israeli conflict and by a tradition in the Middle East that fosters domination of the ruling group, in most cases an ethnic minority, over other groups in the state. The problem is best articulated by David Shipler who contends that:

> The pluralistic, integrationist approach that has been the standard for American society has no relevance here. In nobody's mind can Arabs and Jews be simply individual human beings, divorced from their identities as Arabs and Jews. Nationhood in the American concept may transcend race, creed, and ethnic origin, but in the Middle East the nation attempts to serve as an embodiment of those traits—not to promote harmony among diversity but to emphasize and express those differences.[67]

Arab-Israeli wars, particularly the 1967 conflict, culminated in an enormous expansion of Israel's boundaries and the inclusion of approximately one million Palestinians within what proponents of the New Zionism and a growing number of Israelis born after 1967 regard as Israel. The occupation of the West Bank and Gaza radically altered the ethnic composition of the Jewish state and exacerbated problems between Arabs and Jews. Within the Green Line that demarcates Israel proper form the Occupied Territories, there are roughly 4.1 million Israelis, fifteen percent of whom are Arabs. Beyond the old boundaries are West Bank-Gaza Arabs who are not Israeli citizens but have been under Israel's military control since 1967.[68] Many of them provide cheap labor in Israel and are integrated in the Israeli economy.

Unlike in Britain, where minority groups may be viewed only as competitors for available resources or as culturally different, in Israel ethnicity and national security are inseparable. West Indians and Pakistanis in Britain or Turks and Italians in West Germany are not perceived as potentially dangerous to those countries' existence, and there is no conflict between the various countries sending and receiving immigrants. In Israel, Israeli Arabs are regarded as serious threats to national security, a perception which permeates the society. They are viewed not in the context of an ethnic minority whose rights must be protected but rather as a potential fifth column.[69] The ascendancy of the military in a country preoccupied with security reinforces this impression.

Although the Arabs are Israeli citizens with the right to vote and serve in the Knesset and in government offices, the realities of the wider Arab-Israeli conflict and terrorist activities in the country undermine efforts by successive Israeli governments to effectuate a more complete integration of them into the life of the country and to foster their economic, social, and cultural advancement.[70] Arabs and Jews remain suspicious of each other, and in an atmosphere of hostility and the understandable obsession with public safety, just being an Arab in appearance is to wear a badge that commands the attention of the security services.[71] The relative ease with which the Falashas, Jews from Ethiopia, have been accepted as part of Israeli society demonstrates that ethnicity as such is not the primary cause of Jewish-Arab antagonism. The decision by Israel's Central Elections Committee to disqualify Rabbi Meir Kahane and his extremist Kach Party from running in the 1988 national elections because of racist and undemocratic views distinguishes Israel from West Germany where the neo-Nazi Republican Party has made significant political gains.[72] This does not mean, however, that some of Kahane's views were not represented by other groups.

Preoccupied with their own condition and that of Palestinians in the West Bank and Gaza, Israeli Arabs are unlikely to be primarily concerned with Israel's relations with South Africa. Furthermore, like ethnic groups in Britain, Arabs are too divided ideologically to have an impact on their country's foreign or domestic policies. Arabs run with Jewish-led parties and generally vote for the Communists, the Labor Alignment, the Progressives, and even the Likud-led coalition of parties.[73] Given the fragmentation of Israel's electoral system and the ability of small parties to exercise considerable political influence, the Arabs, who cast roughly nine percent of votes, could win ten seats in the 120-member Knesset and thereby gain pivotal power to determine which major party would lead the coalition government.[74] However, diverse views among Arabs and the security concerns of Israeli Jews render such an eventuality unlikely. It is only within the context of national security that ethnicity influences Israel's South Africa policies.

## THE EVOLUTION OF ISRAEL'S RELATIONS WITH SOUTH AFRICA

Israel's relations with South Africa grew gradually between 1948, when Israel was created and the Afrikaner government implemented apartheid, and 1973, when Israel became increasingly isolated in the international community. From 1973 to 1987 Israel intensified its connections, cooperating with Pretoria on various military projects and expanding trade and cultural ties. Israel's decision in 1987 to join the United States, Western Europe, Japan, Canada, Australia, and many Third World countries in imposing sanctions against Pretoria marked a retreat from what seems to have been Israel's alliance with South Africa. National security concerns of the Israeli government and its strategy for dealing with perceived threats determined, to a large extent, Israel's South Africa policy.

### Israel and South Africa, 1948–1973

The period between 1948 and 1973 may be subdivided into three stages for analytical purposes. The first stage lasted from 1948 to 1961, the second from 1961 to 1967, and the third from 1967 to 1973. During the first stage, when the Afrikaners were consolidating their electoral victory by implementing legislation depriving blacks of basic rights, Israel established limited diplomatic relations with Pretoria.[75] The Jewish experience with the recent Holocaust led the newly created state to strongly condemn apartheid and to develop ties with emerging nations in Asia and Africa. Israelis were primarily interested in countering Egypt's hostility and its attempts to isolate the Jewish state diplomatically by persuading African and Asian governments not to recognize Israel as a sovereign entity. Israel responded by establishing diplomatic relations and weaving a web of political, military, economic, and cultural relationships with as many countries as possible.[76]

Many newly independent countries regarded Israel as a model and were impressed with its achievements. In a world where anti-colonial sentiments were strong, Israel enjoyed certain advantages. Israel was not a colonial power, it was too small to threaten the emerging states' independence, and its mixed economy appealed to many of the former colonies who equated capitalism with political, economic, and cultural subjugation. Israel's advanced technology, its experience with many of the same problems with which African and Asian states were confronted, and its ability to provide technical assistance and investment capital influenced many states to develop political and economic links with that country.[77] Trade and diplomatic ties were established with Ghana, Liberia, Ethiopia, Nigeria, Sierra Leone, and Senegal between 1948 and 1961, and Ghana, Liberia, and Ethiopia resisted Egyptian attempts to obtain an anti-Israeli declaration from the Accra conference of Independent African States held in Ghana in 1958.[78]

During the second stage, from 1961 to 1967, Israel adopted a strong anti-apartheid stance, even as Arab states exerted considerable pressure on the Africans to sever diplomatic ties with Israel. In July 1961 the Jewish state joined Upper Volta (Burkina Faso) in issuing a statement condemning apartheid and, shortly thereafter, Israel and the Netherlands were the only two Western countries that voted to censure Eric Louw, South Africa's Foreign Minister, for a speech to the U.N. General Assembly which they deemed to be offensive. Israel further distanced itself from the apartheid regime by voting in favor of sanctions against it in November 1961.[79] South Africa retaliated by refusing to approve routine transfers of South African Jewish donations to Israel. Nevertheless, Israel voted for additional sanctions in 1962, and in 1963 it withdrew its ambassador, downgrading its representation to the consular level. When Israel voted with the U.N. majority in 1966 to revoke South Africa's mandate over Namibia, its relations with that country were significantly diminished, and by 1967 real contacts had dwindled to a mere trickle.[80] In black Africa, Israel had succeeded through its anti-apartheid policies in frustrating Arab efforts to isolate it. However, the Six Day War in 1967, in which Israel captured and occupied part of Egypt's territory, created serious dilemmas for Israel and the African states.

The third stage, which commenced after the Six Day War, was marked by South African overtures toward Israel and the adoption of resolutions on the Arab-Israeli conflict by African states in keeping with their obligation to promote African solidarity under the charter of the Organization of African Unity. Israel had seized African territory, and despite the African countries' reluctance to criticize an ally, they had to support Egypt, a member of the OAU. In light of the OAU's provision that the borders of member-states should not be violated, Arab states were successful in persuading African governments to vote in favor of implementing U.N. Council Resolution 242, which held that Israel had illegally seized Arab territory. Nevertheless, given the benefits derived from their alliance with Israel, African states endeavored to initiate a Middle East peace process in 1972.[81] South Africa, on the other hand, feeling the effects of growing international isolation, viewed emerging strains between Israel and black Africa as providing an opportunity for it to reestablish trade and diplomatic relations with the Israelis. Pretoria permitted South African Jews to transfer an extra $20.5 million to Israel and supplied various military weapons to Israel following France's decision to impose an embargo on shipments of arms to that state.[82] Israel's policy during this transition period was ambiguous. Israel evinced reduced enthusiasm for supporting strong anti-apartheid measures but continued to support liberation movements in southern Africa until 1971 when its financial contributions to the OAU's Liberation Committee were rejected. The major shift in Israel's policy came in the aftermath of the Yom Kippur war and the Arab oil boycott of 1973.

## Israel's South Africa Policy, 1973–1989

During the 1973 war the problems of southern Africa became entangled in the Arab-Israeli conflict, and the foundations for contemporary Israeli-South African relations were built on the ensuing developments. By 1973 the African wars of liberation had emerged as extremely important issues to that continent's leaders. Nigeria, Tanzania, Zambia, Ghana, and other major states embraced removing white minority rule and colonialism as major foreign and domestic policy objectives. The Portuguese colonies of Angola and Mozambique were deeply involved in a struggle that was attracting international attention. Thus, when Portugal allowed American planes transporting military supplies to Israel during the Yom Kippur War to land in the Azores, Arab leaders had little difficulty in convincing the Africans that Israel was cooperating with white minority regimes in southern Africa. This perception was strengthened by South Africa's political support for Israel, the participation of approximately eight thousand South African Jews in the war effort, and by the fact that the Jewish community in that country had raised more money per capita for Israel than any other Jewish community in the world.[83]

Although factors such as feelings of Islamic solidarity among Africa's Muslims—estimated at one-fifth of the continent's population—and growing sympathy for the Palestinians in light of Israel's military superiority in the Middle East played a crucial role in shifting alliances, the Arab oil embargo was principally responsible for changing the political dynamics between Israel and Africa. Escalating petroleum prices and the willingness of Arab leaders to use their newly acquired power was a surprising and catastrophic development for Western Europeans and other industrialized societies. The Europeans responded by reducing their support for Israel and taking Arab views into their foreign policy calculations. From Israel's perspective, Europeans had become unreliable.[84]

African states which had enjoyed many tangible benefits from their collaboration with Israel were persuaded and coerced into relinquishing their ties with the Jewish state. The Arab League threatened to retaliate with an oil embargo against African countries which failed to comply with its efforts to ostracize Israel and offered financial incentives to those adopting a pro-Arab stance. By the end of 1973 only Swaziland, Lesotho, Botswana, and Malawi, all closely integrated into the South African economy, maintained ties with Israel. Stung by radically altered circumstances, Israelis became almost obsessive about the military aspects of national security and concluded that their interests could be best safeguarded through developing closer relations with Pretoria. Ironically, Israel's decision to reinstate its diplomatic representation in Pretoria in early 1973, the visits by senior Israeli officials Moshe Dayan and Haim Herzog to South Africa, and increasing trade between the two countries inadvertently bolstered the Arabs' case against Israel.[85] But the Arab success in convincing the Africans to isolate Israel ultimately strengthened Israeli-South African links and resulted in the loss of the valuable technical assistance that Israel had provided for the Africans.

The African states' support for the infamous U.N. resolution in November 1975 which equated Zionism with racism and apartheid influenced Israel to sharply increase its contacts with South Africa. But developments in Israel were also instrumental in changing that country's foreign policy. The surprise attacks by Syrian and Egyptian forces on Yom Kippur led to the establishment of a commission to study the state of Israel's military intelligence and preparedness on the eve of the war and prompted the resignations of senior military officers. When Golda Meir resigned in April 1974, Yitzhak Rabin, the first former professional soldier to become Prime Minister, formed a new government. After the National Religious Party rejoined the coalition government in October 1974, the question of "who is a Jew" resurfaced.[86] A combination of external and internal events were clearly pushing Israel closer to Pretoria and away from the ideas of Ben-Gurion, Golda Meir, and other labor leaders. Rabin, who had long advocated lowering Israel's high costs of developing military weapons by exporting arms to South Africa and elsewhere, met with South Africa's Prime Minister John Vorster when the latter visited Israel and signed an agreement to promote closer cooperation between the two states. A joint ministerial committee, to meet at least once a year, was formed to oversee implementation of the pact.[87] Arab states immediately publicized the joint economic and military interests binding Israel and South Africa and consistently labeled them as the common enemy of both Africa and the Arabs.[88] The emergence of the New Zionism, embodied in Begin, Israel's Prime Minister in 1977, and Israel's growing international isolation combined to allow Begin virtually unchallenged freedom domestically to expand trade, military, and diplomatic connections with South Africa, a move which further alienated Israel in the world community. This isolation was viewed by proponents of the New Zionism as evidence of the righteousness of their cause. Only the possible loss of U.S. military assistance and pressure from American Jews would counterbalance the power of Israel's religious fundamentalists and alter its economic and military ties with South Africa.

## ISRAEL'S ECONOMIC INTERESTS IN SOUTH AFRICA

Escalating costs of national security and serious economic difficulties prompted Israel to pursue an expansion of its trade and investment activities in South Africa. As in the cases of Japan, West Germany, and Britain, international trade is extremely important to Israel's economy and security. However, unlike Britain and West Germany, Israel did not attempt to justify its economic transactions with Pretoria in terms of morality. No effort was made to demonstrate how trade would contribute to the non-violent abolition of apartheid; Israel's preoccupation with its own survival seemed to outweigh all other considerations. In this respect, Israel's behavior more closely resembles Japan's relationship with Pretoria, despite Japan's anti-apartheid rhetoric.

According to Israeli officials, the Jewish state's major economic objectives in South Africa include: (1) protecting the right of the Jewish community in South Africa to invest in Israel; (2) the importation of coal at low prices with liberal credit; and (3) maintaining Israeli fishing rights in South African waters.[89] The dominance of military factors in Israel's economic life augments Israel's determination to protect these economic goals. As the chapters on Britain, West Germany, and Japan show, countries are unlikely to support measures that could be detrimental to their interests.

While the Commonwealth, the European Community, Canada, and the United States were debating what kinds of sanctions should be implemented against apartheid in 1986, Israel, though stating that it "would join whatever decision will be taken by the mainstream Western countries," sent a high-level delegation headed by Immanuel Sharon, director general of the Finance Ministry, and senior officials from the Treasury, the Trade Ministry, and the Chief Scientist's office to South Africa to renew trade and credit agreements between the two countries.[90] The timing of this mission raised the possibility that Israel, along with other countries, would play a crucial role in undermining the effectiveness of international economic sanctions against Pretoria.

As Western countries appeared more likely to adopt limited sanctions against South Africa, Pretoria sought to diminish their impact by encouraging joint ventures between Israeli and South African firms as well as by developing stronger economic ties with Taiwan and Korea. Israel's preferential access to both EC and U.S. markets appears to be an important consideration in Pretoria's decision to establish closer ties with that state. Products manufactured in Israel or with an Israeli-added value of forty to fifty percent are eligible for duty-free entry into the EC, and more than three thousand Israeli-manufactured products may be exported to the United States under the Generalized Preference System. Furthermore, in 1985, in an effort to assist Israel's ailing economy, the United States signed a Free Trade Area agreement with Israel that essentially reduced trade barriers by removing tariffs on trade between them.[91] This effectively allows products from joint ventures between Israel and South Africa to enter Western European and U.S. markets and encourages South Africa to ship semi-finished products such as steel and iron to Israel to be fully processed there in order to qualify for an Israeli certificate of origin.[92] However, in light of the unwillingness of Western Europeans to reduce trade with South Africa and their tendency to circumvent their own restrictions, Israel's role in defeating the aim of sanctions is not as significant as it might appear.

Obtaining accurate data on various countries' trade with South Africa is extremely difficult, if not impossible. Nevertheless, available trade figures suggest Israel's imports from South Africa, excluding diamonds, gold, and goods intended for re-export, amounted to $171 million in 1984 and $203 million in 1986, roughly three percent of all imports. Exports to South Africa which stood at $104.4 million in 1984 declined to $64.6 million, down from 1.2 percent in 1984 to 0.7 percent in 1986.[93] However, when military sales, diamonds, and gold are included, trade figures are radically different. For example, the value of Israel's military sales to South Africa was estimated at between $125 million and $800 million in 1987, just prior to Israel's imposition of sanctions against Pretoria.[94] Similarly, the complex nature of international trade obscures revenues received from the diamond trade. Israel cuts and polishes about half of the world's diamonds. Diamonds from South Africa are sold through the Central Selling Organization in London, part of the De Beers conglomerate in South Africa. Many countries, including India, the Soviet Union, and other vocal critics of apartheid, are generally believed to use the Central Selling syndicate, which has a monopoly on the world market for uncut stones. Polished diamonds constitute Israel's largest export item, valued at $1.6 billion in 1986. This industry employed about 15,000 people and earned over $300 million in foreign exchange in the early 1980s, making it the second largest non-military related source of foreign ex-

change after tourism.[95] The secrecy surrounding trade between many countries and South Africa militates against an accurate analysis of economic
ties. Nevertheless, available evidence indicates that commerce between
Israel and South Africa may be almost as significant as trade between
South Africa and West Germany or Britain.

From 1965 to 1987 there was a sharp increase in non-military trade
between Israel and South Africa. Israel's exports to South Africa rose
from $2.7 million in 1965 to $28 million in 1974, and its imports from
South Africa climbed from $4.3 million in 1965 to $43.1 million in 1974.
By 1978 the value of South African exports had risen to $51 million,
while Israel's exports reached $37 million.[96] South Africa facilitated trade
with Israel by granting it a $42.5 million line of credit in 1978 to purchase
South African products, removed some import restrictions on Israeli
goods, and allowed Israeli fishermen to increase their catch in South
African waters at a time when its own fishing fleet was attempting to
gain greater access to the more profitable Chilean fishing grounds.[97]

South Africa supplies Israel with steel, coal, paper, iron, tobacco, timber,
pesticides, canned fruit, sugar, asbestos, and, as mentioned previously,
diamonds. Israel also imports semi-finished products from South Africa
for export to many African countries that fully support sanctions against
Pretoria in international forums.[98] But the reality is far more complex
than the anti-apartheid rhetoric would suggest. Israeli non-military exports
to South Africa include potash from the Dead Sea, base metals, animal
feed, paper products, and high technology. The exchange of technical
knowledge is a major component of Israeli-South African trade. In 1983
Barlow Rand of South Africa and Degem Systems of Israel formed a
joint venture to work on computer-assisted instruction. This involved
developing software, providing teacher training, and creating specific
courses appropriate for South Africa's curriculum requirements. There
was also a Technology Exchange Agreement to expand research and teach-
ing at the Laser Centre of the Faculty of Mechanical Engineering of the
Technion-Israeli Institute of Technology in Haifa.[99]

Like Britain and West Germany, Israel allows its business enterprises
to form joint ventures with their South African counterparts. The close
relationship between the companies and the Israeli government brings
that country into direct commercial contacts with South Africa, which
also has many state-owned enterprises. South African investors are attracted to Israel because it has free trade arrangements with the European
Community and the United States, a fact Israel does not overlook. For
example, the Mayor of Eilat, a free trade zone in southern Israel, spent
ten days in 1986 in South Africa visiting South African companies and
local Jewish leaders to discuss investing in Eilat.[100] Until 1987 South Africa
permitted the local Jewish Community to invest approximately $20 million
a year in Israel, far less than what Jews wanted to invest. But South
Africa allowed investment beyond the specific quota if such investments

would benefit South Africa's economy through the use of raw materials.[101] However, disinvestment activities by Western multinational companies, a sharply depreciated South African rand, the country's indebtedness, and general economic problems and uncertainties significantly reduced South Africa's readiness to encourage the additional outflow of scarce capital.

Private Israeli firms increased their investments in the homelands, two of which, Ciskei and Bophuthatswana, have commercial offices in Tel Aviv. About ten Israeli companies set up joint ventures in computers, agriculture, and textiles in Ciskei, and a housing contract was signed with Bophuthatswana, whose leader, Chief Lucas Mangope, visited Israel in 1983. Trade missions from the various homelands were encouraged to visit Israel by the Israel-South Africa Chamber of Commerce, which usually sponsored the visits.[102] These activities were generally regarded as direct Israeli support for South Africa's policy of depriving blacks of their right to South African citizenship. In contrast to Britain and West Germany, Israel does not encourage its companies to follow the equivalent of the Sullivan Principles or the EC Code of Conduct, a fact contrary to Israel's anti-apartheid statements. Like Britain and West Germany, Israel does not perceive black African states as having sufficient leverage to alter its relations with Pretoria, especially in light of their decision in 1973 to isolate Israel diplomatically.

Israel's relations with black Africa clearly highlight the complexities of anti-apartheid politics, the connections between domestic interests and foreign affairs, and the chasm between declaratory policies and actual behavior. Despite Israel's ostensible exclusion from Africa because of its occupation of African territory during the Middle East conflicts and its subsequent collaboration with South Africa's white minority regime, many African states maintained unofficial ties with the Jewish state while they officially condemned it.[103] Israel's growing cooperation with Pretoria in areas widely regarded as essential to the perpetuation of white control did not prevent it from maintaining and extending its economic interests and opening dialogue with African states. And since several African countries, particularly the Frontline States, have economic relations with South Africa, many Israeli leaders dismiss criticism from officials, such as Yosef Beilin and David Kimche, who contend that Israel's ties with Pretoria damage its relations with black Africa. From their perspective, it was not the Israel-South Africa connection that was responsible for the continued absence of links between Israel and black Africa; Arab pressure was the primary cause.[104] Consequently, Israeli leaders concluded that their collaboration with South Africa would not be an obstacle to the resumption of diplomatic ties with African states, especially in light of rapidly falling oil prices in the 1980s and OPEC's ineffectiveness, a reduction in Arab aid, and serious economic problems in Africa.

Israel's strategy yielded a major breakthrough in Africa when diplomatic ties were reestablished with Zaire in 1982, followed by Liberia (1982), Ivory Coast (1986), Cameroon (1986), and Kenya (1988). Friendship associations were also formed with Mauritius, Ghana, Sierra Leone, Liberia, and Kenya.[105] Trade between Israel and black Africa actually increased during the period when Arab states were most successful in their efforts to isolate Israel diplomatically. From 1971 to 1982, Israel's exports to black Africa rose from about $40 million to roughly $120 million, reaching four percent of Israel's total exports. These exports have been mainly chemicals, fertilizers, textiles, electronic equipment, machinery, and rubber and plastic products. Imports include coffee, cocoa, wood, skins, and diamonds. Israel's principal trading partners include Nigeria, Ethiopia, Kenya, Zambia, Zaire, Tanzania, Ivory Coast, and Gabon.[106] In addition, Israeli firms are involved in several countries. For example, Solel Boneh (construction and road building), Tahal (water engineering and irrigation), Agridan (agricultural development), and Federman Brothers (hotel building) have projects throughout Africa. And similar to Japan and West Germany, Israel permits its businessmen to play a political role, meeting with political leaders, diplomats, and other businessmen.[107] Available evidence suggests that black African states, despite their rhetoric, are not willing or able to significantly alter Israel's economic relations with South Africa, although they could have an impact on military cooperation between the two countries, due largely to American opposition to the sale of military weapons to Pretoria.

## MILITARY COOPERATION WITH SOUTH AFRICA

Until the U.S. State Department issued its congressionally mandated report on nations that violate the U.N. arms embargo against South Africa, there was much controversy surrounding Israel's military ties to Pretoria and denials by the Israeli government of any involvement in supplying arms to South Africa. However, faced with the possibility of a congressional debate on its relations with South Africa and the impact that would have on its military aid from the United States, the Israeli Cabinet, after much discussion, decided to adopt sanctions against Pretoria, including refraining "from new undertakings in the realm of defense."[108] Although this statement left unclear the extent to which military cooperation would continue under existing arrangements, it marked a radical departure from the previous government policy of dismissing any suggestions of arms trade between the two countries. Among the nonsuperpowers, Israel is unique in its willingness to violate the arms embargo. While companies in Germany and Britain sold military weapons to South Africa, their actions were not overtly approved by their governments and, as we have seen, violators were prosecuted for infringing the law. But neither West Germany nor Britain was confronted by the security and economic problems that plagued Israel.

Following the Yom Kippur War, the arms race between Israel and its neighbors rapidly escalated. Between 1973 and 1984 Israel imported and produced roughly five hundred aircraft, two thousand new battle tanks, almost three thousand armored personnel carriers, sixteen missile boats, three submarines, and many different types of missiles.[109] Similarly, Syria doubled the number of its aircraft and increased the number of tanks, armored personnel carriers, and anti-aircraft defense systems. Ironically, American aid provided under the Egyptian-Israeli peace treaty enabled Egypt, as well as Israel, to buy significant quantities of weapons from the United States and other countries.[110] Also between 1973 and 1984, Israel emphasized co-production and other mutually beneficial arrangements to lower the costs of research and production and to obtain badly needed financial resources for its own military and economic schemes. In 1977, for example, Israel approved licensing and co-production agreements for Reshef class boats to be built in Durban, South Africa, in addition to six previously bought by South Africa's navy.[111] An important aspect of the military ties between the two states involves sharing intelligence and technical knowledge.

Israel's own security concerns, its perception of the ANC as the PLO's equivalent, and the general tendency among many black South Africans to equate their struggle for basic human rights with that of the Palestinians combine to influence the Israeli government to cooperate with Pretoria in the area of intelligence gathering. It is generally believed that South Africa has access to Israeli sources in Africa and the United States, while Israel has access to South Africa's Silvermine facility, an ultramodern surveillance center for naval vessels and aircraft.[112] The closeness of the collaboration between Israel and South Africa was revealed in 1986 when Jonathan Pollard was convicted of spying on the United States for Israel and sentenced to prison for life. According to Benjamin Joseph, former U.S. Defense Secretary Caspar Weinberger reportedly prepared a sworn affidavit in which he detailed how Pollard had gravely compromised American intelligence operations against South Africa.[113] Information given to Israel was passed on to South Africa. This development clearly worried U.S. government officials and was probably responsible for the insidious erosion in what appeared to be the unquestioning American support of Israel.

An important corollary of intelligence sharing is training. While it is difficult to corroborate training activities, available evidence indicates that Israel assists South Africa with different aspects of military training. South Africans have graduated from Israeli military schools, and Israeli military advisers serve in South Africa as instructors and models for local ground forces.[114] Many Israelis have been involved in South Africa's regional military operations. For example, it is generally believed that strategies used by the South African Defense forces in their invasion of Angola and attempts to destabilize neighboring states follow Israeli strategies against the PLO and the Arab states.[115] Furthermore, Israeli officers regularly lectured their South African counterparts on combat to be used against Soviet aircraft in Angola.[116] It is also alleged that the Mossad, Israel's intelligence agency, shares information on ANC activities with South African officials, giving the latter early warning of changes in ANC strategy and tactics as well as detailed lists of recruits, their special skills, and other pertinent data.[117] A logical outgrowth of intelligence-sharing and training is technical cooperation.

Technical and research collaboration between Israel and South Africa has significantly enhanced the latter's ability to produce many of its own weapons, to lengthen the production run and lower the unit cost, and to protect its borders against guerrilla attacks. Israelis have assisted South Africans with updating the equipment of their Mirages and have supplied the necessary spare parts. More important, Armscor, South Africa's state-owned arms manufacturer, produces weapons that are virtually identical to those made in Israel. For example, South Africa's Scorpion ship-to-ship missile is derived from Israel's Gabriel missile, and the Cheetah is believed to incorporate electronics developed when Israel produced the Kfir fighter plane.[118] Israel's efforts to make the Lavi aircraft is another example of technical cooperation and cost-sharing with South Africa. Even prior to securing funding from Washington for producing the Lavi, Israeli Defense Minister Ezer Weizman discussed cost-sharing with the South Africans.[119] When the high cost of developing and manufacturing the plane, as well as possible duplication of what the United States was doing, eventually forced the Israelis to abandon the project, South Africa tried to attract the unemployed aircraft workers to relocate to that country by offering salaries of $7,000 a month and generous transportation and housing allowances.[120] However, there is no evidence to suggest that Israelis accepted the offer. In addition to cooperating on technical and other matters, Israel is involved in direct arms sales to South Africa.

National security concerns influenced Israel, as well as Britain, to form a strategic alliance with South Africa. Initially, Israelis provided weapons which could be used only against external threats. Similar to Britain, Israel's perception of the Soviet threat in the Indian Ocean and the inaccessibility of the Suez Canal to its ships influenced that country to supply Reshef missile boats and Gabriel missiles to the South African navy. According to Israel's first ambassador to Pretoria, Yitzhak Unna, protecting the freedom of the seas was a major consideration in his country's decision to sell the weapons. They could not be used for riot control, and only South Africa permitted Israeli vessels to use its ports and refueling facilities.[121] Other military sales included Uzi sub-machine guns, Kfir jet fighters, light-weight Scorpion helicopters, the Merkava tank, military refueling planes, remotely piloted drone aircraft for reconnaissance activities, 115mm howitzer cannon, and electronic and counterinsurgency systems.[122] Another controversial aspect of the collaboration between Israel and South

Africa is in the area of nuclear weapons. Enough evidence exists to support the assumption that South Africa is working on nuclear weapons, and that Israel already has the capability to make them. What was more difficult to assess until late 1989, when the U.S. government made public that Israel was helping South Africa develop missiles with a range of nine hundred miles, was the level of cooperation between these countries. It is generally assumed that Israel is providing South Africa with technical expertise in exchange for uranium, and Israel does not formally deny working with the South Africans on nuclear weapons.[123] Military and economic relations are to some extent influenced by family and cultural ties between the two states.

## FAMILY AND CULTURAL TIES

Israel shares with Britain deep family and cultural links to South Africa. Both countries often justify their foreign policies toward South Africa on the basis of how certain decisions would affect family members or individuals who are entitled to Israeli or British citizenship. Both countries essentially favor the status quo in Pretoria in order to protect those who identify with these states. Israel has often argued that its concern for the approximately 125,000 Jews in South Africa justifies the improvement of relations with the white minority regime.[124] As Chazan observed, "the feebleness of the Jewish argument is corroborated by the fact that Israeli foreign policy has not been subservient to the sensitivities of the Jewish diaspora when other considerations intruded. Israel has not supported the Soviet Union because of its large subjugated Jewish community."[125] While there are many factors complicating Israel's relations with Moscow, this argument is basically valid. Labor governments and the founders of the new state consistently condemned apartheid. Shimon Peres, for example, stated long ago that "world Jewry is an Israeli national interest. But when we stand between a local Jewish interest and a basic moral problem we give up the local Jewish interest. Such was the case with apartheid."[126] This position is consistent with both the principles of Judaism and the Jewish experience with discrimination and religious and racial hatred. The rise of Begin and the New Zionists, combined with national security and economic problems and Arab efforts to isolate Israel, contributed to a reversal in Israel's position on South Africa's Jews.

The Afrikaners, who had strongly identified with the Israelites of the *Old Testament* who were in search of the promised land, were not as willing to accept the Jews who settled in South Africa. So prevalent was anti-Semitism throughout Europe in the seventeenth century that the Dutch East India Company did not allow practicing Jews to settle in South Africa; Jews had to convert to Christianity. Although "converted" Jews reached South Africa as early as the second half of the seventeenth century, the first *identified* Jews arrived in 1806 with the British who had occupied the Cape.[127]

The position of South African Jews was ambiguous primarily because of contradictory tendencies within the Afrikaner community in particular and the white society in general. During the early period of white settlement in South Africa, Jews engaged in trade and commerce in rural areas inhabited by Afrikaner farmers. When diamonds and gold were discovered in the latter half of the nineteenth century, many Jews participated in the mining industry and the expansion of trade.[128] But anti-Semitism grew as Jews, the majority of whom had moved from the countryside to settle in urban areas, sent their children to English schools and became more closely allied with the British who regarded themselves as culturally and morally superior to the Afrikaners. By the 1930s Jews were openly attacked by groups such as the Greyshirts who were sympathetic to Nazism, and the number of Jewish immigrants was severely restricted under South Africa's quota laws. As was the case in Germany, blaming the Jews for economic ills had become an intrinsic element of Afrikaner national consciousness.[129] Despite this obvious discrimination against Jews, many Afrikaners actively assisted in creating the state of Israel. General Smuts, a moderate in the South African context, strongly supported the Balfour Declaration, which called for a homeland for Jews in Palestine and coexistence between Jews and Palestinians, on behalf of his friend Chaim Weizmann who became Israel's first president. Many South African Jews backed Begin's violent campaign to end the British mandate over Palestine, and many migrated to the new state of Israel. Prominent politicians and diplomats such as Abba Eban, Michael Comay, Shmuel Katz, and Louis Pincus were born in South Africa.[130] These deep historical links are perpetuated through religious, cultural, and family ties between the two countries.

Israelis established an Israel-South Africa Friendship League in 1968 to promote better relations between the two societies, particularly the Jewish communities. Begin was president of the League when he became Prime Minister in 1977, and Simcha Erlich, former Israeli Finance Minister, Eliezer Shostak, Minister of Health in Begin's Cabinet, and Shmuel Tamir, Begin's Minister of Justice, had prominent roles in the organization.[131] South African Jews, aware of increasing anti-Semitism by Afrikaner extremist movements, have helped to augment the activities of the Friendship League by encouraging Jewish educators, rabbis, and Israel's religious leaders to become more actively involved in maintaining bonds between Jews in Israel and those in South Africa. Begin's decision to appeal to the Diaspora Jewry for support of his foreign and domestic objectives also strengthened relations between the Likud Party and the revisionist Herut faction that had dominated the South African Zionist Federation since the early 1970s,[132] thereby bolstering conservative views on apartheid among some South African Jews.

Israeli officials have supported cultural exchanges during times of serious political turmoil in South Africa when the world community and the South African Jewish community have tried to distance themselves from the apartheid regime. For example, when Israel's National Olympic Committee decided to terminate all sports contacts with Pretoria in 1977 in the aftermath of the Soweto riots and the death of Steve Biko while in police custody, the Israeli government pressured the Committee into rescinding its decision.[133] Similarly, a month after South Africa imposed a draconian State of Emergency in June 1986, Yitzhak Shamir, Israel's Foreign Minister and Alternate Prime Minister under the Likud-Labor coalition agreement, approved a tour of South Africa by the Israel Chamber Orchestra and recommended that two racially segregated choirs from South Africa be allowed to participate in a song festival in Israel.[134] Tourism and other exchanges were also openly encouraged by the government until 1987, when the Cabinet adopted sanctions against Pretoria.

## STRATEGIES

Israel's decision to impose sanctions against South Africa was clearly inconsistent with its policy of collaboration with the minority regime from 1967 to 1987. The heated anti-apartheid debates which occurred in the British House of Commons or in the American Congress were conspicuously absent in the Knesset. Objections to Israel's South Africa policy by David Kimche, Director-General of the Foreign Ministry, and Yosef Beilin, political director-general of the Foreign Ministry and the chief architect of sanctions, were largely ignored by both Likud and Labor members of the Cabinet. Israel's experience with sanctions imposed against it by the Arab states may have contributed to the decision to take a strong anti-sanctions position vis-à-vis South Africa and to Israel's special skills in avoiding trade embargoes. But Israel's early support for sanctions against Pretoria, at a time when Arab sanctions were in effect, and its endorsement of the Jackson-Vanik amendment, which linked Jewish emigration from the Soviet Union to trade with the United States belie the argument that Israel is consistently opposed to sanctions. This point, as we have seen, is also applicable to Margaret Thatcher's position on sanctions. However, unlike Britain, Israel did not articulate its position on sanctions against South Africa until 1987. In fact, only on March 19, 1987, did Israel admit, for the first time, that it had significant military ties with South Africa in defiance of the U.N. arms embargo.[135]

When the inner cabinet of the Israeli government met on March 18, 1987, there were obviously lengthy discussions on that country's relationship with South Africa. It was at that time that Israel issued a statement which contained an admission that there was military collaboration between the two countries. In what appears to be a concession to Pretoria, or a point intended for the domestic audience, Israel stated that the decision to impose sanctions against South Africa "marks the first time that the Israeli government has adopted an explicit overall decision that would impair relations with South Africa. The decision was preceded by deliberations extending nearly six months, in the course of which a complex and delicate set of considerations had to be taken into consideration."[136] Israel's Ministry of Foreign Affairs elaborated on some of the factors which influenced the new policy. These included: (1) concerns about the South African Jewish Community; (2) vital economic interests; (3) Israel's economic problems; and (4) the profound belief that certain policies being practiced by the South African regime were intolerable. According to the Ministry, "what ultimately tipped the scales, however, were long-term moral and political considerations. Were it not for the deeply held belief (that certain South African practices are immoral), no amount of American or European pressure could have persuaded Israel to adopt that kind of decision."[137] Despite these statements, a detailed analysis of how and when the Cabinet reached its decision would probably show that American pressure was the key ingredient that influenced Israel to alter its policy. As noted earlier, relations between Israel and the United States have been adversely affected by the Jonathan Pollard affair. Furthermore, Israel's alleged involvement in the Iran-Contra arms for hostages scandal, and the hard line adopted by the Likud on a wide range of issues led to growing American criticism of Israel's foreign policy. Most important was quiet but consistent pressure from American Jews, many of whom are leading advocates of stronger measures against South Africa. Following intense lobbying by American Jewish organizations and a delegation of black Americans, Israel's staunchest supporters in Congress, it was clear that continuation of the status quo in relation to South Africa could result in a reduction of roughly $3 billion in U.S. military assistance to Israel.[138]

Widespread anti-apartheid activities in the United States in 1985 and 1986 culminated in the passage of the Comprehensive Anti-Apartheid Act over the President's veto. The Congressional Black Caucus, Jews, leading Republicans such as Lowell Weiker, Nancy Kassebaum, and Richard Lugar, and Democrats such as Edward Kennedy supported the anti-apartheid legislation. The emotive nature of this issue in the United States and obvious bi-partisan support in the House and Senate for sanctions against South Africa created a serious predicament for Israeli foreign policymakers. The Comprehensive Anti-Apartheid Act required the President to submit a report to Congress on other countries' relations with South Africa. The State Department report included Israel as one of the countries that circumvented the U.N. arms embargo against Pretoria.

The implications for Israel were apparent form the language and intent of Section 501 of the Comprehensive Anti-Apartheid Act, which states that:

If the President determines that significant progress has not been made by the Government of South Africa in ending the system of apartheid and establishing a nonracial democracy, the President shall include in the report required by subsection (b) a recommendation on which the following additional measures should be imposed: (1) a prohibition on the importation of steel from South Africa; (2) a prohibition on military assistance to those countries that the report required by section 508 identifies as continuing to circumvent the international embargo on arms and military technology to South Africa. . . .[139]

Although American aid to Israel was in jeopardy, perhaps a more important consideration for Israeli policymakers was the information that would emerge from extensive debates on Israel's relationship with South Africa and the impact it would have on American perceptions of the country.

In an almost complete reversal of policy, the Israeli Cabinet adopted measures against South Africa that included: (1) no new investments, unless approved by the Ministry of Finance, the Bank of Israel, and the Ministry of Foreign Affairs; (2) prohibition on the granting of government loans; (3) bringing cultural ties between the two countries into conformity with Israel's basic negative view of the apartheid regime; (4) an end to the promotion of tourism to South Africa by the Government; (5) no new agreements in the area of science; and (6) no visits to South Africa by Israeli civil servants unless approved by an inter-ministerial committee.[140]

Israel's preoccupation with national security and its serious economic problems diminish its ability to allocate substantial resources for black empowerment. Nevertheless, the government committed itself to establishing a fund "to assist in the implementation of training programs in Israel in educational, cultural, and social fields for participants from the black and colored communities of South Africa."[141] The Israeli Ministry of Foreign Affairs Division of International Cooperation works with private organizations that are involved in running community development programs for black South Africans. In July 1986 the Israeli Histadrut's Afro-Asia Institute, with the Foreign Ministry's assistance, conducted a seminar on nation-building for twenty black South African leaders.[142] These efforts are augmented by those of The Marjorie Kovler Institute for Black-Jewish Relations of the Religious Action Center on Reform Judaism. Primarily concerned with strengthening ties between black and Jewish Americans, the Institute donated $100,000 for training black South African medical workers.[143]

While implementation of the provisions adopted by Israel will be difficult to monitor, as developments regarding the attempted transfer of U.S. missile technology to South Africa via Israel demonstrate, their adoption and Israel's commitment to help the black community represent a significant shift and a new beginning in Israel's relations with South Africa. Furthermore, progress toward a peaceful resolution of the Israeli-Palestinian conflict will undoubtedly contribute to greater security for Israel, and thereby lessen its emphasis on the military aspects of national security. More important, Israel's efforts to distance itself from apartheid and to end the bloodshed between Arabs and Jews will help to bring that country's behavior closer to the ideals of Diaspora Jewry. In the final analysis, Israel's strength depends not only on military might but also on its concern for human rights in a world where indifference to suffering has resulted in tragic consequences.

# 6

# SCANDINAVIA

## The Morality of Small States

Compared to Britain, West Germany, Japan, and Israel, the Scandinavian countries of Denmark, Norway, and Sweden have implemented far-reaching sanctions against South Africa and play a leading role in international forums in an attempt to influence the major powers to adopt policies that would force South Africa to abolish apartheid. Norway's Prime Minister Gro Harlem Brundtland was instrumental in convincing Denmark and Sweden to impose a full trade boycott against South Africa in order to set an example for the United States, Britain, and West Germany, and Denmark consistently urged its European Community partners to radically alter their position of favoring modifications in the status quo in South Africa, albeit unsuccessfully. Although Scandinavia's modest economic interests in South Africa may be viewed as a factor motivating Denmark, Norway, and Sweden to strongly oppose racial domination, several other factors combine to shape their South African policies.

Scandinavia's geographic isolation, common history, political orientation, the small size of the three countries, their experiences during World War II when Nazi forces occupied Denmark and Norway, and their cultural and religious beliefs contribute to a policy that emphasizes humanitarianism, the peaceful resolution of conflicts through international organization, and compliance with international law. In all three countries the Evangelical Lutheran Church, though not well-attended, claims over ninety-five percent of the population as members and augments the widely held and strong sense of responsibility for one's actions and concern about others. Cultural factors and political realities reinforce the view that humanitarianism and internationalism are intricately linked with perceptions of national security. Compared to Israel, which is surrounded by hostile countries, the relative isolation of Scandinavia and its international popularity has led to its radically different view of the role of small states. The Hobbesian approach that characterizes Israel's foreign policy is clearly absent. Instead, Norway, Denmark, and Sweden have concluded that the unification of small states might allow them to persuade great military powers to obey international law, thereby protecting their own national security interests. In other words, a foreign policy based on morality is regarded as the most pragmatic approach for small states in a world dominated by power politics. The Scandinavians' emphasis on human rights and the peaceful resolution of conflicts through international institutions has contributed to the emergence of concern about apartheid, a violation of human rights enshrined in the U.N. Charter and the Universal Declaration of Human Rights, as a central foreign policy issue.[1] The self-perceptions and cultural values of the three countries are major factors influencing their policies toward Pretoria.

Although Sweden, Denmark, and Norway are small states, their perceptions of international relations are very similar to those of the leading superpower, the United States. The foundations of American foreign policy were laid during a relatively long period of isolation from the political and military turmoil of Europe, and increasing economic prosperity and an abundance of natural resources reinforced the American myth of exceptionalism and messianic responsibilities. Despite the United States' emergence as a superpower, the view that American power must be used for righteous causes and that its foreign policy must be based on morality still prevails.

Sweden in particular has enjoyed domestic tranquility; its isolation has helped it to avoid entanglement in European wars since the time of Napoleon. Its sense of being exceptional has been strengthened by feats of technological, social, and political creativity that have transformed it during the twentieth century from a society of misery and backwardness into a model for the world.[2] Not surprisingly, in contrast to Norway and Denmark which were occupied by Nazi Germany, Sweden tends to dismiss force and realpolitik as great power arrogance and embraces peace and neutrality as inherent Swedish virtues.[3] But while experience with European conflicts has influenced Denmark and Norway to regard membership in the North Atlantic Treaty Organization (NATO) as being pragmatic, all three Scandinavian countries share the self-image of being the "good guys" of the world, and all three subscribe to the view that morality should be the cornerstone of their foreign policies. Both Scandinavia and the United States generally see the issue of apartheid in moralistic terms and tend to subordinate economic considerations, especially when compared to West Germany, Britain, and Japan. While trade is clearly important, the foreign policies of America and Scandinavia are driven primarily by a sense of fairness and humanitarianism that is deeply embedded in their cultures. Yet Scandinavia's small size, economic prosperity, relative isolation from superpower conflicts, lack of the anti-Communist crusading aspect that characterized U.S. policy, and its socio-political philosophy facilitated its adoption of a South African policy that is far more stringent than that implemented by the United States. Only Canada has taken a strong anti-apartheid stance that is similar to Scandinavia's.

## FOREIGN POLICYMAKING IN SCANDINAVIA

Despite differences among Denmark, Norway, and Sweden, their foreign policies and the domestic contexts which influence them are characterized by a high degree of similarity and by deliberate attempts at consensus within the framework of Nordic cooperation. Their relative geographic isolation and the dominance in all three countries of the Social Democrats and other political parties with leftist and liberal philosophies have had a profound effect on the foreign policy process. Unlike Britain and Germany, which had colonies in Africa and long foreign policy traditions, Scandinavia, with the exception of Denmark which colonized the Virgin Islands, played no significant role in Europe's scramble for overseas territories and, consequently, developed different perceptions of Africans in particular and the Third World in general.

If Britain and Germany rely on realpolitik and embrace morality as an instrument of foreign policy only when it is expedient to do so, the small countries of Northern Europe clearly depend on the great powers' appreciation of morality and a peaceful international environment governed by the rule of law to safeguard their security interests. Although this should not be construed as military passivity on the part of Scandinavians, commitment to morality and international norms is far more prevalent among them than elsewhere in Europe. It may be argued that remoteness and memories of the German occupation of Denmark and Norway have contributed to Scandinavia's insistence on ideal standards in foreign policy, and that emphasis on domestic consensus and the belief that the government should assist individuals to obtain a decent standard of living have helped to shape Scandinavia's role as a bridge builder between developed countries and the Third World on the one hand, and between capitalist and socialists states on the other.[4] Yet Scandinavian foreign policy reflects the dichotomy between adaptability and rigidity, consensus and individualism, and idealism and pragmatism evident in all three countries.

During the 1930s when the world was suffering from the economic hardships associated with the Great Depression, the Scandinavians, led by Sweden, adopted social programs that represented a compromise between various classes and between capitalism and communism. Known as the "Middle Way" or the Swedish model, these social reforms spread throughout the Nordic countries and were carried to Germany and Austria by politicians from these countries who had lived in exile in Sweden during World War II. Through the efforts of Willy Brandt, Herbert Wehner, Bruno Kreisky, and other Social Democrats, the idea of Sweden as a model for the reconstruction of Europe was firmly embedded in the Continent's political landscape.[5] But Scandinavians' willingness to experiment and adapt to changing realities is counterbalanced by their view of politics as a serious enterprise that is characterized by an ethos of responsibility, competence, and a sustained effort of political socialization,[6] a consequence of which is a general domestic consensus on foreign policy initiatives and a deliberate combination of idealism and realism.

Essential to understanding the South African policies of Denmark, Norway, and Sweden is the realization that what might appear to be contradictions between idealist and realist tendencies are carefully managed. The Social Democrats and their allies who have dominated Scandinavian politics since World War I operate in a political environment shaped by the pragmatism deeply rooted in the cultures of the three countries. Thus, while the idealist tendencies of the Socialists in international affairs receive considerably less scrutiny than their domestic politics, there is an obvious coexistence between idealist and realist elements in Scandinavia's foreign policies. As Paul Cole observed, the socialist and liberal parties formulate declared policy in a more idealistic manner than do the conservatives. This is in contrast to operative policy, which usually does not reflect a particular political style. Rather, it reflects realism.[7] This pragmatism, however, influences Denmark, Norway, and Sweden to pursue slightly different foreign policies, despite numerous similarities among them.

The geographic location of the Scandinavian states and their remembered experiences play a decisive role in the formulation of their foreign policies. Sweden's ability to avoid involvement in Europe's conflicts, partly because of its remoteness, reinforces the commitment in that country to neutrality and military preparedness. Consequently, Swedish participation in the international arena avoids entangling alliances, such as membership in NATO or the EC, focusing instead on U.N. activities and political engagements in foreign policy issues outside Europe,[8] especially in southern Africa and Central America. Norway and Denmark, on the other hand, have been forced by their geographic proximity to Western Europe and historical experiences to adopt a dual foreign policy: one for the Nordic region, including Scandinavia, Finland, and Iceland, and another for the continental European states and Britain with which they have formed military alliances and, in the case of Denmark, an economic alliance as well.[9] Nevertheless, the Scandinavian countries' relations with South Africa are all strongly influenced by their humanitarian beliefs.

## HUMANITARIANISM AND FOREIGN POLICY

South Africa's repugnant practices are in direct contradistinction to the humanitarian impulses of the Scandinavians, whose strong sense of community militates against toleration of great inequalities among individuals. Influenced by the ideas of the Enlightenment and the French Revolution, Scandinavians have embraced social liberalism, humanitarianism, equality, social security and justice, and an emphasis on social harmony and order among all segments of society as cornerstones of domestic as well as foreign policy. Just as America's pluralism and political philosophy provide the context for U.S. foreign policy, Scandinavia's egalitarian ideology which focuses on questions of equity in the human condition has likewise structured its attention and approaches to international affairs.[10] But whereas the American ideology of equality is principally concerned with providing individuals with equal opportunity to achieve their objectives, the Scandinavians reject the assumption implicit in the American view that all people are created equal and therefore have similar ability to take advantage of opportunities in society. Instead, the Norwegians, Swedes, and Danes display a greater degree of solicitousness toward the disadvantaged members of their communities. While in Britain and the United States humanitarian efforts are often motivated by utilitarian concerns and are plagued by suspicion and condescending attitudes toward economically deprived citizens, Scandinavians tend to regard the disadvantaged as frail and vulnerable members of a closely-knit family.[11] The competitiveness of American society is in sharp contrast with Scandinavians' emphasis on kindness and helping others. Although there is competition in these societies, it is overshadowed by the belief that the glory of a nation is to be assessed by the level of decency in human relations that it achieves.[12] Not surprisingly, their foreign policies, especially toward South Africa, reflect these values.

Although it may be argued that Scandinavians' passion for good causes such as South Africa and the plight of the Third World emanates from a bad conscience, brought on by the contrast between their own economic prosperity and the terrible conditions under which Africans must live,[13] Scandinavia's foreign policy behavior is consistent with the generally accepted assumption that external relations are to a large degree an extension of domestic realities. As the concept of "middle way" was made operational within Sweden, Denmark, and Norway, economic conditions in poor countries began to attract widespread public attention. Humanitarians such as Fridtjot Nansen and Count Folke Bernadotte, the emergence of missionary revivalist movements, and awarding the Nobel Peace Prize to Albert Schweitzer for his work in West Africa helped to dramatize the problem of world poverty and contributed to its emergence as a cardinal component of Scandinavian foreign policy. While the general issue of poverty was important, it was racial discrimination in South Africa and the brutal efforts of the government to destroy what had been integrated communities that outraged the Scandinavians. Herbert Tingsten, editor of *Dagens Nyheter,* and other writers were instrumental in publicizing the inhumane nature of apartheid and generating public discussion in the early 1950s.[14] Apartheid's emphasis on legislated inequality and separateness, and its implementation so soon after both Denmark and Norway had been occupied by the Nazis whose doctrine of racial superiority culminated in the Holocaust, stood in direct contrast to Scandinavia's sense of community and adherence to human rights and international law. From the latter's perspective, an integrated world community as a step toward international peace required the removal of gross inequalities not only among individuals within countries but also between nations.[15] The elimination of racism was regarded as an integral part of this endeavor.

Compared to Japan and West Germany, which view economic growth in terms of national security, or Israel, which focuses on military might in order to ensure its survival, Scandinavian countries, while not overlooking economics and military power, take a more comprehensive approach to security. Unlike the United States, which generally disregards the socio-economic causes of conflicts, especially when Cuba or the Soviet Union is involved, Scandinavia focuses on social justice when assessing international security issues. But relying on the provision of substantial amounts of development assistance as a major part of the strategy for resolving conflicts highlights the fact that small states generally lack the ability to project military power outside their immediate area; they are not expected to do so. Consequently, they tend to transform the thorny issues of international order into questions of distributive justice, causing considerations of power and influence to be overwhelmed by concerns about human rights and economic welfare.[16] This approach is consistent with their reliance on international institutions and the peaceful resolution of conflicts to protect their security interests.

## INTERNATIONALISM AND NATIONAL SECURITY

Participation in international forums and support for international law provide small states with an opportunity to exert influence disproportionate to their size. Furthermore, as Norway's Foreign Minister Thorvald Stoltenberg put it, "a small country's possibilities of exercising influence in international affairs depend on a world community in which the will of the strongest does not prevail. International cooperation . . . gives us an opportunity to participate in decisions which would otherwise be made over our heads."[17] From Scandinavia's viewpoint, viable international institutions such as the United Nations increase the likelihood that a more organized and unified world community will emerge to reduce conflicts stemming from narrow perceptions of national interests. Combined with their tradition of humanitarianism, this view of world affairs undoubtedly influenced Scandinavians to regard themselves as natural mediators, guardians of the coveted Nobel Peace Prizes, and leaders in the struggle for world peace. Not surprisingly, Scandinavians such as Fridtjot Nansen, who gained prominence as the conscience of the world in the League of Nations, and Trygve Lie and Dag Hammarskjöld, who became the first two secretaries-general of the United Nations, have significantly contributed to the pervasive assumption that Scandinavians are dedicated to the achievements of world peace.[18] If security interests forced Israel, another small state, to elevate military strength above concerns about morality and international organizations, encouraging diplomacy clearly furthered Scandinavia's security interests. The crucial and obvious difference between Israel and Scandinavia is that the former is surrounded by countries with which Israel has fought since its inception in 1948, and the latter's geographic remoteness reduces the possibility of military attacks. These radically different circumstances have led to the selection of different instruments for achieving foreign and domestic policy objectives. In Sweden in particular and in Scandinavia in general the politics of internationalism has replaced earlier notions of national identity, growing into an ideology shared by most Scandinavians.[19] The fact that Sweden and Norway had succeeded in terminating their political association through diplomacy was not an inconsequential factor in shaping their general approach to international conflicts. In 1905, when the Norwegian Storting (parliament) responded to growing nationalism in the country and to opposition to Swedish control by declaring dissolution of the Swedish-Norwegian Union, Sweden acquiesced to the demand of the vast majority of Norwegians for separation. But international activism as official government policy is a direct response to the two World Wars. Scandinavians, decisively influenced by totalitarianism, Nazism, and the brutality of war, articulated the view that small states could unite in order to persuade great powers to observe international law. Sweden in particular believed that its neutral status in both wars positioned it to assume an active role in promoting international peace through its support for the United Nations, international economic cooperation, and human rights in other countries.[20] Denmark also approved the formation of an international security organization following its experiences under German occupation. A Danish delegation participated in the U.N. founding conference at San Francisco, and its Foreign Minister assured the first General Assembly that Denmark would be responsible for helping to maintain an international security system.[21] When the debates in the United Nations shifted to the issue of apartheid, the Scandinavians were regarded as natural allies of the anti-apartheid movement and the Third World.

By taking a strong anti-apartheid position, the Scandinavians also enhance their international visibility. Norway's seat on the Security Council
provided it with an unusual opportunity to serve as a bridge between
industrialized countries and the Third World, and to simultaneously put
into practice domestic anti-apartheid sentiments.[22] Furthermore, by having
the responsibility within the United Nations of heading the committee
which monitors the international supervision of the oil boycott against
South Africa, the Norwegian government could convincingly assert its
lack of involvement in efforts to circumvent the embargo. While a strong
anti-apartheid stance is compatible with Scandinavia's foreign policy goals,
it also poses some policy dilemmas. For example, the Scandinavians' preference for a peaceful resolution of the South African problem generally
influences Denmark, Norway, and Sweden to oppose U.N. resolutions
calling for armed liberation in southern Africa. Yet their belief that Africans
should protect themselves against Pretoria's aggression leads them to
support and make generous financial grants to liberation movements on
purely humanitarian grounds.[23]

## THE CABINETS AND FOREIGN POLICY

Although policymaking in Scandinavia varies slightly from one country
to another, common features include: the widespread use of official commissions of inquiry to maintain open communication between the governments and interest groups on a wide range of policy initiatives; a strong
emphasis on consensus; flexibility and adaptability in policymaking in
order to achieve consensus; small ministries composed of elite bureaucrats;
and a highly rigid and structural way of managing the politics of policy
development.[24] Contradictions between adaptability and rigidity are carefully managed and accepted in societies that elevate consensus and community above factionalism and individualism. Furthermore, their electoral
systems, based on proportional representation, function in a way that
avoids having governments that are made moribund by a multitude of
small extremist parties, as is the case in Israel. In Norway, for example,
each party receives a percentage of the seats in parliament corresponding
with its share of the votes. Compared to Israel, where small parties exercise
disproportionate power, the Norwegian system reduces this possibility
by favoring bigger political parties. In other words, large and moderately
large parties obtain a numerically higher representation in the Storting
(parliament) than would accurately correspond in mathematical terms to
their electoral support.[25] As in other parliamentary systems, less faction-
alized representative bodies facilitate the policymaking role of the prime
ministers and their cabinets.

The prime ministers, like their counterparts in Britain, Canada, and

Israel, are primarily responsible for articulating, formulating, and implementing their countries' foreign policies. Members of parliament, unlike members of the U.S. Congress, do not generally have a decisive or direct impact on foreign relations. Scandinavian prime ministers represent majority parties or a majority composed of coalitions in parliament. In Sweden the cabinet as a whole is responsible for all government decisions, although in practice many routine matters are decided by individual ministers, and the prime minister's role in determining foreign policy is widely accepted. Nonetheless, the principle of collective responsibility is reflected throughout the government.[26] While Denmark's constitution provides the monarch with the power to appoint and dismiss cabinet members, it is the dominant party in the Folketing (parliament) that ultimately determines the government's fate. As in Britain and Canada, a prime minister with a disciplined majority in the Folketing is able to galvanize support for various policies in the legislature. Despite the fact that members of parliament are constitutionally permitted to introduce legislation, the vast majority usually defer to the superior expertise of the cabinet in general and the Foreign Ministry in particular. Although Norway's constitution empowers the king to appoint the cabinet, in practice, leaders of the majority political party in parliament tell the king who should be elected for cabinet positions.[27] Here, too, the cabinet's responsibility for foreign policy is unchallenged. The deeply rooted tradition of the government consulting citizens throughout Scandinavia engenders consensus which, in turn, buttresses support for foreign policy initiatives taken by the cabinet.

## CONSENSUS THROUGH CONSULTATION

Scandinavia's South Africa policies must be analyzed within the context of cultures that emphasize the importance of consensus and consultation among various groups in society. The basic character of the Scandinavians, more than any other factor, brings them into direct conflict with the practices of the South African government. The ethnic and cultural homogeneity of Denmark, Sweden, and Norway no doubt contributes to domestic harmony, whereas South Africa's ethnic and cultural diversity makes conciliation more problematic. But the essential difference is that while Scandinavians stress community for all citizens, Afrikaners have always applied the concept and practice of community to their own specific group in an effort to exclude all others, including English-speaking whites. Historical factors also clearly account for incongruities between the two societies. If separateness ensured the Afrikaners' survival, community was viewed as the paramount virtue in Scandinavia, an arrangement that would protect the interests of all citizens.

While all three Scandinavian countries respect individual rights, the extreme individualism so pervasive in American society is kept in check by a political ethos which subordinates individual claims in favor of group objectives. If one accepts the argument that economic attitudes and individualism are interrelated, then Harry Eckstein's view concerning the predominance of noneconomic attitudes in Norway as they relate to that country's strong sense of community, especially after the Nazi occupation, is plausible. Eckstein asserts that "the first and foremost indicators of a deep sense of community in Norway are a set of behavior patterns that involve unconditional noneconomic attitudes both toward other persons and institutions that embody otherness, and certain tendencies in behavior that prevent or suppress interpersonal hostilities."[28] While economic competition obviously exists, societal norms of cooperation diminish the probability of it becoming the dominant mode. Of direct relevance to Scandinavia's South Africa policy is the fact that consensual norms assist in elevating foreign policy above party strife. Denmark, Norway, and Sweden have succeeded in achieving general agreement among all major political parties on policy toward Pretoria. In Scandinavia in general, and in Sweden in particular, most foreign policy issues are not discussed in parliament or during election campaigns but are resolved through consultations in informal leadership conferences, and in Sweden by the Riksdag's (parliament) Advisory Council on Foreign Affairs.[29] Encouraging the involvement of all relevant groups in these consultations is essential to attaining consensus on the countries' policies on apartheid.

Distinctive to Scandinavia is the institutionalized practice of consulting interest groups on a myriad of public policy issues, and the systematic incorporation of these groups into the legislative and administrative processes. Almost every conceivable aspect of social, economic, and political life has its formal organization, and the relationship between these groups and the government is formalized through rules and practices of communication prior to making foreign policy, and through representation in the plethora of consultation and decision-making bodies.[30] In Sweden, for example, interest groups and anti-apartheid organizations are generally regarded as essential participants in the foreign policy process, and relevant groups as well as government ministries and agencies are given preparatory drafts of proposed legislation for comment, which helps to reinforce cooperation and consensus-building. The various anti-apartheid organizations carry their own legacy of past involvement in the formulation of particular policies, a busy schedule of ongoing consultations, and a well-justified expectation that their opinions will be solicited and taken into consideration in the future.[31] The small size of the Scandinavian countries encourages politicians, administrators, and anti-apartheid group leaders to develop less adversarial relationships. To a much greater degree than is the case in Britain, the various participants in the policymaking process place considerable stress on the social skills of cooperation, not pushing advantages too far, avoiding outright confrontation, and not casting anyone in the role of a permanent loser.[32] Like Japan, Scandinavia's sense of community motivates all groups to make concessions in the interest of the larger society and to facilitate future negotiations. Although this approach may be regarded as idealistic within the American context of policymaking, it is extremely pragmatic in Scandinavia, where it is very difficult for an interest group to achieve its goals by ignoring the concerns of others. Within the multi-party framework that exists in Denmark, for example, a coalition must be formed of several interests and parties to secure passage of a particular program.[33] Commissions of inquiry function to work out differences among groups.

Commissions of inquiry are generally associated with the Swedish tradition of consultations by the central government with royal governors who were based in outlying provinces. As the pressures prompted by Sweden's industrialization and democratization forced the central government to deal with disaffected groups, these commissions became an integral part of the policymaking machinery. Today commissions of inquiry constitute an extension of the relatively small permanent ministerial staffs through which individuals with specialized political, administrative, interest group, and professional roles can collaborate to find acceptable solutions to particular problems.[34] Consequently, anti-apartheid groups, with their large, specialized research departments, have direct access to joint decision making forums. Under these circumstances public opinion on South Africa is taken into consideration by governments throughout the process of policy formulation and implementation.

## PUBLIC OPINION AND FOREIGN POLICY

Compared to Britain, West Germany, and Japan, where public opinion has relatively little impact on these countries' South Africa policies, public opinion in Scandinavia is a decisive element in foreign policymaking, a fact attributable to the latter's policymaking style, emphasis on consensus, and tendency toward conformity. As Erik Allardt observed, people are easily moved and mobilized by the same events; the public tends to become a mass easily shifting its focus of attention. Letters to the editor and human interest stories are uniformly humanitarian and stress the importance of being sympathetic with the underdog.[35] This is especially true of Sweden where social conformism tends to be greater. Disagreement, when it occurs, is usually about intensity of feelings regarding apartheid rather than opposition to efforts to abolish it. The ruling Social Democrats and their governing partners have decisively shaped and reinforced public opinion on the apartheid issue. Attitudes of individual citizens toward foreign policy tend to be strongly correlated with left-right positions on domestic issues such as state control over economic activities. Since the public generally subscribes to the view that foreign policy is an extension of domestic policy, the ideological and philosophical orientation of the predominant political parties continues to be an important, if not determining, factor in the formulation and content of Scandinavia's foreign policy in general and its South African policy specifically.[36]

The anti-apartheid movement is very strong throughout Scandinavia. Among the range of groups that supports the aims of the anti-apartheid movement are political parties, religious organizations, the trade union movement, youth and women's organizations, and groups such as the Isolate South Africa Committee and the Africa Groups in Sweden. All parliamentary parties, except the Conservatives, voted for the trade embargo adopted by Sweden, the Scandinavian country with the most economic interests at stake in South Africa.[37] In Norway—the leading advocate in Scandinavia of sanctions against Pretoria— public opinion is decidedly against apartheid. Not only do Norwegians consider apartheid to be a flagrant and methodical suppression of fundamental human rights, they also regard racial confrontation in South Africa as a potential danger to international peace and security. Consequently, public opinion is fully supportive of the Norwegian government's position that continued pressure on the white minority regime and continued assistance to black South Africans are essential ingredients of a nonviolent approach to abolishing apartheid.[38] Both Sweden and Denmark concur with Norway.

Sweden, as mentioned previously, emerged as a leading advocate of humanitarian efforts in the Third World in the early 1950s, and its writers focused much of their attention on racial discrimination in South Africa. In no other European country, including Britain, was so much newspaper space given to the description and discussion of apartheid as in Sweden. The problem of race relations also received much attention in Denmark. Youth organizations in Denmark as well as in Sweden and Norway initiated an anti-apartheid campaign in 1963; they called for a boycott against South African products, distributed information on the nature and consequences of apartheid, and attempted to enlist assistance for black South Africans. During the same year approximately one hundred members of Denmark's parliament (the Folketing) appealed to Danish citizens to comply with the boycott, and the trade union organization pressured the government to seek renewed action in the United Nations against Pretoria and asked consumers to avoid purchasing South African products until apartheid was abolished.[39] Public opinion on apartheid has intensified, and the Scandinavian countries are clearly in the forefront of international efforts to encourage peaceful change in South Africa. Cooperation among them helps to augment their opposition to racial discrimination and enables Denmark to represent the views of Norway and Sweden in the European Community.

## SCANDINAVIAN COOPERATION AND FOREIGN POLICY

Scandinavia, together with the other two Nordic countries, Finland and Iceland, is a distinct region of Europe, one characterized by considerable ethnic, cultural, linguistic, and religious homogeneity. After complete separation from the Holy See in 1517, the Scandinavians overwhelmingly adopted Lutheran Protestantism as the state religion in all three countries. Because they were not under the direct political and administrative control of the Holy Roman Empire, they were relatively unencumbered in their efforts to create their own independent cultural institutions following their break with Rome.[40] While it is difficult to fully explain the emergence of common characteristics such as their emphasis on responsibility, competence, consensus, and the community, extensive interaction between the three countries, common agrarian backgrounds, the absence of an agrarian-based Junker class, similar climatic conditions, and the early standardization of vernacular scripts are all contributing factors. Although not all Scandinavians understand each other's language, educated people in Denmark, Norway, and Sweden apparently have no difficulty communicating; linguistic unity exists in university settings, the research environment, the foreign service, and in the commercial world.[41] Cultural and linguistic similarities and geographic remoteness significantly enhanced cooperation among the three states within the framework of the Nordic Council.

The Nordic Council Statute, which governs cooperation between Denmark, Norway, and Sweden, was first proposed in 1938 by the Danish Foreign Minister Peter Munch and again in 1951 by Hans Hedtoft at a meeting of the Northern Inter-Parliamentary Union. Specific plans for a permanent regional organization to promote Scandinavian cooperation were debated by parliamentary groups and the foreign ministers of the Nordic countries in 1952 and were approved by them later that year. The Nordic Council Statute was adopted not as a treaty but as identical domestic legislation by the five states.[42] An underlying reason for encouraging Nordic cooperation was to strengthen the small states vis-à-vis the great powers. To some extent, the Scandinavians subscribed to the view that small countries are usually at a disadvantage in collaborative efforts with great powers. Furthermore, an independent Nordic Council would enable the small countries to pursue foreign policies that were largely independent of those of the great powers.

But the experiences of Norway and Denmark during Nazi occupation left them less enchanted than Sweden with isolation, and the latter's neutrality throughout the war engendered strains in its relationship with the former two. Norway and Denmark felt helpless without the support of allies, partly because their geographic proximity to Britain and Western Europe increased their vulnerability to attack. Consequently, when given the choice in 1949 to join NATO, Norway and Denmark elevated their security interests above Nordic solidarity with Sweden and became NATO members.[43] However, only Denmark joined the European Community, an organization often regarded as the economic component of Western security.

Despite the view that Denmark's participation in the E.C. influences it to pursue a more moderate South Africa policy, especially when compared to Norway and Sweden, Denmark has attempted to satisfy both domestic public opinion and that of the other two countries by adopting a foreign policy which can be perceived as being both Nordic and European. Although Denmark officially represents its own interests within the context of European Political Cooperation, its membership in both the Nordic Council and the E.C. inevitably leads to indirect communication between the two groups.[44] Denmark has consistently supported stronger measures against South Africa in the E.C. and continues its attempts to persuade West Germany and Britain that economic sanctions can be used as policy instruments vis-à-vis Pretoria. For Japan, Britain, and West Germany, economic considerations are clearly more decisive factors influencing their South Africa policies than they are in Scandinavia's case.

## ECONOMICS AND FOREIGN POLICY

Among the nonsuperpowers, Sweden and Canada enjoy the distinction of being virtually unaffected economically by the destruction caused by World War II. Both Denmark and Norway became unwillingly entangled in the war and, consequently, suffered serious losses. It is not coincidental that countries such as Britain, West Germany, and Japan, whose economies were severely damaged, made economic reconstruction the paramount foreign policy objective and continue to aggressively defend the right of private enterprise to engage in trade and commerce with countries that may have unpopular and oppressive governments. Yet economic factors were not predominant in Norway's or Denmark's South Africa policy calculations, despite the fact that the state's role in economic activities resembled that of Germany and Japan, both of which adopted a modified traditional economic liberalism. Mass emigration from Scandinavia to the American Midwest and the small markets of Denmark, Norway, and Sweden combined to force Scandinavians to rely on the state and other collective arrangements for economic benefits. Perhaps what partially accounts for the relative insignificance of economic considerations in Scandinavia's South Africa policy is a number of interrelated factors, including their humanitarian traditions, their geographic remoteness, domestic sources of minerals and raw materials, their lack of historical ties to South Africa, and their noninvolvement in the scramble for colonial possessions outside of Scandinavia, with Denmark's acquisition of what are now the American Virgin Islands as the exception. But the lack of colonial territories does not mean that Scandinavians did not share the benefits of empire. As Bernt Hagtvet and Erik Rudeng put it, commercially, from the High Middle Ages on, the process of give-and-take meant learning to find an advantageous role in the various Hanseatic, Italian, Spanish, Dutch, and British attempts at creating world systems of trade. Scandinavians could benefit from the spinoffs of conquest and exploitation without having to get their hands dirty in major colonial undertakings.[45] For example, Sweden, the least affected of the Scandinavian countries by European politics and violence and more economically secure than its Nordic partners, viewed itself as a model of political morality and became the leading advocate of greater concern for the Third World in general and southern Africa in particular.

Since the Napoleonic wars, Sweden has remained a peaceful country. With a prosperous industrial base created in the mid-nineteenth century and a culture which facilitated cooperation and compromise between labor and management, Sweden was positioned to capitalize on technological breakthroughs and on its highly efficient industry after Europe's devastation in World War II. This material base allowed it to rise to the status of a small state with the freedom of action of a greater power.[46] Sweden's considerable diversity of mineral resources augmented its industrial capabilities and allowed it to implement foreign policies that indeed reflected its commitment to morality and humanitarianism. Neither Denmark nor Norway was economically positioned to pursue similar policies until much later. Although Norway has important natural resources, its economic structure differs from Sweden's in that it lacks the diversity and technological advantages enjoyed by its neighbor. Until Norway's oil boom in the early 1970s, the country could not afford to follow Sweden's more liberal approach to the Third World. Denmark found itself in a similar situation. In addition to the fact that Denmark's geographic proximity to Europe exposes it to less Nordic influences, that country has long suffered serious economic difficulties. Its membership in NATO as well as in the EC mitigates the more radical tendencies that are generally associated with Sweden and Norway.[47] But while Sweden's weakening economy may ultimately moderate its approach to the Third World, its relatively insignificant economic interests in South Africa, its growing commercial ties with the Frontline States, and the predominance of cultural values make a major shift in its South Africa policy unlikely.

Although Scandinavia as a whole continues to enjoy economic prosperity, both Denmark and Sweden are experiencing economic difficulties. With declining exports and a wide array of public services, both countries have borrowed extensively to finance government expenditures. After more than twenty-seven years of current account deficits, Denmark's foreign debt exceeded forty percent of its Gross Domestic Product, and interest payments on the national debt accounted for over four percent of the country's GDP in 1988.[48] Sweden depends on exports for about thirty-five percent of its GDP, twelve percent of which went to West Germany (which also employs approximately one hundred and eighty thousand Swedes), fifty-seven percent to Western Europe, and twelve percent to the United States in 1985.[49] In light of Sweden's dependence on Western European markets, its ability to resist being formally integrated into the EC as a full member as Europe moves toward 1992 is likely to diminish. Full membership in the EC would undoubtedly affect Scandinavia's South Africa policies, as Sweden would be pressured to harmonize its foreign policy with that of its EC partners. However, given the problems which currently plague attempts at foreign policy coordination in Western Europe, Sweden's predilection for an independent foreign policy would not necessarily be compromised.

## ETHNICITY AND FOREIGN POLICY

Compared to Britain, Japan, West Germany, and Israel, ethnicity does not play an important role in the foreign policies of the essentially racially homogeneous Scandinavian countries. Finnish and Lapp minorities in the north and the approximately one million resident aliens from Finland, Greece, Turkey, Yugoslavia, and elsewhere have been generally integrated in Sweden, Denmark, and Norway. Nevertheless, there are indications that ethnicity is emerging as an issue in domestic politics throughout Scandinavia. Declining economic conditions have forced the three countries to adopt more restrictive immigration policies. In Denmark, an immigration law introduced in 1986 allows frontier police to deny entry to individuals who have not obtained a visa from a Danish embassy or who have arrived from a third country. As a result of these regulations, the number of refugees entering Denmark decreased from nine thousand in 1986 to less than two thousand in 1987.[50] Although Sweden continued to accept about eighty percent of all refugees arriving at the border in 1987, public opinion seemed to be divided on this policy.

More extreme responses to refugees came from minor political parties in Norway where King Olav appealed for toleration. Until the mid-1980s few refugees attempted to settle in Norway, but during the first ten months of 1987 the number reached over six thousand, due in part to political and economic problems in the Middle East, South America, and Yugoslavia. Political parties such as the Progress Party in Norway, headed by Mogens Glistrup, and the Faelleskurs (common cause) in Denmark, led by the chairman of the seamen's union, Preben Moeller Hansen, ran on platforms which included calls for restricting immigration.[51] Despite the ability of these parties to increase their number of seats in parliament, ethnicity is likely to remain extraneous to Scandinavia's South Africa policy.

## SCANDINAVIA'S RELATIONS WITH SOUTH AFRICA

Unlike Britain and West Germany, which have deep historical and familial ties to South Africa, Scandinavia has virtually no links to Pretoria. Consistent with their geographic isolation and humanitarian philosophy, Denmark, Norway, and Sweden were only indirectly involved in Africa through the missionary activities of the Evangelical Lutheran, Baptist, and Pentecostal churches in the late nineteenth century. Many of the missionaries combined social welfare work with proselytizing in eastern and southern Africa, and during the two World Wars they replaced German Lutherans in the former German colonies of Tanzania and Namibia. Swedish commercial interests which followed missionary activities were concentrated primarily in South Africa where, due to its relatively advanced economic development, there was demand for Swedish industrial products.[52] Given Sweden's technological breakthroughs and its strong economy, it is not surprising that among its Scandinavian partners Sweden continues to have the largest economic interests at stake in South Africa.

Approximately one thousand Danes and roughly four hundred Norwegians live in South Africa, many of the latter being seamen who worked on Norwegian ships that until recently transported about a third of South Africa's oil imports. There is also a small number of Norwegians living in South Africa who are descendants of Norwegians who settled in Natal over a hundred years ago. Although both groups claim Danish and Norwegian citizenship respectively, their impact on their countries' South Africa policies is virtually nonexistent, especially when compared to Britain's or Israel's concern for South Africans who are entitled to citizenship in those countries. Nevertheless, Norway maintains a consul in South Africa to provide assistance to Norwegian seamen and their ships. Scandinavia's economic links with South Africa are also relatively insignificant.

## SCANDINAVIA'S ECONOMIC INTERESTS IN SOUTH AFRICA

Commercial relations with South Africa have never been of critical importance to the Scandinavian countries, and their consistent commitment to international law and human rights has propelled them to the forefront of international efforts designed to persuade Pretoria to terminate apartheid. Among the nonsuperpowers Scandinavia stands out as the leading advocate of sanctions. Unlike the Frontline States which condemn Britain and others for trading with South Africa even as their own economic ties with Pretoria remain unchanged, Scandinavia has implemented the most far-reaching and comprehensive sanctions against apartheid. While countries such as Japan, Taiwan, Spain, Argentina, and Chile actually increased trade with South Africa in 1987, Denmark, Norway, and Sweden experienced the largest declines in both imports from and exports to South Africa. By 1989 the level of commercial transactions between Scandinavia and South Africa was insignificant, especially in the cases of Denmark and Norway. The following analysis of Scandinavia's economic links with South Africa is therefore primarily concerned with the period prior to the almost total trade boycott implemented by the former in 1986. As noted earlier, cultural factors in Scandinavia facilitated the adoption of strong economic measures against South Africa, despite economic arguments for continuing commercial relations.

Norway's imports from South Africa amounted to an estimated $25 million in 1986, a figure which represented less than 0.5 percent of total Norwegian imports. Products purchased from South Africa included manganese ore, phosphate, and copper and nickel mats. Exports to South Africa, estimated at $51 million in 1986, or less than 0.5 percent of total Norwegian exports, were mainly fish and inorganic chemicals.[53] Of greater importance to Norway's economy was the revenue derived from shipping oil and other products to South Africa.

Before parliament approved a ban on the transportation of oil to South Africa by Norwegian ships, Norway's shipping industry carried about one-third of South Africa's oil imports. It was estimated that a full boycott on such trade with Pretoria would result in an annual loss of $540 million, would idle roughly seventy ships, and create unemployment for almost two thousand Norwegian seamen. Shipping company employees, brokers, and business people associated with the industry were also vulnerable to severe financial losses, despite compensatory benefits provided by the government.[54] However, when parliament approved the trade boycott in March 1987, it left a potential loophole for the oil-shipping industry by exempting Norwegian-owned tankers whose destination is decided at sea. Since oil cargoes are often resold after the voyage begins, Norwegian tankers could continue transporting oil to South Africa without technically violating the embargo. However, Norway's severe restrictions on trade with Pretoria render this potential violation relatively insignificant, especially when compared to the actions of the other nonsuperpowers.

Like Norway, Denmark's aggressive sanctions policy resulted in an almost total elimination of commercial transactions with Pretoria by 1989. By 1986 Danish trade with South Africa accounted for less than 0.4 percent of all its exports and imports. There was a precipitous drop in Danish trade with Pretoria between 1985 and 1987 (see Table 8). In 1985 imports from South Africa were valued at $160 million, and during the first half of 1986 that figure sharply declined to $90 million. Exports followed a similar pattern, decreasing from $57 million in 1985 to less than $35 million in the first half of 1986.[55] Leading exports included machinery and equipment, chemicals, foodstuffs, and medical supplies (which are unaffected by the ban). Major imports were coal, raw phosphate, processed fertilizers, fruit and vegetables, vermiculite, and tanning extracts. Due to limited availability of alternative supplies of raw phosphate, vermiculite, and tanning extracts, Denmark decided to continue importing these items, valued at $10 million, until the end of 1988. Although several Danish companies continued their South African operations after the trade ban was introduced in 1986, other firms sold their interests and terminated their business activities there. Firms remaining in South Africa are required to adhere to guidelines which are designed to empower black South Africans. But Denmark's membership in the EC mitigates the impact of comprehensive sanctions because South African products cannot be completely barred from Denmark once they enter other EC countries.

Compared to Denmark and Norway, Sweden's interests in South Africa had been relatively significant. However, due to pressures generated by Norway through Scandinavian cooperation and the Nordic Council, Sweden's trade has also declined. Between 1980 and 1986 Sweden's trade with South Africa comprised a minuscule proportion of its overall interna-

TABLE 8
**Biggest Percentage Changes in Trade with South Africa**

1987 compared to 1983–85 average
changes of more than 40% (by value)

| Imports from South Africa | | Exports to South Africa | |
|---|---|---|---|
| Country | % Change | Country | % Change |
| *Increases* | | *Increases* | |
| Argentina | 203 | Turkey | 161 |
| Taiwan | 146 | Taiwan | 99 |
| Turkey | 132 | Ireland | 61 |
| Brazil | 119 | | |
| Portugal | 91 | | |
| Mauritius | 86 | | |
| Spain | 84 | | |
| Chile | 75 | | |
| Greece | 48 | | |
| Japan | 44 | | |
| | | | |
| *Decreases* | | *Decreases* | |
| New Zealand | − 42 | Greece | − 44 |
| U.S.A. | − 42 | Denmark | − 78 |
| Ireland | − 50 | Norway | − 91 |
| Sweden | − 60 | Finland | − 98 |
| Norway | − 75 | | |
| Denmark | − 96 | | |
| Finland | − 97 | | |

*Source:* Commonwealth Experts Group, *Statistics on Trade With South Africa* (1988).

tional commercial activities, accounting for 0.6 percent of exports and 0.2 percent of imports in 1980, and dropping to 0.3 percent of exports and 0.1 percent of imports in 1986. In 1985 Swedish imports, mainly metals and ores, were valued at $48 million while exports, primarily machinery, steel, and trucks, stood at $114 million.[56] However, Swedish firms operating in South Africa play an important role in the mining industry and other sectors of the economy. Alfa-Laval, for example, directly assisted South Africa's SASOL industry in solving its construction problems as recently as 1986. In 1987, however, Alfa-Laval, due to pressure from the Swedish government, announced an end to its business contacts with SASOL. Another company, Scania, continued to sell trucks to South Africa and ASEA, which merged with the Swiss-based Brown Boveri Corporation in 1987, and continued to supply South Africa with advanced technology, despite its decision to sell its shares to South African interests.[57] Concerned about the domestic economic implications of a trade boycott against South Africa, a special interdepartmental working group, composed of representatives from the Ministry for Foreign Affairs, the Cabinet Office, and the Ministries of Labor, Finance, and Industry, was appointed in 1986 to review the consequences for Sweden's economy of a termination of economic links with Pretoria. Consistent with the practice of obtaining consensus through consultation, the working group developed extensive contacts with trade unions, the companies affected, and various experts. From the companies' perspective, the 2,500 persons employed in production for the South African market would be negatively affected by the embargo. However, since more than half of them were employed by companies with relatively few sales to South Africa, it was estimated that only eight hundred jobs would be lost as a result of sanctions. Although the firms supplying the South African mining industry and the specific regions and towns dependent on these companies would clearly suffer, the working group concluded that "the overall effects on unemployment were not thought to be such that they could not be dealt with essentially by normal methods used in labor markets and regional development policies."[58] While the number of jobs at risk was substantially smaller than in Britain's case, what clearly distinguishes Sweden's approach to South Africa from Britain's is the former's willingness to place humanitarian concerns above economic interests and to involve all affected parties in the decision making process. The Swedish Labor Market Board, various government ministries, the Nordic Institute for African Studies, the Isolate South Africa Committee, and church organizations collaborated in finding solutions to the labor problems caused by the government's sanctions policy.

Scandinavia's economic ties to black Africa, though not a dominant consideration, nonetheless appeared to be a factor in its South Africa policy. Sweden, Denmark, and Norway are very active in the Frontline States of Tanzania, Zambia, Zimbabwe, Mozambique, and Botswana. Even though markets in these countries for Sweden's exports are small compared to South Africa's, Sweden in particular has taken considerable interest in the long-term commercial opportunities offered by the region. Consequently, much attention is given to SADCC as an alternative market, and Scandinavia has decided to concentrate its provision of financial and technical assistance in the member states. Partly due to ideological reasons, particularly its commitment to the social welfare state, Scandinavia has long had close political and economic ties with black Africa, and its trade with these countries far exceeds its current levels of exports to and imports from South Africa. Scandinavia's principal trading partners on the continent include Algeria, Morocco, Liberia, Tanzania, and Kenya. Its major exports are chemicals, medical products, paper, manufactured products, automobiles, and building materials, while imports include vegetables, fruit, coffee, cocoa, cotton, rubber, phosphates, petroleum, and other mineral resources.[59] These markets, however are relatively unimportant since much of Scandinavia's economic relations are with industrialized European countries and North America. Thus, economic calculations do not appear to significantly influence Scandinavia's choice of strategies for effectuating change in South Africa.

## SCANDINAVIA'S STRATEGIES

Although Scandinavia's minimal economic interests in South Africa obviously facilitated its decision to impose comprehensive sanctions against the minority regime, the myriad of cultural, political, and geographical factors discussed earlier in the chapter undoubtedly outweighed economic considerations. Humanitarian instincts, a wider commitment to international law and organizations, and deeply rooted feelings of solidarity with the Third World assumed greater priority in Scandinavians' perception of their national interests. Just as purely economic factors do not prevent the United States from imposing sanctions against the Soviet Union, Cuba, or Nicaragua, commercial transactions are not always paramount in the hierarchy of other countries' national values. Perhaps no other international conflict is of greater interest to the Scandinavians than apartheid. This problem, which is viewed as requiring a nonviolent solution, allows the Scandinavians to fully apply the foreign policy instruments available to small states.

### Sanctions

Denmark, Norway, and Sweden subscribe to the view that since the policy of trying to abolish apartheid through dialogue with Pretoria has failed, external pressure must be applied to South Africa in order to end apartheid through peaceful means. As Sweden's Prime Minister Olof

Palme put it, shortly before he was assassinated in 1986, "it is by taking joint responsibility that we can contribute towards abolishing the apartheid system. This system can live on because it gets support from the outside. If the support is pulled away and turned into resistance, apartheid cannot endure. If the world decides to abolish apartheid, apartheid will disappear."[60] This approach sharply contrasts with Margaret Thatcher's assertion that sanctions are ineffective and counterproductive. However, it is clear that the reforms instituted in South Africa are undoubtedly influenced by a combination of internal protests and international pressures.

Unlike Britain and West Germany, Scandinavia was an early advocate of sanctions as a way of inducing change in South Africa, despite strong opposition to such measures from many Western European countries and the United States. But Sweden's position on the actual implementation of sanctions, at least until 1987 when Norway's Prime Minister Gro Harlem Brundtland influenced the Nordic Council to follow her decision to impose a full trade boycott against Pretoria, was that punitive economic measures against South Africa should occur within the framework of the U.N. Security Council. Noting that this approach is an essential principle of Swedish foreign policy, the Ministry for Foreign Affairs asserted that "this policy is founded on Sweden's strong support for the U.N. Charter and our declared policy of nonparticipation in alliances in peacetime with a view to neutrality in war. Sweden has consistently rejected proposals that we should participate in sanctions outside the framework of the United Nations. Our position in this matter is guided by considerations of both international law and security policy."[61] Among the reasons advanced by Sweden to bolster its position were: (1) the U.N. system provides an important safeguard against countries being involved in economic warfare between the major powers; (2) only concerted measures, supported by South Africa's principal trading partners, could achieve effective results; and (3) it would be undesirable from a strategic viewpoint for the U.N. to risk undermining its credibility by entangling itself in a situation in which it cannot take sufficiently vigorous action.[62] Yet Sweden's policy of only imposing sanctions in accordance with such a decision by the Security Council was tantamount to taking extremely limited actions against Pretoria, simply because any proposal for comprehensive economic sanctions against South Africa in the Security Council was guaranteed to be vetoed by either Britain or the United States. Nevertheless, Scandinavian countries provided momentum for the wide-ranging economic measures that were implemented against apartheid in 1986 and 1987. Sweden's policy position came under increasing pressure from Denmark and Norway through the broader framework of the Nordic Council.

As early as 1963 the Scandinavian countries developed a common policy on apartheid and committed themselves to maintaining a common Nordic position in the U.N. In accordance with their view that they would only comply with sanctions approved by the U.N. Security Council, Denmark,

Norway, and Sweden refused to support U.N. General Assembly resolutions that called for severing diplomatic and economic links with South Africa but readily enforced the Security Council's arms embargo against Pretoria in 1963. When Denmark voted in favor of a resolution proposed by African and Asian countries in 1965 without consulting its Scandinavian partners, the matter was discussed and quickly resolved in the Nordic Council.[63] Subsequent anti-apartheid actions have taken place within the context of Scandinavian cooperation, and increasing violence in South Africa has prompted the Nordic Council to initiate its own sanctions against Pretoria. In response to the deteriorating situation in South Africa following the Soweto riots in 1976, the Foreign Ministers of Norway, Denmark, Sweden, and Finland announced the adoption of a Nordic program of action in March 1978 that included measures to: (1) discourage Scandinavian investments in South Africa; (2) discourage sports and cultural contacts; (3) increase humanitarian assistance to the victims of apartheid; (4) require visas for South African visitors; and (5) provide additional economic aid to the Frontline States in order to diminish their dependence on South Africa.[64] Each country, through its domestic legislative and executive processes, was responsible for implementing these measures. Both Denmark and Norway applied additional restrictions to a range of exports in 1978 and 1979. In Denmark's case, these included a ban on the sale of military equipment to South Africa and on the transportation of such cargoes by Danish vessels; a prohibition against the transfer of nuclear weapons technology; the withdrawal of the official Danish trade delegation from South Africa; and the revocation of the export credit insurance program for Danish companies operating in South Africa.[65] Similarly, Norway decided to withdraw government credits for Norwegian exports to South Africa, to stop issuing currency licenses for Norwegian investments in South Africa, and to cease promoting exports to South Africa through the Norwegian consul-general in Cape Town.[66] Between 1979 and 1989 Scandinavian countries implemented several restrictions on trade with and investments in South Africa through the Nordic Council as well as through individual member states.

Contending that apartheid constitutes a serious threat to international peace and security, the Nordic Foreign Ministers met in October 1985 and endorsed several unilateral measures for Denmark, Norway, Sweden, and other Nordic countries to implement on a national basis. Many of the recommended actions reinforced steps already taken against South Africa. The new measures included prohibition of (1) the importation of Krugerrands; (2) leasing to enterprises in South Africa; (3) new contracts in the nuclear field; (4) granting new loans to South Africa; (5) the exportation of computer equipment which might be used by the South African armed forces and police; and (6) the transfer of patents and manufacturing licenses to South Africa.[67] On June 27, 1987, the governments of Norway, Denmark, and Sweden decided to terminate their air agreements with

South Africa, and on September 1, 1985, the Scandinavian Airline System discontinued its flights to South Africa, although it maintained a sales office in the country. The South African Airways also stopped flying into Scandinavia but continued to operate a sales office in Copenhagen. Among the Scandinavian countries, Norway was the one most responsible for initiating sanctions against South Africa that were later adopted by its Nordic partners and took steps beyond those endorsed by the Nordic Council.

Following a wide-ranging debate on apartheid in the Norwegian Storting in February 1984, an interministerial group, set up in the spring of that year, reviewed existing Norwegian actions against Pretoria and considered possible new measures for Norway to initiate either unilaterally or in cooperation with its Scandinavian allies. The group's report, presented to the Ministry of Foreign Affairs in December 1984, specified that any new sanctions would have to have tangible effects on the apartheid regime, a recommendation accepted by Asbjoern Haugstvedt, Norway's Minister of Trade. In March 1985 Haugstvedt urged the Storting to take initiative, within the context of Scandinavian cooperation, to reach an agreement on the adoption of extensive and binding international economic sanctions vis-à-vis Pretoria, and to attempt to induce other Western countries to enact measures similar to those in the Nordic Program of Action.[68] In the meantime, Norway imposed restrictions against South Africa that were not part of the Nordic Program of Action. As an oil-exporting country whose ships were the primary carriers of petroleum to South Africa, Norway apparently felt a special responsibility to ensure that Norwegian oil was not being transported to South Africa. As early as 1979, during a meeting between the Ministry of Petroleum and Energy and representatives from companies directly involved in oil production on Norway's continental shelf, the oil companies endorsed their country's policy of not selling its petroleum to the apartheid regime. In addition to this restriction, the government reserved the right to subject license applications for exporting ships to an assessment of the political implications of such sales.[69] Although some Norwegian ships violated the prohibition against transporting oil to South Africa, widespread domestic support for stronger measures against apartheid militated against egregious sanctions-breaking activities. By July 1985 Norway had implemented many of the sanctions later endorsed by the Nordic Council, and both Denmark and Sweden took similar actions shortly thereafter.

Denmark's membership in the EC complicates its relationship with the other Scandinavian countries while giving it an opportunity to persuade West Germany and Britain to take actions against apartheid similar to those implemented by the Nordic Council. But because both West Germany and Britain are reluctant to jeopardize their significant economic interests in South Africa by altering the status quo, Denmark's policies toward Pretoria are very different from the EC's. Apart from putting into effect the sanctions recommended by the Nordic Council, Denmark, like Norway, passed extensive anti-apartheid legislation that prohibited the sale and transportation of Danish oil to South Africa and imposed a ban on the imports of South African goods and services into Denmark and on exports from Denmark to Pretoria.[70] On May 30, 1986, the Folketing voted in favor of a bill imposing fines or imprisonment on individuals, including company board members, found guilty of violating sanctions against South Africa. However, unlike in Norway, where members of parliament from different political parties find it relatively easy to vote for strong sanctions because of popular opposition to apartheid, there was considerable disagreement on the wisdom and efficacy of a total trade ban, especially in light of Denmark's shipping interests and its dependence at the time on South African coal for between eighty to ninety percent of its domestic consumption. Consequently, the bill passed by a vote of seventy-six to five, with sixty-five abstentions.[71] Sweden, with relatively more economic interests in South Africa, focused primarily on regulating investments already in that country.

In February 1985 Sweden's Ministry for Foreign Affairs proposed that the government be authorized to prohibit Swedish lending institutions from extending loans to the South African government and from providing security for Pretoria's debts. The Ministry also recommended that Swedish companies be allowed to make replacement and other specified investments, provided that the companies did not use such investments to extend their business activities in South Africa and Namibia. Business enterprises could only make investments to improve employees' working conditions or replace fixed assets. Furthermore, they were required to submit reports on wages and working and social conditions for their employees. These proposals, approved by the Riksdag, entered into force on April 1, 1985.[72] At the end of the same year the Ministry for Foreign Affairs prohibited imports of agricultural produce from South Africa because of that country's extensive utilization of prison or forced labor in the agricultural sector. The Ministry's basic argument in favor of the ban was that "most of the prisoners are convicted of offenses under laws that constitute the very cornerstone of the system of apartheid, and which are only applied to the black majority."[73] Despite the general consensus within Sweden and the other Scandinavian countries on most of the sanctions against South Africa, there was significant opposition to a full trade boycott in both Sweden and Denmark.

When the ban on new investments was seriously debated in Sweden in 1978, the Swedish business community mobilized support to promote the idea that economic growth is instrumental in inducing reforms in South Africa and that sanctions are counterproductive in that they increase black unemployment as well as fueling white intransigence. Business interests, some trade unions—especially the Swedish Metal Workers Union—and the International Council of Swedish Industry contended that any curtailment of business links with South Africa would also hurt Swedish employees.[74] The most serious opposition to a full trade boycott developed in Denmark where Prime Minister Poul Schluter and his coalition government, composed of the Conservative, Liberal, Center Democratic, and Christian People's parties, expressed serious reservations about the May 1986 bill that prohibited trade with South Africa. The Prime Minister argued that unilateral measures by Denmark would not prevent South Africa from receiving various products, particularly oil, because other countries would view Denmark's action as an opportunity to increase their business activities with Pretoria. Furthermore, from Schluter's perspective, restrictions on trade would hurt those businesses for which the transitional period suggested by the bill's sponsors was inadequate and would cause substantial economic losses and layoffs of Danish wage earners in the affected companies, while having no harmful effect in South Africa.[75] Despite these objections, the bill was passed in the Folketing by a majority that included the opposition Social Democratic, Social People's, left Socialist, and centrist Radical-Liberal parties. Less controversial were strategies designed to empower black South Africans and assist the Frontline States to decrease their vulnerability to violent as well as nonviolent sanctions imposed against them by Pretoria.

## Black Empowerment

Scandinavia's commitment to the United Nations and its reliance on international organizations in general to protect its interests inevitably influenced it to devote increased attention to Pretoria's systematic denial of human rights for blacks. The probability of violence emanating from racial discrimination and oppression seemed to be an important factor motivating the Nordic countries to explore possible ways of assisting in the abolition of apartheid. Denmark, Sweden, and Norway, conscious of the growing Afro-Asian membership in the United Nations, persuaded that organization to consider how it could effectively contribute to ending apartheid. The basic challenge was to simultaneously reassure the white population that their future would be secure in a nonracial South Africa with equal rights for all.[76] By 1969 the Scandinavian countries had implemented general policies under which aid and material support was given to help refugees, to finance educational activities, and to assist detainees and victims of political repression inside South Africa. In order to be consistent with their interpretation of the U.N. Charter in regard to the principle of non-interference in the internal affairs of other states, Sweden, Denmark, and Norway channelled their support through the United Nations and voluntary agencies, especially those connected with churches. Between 1966 and 1974 these countries provided approximately two-thirds of the total $2.7 million in contributions for the U.N. trust fund to aid South African exiles, compared to merely $25,000 from the United States and $40,000 from Britain.[77] As conditions in southern Africa deteriorated, Scandinavia's participation in the region intensified, and adherence to a more conservative construction of the U.N. Charter's non-interference clause was significantly modified. Norway in particular became more directly involved in assisting national liberation movements, including the ANC. Because the general tendency in the United States is to perceive the ANC primarily as a Soviet proxy, Scandinavia's contributions to that organization are often conveniently ignored or overlooked. Norway, which enjoys a high international profile, strong domestic support, and solidarity with the Third World on the issue of apartheid, was sufficiently economically secure in 1973—following the discovery of North Sea oil—to augment its opposition to apartheid through its participation in a large-scale conference held under the aegis of the United Nations and the Organization for African Unity in Oslo in April 1973 and in the U.N. Conference Against Apartheid in Lagos in August 1977, which was attended by Norway's prime minister. While stressing that it was essential to endeavor to solve problems in southern Africa by nonviolent means, Norway, as a member of the U.N. Committee on Decolonization, concluded that liberation movements had to resort to other means when the white minority regimes rejected negotiations. Consequently, in 1977 Norway decided to give non-military assistance directly to the ANC at first and later to the Pan African Congress.[78] Sweden and Denmark also shifted their policies on the ANC, although they were more cautious than Norway, partly because of political and economic considerations. Contributions to ANC refugees were initially in the form of deliveries of food, vehicles, clothes, and medicines. Later, however, greater emphasis was given to project cooperation in the areas of agriculture, health, and education. Workshops for training merchants and the maintenance of vehicles are sponsored by Scandinavia, and farms and agricultural equipment have been purchased for the ANC to enable refugees to become self-reliant. The ANC also receives an estimated $20 million for scholarships, training programs, and housing.[79]

Whereas Britain and the United States have avoided direct contacts with the ANC until recently, Sweden has encouraged dialogue with the ANC for over twenty years in an effort to reduce the possibility of widespread violence within South Africa. One week before he was assassinated, Prime Minister Palme delivered a speech at the Swedish People's Parliament against Apartheid in which he praised Oliver Tambo, the ANC's leader, for his struggle to win freedom, pointing out that "his work, his optimism, and his belief in the possibility of change, that it will be possible finally to send apartheid to the lumberroom of history, has been a great inspiration to us all."[80] By legitimizing the ANC as a major participant in efforts to create a non-racial South Africa, the Scandinavian states have made a significant contribution to black empowerment within South Africa itself.

## SCANDINAVIA'S POLICY TOWARD THE FRONTLINE STATES

Sweden and Norway have been the major contributors to SADCC. Both countries have focused primarily on projects that would help to reduce the Frontline States' dependence on South Africa's transportation and communication services, a formidable task given the interdependence of the southern African region. The political platform which guides Scandinavia's foreign policy and aid programs in southern Africa is based on the Nordic initiative for broader economic cooperation between the Nordic countries and SADCC. This initiative was developed by the Finnish Prime Minister Kalevi Sorsa who believed that Nordic countries should begin a program of comprehensive cooperation with selected regional groups of developing states and, in the broader context of North-South relations, try to make the grand design for a new world economic order a partial reality by addressing Third World problems on a more limited scale.[81] But economic considerations were also influential in Scandinavia's decision to allocate about forty percent of its bilateral assistance to southern Africa. In addition to supporting moral causes, the Nordic countries wanted to accelerate the relocation of companies from South Africa to other countries in the region by promoting trade, investments, technology transfer, cultural exchange, and communications between members of the two regional organizations.[82] Sweden, with the largest investments in South Africa among its Scandinavian partners, was the country principally engaged in consolidating links between Scandinavia and southern Africa.

During 1986 and 1987, the Swedish International Development Authority (SIDA) allocated roughly $287 million in bilateral assistance to various countries in southern Africa. The recipients included Tanzania ($68 million), Zambia ($29 million), Mozambique ($43 million), Zimbabwe ($19 million), Angola ($18 million), Botswana ($13 million), and Lesotho ($5 million). SADCC received about $23 million, the ANC $7.5 million, and Swapo $8.4 million. Approximately $12.7 million was given for humanitarian assistance, $6.4 million for nongovernmental organizations, $2.1 million for special programs, and $28.5 million in emergency aid.[83] Swedish bilateral development aid is focused on specific projects within particular countries, and Swedish personnel play a key role in implementing the programs. Many Swedes are (1) employed by companies or work as consultants; (2) long-term staff on a SIDA contract; (3) volunteers sent by an NGO receiving financial assistance from SIDA; (4) short-term employees; and (5) those on contract directly with the host governments. The schemes in which they were involved include telecommunication projects establishing microwave links between SADCC countries; building an international telephone exchange and earth station in Zimbabwe; rural electrification in Lesotho; and many agricultural projects throughout the region.[84]

Given the serious food shortages and starvation in Mozambique, due primarily to political and military problems, Sweden is extremely active in agriculture, providing more than ninety percent of Mozambique's Ministry of Agriculture budget. Based on its underlying assumption that economic growth and social and economic equality in Africa depend to a large extent on rural development, Sweden has concentrated its resources on building primary schools, providing equipment and teacher training, and on rural health projects. A major objective is to support each country's efforts to achieve integrated rural development, to counterbalance the ubiquitous trend toward rapid urbanization to diversify the economy, and to create an alternative to the system of migrant labor, especially in Lesotho's case.[85] For commercial as well as political reasons, Sweden has stipulated that its funds cannot be used to purchase goods or services from South Africa, or for businesses in which South Africans are involved. Instead, southern African countries are generally required to utilize Swedish goods and services in projects that are supported by Swedish funds.[86] But given the interdependence of the region, it is virtually impossible to guarantee that such conditions will be followed. For example, Botswana and Mozambique have violated Swedish aid agreements by buying materials from South Africa simply because these countries are part of the complex regional economic system. Botswana, for example, used materials from South Africa in water projects financed by Swedish aid, despite the restrictions, because South African products were less expensive and because maintenance technicians and operators were reluctant to change from the South African engines and pumps they had been using to unfamiliar equipment.[87] Nevertheless, Sweden is making significant progress in southern Africa and is likely to enjoy substantial commercial benefits from its aid program if there is improved political stability and a decline in the sabotage activities to which South Africa is allegedly linked. As will be discussed in chapter eight, the Frontline States are intricately linked to South Africa, and therefore can influence, or be influenced by, Pretoria, a reality which must eventually be addressed by the major players, including Scandinavia.

Like Denmark, Sweden, and Norway, Canada, as a middle power which is most comfortable when it can clearly distinguish itself from its powerful southern neighbor, pursues a South Africa policy that emphasizes the rule of law in the global community and a strong commitment to human rights. The many cultural, political, and historical similarities between Scandinavia and Canada help to explain why their positions on apartheid are not radically different.

# 7

# CANADA

## The Politics of a Middle Power

Canada's South African policy is strongly influenced by its status as a middle power and by a myriad of cultural, economic, political, and geographical factors. Its choice of policy instruments reflects a deep commitment to human rights, a strong predilection for non-violent solutions to international conflicts, the predominance of moral values over economic considerations on the South African issue, and a preference for compromise agreements in international forums, particularly at Commonwealth meetings. Canada has consistently opposed apartheid and played a crucial role in South Africa's departure from the Commonwealth, despite Britain's efforts to prevent the apartheid regime from being ousted by African and Asian states. Like Americans, Canadians feel strongly about racial discrimination and attempt to eliminate it abroad, partly to preserve racial harmony and tranquility at home and to strengthen ties with Third World countries. Canada's opposition to apartheid enjoys widespread support from all major political parties, traditional elite groups, and the general public. Although Prime Minister Mulroney is a conservative within the Canadian political context, his approach to South Africa is radically different from that of his British counterpart, Margaret Thatcher, a fact which has resulted in occasional public disagreements between the two leaders at Commonwealth summits and within the industrialized countries' Group of Seven. But Canadian foreign policy is not seriously constrained by the economic and political factors that are paramount in Britain's South African policy calculations. Indeed, it may be argued that Canada's minuscule interests in South Africa as well as competition between the two countries for markets for their mineral resources allow Canadian policymakers to adopt economic sanctions against Pretoria without fear of negative economic or political consequences. Like Australia, Canada may actually benefit from South Africa's economic problems. Britain, a resource-poor country, when compared with Canada, is far more dependent on South Africa's minerals. Yet such an analysis of Canadian policy toward South Africa would be misleading. Although commercial interests are an integral component of all the nonsuperpowers' relations with Pretoria, they are obviously more important for some countries than for others. A clear distinction must be made between Japan, West Germany, and Britain on the one hand and Canada and Scandinavia on the other in terms of the relative weight of economic factors in these countries' foreign policy processes. Apart from domestic cultural and political characteristics which allow policymakers to propel Canada into a leadership role in the fight against apartheid, that country's status as a middle power contributes to its formulation and implementation of foreign policies similar to those of Denmark, Norway, and Sweden.

Although former Canadian prime ministers have traditionally argued that Canada should be more assertive on international affairs, they generally followed Western consensus on many issues. While several of them contributed to creating conditions conducive to the new policy orientations that are clearly visible under Mulroney, it may be argued that both Joe Clark, the Secretary of State for External Affairs, and Mulroney are responsible for decisively shifting Canada's position on South Africa from one of caution to one of bold leadership. Both men were educated at St. Francis Xavier University in Nova Scotia, an institution with strong ties to the Third World. Clark, for example, was the first Canadian Prime Minister to visit Africa. To some extent, they exhibit the missionary zeal common to many Canadians on human rights issues. Similar to the Scandinavians, Canadians generally view apartheid as a problem to which a middle power can apply its foreign policy instruments. As Clark put it, "we believe this to be an issue where we have both influence and power, and we have tried to deploy our political influence and our economic power to have the most effect in the fight against apartheid."[1] A strong stance against South Africa is also consistent with Canada's major foreign policy objectives.

## OBJECTIVES OF CANADIAN FOREIGN POLICY

Canada's long history of stability, strong economy, abundant natural resources, historic links to Britain and the Commonwealth, penchant for compromise, cautious and pragmatic approach to international problems, geographic proximity to the United States, bilingual heritage, and its growing concern with multiculturalism combine to determine its basic foreign policy objectives. Canada's history and status as a middle power allowed it to serve as a bridge builder between the United States and

Great Britain until the end of World War II, and to pursue a relatively open and flexible foreign policy, unencumbered by the strategic and ideological concerns of the superpowers.[2] Thus, on the South African issue, Canada's policy closely resembles that of the Scandinavian countries. But while small and middle powers are generally freer than greater powers to implement more restrictive measures against apartheid, their ability to effectuate meaningful changes is significantly limited. It is only through countries such as Britain, the United States, West Germany, and Japan that their objective of bringing substantial international pressure on South Africa can be realized. Both the Commonwealth and the United Nations are important forums for Canadian foreign policymakers because they provide them with opportunities to exert influence on those states with major economic stakes in South Africa that are better positioned to induce Pretoria to consider the benefits of abolishing apartheid. As a middle power that shares the North American continent with the world's leading superpower and Mexico, Canada views internationalism and the strengthening of international institutions as a key foreign policy goal. But unlike Sweden, it does not perceive the United Nations as an alternative to military and economic alliances with the United States and Western Europe, and it would be impractical, if not impossible, to eschew economic and military cooperation with the United States.

Internationalism as a major Canadian foreign policy objective emerged out of the devastation and violence of World War II and was augmented during the 1950s and 1960s when many Western European countries were preoccupied with reconstruction. Under these postwar circumstances, Canada and Sweden were able to enjoy greater influence in world affairs through articulating their commitment to human rights, international law, and the United Nations. For Candadian leaders such as Lester Pearson, internationalism was a way of fusing Canada's security interests with the notion of a global community in which conflicts would be resolved peacefully.[3] This approach to international affairs sprang from Canada's concern for democratic values and human rights but was also a response to decolonization in Asia and Africa.

Promoting social justice abroad is a fundamental objective of Canadian foreign policy that brings it into direct conflict with South Africa's apartheid regime. Within the framework of the general consensus on the importance of human rights which emerged from the ravages of war and the Holocaust, there was great international opposition to colonial domination, especially in countries such as Canada and Sweden which had neither colonies nor colonial aspirations. The legalization of apartheid in 1948 only heightened tensions between Europeans and Asians and Africans because, from the latter's perspective, racial discrimination and the dehumanization of non-Europeans were among the most deleterious aspects of colonialism. Increasingly Africans and Asians evaluated Canada's foreign policy primarily in terms of its position on apartheid and the nature of its relationship with Pretoria. As a middle power concerned with the effects of a precipitous European withdrawal from Africa, the expansion of the Soviet Union, and the possible appeal of communism to colonial peoples—many of whom equated capitalism with oppression—Canada believed that by virtue of its own experience as a British colony and its reputation as an honest broker in international politics it could play a pivotal role in reducing the spread of communism. The perception among Canada's foreign policy elite was that by showing confidence in the emerging states, by adopting imaginative programs of economic assistance, and by serving as a model of a capitalist and liberal democracy, Canada could significantly contribute to containing communism in Africa and Asia.[4] But the middle power's role as peace broker was complicated by difficulties inherent in attempting to balance its interests in maintaining a dialogue with South Africa on the one hand and adopting policies that would clearly demonstrate to Third World countries its abhorrence to apartheid on the other.

Although advocates of a complete severance of links to South Africa would argue that this dilemma is not resolved, Canada's strong anti-apartheid stance under Mulroney marked a major departure from previous attempts to maintain a balanced position on apartheid. However, even prior to Mulroney's open confrontations with Margaret Thatcher on sanctions against South Africa, Canadians had been deeply concerned about moral questions and human rights considerations in relation to apartheid. Since all Canadian governments condemned apartheid since it was implemented in 1948, the debate in Canada has been and continues to be focused on what actions should be taken under the prevailing circumstances.[5] Yet human rights and relations with the Third World must be balanced with Canada's economic ties with the United States.

Fostering economic growth through trade remains a primary objective for a country that relies on international commercial transactions for approximately thirty percent of its gross national product, eighty percent of which is with the United States. Consequently, all Canadian governments have shared concerns about their country's dependence on trade with its neighbor and its overall international competitiveness. The issues of trade, Canada's defense relationship with the United States, and acid rain as a threat to a harmonious natural environment continue to dominate the foreign policy agenda.[6] Despite Canada's improved bargaining position vis-à-vis the United States, due to its increased investments in, and exports of important natural resources to the latter, the expansion of free trade between the two countries became a central issue in the 1988 national elections. The emotion generated by free trade demonstrated Canada's deep concern about its sovereignty and independence.

Another fundamental objective of Canada's foreign policy is the maintenance of its national identity in relations with the United States. While Americans generally perceive Canadians essentially as some of them, failure to distinguish residents of the two countries is viewed differently in Canada. For Canadians, concern about the question of a national "self" is a real one, one that the inequality of the relationship makes inevitable.[7] The long border between the two countries does not diminish significant historical and cultural differences between them, and their approaches to international problems generally reflect these divergent values and attitudes. Heirs of failed European revolutions and descendants of those who rejected the American revolution, Canadians are generally predisposed to be law-abiding and to favor peaceful solutions to conflicts. On the Angolan civil war, for example, Canadians believed that American support for Unita (The Union for the Total Independence of Angola) would only prolong and deepen violence in Angola without helping Namibians achieve their independence from South Africa. This position, similar to that held by Scandinavia and by many African countries, reflects political and cultural values which inevitably shape Canada's external relations.

## CULTURAL FACTORS AND FOREIGN POLICY

Political and cultural factors are of critical importance in understanding how and why Canada formulates foreign policies toward South Africa. Extremely close economic, political, cultural, and historical ties between Canada and the United States often obscure their outstanding and fundamental differences. The ethnic separatist tendencies of the French-speaking Canadians, the desire of English-speaking Canadians to maintain their political and economic dominance, the sometimes uneasy coexistence between capitalism and traditions of statism, American domination of much of the economy, and growing multiculturalism are domestic environmental features which greatly affect Canada's international behavior and distinguish it from that of the United States.[8] Even more salient are historical factors which continue to serve as reference points for Canadian policymakers.

If Americans believe that ordinary citizens have a constitutional right to own guns, designed for military combat, in order to protect their liberties against an oppressive government or foreign invasion, Canadians not only reject this approach but also view government in less antagonistic terms. The revolutionary traditions from which contemporary American thinking has emerged are explicitly repudiated by Canadians, whose political origins are grounded in an acceptance of the "peace, order, and good government" offered by British traditions and institutions and are enshrined in the British North America Act. While Americans embrace their own revolutions as a positive experience, Canada represents failed revolutions. Early Canadian settlers were individuals who escaped the American, French, Scottish, and Hungarian revolutions. Both the French and British Canadians are historically connected with Royalist refugees from France and the thirteen American colonies, a fact which profoundly affects Canada's self-perception and its view of its role in world affairs. Although Canada's status as a middle power undoubtedly influences it to partly rely on international institutions and law to achieve its foreign policy goals, its preference for non-violent solutions is reinforced by its historical experiences.

Unlike the United States, Australia, and South Africa, where many settlers became a law unto themselves, during the settlement of Canada's vast territory the instruments of authority—the military governor, the missionary priest, the railway agent, and even the branch bank manager— arrived ahead of most settlers. A few dozen Mounted Police, Canada's national symbol, managed to maintain law and order over half a continent.[9] Furthermore, Canadians succeeded in working out various compromises with the original settlers and avoided the equivalent of the American Indian wars, the Boer conflicts with the Zulus, or the white Australians' destruction of many aboriginal groups. Misunderstandings and differences between the English and French over two hundred years did not erupt into war as was the case in South Africa between Briton and Boer, or the North versus the South in the American Civil War. Akin to Sweden, Switzerland, Australia, and New Zealand, Canada has had no significant conscription for overseas military service since 1918 and no involvement in any serious international conflict since Korea in 1952.[10] Similar to Sweden, Canada developed its own unique brand of exceptionalism, a feeling that expresses itself through volunteerism, peacemaking, and humanitarianism.

Canada's emergence as a liberal democratic state was accompanied by a strong adherence to egalitarianism and collectivism. The sense of community which characterizes Scandinavian societies is also an integral component of Canadian political culture. Canadians and Scandinavians have emphasized cooperation, as opposed to individualism, in order to ensure the survival of the community in extremely harsh physical environments. In Canada's case, the Tory tradition, based on an organic or collectivist relationship of the individual to the state that emanates from European feudalism, augments cooperative instincts and the feeling that the state should be responsible for the welfare of less fortunate members of society.[11] Thus, while many Americans are deeply suspicious of their government's efforts to assist disadvantaged groups, Canadians have an almost missionary zeal, a conviction that they have an obligation to help poor people at home and abroad. These values are embraced by all major political parties to a greater or lesser degree and provide the foundation for both domestic and foreign policies. As the *Economist* put it, a party carrying a right-wing label can usually win power only by adopting foreign and social policies that would be regarded as "bleeding-hearted" at an international gathering of conservatives.[12] Within the American context, Mulroney's South African policies could hardly be considered conservative. In fact, Canada has solid credentials among the vast majority of Third World states as a proponent of measures to dismantle apartheid. International forums such as the Commonwealth, various Francophone Summits, and the United Nations provide Canadians with an opportunity to communicate their country's distinctiveness and independence, and to simultaneously achieve their foreign policy objectives in relation to apartheid.

## THE COMMONWEALTH AND FOREIGN POLICY

Prior to World War II Canada's role in international affairs was to a large extent defined by its relations with Britain, the United States, and what was known as the white Commonwealth. Apart from the decolonization process, induced by the changing realities of the postwar international system, Canada and Australia had to confront the fact that British power and wealth, severely diminished by war, could no longer be relied upon to safeguard their national interests. The emergence of the Third World as a potent force within newly created international institutions, the rise of the United States as an economic as well as a military superpower, the remarkable economic growth of Japan and West Germany, the challenges to Western and Japanese economic dominance by newly industrialized Asian countries, and momentum toward an economically united Europe seriously undermined old assumptions upon which Canadian foreign policy was premised. From Britain's perspective, these new lineaments meant that the Commonwealth could no longer be expected to play a cohesive role.[13] But if Britain was less than enthusiastic about the Commonwealth, for Canada and Australia this international organization, representing the remnants of the British Empire and Britain itself, was viewed as instrumental in the achievement of their overall foreign policy objectives. No longer anchored to Britain, Canada and Australia became more aware of their connections with former British colonies in Asia, Africa, and the Caribbean and were more adroit at utilizing these ties to improve their international status vis-à-vis the great powers in general and the United States in particular. The Commonwealth continued to be important for Canada which, as a middle power with strong ties to the United States and Britain, regarded the transnational multi-racial institution as being able to uniquely bridge wide diversities between governments and peoples, the industrialized North and the developing South, and the rich and poor areas, and as being instrumental in enhancing cooperation in the world community.[14] Ottawa's penchant for compromise is manifested through its mediation efforts between Britain and the Frontline States on the issue of sanctions against South Africa within Commonwealth meetings, a practice which began in 1961. However, its strong opposition to apartheid often has led it to take positions which are in direct conflict with Britain's.

The Canadian debate on South Africa's racial policies began shortly after the Afrikaners assumed power in 1948 and became intertwined with domestic concerns about civil rights in the early 1950s. Both Liberals and Progressive Conservatives agreed that apartheid was a threat to the Commonwealth because it violated that organization's cardinal principle of equality of all races and non-discrimination. Furthermore, apartheid violated the intent of the U.N. Charter so soon after the Holocaust and worldwide devastation initiated by Nazi Germany. For civil rights activists and defenders of the Commonwealth, such as Progressive Conservative Prime Minister John Diefenbaker, South Africa's race laws were inadvertently facilitating the spread of communism and diminishing the Commonwealth's ability to serve as a bulwark against Soviet expansion in Africa.[15] South Africa's reluctance to admit that apartheid was inconsistent with Commonwealth principles and its general lack of enthusiasm for continued membership in that organization forced Canadian policymakers to reassess their policy of attempting to moderate South Africa's apartheid policy through quiet diplomacy and abstaining on U.N. resolutions that were directly critical of it.[16] Despite his deep aversion to racism, Diefenbaker was not anxious to expel South Africa from the Commonwealth in 1961. However, pressure on Ottawa from African and Asian leaders eventually influenced him to join the Afro-Asian bloc within the Commonwealth to oppose Britain's Prime Minister Macmillan's efforts to prevent South Africa's expulsion from the organization. Even though no longer a Commonwealth member, South Africa continued to enjoy trade preferences with both Britain and Canada. However, South Africa's new status prompted Ottawa to abandon some of its earlier hesitation about intervening in the domestic affairs of a fellow Commonwealth member. In light of the growing weight of African and Asian countries in the United Nations, Canada was inclined to view adoption of a more critical stance on South Africa as being consistent with its overall foreign policy objectives.[17]

Canada and Australia have emerged as major proponents of sanctions against Pretoria in alliance with Third World Commonwealth members and the Scandinavian countries. An excellent example of this leadership is the pivotal role played by Clark and Mulroney at the 1985 Commonwealth meeting in Nassau and at subsequent summits. Mulroney advocated "a common program of action to enable Commonwealth countries to signal together without exception that worldwide pressure against South Africa will be sustained until apartheid is ended."[18] But the Commonwealth, so important to Canada, risked being dismantled because of fundamental differences among its members. Britain, for example, was no longer strongly committed to the Commonwealth, partly because its power and interests were altered by postwar realities. Furthermore, of all the Commonwealth states, with the exception of the Frontline countries, Britain had the most to lose by imposing economic sanctions, and the contradictions between the rhetoric of the Frontline States favoring sanctions and the reality of their continued economic relations with Pretoria did not escape Margaret Thatcher's notice. The challenge confronting Canadian policymakers was how to maintain the effectiveness of an institution they valued and simultaneously obtain Britain's cooperation in Ottawa's efforts to remain in the forefront of countries which opposed apartheid.

## THE PRIME MINISTER, PARLIAMENT, AND FOREIGN POLICY

As in the British parliamentary system of government, the Canadian prime minister represents the majority party in Parliament and is principally responsible for the formulation of both domestic and foreign policies. Each prime minister brings his own personal style of governing to the office and may consult most party members infrequently if he believes that his party is disciplined enough to push his various programs through Parliament under the guidance of a select group of parliamentarians who maintain direct contact with him. The cabinet, headed by the prime minister, is the primary policymaking group in parliamentary systems, as we have seen in the cases of Britain, West Germany, and Israel. This small group of decision makers is reinforced by a cadre of key unelected political and public service advisers, known collectively as the mandarin class.[19]

Because these deputy ministers, assistant deputy ministers and high level advisers are effectively the leaders of various government bureaucracies, they exercise tremendous power and may actually frustrate the prime minister's foreign policy endeavors. Linda Freeman, for example, claimed that in late 1987 an internal struggle had developed over Canada's South Africa policy between Mulroney and some senior officials, including Clark, in the Department of External Affairs and that Mulroney had to rely on the strategic support of Ambassadors Stephen Lewis at the United Nations, Roy McMutry in London, and Roger Bull in Harare.[20] Although Mulroney's leadership on apartheid remained undiminished, by 1989 it was clear that a combination of factors, largely beyond Canada's control, had reduced the government's strong support of comprehensive economic sanctions. Perhaps the most obvious cause of Canada's sanctions fatigue was the refusal of South Africa's major trading partners to make apartheid a major foreign policy issue and to impose sanctions that would have a substantial impact on their economic interests.

Given the general domestic consensus on apartheid, the prime minister experienced little opposition to his policies from Parliament. However, even if there were divergent viewpoints on South Africa within Parliament, the nature of that institution's role in the foreign policy process would limit their impact on the prime minister's ability to conduct his country's international affairs. While Parliament has the right to compel debate and force elaboration and clarification by questioning the prime minister and his cabinet on foreign policy matters, as is the case in Britain, the prime minister's authority in external relations is enshrined in tradition and supported by his majority party in Parliament. In fact, the very nature of foreign policymaking in Canada places large constraints on the legislature's participation in the process.[21] Through its representation of and communication with various segments of the voting public and its control over government spending, the legislature exercises limited influence on foreign policy. But since executive and legislative functions are fused within the Cabinet, Parliament plays a relatively unimportant role, especially when compared to its U.S. counterpart. In addition to the prime minister's personal influence on foreign policy, economic factors also have an impact.

## ECONOMIC FACTORS AND FOREIGN POLICY

Exploitation of resources such as forest products, oil and gas, minerals, agriculture, and fisheries is essential to the overall strength of Canada's economy. Dependent on foreign trade for roughly thirty percent of their income, Canadians are very sensitive to problems of oversupply, protectionism, international competition for markets, and the overall performance of other large industrial countries, especially the United States, with which Canada conducts approximately eighty percent of its international trade. Although Canada enjoyed five years of uninterrupted economic growth following the 1981-82 recession—during which the economy expanded at an average annual rate of 4.2 percent, the highest in the Western industrial world and Japan[22]—the relatively strong domestic demand for Canadian products and modest growth in demand abroad for Canadian exports resulted in a significant decline in Canada's trade surplus with the United States and a widening trade deficit with other countries. Canada's surplus in merchandise trade steadily declined from $20.7 billion in 1984 to about $17 billion in 1985.[23] With unemployment at 7.6 percent of the labor force in early 1989 and consumer spending decreasing due to higher interest rates, the Canadian economy was considerably less robust in 1989 than during the previous five years. The economic implications of the free trade agreement with the United States remained uncertain, despite the optimism of many Canadians. As trade became more central to Ottawa's foreign policy, the relationship between business and government received greater scrutiny, especially in light of the practices of countries such as Japan, Britain, Sweden, and West Germany which encourage close cooperation between the public and private sectors.

The conflictual relationship between the Canadian business community and the government and the failure of the former to demonstrate strong support for and to actively participate in broader foreign policy initiatives can be attributed to a wide variety of cultural, political, and economic factors. Clearly, business was not required to play the major role in Canada as it did in Japan, West Germany, and Great Britain, especially during their postwar economic reconstruction. Consequently, the Canadian government's autonomy was essentially unaltered, and federal as well as state bureaucrats were less sympathetic to private enterprise than their Japanese or West German counterparts were.[24] Another reason for this relatively adversarial relationship is the fragmentary structures of governmental authority and the different roles managers on both sides are required to play in the broader societal context. Unlike in Japan where the boundaries between business interests and foreign policy are less clearly defined, policymaking in Canada involves consideration of broader interests and balancing a myriad of viewpoints.[25] Under these circumstances, the impact of business interests on government decision making is severely diluted. Perhaps a more fundamental explanation for this lack of close cooperation and consultation is the deeply rooted populism which characterizes federal-state relations in Canadian politics. Rather than collaborating with government to achieve national objectives, business tends to by suspicious and assumes it is powerless to initiate alternative policies. When the populist element of the business community's relationship with the government is projected onto foreign economic policy, business assumes a recalcitrant and passive posture, relying heavily on Ottawa to carry out responsibilities that advance business interests while reserving the right to denigrate and undermine the state from the sidelines.[26] This situation is exacerbated by interdependence between Canadian and American commercial interests, and the vulnerability of the former to pressure from the latter, both of which combine to diminish the ability or willingness of Canadian business interests to strongly identify with their government's foreign policy objectives.

In order to improve cooperation between the business community and Ottawa in international trade, the government created an international trade advisory structure in 1986—similar to the Advisory Committee on Trade Negotiations in the United States—to facilitate the flow of information between the public and private sectors.[27] Two major components of the advisory structure are the International Trade Advisory Committee (ITAC) and the Sectorial Advisory Groups on International Trade (SAGIT). ITAC, the senior committee and principal source for private sector advice to the federal government, is responsible for broad national issues relating to such aspects of international trade policy as access, marketing, trade agreements, finance, government support, and export programs and policies. It is composed of prominent Canadians who represent large and small companies, consumers, and labor. SAGITs, on the other hand, are responsible for sectorial views on issues emanating from trade negotiations and are made up of representatives from all sectors of the economy.

Both groups report directly to the Minister for International Trade.[28] While these efforts may eventually result in closer collaboration between government and private enterprise, their influence on Canada's South Africa policy is unlikely to be significant due to similarities between the two countries' economies.

Compared with Britain, Japan, and West Germany which depend on raw materials from South Africa or have large investments there, Canada actually competes with South Africa for markets as well as investment capital, a factor which, however tangentially, influences its foreign policy. Canada has been actively encouraging foreign investments, partly to offset the substantial flow of funds from that country to the United States, and to compensate areas, such as venture capital directed at small and medium enterprises, where the Canadian financial industry was weak.[29] Under these circumstances, it is not advantageous for Ottawa to promote investments in South Africa. In fact, one could argue that divestments from South Africa could create economic opportunities for Canada. Similarly, sanctions against South Africa's raw materials may also help to reduce Canada's stockpiles of minerals by opening up new export markets or by helping to expand shares in existing markets. For example, as various countries banned imports of South African coal, production and exports of Canadian coal increased sharply in 1988. Output reached about seventy million tons, forty-five percent of which was exported. Exports actually increased by 19.5 percent over the previous year.[30] Apart from economic benefits to Canada which inadvertently accrue as a result of comprehensive sanctions against Pretoria, the government's South Africa policy is strongly supported by Canadian public opinion.

## PUBLIC OPINION AND FOREIGN POLICY

The foreign policymaking process in parliamentary systems of government, with power concentrated in the Cabinet and the bureaucracy, determines to a large extent the ability of public opinion to influence decisions. More specifically, the leadership style, knowledge, and personality of the Prime Minister can facilitate or frustrate attempts by relevant publics to shape particular foreign policies. The Prime Minister may enter office with extensive knowledge of foreign policy and a predisposition to support policies favored by the general public. His beliefs and perceptions of political circumstances may lead to either an open or closed style of government, with more or less attention given to public opinion.[31] But where an issue is extremely important to a large segment of the population, including relevant elites, and if there are no major strategic or economic national interests at stake, few Prime Ministers would deliberately ignore public opinion. The very nature of the democratic process makes foreign policy responsive over time to changes in public mood or climates of opinion.[32] Furthermore, the emotive nature of apartheid reduces the likelihood that a Prime Minister would gain politically by disregarding public opinion.

Canada's foreign policy establishment has long been aware of the fact that most Canadians regard apartheid as contrary to their basic values and a violation of democratic principles. Perhaps no other foreign policy issue, with the possible exception of free trade with the United States, has generated more debate within the ranks of successive Canadian administrations and among the general public than apartheid. All major political parties favor strong measures against South Africa. Not surprisingly, the influence of ordinary citizens on Canada's South Africa policy has been effective and evident. In fact, according to Douglas Anglin, "never before has a Canadian government revealed such a preoccupation with the nuances of public opinion."[33] Since many Canadian leaders come from church backgrounds and from families in which their fathers were often involved in missionary work, churches in Canada, which play a highly visible role in all aspects of policy, have been able to effectively argue the immorality of apartheid and to persuade the government to take their concerns into consideration, especially in the absence of serious opposition from the business community.

Church groups representing the major denominations have involved themselves in efforts to convince Ottawa to elevate human rights to a central foreign policy concern. By combining their resources and through inter-church coalitions represented by the Taskforce on the Churches and Corporate Responsibility, the Anglican Church of Canada, the United Church, and other denominations have had a tremendous impact on Canada's South African policies. In many cases, the Taskforce on the Churches and Corporate Responsibility has initiated policies which are later endorsed by the government.[34] Churches have also been primarily responsible for keeping the general public informed on apartheid through various publications and by cultivating strong ties with the media. Other anti-apartheid organizations include labor groups, the Toronto Committee for the Liberation of Southern Africa, and student groups at major Canadian universities. The Canadian Labor Congress advocated the withdrawal of any government support for trade with Pretoria, and students at McGill University were in the forefront of the divestment campaign.[35] While Canadian public opinion undoubtedly influences foreign policy, ethnic groups have not yet demonstrated that they are capable of having a similar impact. Nevertheless, ethnicity does play a part in the overall formulation of Canada's South Africa policy.

## ETHNICITY AND FOREIGN POLICY

The growing ethnic diversity of Canadian society and that country's desire to promote a non-racial image of itself internationally, and within the

Commonwealth especially, have fostered increased domestic opposition to racism in South Africa. Although ethnic groups do not exercise as much influence on Canadian foreign policy as do blacks and Jews in the United States do on American policy, the fact that racial discrimination is an emotional issue affecting many Canadians diminishes the need for specific ethnic groups to advocate on their own for radical changes in their country's South Africa policy. Furthermore, Canadians are seriously grappling with racial injustices and the question of aboriginal rights and view apartheid within the context of their own experiences. Canadian Jews in particular tend to perceive apartheid primarily in terms of Kristall-nacht and the Holocaust, often recalling how most of the world ignored the suffering and extermination of six million people. The feelings of many Canadian Jews were articulated by Sheila Finestone, member of Parliament, who argued that lessons from the Holocaust have implications that should be taken into consideration by foreign policymakers. Finestone stated that, "we must stand tall and firm as Canadians in active remembrance, with fidelity to memory and fidelity to truth. The Holocaust must stand for more. It must be a lesson for all mankind. If ever there was a lesson to be learned, it is that one. When racism rears its ugly head, it is time to stand up and be counted."[36] Increasing immigration from Asia, the Caribbean, and other areas outside Western Europe reinforces Canadian efforts to resolve racial conflicts at home and abroad. As Britain dismantled its colonial empire after World War II, Canada began to assume a greater role within the Commonwealth. As part of its strategy to consolidate Canadian power and influence within the Commonwealth and to merge rhetoric and practice, Ottawa made agreements in the late 1950s with India, Pakistan and Ceylon that provided for the admission into Canada each year of at least one hundred and fifty Indians, one hundred Pakistanis, and fifty citizens from Ceylon for permanent residence.[37] Despite this development, immigration policies encouraged Northern and Western Europeans to settle in Canada while, at the same time, systematically excluding blacks on the grounds thay they were "unassimilable and unsuitable for reasons of climate."[38] However, by 1974 immigration from Western Europe was sharply reduced as economic conditions in the various countries improved, and the number of Asians and blacks admitted as permanent residents steadily grew. But unlike in Britain, where immigrants from various Commonwealth countries have been targets of racial discrimination, overt discrimination in Canada is relatively rare, partly because of cultural factors and the selectiveness of Canadian immigration policy.

Canadian society, characterized by binationalism and ethnic pluralism prior to the influx of non-European residents, was socially and culturally equipped to absorb small numbers of well-educated and skilled professionals from Asia and the Caribbean. Teachers, doctors, nurses, and various technicians from these areas generally obtain appropriate employment upon arrival and are integrated into the mainstream of Canadian life. In Britain, on the other hand, many immigrants were unskilled laborers who were needed to help rebuild a devastated country that had lost a large proportion of its labor force during World War II. Furthermore, as large numbers of relatively uneducated West Indians and Asians settled in segregated areas in major industrial cities such as Birmingham and Manchester, white workers felt threatened by the growing competition for available employment opportunities. As Jeffrey Reitz observed, racial conflict in Britain was aggravated by institutionally-derived negative perceptions of immigrants as a potential burden, whereas in Canada the more positive institutionally-sanctioned perceptions of immigrants as an economic asset helped to dilute racial conflict.[39] In addition, Canada's experience with the aboriginal peoples and its commitment to redress past wrongs and entrench native rights in the Constitution, as well as its proximity to the United States where civil rights issues dominate domestic politics, contributed to rendering racial discrimination a more sensitive issue in both domestic and foreign policy. By taking a strong stance against apartheid, Canada strengthens its credibility among Commonwealth members and the Third World while demonstrating its commitment to racial equality to domestic constitutents. Having few investments, insignificant cultural links, and no major strategic and security interests in South Africa, Canada is relatively unencumbered, especially when compared to Britain, in adopting an unambiguous anti-apartheid foreign policy.

## CANADA'S RELATIONS WITH SOUTH AFRICA

Canadian missionaries, physicians, teachers, and explorers established contacts with Africa during the nineteenth and early twentieth centuries, but direct Canadian offical contacts with South Africa were virtually nonexistent until after the Boer War of 1899. As a member of the British Empire, Canada was expected to share some of the responsibilities of empire. Yet Canadians were not enthusiastic about fighting in distant wars in order to protect British interests, especially if their participation in such conflicts would exacerbate problems between French Quebec and the English-speaking provinces. This was precisely the dilemma confronting Canada in 1899 when British imperialist interests and the historical antagonism between the British and the Boers culminated in war in the Transvaal. Although nationalistic instincts and sympathy among French Canadians for the Boers' aspiration to maintain their independence in their own Republics exerted considerable pressure on the Canadian government to avoid being drawn into the war, there was sufficient support for Britain among English-speaking Canadians and opposition political parties to influence the government to send approximately seven thousand troops to the Transvaal.[40] However, when compared to Australia, which had a much smaller population but sent more than twice as many men, Canada's efforts were minimal. Moreover, many Canadian recruits were newly-arrived British immigrants, having come during the 1890s, and thus more likely to share British opinions on the treatment of the *Uitlanders* (foreigners) in the Transvaal, the issue that precipitated the war.[41] Since the conflict was principally a British problem, Canadians paid relatively little attention to South Africa until 1946. The radical transformation of the international political and economic system in the aftermath of World War II profoundly affected Canada's relations with South Africa, and the racial problem which was previously perceived in terms of Anglo-Boer rivalry emerged as the pivotal issue around which Canadian policy evolved. While South Africa showed little concern for the Commonwealth or the United Nations, Canada not only held both institutions in high esteem but also regarded them as vital to the politics of a middle power. However, until South Africa's departure from the Commonwealth in 1961, Canadian policymakers struggled with the dilemma of reconciling their country's interests in maintaining economic and diplomatic relations with Pretoria on the one hand and its aversion to racism, its support for the United Nations and a multiracial Commonwealth, and its desire to contain the spread of communism throughout Africa and Asia on the other.[42] While Canada's remoteness from South Africa, its political culture, its growing reputation among Third World countries and in the Commonwealth as an honest peace broker, and the collapse of Portugal's empire and increased violence in South Africa influenced its policy toward Pretoria, Canada's negligible economic, military, and cultural ties with South Africa also played a role.

## CANADA'S ECONOMIC TIES WITH SOUTH AFRICA

Structural similarities between the Canadian and South African economies militated against the development of extensive trade and investment links between the two countries. Unlike Britain, West Germany, and Japan which are highly dependent on South Africa's raw materials and markets, Canada's abundant resources, its relatively weak manufacturing sector, and economic interdependence with the United States greatly reduced the necessity of economic interaction with South Africa. Indeed, the fact that Canada and South Africa both exploited natural and agricultural resources for export created a certain degree of competition between them for increasingly tight international markets. Consequently, the volume of their trade with each other remained small, though not unimportant.

Shortly after the Boer War Canada attempted to promote exports of mainly manufactured products to British South Africa through the extension of the British Preferential Tariff in 1907 and the establishment of trade offices in Cape Town and Durban in 1907 and 1911, respectively. Although the Durban office was closed in 1913, due partly to its limited utility, trade ties were formalized with the newly independent South Africa in the Canada-South Africa Trade Agreements of 1932 and 1935. In 1935 a trade office was opened in Johannesburg to facilitate expanding economic relations emanating from these trade agreements.[43] Further Canadian efforts to increase trade occurred through the Promotional Projects Program (PPP), the Program for Export Market Development (PEMD), and the Export Development Corporation (EDC). Canadian trade visits, missions, and fairs have been encouraged under PPP since 1947, and beginning in 1968 the private sector, through PEMD, financed several projects designed to stimulate exports to South Africa. The EDC, a government organization, provided insurance and financing for export purposes, especially for high-risk commercial ventures.[44] But given the nature of business-government relations in Canada, the degree of cooperation between them remained inconsequential, particularly when compared to similar efforts by the British, West German, and Japanese governments.

Canada's trade with South Africa, miniscule even before that country imposed wide-ranging economic sanctions against Pretoria in 1985, represented approximately one percent of total exports and imports respectively between 1978 and 1985. Major imports included fresh and tinned fruit, sugar, wines, chromium, uranium, manganese, iron and steel alloys, scrap metal, sheets, plate, and manufactured goods. Many of these products were excluded after 1985 due to Canadian sanctions. Major exports included sulphur, wheat, wood pulp, motor vehicle parts, office machines and equipment, and paper. Prior to 1985 the Canadian government, consistent with its view that free trade with all countries would eventually contribute to political liberalization, refused to impose meaningful economic sanctions against Pretoria and did not discourage Canadians from expanding trade. Despite controversy within the government about the efficacy of sanctions in inducing political change, Mulroney, Clark, and Stephens vigorously supported sanctions in 1985. However, from 1985 to 1986 Canada's trade with South Africa increased as Canadian companies, remaining undeterred by the government's unilateral decision to terminate its loan program and insurance for business deals with South Africa and to impose an embargo on air transport cargo, stockpiled wine, chrome, and manganese in anticipation of further trade restrictions. Far more difficult to explain was the government's wheat marketing board's decision to increase the sale of Canadian red spring wheat to South Africa from one ton in all of 1985 to sixty thousand tons in the first six months of 1986, at the same time that Mulroney called for tough sanctions.[45] Although this descrepancy between declaratory and actual policy may be attributed to Canada's heavy dependence on trade, it is also likely that the government's enthusiasm for coercive economic measures was not fully shared by members of the Canadian bureaucracy and the Depart-

ment of External Affairs. Nevertheless, Canadian imports from South
Africa declined dramatically from $256 million in 1986 to $106 million
in 1987, or by fifty-nine percent. Similarly, the total value of exports
dropped from $137 million in 1986 to $88 million in 1987, or by thirty-five
percent.[46] While reduced sales of wheat and sulphur, two commodities
not covered by sanctions, accounted for most of the export reduction,
economic restrictions also contributed to the sharp decline in Canada's
trade with South Africa, a decrease surpassed only by the Scandinavian
countries. Prior to the ban on imports of uranium from Namibia's Rossing
mine, that aspect of Canadian trade with South Africa was very controversial and of great concern to anti-apartheid groups.

In April 1972, Canada, France, South Africa, Australia, Britain, and
various company representatives formed the Uranium Market Research
Organization, an international uranium cartel, to control the world price
and supply of uranium through a complex scheme of price-fixing, bid-
rigging, and the allocation of markets following the U.S. government's
decision to prevent imports of uranium from foreign countries.[47] Major
objectives of the cartel, a precursor of OPEC, were to ensure a satisfactory
price for uranium, to stabilize prices, and to eliminate undesirable competitive practices—which resulted in extremely depressed uranium prices—by
the Nuclear Fuels Corporation of South Africa. Although details of the
bargaining process among cartel members remain elusive, it is assumed
that Canada "must have made some political concession to South Africa
in order to acquire its support, for uranium mining in South Africa was
never as seriously threatened by American protectionist policies as it
was in Canada."[48] Despite Ottawa's support for an independent Namibia,
both in the United Nations and in the Western Contact Group, the government permitted the import, processing, and re-export of uranium from
Rossing until 1985. Mined by Rio Algom, a subsidiary of the British company Rio Tinto Zinc, the uranium was processed by Eldorado Nuclear
Ltd., a Canadian government corporation, and mixed with other ores
before being re-exported as uranium hexafluoride.[49] In addition to trade,
there was also a relatively insignificant amount of Canadian investments
in South Africa, representing less than one percent of total direct foreign
investments in that country prior to Ottawa's ban on new investments
and divestment by companies already there between 1985 and 1987. By
early 1988 half of the twenty-four Canadian companies abandoned all
commercial ties with South Africa, five of the remaining firms were considering disinvestment, and total Canadian investment was roughly $100
million.[50]

In light of Canada's need for investment capital, the government has
been far more interested in attracting foreign investment to the country
than in encouraging Canadian firms to export capital to South Africa.
Nevertheless, several Canadian corporations and their subsidiaries invested in a number of major industrial fields, including: mining, explora-

tion, and the supply of mining equipment; agricultural machinery; heavy road machinery and construction equipment; textiles, leather goods, and business forms; and automobile manufacturing and consulting engineering services. Many of these companies, which have strong connections with other multinational corporations, have reputations in Canada and elsewhere for their efficient organization, advanced technology, effective business techniques, and competent administration in the various industrial sectors in which they operate.[51] Despite the relatively low level of investment, many Canadian anti-apartheid groups have been concerned about the dual use of mining and other types of equipment for both civilian and military purposes, as well as about possible cooperation between Canadian companies and the South African government. The Taskforce on the Churches and Corporate Responsibility and the International Defence and Aid Fund for Southern Africa, for example, were concerned about corporations such as Rio Algom, Alcan, Falconbridge, and Texasgulf that were directly or indirectly linked to various activities in which the South African government was involved or benefited from. Canada's refusal to cancel foreign tax credits available to these corporations, which were operating in Namibia even after the International Court of Justice declared South Africa's control over Namibia to be illegal, was viewed as implied official Canadian recognition of South Africa's claim to have legal jurisdiction over Namibia.[52] Similarly, the Taskforce on the Churches and Corporate Responsibility regarded Alcan's twenty-four percent investment share of Hulett Aluminum fabricating company, part of a group controlled by the Anglo-American Corporation, as directly undergirding the structures of apartheid because Hulett, as the leading South African aluminum fabricator, was involved in supplying of products for military purposes.[53] Rio Algom's participation in uranium mining at Rossing, the development of which was partly financed by the South African government's Industrial Development Corporation, Bata Shoe Company operation in the homeland of Kwa-Zulu, and Massey-Ferguson's association with Perkins, a British subsidiary, were viewed as additional examples of cooperation between Canadian firms and Pretoria. Perkins was directly linked to the South African government because of its fifteen-year contract, negotiated in 1979, in partnership with Daimler-Benz of West Germany, to transfer diesel engine technology to the Atlantis Diesel Engine Company, owned by the South African government and responsible for ensuring Pretoria's self-sufficiency in diesel engines.[54] While the complex operations of multinational corporations and secrecy in South Africa make it extremely difficult to accurately assess the degree of collaboration between foreign firms and Pretoria, available evidence does not indicate significant involvement by Canadian companies in South African politics. Like their Scandinavian counterparts, Canadian firms largely support their government's position on apartheid, at least to the extent of not being actively opposed to it.

Most companies comply with the voluntary Code of Conduct recommended by Ottawa to ensure fair and equal treatment in the workplace for all employees. However, in light of their limited investments in South Africa, they are unlikely to have a major impact on labor-management relations or equal employment opportunities in South Africa. In 1988 the nine Canadian companies which issued reports to John Small, the Code's administrator, and the Canadian Embassy employed a total of 3,084 blacks, or one-twentieth of one percent of the labor force.[55] In 1985 approximately twenty thousand blacks worked for Canadian businesses. The sharp decrease from 1985 to 1988 indicates significant divestments by Canadians. While operating in South Africa many firms negotiated with trade union representatives, although the small size of these enterprises encouraged informal and direct personal contacts between management and labor. Several companies provided medical insurance plans which allowed their employees flexibility in obtaining better medical services and, in some cases, medical health clinics were established at the workplace to provide additional care for employees. Companies also rented houses to employees, with the option to buy, and offered loans for houses, durable goods, and automobiles.[56] Overall, Canadian firms adhered to the basic principles of the voluntary code. Likewise, the Canadian government has complied with the U.N. arms embargo against Pretoria, with a few notable exceptions.

## MILITARY TIES

As a middle power that emphasizes non-violent resolution of conflicts and values the United Nations and the Commonwealth as international forums through which it can achieve its broader foreign policy objectives, Canada, like Scandinavia, supported early the U.N. arms embargo against South Africa. Canadian policy against military sales to Pretoria was implemented in August 1963, although exceptions were made for the sale of spare parts for equipment supplied to South Africa before that date. In 1964 the Canadian government embargoed the sale of ten thousand four-wheel trucks by Ford of Canada to South Africa on the grounds that they might be used by the military. However, when Britain decided to sell the trucks to South Africa, Ottawa revised its policy. Instead of focusing on the equipment's capabilities, emphasis was now on intended use.[57]

Britain's Conservative Party, led by Harold Macmillan, had refused to implement the arms embargo, partly because of substantial support within the Cabinet and in Britain in general for South Africa. Although the new Labour government under Harold Wilson agreed to observe the boycott when it came to power in 1964, by 1970 the Conservatives resumed political control and reversed Labour's policy. Britain's resumption of arms sales in early 1970, for a number of reasons discussed in chapter two, created serious strains within the Commonwealth and influenced Canada, in an effort to prevent the Commonwealth's disintegration, to seek a compromise between Tanzania's Julius Nyerere and Zambia's Kenneth Kaunda, who strongly opposed the decision, and Britain. But Canada's economic interests, however minuscule, complicated its role as a peace broker and may have contributed to its abstention on the General Assembly resolution calling for the arms embargo to include provision of parts, military investments, and training of military personnel, among other things.[58] However, Canada's image and interests in the Commonwealth seemed to be decisive factors in its decision to extend the embargo to spare parts in November 1970. Canada itself had been criticized by African leaders for selling spare parts. Canada's Prime Minister Pierre Trudeau dispatched Ivan Head, his special foreign policy adviser, to Zambia and Tanzania, and Mitchell Sharp, Minister of External Affairs, met with Sir Colin Crowe, Britain's High Commissioner to Canada, to express Canada's opposition to arms sales to South Africa. Consensus among the Liberals, Progressive Conservatives, and the New Democratic Party substantially strengthened Trudeau's negotiating position within the Commonwealth. Instead of stating the problem in terms of preventing British arms sales, the Canadians presented it as an effort to preserve the Commonwealth as a viable organization, thus avoiding direct confrontation with Britain's conservative government.[59] Despite Canada's strong adherence to the arms embargo, especially when compared to Israel, Britain, and West Germany, significant loopholes remained in its policy.

Ottawa's decision not to ban exports of dual-purpose equipment on the basis of performance characteristics has been criticized by anti-apartheid groups in general and the Taskforce on the Churches and Corporate Responsibility in particular. Under the end-users policy Canada permitted Control Data of Canada to sell several computer systems to South Africa's state-owned steel industry, a major supplier for the armaments industry.[60] However, in a notice to exporters in February 1986, the government indicated that it would restrict exports of sensitive equipment, such as computers, to various South African agencies directly involved in maintaining apartheid in order to comply to the fullest extent possible with the U.N. arms embargo. For exports of sensitive equipment to non-government customers, Canada requires a statement from the end-user that the equipment is solely for civilian purposes.[61] Difficulties involved in ensuring compliance with this policy in South Africa are obvious. The most serious violation of the embargo occurred between 1976 and 1978 when Space Research Corporation, a company literally straddling the Quebec-Vermont border and owned partly by the South African parastatal arms corporation, exported from Canada to South Africa a radar tracking system, fifty thousand long-range artillery shells, and two 155mm cannons through third countries.[62] Senior officials of the company were tried, convicted, and fined by Canada and the United States. Ottawa's anti-apartheid strategies are similar to those adopted by Scandinavia, but with greater emphasis on communication with South Africa.

## STRATEGIES

Unlike Britain, which has consistently opposed economic sanctions as an appropriate foreign policy instrument vis-à-vis Pretoria, Canada's position has evolved from strong advocacy of free trade with all governments to ardent support for comprehensive economic measures against South Africa. Furthermore, compared to Britain where there are serious divisions within Parliament on questions of strategy against apartheid, major political parties in Canada differ only on the extent and timing of sanctions, and on the issue of the ANC's recourse to armed resistance. Liberal Party leader John Turner called for full economic sanctions, and Gerald Caplan, former Federal Secretary of the New Democractic Party, urged the adoption of an all-party consensus on South Africa. Mulroney, Turner, and Caplan agreed on Canada's strategy of imposing economic sanctions against Pretoria and aiding the Frontline States.[63]

The underlying assumption of Canada's policy is that South Africa can be influenced to abolish apartheid peacefully if governments apply sufficient economic pressure. But Canada's relatively small stakes in South Africa have diminished its ability to present Pretoria with a credible threat when acting alone. Consequently, Mulroney has attempted to enlist Britain's support within the context of the Commonwealth and that of the United States, France, West Germany, Japan, and Britain within the context of the Economic Summit of major Western industrial countries, albeit without much success. Countries with substantial economic interests in South Africa perceive the moral issues of apartheid as secondary to their major national interests, which are closely connected with the principle of free trade. Although Canada's strategy of strongly supporting sanctions is effective in terms of its interests in the Commonwealth, Mulroney is constrained by economic realities within the Economic Summit. As Kim Nossal observed, Canadian activism on the South African issue at these meetings jeopardizes the maintenance of Mulroney's influence in summit circles.[64] By 1988 it was clear that, despite Canada's position on sanctions, there were definite indications of "sanctions fatigue."

## SANCTIONS

Prior to 1985 the Canadian government's main argument against comprehensive sanctions was that, due to the size of the South African economy, they would be largely ineffective and would hasten rather than avert racial conflict. However, limited measures such as a voluntary embargo on the sale of military equipment (1963) and the sale of spare parts (1970) were imposed, and in 1977 Canada voted for a mandatory arms embargo against Pretoria and ended its active promotion of trade with the minority regime. Trade Commissioners were withdrawn, the Consulate General in Johannesburg and the Consulate in Cape Town were closed, the use of the Export Development Corporation's Government account for financing and insuring trade with South Africa was suspended, and the facilities for insuring Canadian investments in South Africa were also withdrawn. By 1970 Canada had terminated the preferential tariff treatment accorded to South Africa under the Canada/South Africa Trade Agreement of 1932.[65] The election of Mulroney as Prime Minister in 1984, escalating violence, and government brutality in South Africa prior to the imposition of the July 1985 State of Emergency combined to influence a major change in Canada's position on sanctions. Secretary of State Joe Clark announced that "it is part of our duty to make clear to South Africa that Canada is prepared to invoke total sanctions if there is no change."[66] Although Canada refrained from imposing total sanctions, despite support from anti-apartheid groups and both opposition parties for severing diplomatic ties and placing a total ban on everything, it adopted several measures that strengthened its opposition to apartheid.

In July 1985 Ottawa imposed an embargo on the sale of computers to South Africa, abrogated double taxation agreements, prohibited the sale of Krugerrands, banned loans to the South African government, outlawed the sale of crude oil and refined petroleum products to Pretoria, terminated air transportation between the two countries, and assigned an officer charged with responsibility for labor affairs at Canada's embassy in South Africa to maintain direct contact with "authentic opposition African leaders who are agents of reform."[67] On June 12, 1986, when the South African State of Emergency was extended and new draconian measures introduced, Joe Clark announced a ban on the promotion of tourism between Canada and South Africa and contacted tourism operators and media representatives in an effort to obtain their compliance. In early November 1986 the Toronto office of the South African Tourism Board closed at Clark's request. Following the meeting of Commonwealth leaders in London in August 1986, Canada decided to fulfill its promise to get tougher with Pretoria by banning imports of agricultural products, uranium, coal, iron, and steel from South Africa. Although the Canadian government continued to urge firms remaining in South Africa to comply with the voluntary Code of Conduct and did not encourage divestment, when Falconbridge increased its holdings in Western Platinum of South Africa, Clark communicated his disapproval to William James, the company's chairman. This action, combined with political pressure from anti-apartheid groups, influenced Falconbridge to divest its holdings in early February 1987.[68] But Canada's inability to convince Britain to change its position on sanctions significantly diminished the effectiveness of its own economic measures against Pretoria and discouraged officials in the External Affairs Department from advocating additional sanctions. While Canada's strong position against apartheid is obvious, it is also clear that Canadian policymakers are not oblivious to their country's national interests and have carefully balanced their interest in the Commonwealth with their concern about economic growth at home. One view is that Canada used sanctions as convenient tariff measures and as low-cost techniques for showing friendship toward the Third World and the Commonwealth.[69] The basis of this argument is that banned South African products such as fresh fruit, wine and liquor, sugar, and other agricultural products can be easily obtained elsewhere. Apples and raisins are purchased from Canadian, American, and Australian growers, and sugar is imported from Cuba, Australia, and Swaziland. Furthermore, sanctions against Pretoria may directly benefit Canadian industry by eliminating competition from South African companies that produce uranium, coal, iron, steel, and gold coins. For example, Canada, the third largest producer of gold, promotes its own gold coin, the Maple Leaf. Maple Leaf sales, which reached 1 million ounces in 1983, climbed to 1.9 million ounces in 1985 after Canada banned the sale of Kruggerands and other countries took similar actions.[70] However, chromium, manganese, and various platinum group metals continued to be imported in 1989, partly because Canada "did not have other convenient suppliers for these raw materials."[71] Similarly, Canada continued sulphur exports to South Africa for use in that country's fertilizer industry. A proposal from the Committee Against Racism to terminate these exports and to assist the Frontline States to reduce their dependence on Pretoria by helping them to produce their own fertilizer was rejected by External Affairs officials on the grounds that a surplus of sulphur on the world market made it relatively easy for South Africa to diversify its sources. Moreover, the Frontline States had not requested assistance to decrease their dependence on South African fertilizer.[72] Canada's credibility on this issue is strengthened by its substantial support for and involvement in the Frontline States and these countries' historical interdependence with South Africa.

Despite Canada's leadership on the sanctions issue, two developments in 1988 and 1989 indicated not only sanctions fatigue among Canadians but also serious rifts within the Department of External Affairs on enforcing measures strongly supported by the Prime Minister. In 1988 federal grants totaling $7,204 were given to Boart Canada Inc., of Mississauga and Longyear Canada of North Bay, two South African-controlled companies, for export promotion.[73] The second case was far more embarrassing for Canada and its External Affairs Minister. In early February 1989 it was disclosed at a Commonwealth meeting in Harare that the Bank of Nova Scotia had extended a $600 million loan to Minorco, a South African company based in Luxembourg and largely controlled by the Oppenheimer family of South Africa, in its bid to acquire the British mining company Consolidated Gold Fields, which has significant operations in South Africa. The loan was approved by the Canadian government, even though Ottawa strongly advocated banning loans to either the public or private sector in South Africa. Clearly embarrassed by the disclosure and its timing, Clark defended the loan on the grounds that it did not violate Commonwealth law or Canadian law. "This is a South African-controlled company that is not in South Africa. It is in Luxembourg."[74] Although international banking and the operations of multinational corporations are complex, it is unlikely that the Canadian government was unaware of Minorco's connections and the political implications of approving the loan. These developments focused attention away from broader Canadian efforts aimed at black empowerment and at reducing the Frontline States' vulnerability vis-à-vis South Africa.

## BLACK EMPOWERMENT

Until 1984 Canadian foreign policymakers subscribed to the view that economic growth in South Africa was not only beneficial to foreign investors but would also contribute to undermining apartheid's structures because, from their perspective, industrialization was incompatible with white minority rule. However, increasing oppression during periods of rapid economic growth in South Africa engendered skepticism among some Canadians about the correlation between industrialization and respect for human rights.[75] Yet adoption of the opposite assumption, that economic hardship would force Pretoria to abandon apartheid, appears to be equally spurious. Nevertheless, as political pressures obscured more complex aspects of apartheid, Canada shifted its position from being an advocate of black empowerment through economic improvements for all South Africans to being an ardent supporter of economic coercion against the white minority regime. Current empowerment efforts involve educational assistance, funds for community projects, contacts with black leaders, and developing ways to counteract South Africa's disinformation campaign.

In 1983 Canada established a scholarship program for black South Africans with the objective of contributing to the building of black social, economic, and political institutions and preparing blacks to exercise their full rights as citizens in a non-racial South Africa.[76] By 1987 the program, for which Canada allocated $7 million, consisted of four components: (1) scholarships in South Africa administered through the Educational Opportunities Council; (2) scholarships for blacks to study in Canada; (3) a Canadian Education Fund to support local educational initiatives of nongovernmental organizations within South Africa; and (4) labor training and education. In addition, the Canadian Embassy in South Africa was responsible for managing the disbursement of $350,000 in Mission Administered Funds to self-help projects in the black community that are primarily concerned with assisting women.[77] Although an important aspect of Canada's apprach to black empowerment included contacts with black leaders, unlike the Scandinavian countries which provide large amounts of humanitarian aid to the ANC, Ottawa was reluctant to go beyond raising the level and frequency of its contacts with exile opposition groups, partly because Canadians rejected the ANC's strategy of armed struggle as an instrument of change. Nevertheless, Canada indicated that it understood the feelings of the victims of apartheid, held apartheid responsible for causing violence in South Africa, and expressed its opposition to violence on all sides.[78] It also favored maintaining communication with Pretoria and attempted to increase the amount and flow of information to South Africa.

Although Canada has always condemned apartheid, it believed that total isolation of South Africa, instead of encouraging change, would breed defiance and increase racial hatred and oppression. Furthermore, through diplomatic relations with Pretoria, Canadian Embassy personnel could not only monitor developments and communicate their country's support for social and economic change but also identify, supervise, and monitor projects designed to empower blacks. Moreover, the frequent imposition of travel restrictions on South Africans who oppose apartheid meant that Ottawa could maintain contacts with opposition leaders primarily through its Embassy.[79] But Canadian policymakers also contended that more communication, not less, with all South Africans would frustrate Pretoria's deliberate strategy of perpetuating fear and hatred through censorship within South Africa and propaganda at home and abroad. As Clark put it, "among some within South Africa, the resistance to change is intensified by fear, including the fear that they will be torn up from their roots, and that the strong economy they have created will be destroyed. That combination of power and fear is formidable, both in itself, and in the reaction it inspires."[80] Apart from Clark's implied reservations about coercive sanctions that would destroy South Africa's economy, this statement underlines Canada's counter-strategy of decreasing the effectiveness of Pretoria's censorship.

The basic objectives of Ottawa's program to counteract South Africa's disinformation campaigns are to: (1) circumvent the barriers to accurate news reporting from South Africa; (2) penetrate the South African press censorship maze and government news monopoly to correct distorted perceptions of reality within South Africa; and (3) discredit Pretoria's propaganda and "sensitize the international public to its insidious nature."[81] Yet Canada's strategy, which was endorsed by the Commonwealth Committee of Foreign Ministers on Southern Africa, is in direct conflict with the general goal of anti-apartheid groups to isolate South Africa (see Table 9). Canada's pragmatic approach is unlikely to be easily reconciled with the views of more ideological anti-apartheid activists. Nevertheless, its relationship with the Frontline States has buttressed its credibility among Commonwealth members and anti-apartheid groups.

## CANADA AND THE FRONTLINE STATES

The Commonwealth's importance to Canadian policymakers influences them to adopt a strong position against Pretoria's efforts to destabilize neighboring states, the majority of which are Commonwealth members and major recipients of Ottawa's bilateral aid disbursements. Although the Canadian government did not establish direct relations with the various countries until after their independence in the early 1960s, Canadian teachers, missionaries, physicians, and nurses were involved in the region beginning in the late nineteenth century, thereby laying the foundation for contemporary Canadian ties to the Frontline States. Like Scandinavia, Britain, and West Germany, Canada emphasizes (1) rehabilitation of regional railroads to lessen the Frontline States' vulnerability to South Africa's sanctions; (2) agricultural and rural development; and (3) increasing its level of trade with the region. This approach not only demonstrates Canada's opposition to apartheid but also allows it to effectively compete with South Africa for markets in southern Africa, thereby strengthening its manufacturing base.

Approximately seventy percent of Canada's $40 million aid program in 1988 to the Southern African Development Coordination Conference (SADCC)—to which Botswana, Zimbabwe, Zambia, Swaziland, Lesotho, Mozambique, and Malawi belong—was allocated for infrastructural projects, the generation and transmission of power, agriculture, and the development of telecommunications. Projects funded by Canada included the building of the National Resource College in Malawi and the training of several staff members; provision of steel rail and associated materials and equipment to rehabilitate the Nacala Railway in Mozambique; the establishment of a regional Food Industry Advisory Unit within Zimbabwe's Ministry of Agriculture to increase food through installation of more efficient collection, storage, marketing, and processing systems; and the development of energy interconnectors in the SADCC region. Canada also provides individual countries with significant amounts of bilateral assistance. For example, Zambia, with one of the most precarious economies in the area, has received about $15 million annually, beginning in 1985.[82]

But unlike Britain, which provides limited military assistance and training for soldiers from Zimbabwe and Mozambique, Canada has remained opposed to any military presence in the region, although there is confusion about its actual policy. In late 1988 following a meeting with Mulroney in New York, Zimbabwe's President Robert Mugabe announced that Can-

TABLE 9
**Strategic Programs and Activities**


I. GENERAL PUBLIC

A. *Inside South Africa*
  1. Direct Mail Programs

     a) Dissemination of Western
        newspapers into South Africa
     b) Targetted mailings of
        publications into South Africa
     c) Assistance to NGOs
        (Non-governmental
        organization) to use direct
        mail

  2. Shortwave Radio

     a) National shortwave
        programming
     b) Commonwealth shortwave
        programming

  3. Public Affairs Program
     a) Embassy public affairs
        program
     b) Assistance to NGOs
     c) Visits/Speakers program


B. *Outside South Africa*
  1. Public Education Program
     a) Information collection and
        dissemination
     b) Assistance to NGO
        information activities


  2. Visitors/Speakers Program
     a) Program augmentation and
        coordination
     b) Public relations support
     c) Public panels/seminars


II. THE MEDIA

A. *Inside South Africa*
  1. Program for South African
     Journalists
     a) Commonwealth Journalism
        Award
     b) Commonwealth fellowships
        for working journalists
     c) Commonwealth scholarships
        for South African schools of
        journalism


  2. Program for South African
     Media
     a) Legal Advisory Fund
     b) Support for Alternative Press
     c) Funding for Anti-Censorship
        Action Group
     d) Twinning of newspapers


B. *Outside South Africa*
  1. Seminars for Journalists/Editors
     (works in concert with
     Visitors/Speakers Programs)
     a) Speakers
     b) Briefings
     c) Use of South African
        journalists

  2. New Sources of News
     a) South African News and
        Information Digest
     b) Compendium on South
        African news sources

3. Exhibits
   a) Audio-visual exhibit
   b) Archival audio-visual material

4. Special Events
   a) International televised events
   b) Solidarity days

5. Mobilizing Sport/Entertainment
   Industry
   a) Entertainers/Sports
      personalities as
      spokespersons
   b) Influence programming
   c) Funding for artists

*Source:* Government of Canada, *A Strategy to Counteract South African Propaganda and Censorship* (Ottawa, 1988).

ada had promised military assistance to the Frontline States in order to protect various projects against sabotage. The confusion emanated from a statement issued by Joe Clark which promised logistical support in the form of fuel, clothes, and food for project workers and support for training personnel from the Frontline States as part of the military training program for Commonwealth personnel that was initiated in 1966, long before SADCC was created.[83] The extent to which resources allocated for project workers were diverted for use by military personnel remains unclear. Increasing Canadian investments in and trade with southern Africa will undoubtedly create additional pressures on Canadian policymakers to implement policies aimed at protecting business interests.

Since about eighty percent of Canada's bilateral aid to the Frontline States has been tied to the purchase of Canadian goods and services, development assistance not only has helped SADCC countries but also has created export markets for railway rolling stock, telecommunications equipment, and power generators manufactured in Canada.[84] Canadian firms, like their Scandinavian counterparts, are directly involved in programs supported by their government. In 1987 a Canadian business delegation, composed of the Canadian Export Association, the Ontario Mining Equipment and Serivces for Export Association, Hawker Siddeley, Varity Corporation (formerly Massey Ferguson), and S. R. Telcom, attended an Investment in Production workshop in Gaborone sponsored by

SADCC. The main objective was to explore trade and investment opportunities and to safeguard their current market shares. In 1985 Canadian total trade with SADCC was more than $61 million, with exports accounting for $50 million and imports for $11 million.[85]

The interdependence which characterizes the relationship between the Frontline States and South Africa will continue to complicate Canada's South Africa policy and influence policymakers to reassess the implications of actions against apartheid for their own business interests in neighboring states. While Canada has been in the forefront of those adovcating stronger sanctions against Pretoria, the Frontline States, which have urged countries to impose comprehensive economic measures against South Africa, continue to trade with the apartheid regime, a reality which clearly demonstrates the dilemmas of interdependence.

# 8

# THE FRONTLINE STATES

*Dilemmas of Interdependence*

Relations between the Frontline States and South Africa mirror the contradictory nature of and tensions within the apartheid society as well as the chasm between Pretoria's neighbors' rhetoric against apartheid and their reality of extensive economic interdependence with the white minority regime. Products of European power politics and imperial ambitions, the Frontline States' economic and political destinies are inextricably intertwined with South Africa's, a country whose system of racial discrimination is anathema to all of them. Historical realities which welded the fate of Botswana, Lesotho, Swaziland, Mozambique, and Zimbabwe to developments in South Africa, a fact which none of these regional actors can ignore, continue to influence relationships that have long been characterized by resolution on the part of the Frontline States to be independent on the one hand, and by South Africa's determination either to incorporate most of them or to perpetuate their dependence on it on the other. But as long as South Africa maintains white rule, that society as well as its neighbors will suffer from ongoing violence and instability that will inevitably create economic difficulties for the entire region. Thus, by preserving apartheid and destabilizing its neighbors, the South African government inadvertently undermines prospects for peaceful change and economic growth at home. Contradictions between the various countries' declaratory and actual policies emanate from this complex interdependence as well as from domestic political and economic realities. Nowhere is this more obvious than on the issue of sanctions against Pretoria.

While the trend toward greater global economic interdependence makes sanctions an attractive foreign policy instrument to some governments, the imposition of sanctions against South Africa clearly demonstrates the problems involved in making them effective and limiting their impact to the target state. If anti-apartheid groups conveniently ignore the implications of sanctions against South Africa for the neighboring states, many governments use regional interdependence as a reason for inaction and as a justification of the status quo in South Africa, despite their anti-apartheid rhetoric. Yet it is clear that comprehensive economic sanctions against Pretoria would have serious economic and political consequences for the entire region, one that shows the greatest promise for economic development in Africa, and one where geography and history have conspired to create bonds of interdependence. And, as analysis of the Frontline States' policies toward South Africa shows, such sanctions may actually work against efforts to reduce neighboring countries' dependence on South Africa. In other words, comprehensive economic sanctions against Pretoria could undermine the twin strategies of black empowerment and of building up the Frontline States. As Roger Martin put it, like most hard issues of government, it comes down to a question of resource allocation and how the West's limited influence can be best deployed to help southern Africa.[1] But the Frontline States' support of sanctions within the Organization for African Unity (OAU), Commonwealth meetings, and elsewhere, even as they continue their own beneficial economic relations with South Africa, helps to frustrate attempts by the nonsuperpowers to develop pragmatic South African policies and provides Pretoria with an effective argument against sanctions in general. However, rather than dismissing sanctions as ineffective foreign policy instruments, the debate highlights the need for fine tuning and carefully targeting sanctions against South Africa in order to avoid seriously damaging the region's fragile economic systems, thus shifting the balance of power toward the Frontline States.

In addition to showing the complex issues surrounding the imposition of comprehensive sanctions against South Africa, an examination of the Frontline States also demonstrates contradictions in South Africa's policies and their own practices at home, a point not overlooked by white South Africans. Despite their opposition to apartheid, many of the Frontline States see a racial conflagration in South Africa as having negative implications for them and are therefore reluctant to take actions inconsistent with their interest in gradual change. Furthermore, by focusing international attention on apartheid, they have successfully avoided having their own human rights records scrutinized and publicly criticized. Similarities between South Africa's treatment of blacks and the neighboring states' leaders' approaches to rival ethnic groups are partially explained by historical factors. Apart from the personalization of power throughout Africa and the leaders' determination to keep it, contemporary perceptions of human rights were shaped by anti-colonial struggles, which were essentially for equality between Africans and Europeans and not necessarily for equality betwen blacks. Zimbabwe's President Robert Mugabe's treatment of his rival, Joshua Nkomo, is an obvious example. Thus, for many black African leaders, racism is anathema but ethnicity is accepted as a political and social reality. While white South Africans attempt to justify apartheid by comparing developments elsewhere in Africa to the situation in South Africa, obvious similarities obscure fundamental differences between apartheid and ethnicity. Whereas urbanization, Westernization, and anti-colonial movements brought different ethnic groups together, thereby eliminating many negative aspects of ethnicity in Africa, apartheid is a legal system deliberately designed to forcibly separate people along racial as well as ethnic lines. Nevertheless, African leaders' failure to respect human rights weakens the credibility of their argument against apartheid and inadvertently strengthens the status quo in South Africa.

This chapter shows that the Frontline States play a pivotal role in various countries' efforts to abolish apartheid. South Africa's position as the region's economic and military superpower, the fragile nature of many southern African economies, the economic interdependence of the region, and the historical and cultural ties between the Frontline States and South Africa combine to complicate the foreign policies of many nonsuperpowers toward Pretoria. An examination of the relationship between South Africa and Botswana, Zimbabwe, Swaziland, Lesotho, and Mozambique provides a more comprehensive and realistic view of the efficacy of strategies employed by Western countries to help abolish apartheid peacefully.

## INFLUENCES ON FOREIGN POLICYMAKING IN THE FRONTLINE STATES

The foreign policymaking process in southern Africa is influenced principally by political and economic problems which are common to much of Africa. Unlike the other nonsuperpowers, which have democratic governments, the Frontline States, with the exception of Botswana, are dominated by individuals who are unwilling to implement democratic principles or to provide for the orderly transfer of power. Contemporary African politics is characterized by violent upheavals, reliance on military force to obtain compliance, widespread corruption, and the personalization of power. These realities complicate Africa's long declared policy of opposing white minority rule and supporting human rights in South Africa. The fact that many governments are preoccupied with their own survival certainly diminishes their ability to move beyond anti-apartheid rhetoric and take concrete steps that would clearly demonstrate their commitment to respect for human rights for all individuals, regardless of race. In Zambia, for example, serious economic problems and potential political instability, ever since the attempted coup in October 1980, forced Kenneth Kaunda not only to limit his criticism of Pretoria but also to accept South African assistance in one form or another.[2] Similarly, conflicts within Lesotho's Basotho National Party between those who favored collaborating with Pretoria and those who advocated distancing Lesotho from South Africa and strengthening its ties with the ANC and Eastern bloc countries culminated in a coup in 1985 in which South Africa may have played a role. The military officers who executed the coup claimed that they did so independently of South Africa, and it is generally believed that they had long been planning to take such action in response to increasing domestic conflicts.[3] But the violence that has characterized Mozambique's domestic politics since independence represents an extreme case of destabilization and demonstrates South Africa's strategy of undermining the Frelimo government by supporting the ruthless insurgent Mozambique National Resistance Movement, or Renamo. Zimbabwe has been far more successful than Mozambique in bringing together rival groups, albeit at the cost of ending multi-party democracy.

Following the end of white minority rule in Rhodesia (now Zimbabwe), former guerrilla organizations which united to fight the Ian Smith regime divided along ethnic lines. Mugabe, representing the largest ethnic group, the Shona, became the leader of Zimbabwe, and Joshua Nkomo formed the opposition party, backed by his ethnic group, the Ndebele. Between 1980 and 1983 former guerrillas associated with Nkomo's Zapu (Zimbabwe African Peoples Union) party decided to engage in armed resistance against Mugabe's government, partly because of its failure to implement promised land reforms. In response, Mugabe unleashed the Fifth Brigade, composed solely of members of Mugabe's Zanu (Zimbabwe African National Union) party, to eradicate the dissidents, a process during which over two thousand civilians were brutally murdered.[4] As the dissidents continued their violent campaign throughout Matebeleland and the Midlands, killing approximately seventy white farmers, Mugabe outlawed opposition activities and accused South Africa of assisting the rebels. In an attempt to unite the country and help reduce support for the dissidents, Mugabe and Nkomo agreed to merge their rival nationalist parties. While Nkomo was not included in the government, Mugabe had achieved his objective of moving the country toward a one party state. Assured of Nkomo's support, he offered amnesty to the dissidents in 1988 and succeeded in convincing the majority of them to surrender.[5] By consolidating his power within Zimbabwe, Mugabe essentially became the sole spokesman for his country.

Public opinion, anti-apartheid groups, parliament, and other actors associated with foreign policymaking in the countries discussed in previous chapters are clearly absent in the vast majority of the Frontline States. Only in Botswana have voters selected their national and local representatives in essentially competitive elections. Violence has never played a significant role in elections, and the ruling party does not prevent opposition politicians from making speeches highly critical of the government.[6] But functioning constitutional processes in Botswana are an exception in a region where leaders such as Malawi's Hastings Banda and Zambia's Kenneth Kaunda have retained their grip on political power since their countries' independence in the mid-1960s. Under these circumstances, foreign policy is determined primarily by leaders who generally disregard public opinion. Yet, foreign policymaking in Africa reflects both the agony of state formation as well as the arrogance of power. More important, it underscores not only problems of political development but also deteriorating economic conditions which force Africans to focus on their own survival, thus leaving their leaders unrestrained freedom to personalize foreign policy. But the leaders themselves must formulate external relations within the context of domestic economic conditions, a reality which engenders sharp divergences between rhetoric condemning apartheid and actual policies that perpetuate economic ties with South Africa.

Economic factors of paramount importance in the foreign policy calculations of the Frontline States serve to limit choices available to decision makers. Throughout Africa dismal economic conditions have rendered many states marginal in the global economic system and have undoubtedly diminished their effectiveness in international politics. Mismanagement, corruption, mass starvation in Mozambique in particular and malnutrition in southern Africa in general, wasteful expenditures of public funds, and poor leadership undermine the Frontline States' ability to effectively contribute to efforts designed to terminate minority rule in South Africa. In 1989 the vast majority of South Africa's neighbors, as well as South Africa itself, were deeply in debt, reflecting a trend common to Africa as a whole. The overall growth of 2.5 percent in the continent's gross domestic product in 1988, an improvement over the 1.3 percent growth experienced in 1987, was insufficient to reverse Africa's inexorable economic decline, partly because of staggering annual population growth rates of over three percent. Furthermore, the predominant agricultural sector remained stagnant, prices for export commodities such as cocoa, coffee, tea, oil, and copper declined, and Africa continued to fall further behind the rest of the world, a trend that is likely to persist.[7]

Zimbabwe, with the second strongest economy in southern Africa, can play a crucial role in the economic development of the whole region and effectively compete with South Africa for markets, thereby reducing South Africa's economic dominance and hence its leverage vis-à-vis the Frontline States. But Zimbabwe's economic performance symbolizes a myriad of contradictions. Due in part to sanctions imposed against Ian Smith's Rhodesian regime, the manufacturing sector tripled production, reaching over twenty-six percent of the national product in 1980, and made over six thousand products.[8] For the first six years after independence, except for two years of drought, the economy grew phenomenally, despite a large exodus of white experts. By the end of 1986 Zimbabwe's success was fading and the country was plagued by a severe housing shortage and an annual urban growth rate exceeding six percent. As shantytowns sprang up around urban centers, the government adopted a policy of bulldozing them and using the army to forcibly remove squatters and relocate them on state farms.[9] Mugabe's socialist rhetoric, despite his many pragmatic policies, and his increased subsidization of parastatals exacerbated Zimbabwe's economic problems and discouraged foreign investments. The government's decision to reduce foreign currency allocations for imports in order to save hard currency substantially decreased the country's output of goods and services between 1986 and early 1988.

Although agricultural productivity contributed to an impressive 6.5 percent growth in GDP in 1988, foreign investment remained negligible. Despite major disinvestment by Western companies in South Africa from 1985 to 1987, there is no evidence to indicate that the Frontline States in general and Zimbabwe in particular benefited from South Africa's poor investment climate. On the contrary, Zimbabwe has also been faced by disinvestment and is unable to convince the international community that it offers a stable and profitable environment for foreign capital. In an attempt to reverse the decline, Finance Minister Bernard Chidzero introduced a broad liberalization program designed to remove bureaucratic and financial barriers to foreign investment. In addition to centralizing administrative services relating to attracting investments, the current policy on remittances of profits and dividends abroad was changed. Instead of allowing foreign companies to remit only twenty-five percent of after-tax profits, or fifty percent for businesses that had invested since independence, the revised policy would permit firms engaged in "priority projects" to remit all after-tax profits.[10] Given the large number of high school and college graduates who are underemployed or unemployed, policymakers will face continuing pressure to improve Zimbabwe's economic performance. Rapid population growth and the country's inability to provide free education are clearly diminishing current economic achievements. For example, in 1983 there were about twenty thousand high school and university graduates entering the job market; in 1991 that number is expected to reach thirty thousand, at a time when only twelve thousand new jobs are being created annually.[11] Zambia's economic situation is even more dismal.

Historical and political factors are largely responsible for Zambia's economic decline. With approximately sixty million acres of rich agricultural land and abundant water supplies, Zambia rivals the Sudan as a potential breadbasket for much of Africa. Yet the country is now a net importer of food, including maize which is consumed by Zambia's poor majority. One reason for the current food crisis is the colonial division of labor, as it were, among Zimbabwe, Malawi, and Zambia, all members of the Central Africa Federation. British economic interests, particularly the British South Africa Company which colonized the area, focused on developing rich copper deposits in Zambia, while emphasizing agricultural development in Zimbabwe where there was a large number of white settlers. Malawi was essentially regarded as a source of cheap labor for South Africa's mines and farms. These historical factors continue to influence contemporary economic life in all three countries, to a greater or lesser extent, and partly explain Zambia's dependence on copper for over ninety percent of its foreign exchange earnings. Copper's dominance in the economy oriented the government's financial policies away from the agricultural sector, as is the case in so many African countries. Consequently, this change led to mass migration from agricultural areas to urban centers, where government subsidies are more readily available. The net result is that Zambia is the most urbanized country in black Africa, with a third of its 6.5 million people crowded into four major cities. Growing urbanization not only deprives the agricultural sector of labor but also escalates pressure on the remaining farmers to produce food for urban consumers.[12]

Falling copper prices in the late 1970s, rapid population growth (averaging around 3.6 percent a year), and serious political and economic mismanagement have combined to create economic stagnation and an actual decline in both per capita income and the number of jobs since the late 1970s. There were 369,000 jobs in 1977, 365,290 in 1984, and 360,540 in 1986.[13] Just to rehabilitate existing industries, the government was forced to borrow from private companies and banks, foreign governments, and international institutions. Interest and principal payments on Zambia's $5 billion foreign debt left the government with roughly half of its export earnings. Like many other African and Latin American countries, Zambia turned to the International Monetary Fund for credit to repay previous debts and maintain imports. As a precondition for IMF assistance, the government agreed to (1) abolish fixed prices for almost all goods; (2) give parastatal companies more autonomy; (3) relax foreign exchange controls; and (4) cut government spending.[14] Attempts to eliminate government price controls and subsidies led to major food riots and threatened Kaunda's political domination of the country. Instead of facing up to difficult economic choices, Zambia tried to be classified as a "least developed country" within the U.N. system in order to obtain more foreign aid. By 1989 it was clearly moving toward that objective. Botswana was the only country which enjoyed significant political development and economic growth.

Botswana, one of Africa's few democracies, has experienced one of the highest growth rates in the world since 1965 and, proportionately, has the largest foreign currency reserves in the world, enough to cover approximately three years worth of imports. In a region where there is a net decline in economic growth, still, for each of the past twenty-five years annual economic growth has averaged between eight and eleven percent, and per capita income has climbed from $100 in 1968 to over $1,600 in 1989. Instead of having a deteriorating infrastructure, Botswana upgraded its public utilities, transportation and communication systems, and allocated about a third of its budget to education, health, social services, housing and regional development. These improvements are funded by the country's natural resources, especially diamonds, copper, and nickel. Beef exports are also a very important contributor to overall economic development.[15] Although wealth continues to be unevenly distributed, Botswana is not experiencing the mismanagement and widespread corruption found throughout much of Africa. Unlike Nigeria, which squandered its oil wealth, Botswana appears to be far more disciplined and future-oriented. However, rapid population growth, averaging between three and four percent a year, threatens to reverse many of Botswana's achievements. With almost half of its citizens under twelve years of age, the country is likely to double its current population by 1995. Furthermore, of the approximately eighteen thousand people who enter the job market annually, only twenty percent of them find employment in the formal sector of the economy, making work in South Africa an attractive option.[16] Nonetheless, economic growth provides Botswana with a relative degree of freedom to maneuver vis-à-vis South Africa and to avoid Lesotho's predicament. History, geography, and economic circumstances have conspired to make independence for Lesotho virtually meaningless.

Totally surrounded by South Africa, Lesotho's economy is profoundly linked to the vicissitudes of its powerful neighbor. Traditionally a labor reserve for South Africa's mining and agricultural industries, about eight out of ten employed Basutos work in South Africa. Consequently, any major change in that country's labor sector inevitably affects Lesotho. Higher wages in South Africa have contributed to the migration of highly educated Basutos to South Africa's nominally independent homelands where they function in various professional and administrative capacities. In an attempt to arrest the outflow of talented people, Lesotho has been strongly influenced to increase government salaries, as it did in 1984. Similarly, tripartite boards determine minimum wages for commerce and industry. Despite these efforts, real wages for workers in Lesotho have increased only by two or three percent, whereas those of migrant miners in South Africa quadrupled in the 1980s.[17] While Lesotho is by far the most dependent of all the Frontline States on South Africa, historical factors created the often ignored but inescapable reality of cooperation, to a greater or lesser extent, among all the southern African countries.

## HISTORICAL TIES BETWEEN THE FRONTLINE STATES AND SOUTH AFRICA

Britain's reluctance to acquire political control over Lesotho, Swaziland, Botswana, and to a lesser degree, Zimbabwe, South Africa's determination to incorporate them into its territory, and these countries' resolution to remain free of Pretoria's domination combine to shape the cooperation, tension, resistance, and interdependence which characterize their contemporary relations with South Africa. Their geographic proximity to the white minority-ruled country has paradoxically resulted in greater opportunities for their people while simultaneously creating unnecessary humiliation, hardship, and suffering. Their experience reflects, in microcosm, the greater social, economic, and political burdens of the black South African majority in their own troubled land. But it also vividly demonstrates clashes between the Boers and the British and the former's desire to remain independent, albeit at an extremely terrible cost to Africans they encountered. As Boer trekkers moved from Cape Province to the interior where they could establish their own political and social systems, based on their religious beliefs and perceptions of their relationship with Africans, they encroached on land controlled by the Basuto and Swazi. The historic pattern of conquest and resistance, initiated by Shaka, the great and ruthless Zulu military strategist, was repeated as Boer and African clashed in the late 1830s. Appeals by Moshoeshoe, leader of the Basuto, to the Cape Government for British assistance were ignored until 1868 when Britain's Queen Victoria granted British protection. However, Britain's decision to annex Lesotho to Cape Colony without consulting the Basuto, and its refusal to allow them representation in Cape Parliament, even though their taxes were arbitrarily doubled, culminated in the eight-month Gun War which cost the Cape Government nearly five million pounds. Eventually the Imperial Government in London grudgingly yielded to the persistent demands of the Cape Cabinet, and Lesotho became a Crown Colony in 1884.[18] One year later Botswana, the missionaries' road to central Africa, also came under British control. Transvaal Boers extended their domination over parts of the country and its huge herds of cattle, and Cecil Rhodes regarded it as the gateway to what he imagined to be central Africa's equivalent of South Africa's rich gold fields. Confronted with these expansionist schemes, Botswana leaders, like their Basuto counterparts, turned to London for protection. The Swazi case is more complex.

From the late 1830s to 1906 Britain's policy toward Afrikaner control of Swaziland vacillated from indifference to ambivalence. Britain seemed unconcerned about the Boers' encroachment on Swaziland's agricultural and pasture lands until the Transvaal Republic, in an effort to frustrate British imperial designs, planned to construct a coastal railway through Swaziland to the Indian Ocean. Kruger's decision to exploit Anglo-German tensions by encouraging German involvement in South African politics influenced Britain to deny the Transvaal control over Swaziland as well as to prevent that Republic from gaining access to the sea. However, in 1894, shortly before the Boer War, Britain recognized the Transvaal's right to establish a protectorate over Swaziland. But the conflict between Briton and Boer in 1899-1902 resulted in Swaziland being placed under the administration of the British governor of the Transvaal and becoming a British Protectorate in 1906.[19] Nevertheless, during the formation of the Union of South Africa, realized in 1910, it was explicitly acknowledged that Botswana, Lesotho, and Swaziland, also known as the High Commission Territories, would eventually be incorporated into South Africa. The fact that these three territories' posts, telegraphs, currency, banking, and customs and tariffs were operated by South Africa, and that they depended on South Africa for employment, educational opportunities, information, and various economic benefits, especially agricultural subsidies for white farmers, suggested that closer political association with South Africa was a logical extension of the current relationship. But while South African authorities apparently viewed Botswana, Lesotho, and Swaziland essentially as "native reserves," the three countries strongly resisted incorporation.[20]

South Africa's implementation of the Native Land Act in 1913, depriving blacks of their land and forcing them into "native reserves," marked the beginning of the inexorable movement toward the creation of the apartheid state, much to the dismay of British Liberals who had assumed that British civilizing influences would predominate in the newly formed Union of South Africa. The growth of Afrikaner nationalism, the rise of proponents of strict racial segregation such as J. B. M. Hertzog, Daniel F. Malan, and H. F. Verwoerd, and the substantial number of Afrikaners sympathetic to Nazi Germany, partly because they were anti-British to begin with, caused Britain to rethink its policy on the High Commission Territories. When the National Party gained control of the political process in the 1948 elections and introduced apartheid as the legal foundation of South Africa, Afrikaners attempted to justify their policy of separate development in terms of the relationship between Pretoria and its small neighbors. But Britain's painful experience with Nazi Germany, the horrifying Holocaust, the escalation of nationalism in Asia and Africa, and the subsequent emergence of new states clearly prohibited the possibility of Britain allowing South Africa to formally control the Territories. The idea of strict racial segregation, though widely practiced, was now regarded as an anachronistic evil which had culminated in Hitler's extermination of six million Jews. Furthermore, developments in the rest of Africa strengthened the Territories' resolve to resist being pulled into a political alliance with the apartheid regime. Consistent with Churchill's promise in 1954 that there could be no question of transferring the Territories to South Africa until the inhabitants had been consulted and until the British Parliament had expressed its views, Britain began to prepare the Territories for independence. These developments and South Africa's withdrawal from the Commonwealth in 1961 forced Pretoria to abandon its objective of formal incorporation and to treat Botswana, Lesotho, and Swaziland as foreign states, even if their sovereignty was greatly compromised.[21] Compared to the Territories, Zimbabwe was relatively economically and politically independent of the Afrikaner Republics as well as the Union of South Africa.

Zimbabwe, formerly Southern Rhodesia, was colonized by the British South Africa Company, headed by Cecil Rhodes. As early as 1878 Rhodes had planned to expand British control over the interior, partly to prevent a rapidly declining Portugal from linking up Angola and Mozambique by occupying the area in between the two colonies. But Rhodes was also motivated by his personal ambitions and the hope that the land which was named for him would yield gold and minerals to rival the wealth of South Africa. Through negotiations in 1888 with Lobengula, King of the Ndebele, Rhodes obtained the Rudd concession which gave him a monopoly over mineral rights in the area under the king's jurisdiction. Although Lobengula repudiated the treaty and appealed to Britain to prevent Rhodes's encroachment, the South Africa Company was able to obtain "permission" from Britain to settle and administer an area immediately north of the South African Republic (the Transvaal) and west of the Portuguese Dominions.[22] By 1890 Rhodes's Pioneer column, consisting of two hundred settlers and five hundred police, had established a fort at Salisbury, triggering sustained efforts by the Ndebele, the Shona, and other ethnic groups to repel the invasion of their territory. Defeated by 1897, the Africans were unable to prevent the increasing numbers of whites from settling in what became known as Rhodesia. From 1897 to 1980, when Southern Rhodesia became Zimbabwe under black rule, the minority white population effectively controlled the country and forced blacks into subservient roles in the economy and into segregated townships and reserves.

Until 1923 when white settlers were given the choice of remaining under the administration of the South African Company, governing themselves, or joining South Africa, the general assumption was that Southern Rhodesia would be incorporated into South Africa because of the historical, cultural, and economic links between the two countries. However, when a small majority of white settlers voted in favor of self-government, company rule was dissolved and Southern Rhodesia became a largely self-governing colony under nominal British control, while Northern Rhodesia, now Zambia, remained a colony in the traditional sense. In 1953 when Southern Rhodesia, Northern Rhodesia, and Nyasaland (now Malawi) were united to form the Central African Federation, the predominantly agricultural Southern Rhodesia was the main beneficiary of this arrangement. By 1963 it experienced significant industrial growth with manufactured goods replacing agriculture as the main sector of the economy. Several factors accounted for this rapid development: (1) the upsurge of business confidence and agricultural productivity as a result of the newly-created Federation with its capital in Salisbury; (2) direct and protected access for Southern Rhodesia's products to markets in the Federation; (3) increased European immigration to Southern Rhodesia, which provided capital and technical skills; (4) Salisbury's initial industrial advantages which influenced new investments to locate in Southern Rhodesia; and (5) the deliberate policy by the central government of shifting revenues and development projects to Southern Rhodesia.[23] As the country became more industrialized and organized, strict racial separation became less attractive to many whites. Undoubtedly the presence of Scottish missionaries had a moderating effect on white racial attitudes; yet whites refused to share political and economic power in any meaniful way and implemented legislation designed to perpetuate the inferior legal and social status of blacks. While Southern Rhodesia's strong manufacturing sector and agricultural productivity contributed to its relative independence vis-à-vis South Africa, transportation links, trade, and moral solidarity between white minorities in both countries created a degree of interdependence which is still evident today, although in altered form.

## ECONOMIC TIES BETWEEN THE FRONTLINE STATES AND SOUTH AFRICA

The Frontline States' strong position in favor of sanctions against South Africa in forums such as the Commonwealth, the Nonaligned Movement and the United Nations has not been consistent with their actual behavior. Although the level of political and diplomatic cooperation has decreased, regional economic interaction has increased, and various trade agreements have been renegotiated and extended. Much of the trading occurs within the framework of formal agreements such as the longstanding Southern African Customs Union, the 1981 South Africa-Malawi Agreement, the 1984 Rcpmosa Agreement (proposing agricultural linkages and development aid between South Africa and Mozambique), and the 1986 South Africa-Zimbabwe Trade Agreement.[24] The Frontline States' rhetoric does not obscure the reality of their dependence on South Africa for a wide range of agricultural products such as grains, cereals, dairy products, vegetables, fruit, and processed foods. Widespread starvation in Mozambique, caused largely by Renamo's violent and brutal activities in the countryside, underscores the region's vulnerability to a reduction in South Africa's food exports. Historical developments in southern Africa determined, to a large extent, South Africa's current dominant position in relation to its neighbors, and in Africa in general.

South Africa's industrial development, influenced primarily by the vast inflow of Western capital to exploit rich deposits of gold discovered in 1886 in the Witwatersrand reef in the Transvaal, made that country an exception in Africa. With only thirty percent of southern Africa's population, South Africa generates about three-fourths of the region's Gross Domestic Product and two-thirds of its exports. It produces most of the region's coal, iron, wheat, maize and electric power and controls vital transportation routes. Angola, which is the only oil producing country in southern Africa, refines roughly 4.4 percent of oil consumed in the area, whereas South Africa, with no oil reserves, a point emphasized by proponents of sanctions, refines approximately eighty-four percent of the region's oil supplies and exports oil to Botswana, Lesotho, Swaziland, and Malawi.[25]

South Africa's economic dominance is often overemphasized by Pretoria and anti-sanctions proponents and conveniently ignored by governments and individuals who subscribe to the assumption that economic sanctions will induce political change in South Africa. The logic of interdependence, which makes both sides vulnerable to interruptions in economic transactions, challenges both views. Given the fact that economic sanctions are hurting the South African economy, it is understandable why each side takes its respective position. Pretoria stresses its pivotal role in the area while downplaying its dependence on regional markets and labor. In 1985, for example, the South African government alluded to the interdependence of the region's economies in pointing out the implications that sanctions against that country would have for the Frontline States. The arguments made included the following: (1) employment of both legal and illegal workers in South Africa relieves the pressure on the neighboring countries' labor markets to an enormous extent, thereby contributing to their social and political stability; (2) if employment opportunities were reduced by outside forces, such as sanctions, South Africa would give preference to its own citizens; (3) since the two largest public sector borrowers of capital from abroad are the Electricity Supply Commission and South African Transport Services, international sanctions which exclude South Africa from foreign capital sources inevitably have negative economic effects on Botswana, Lesotho, Swaziland, and Mozambique because of their dependence on South Africa for electricity and transportation; and (4) because South Africa's own design, construction methods, as well as maintenance and repair procedures, are used by regional airlines, they are highly dependent on that country for maintenance.[26] The soundness of these arguments is clear: Pretoria can employ substantial leverage against its neighbors, which it does occasionally. But South Africa is also dependent on the Frontline States and is therefore vulnerable to its own sanctions against them. Similar to many Third World countries, South Africa relies on mineral exports to Western countries for most of its foreign exchange. Any reduction in these exports would profoundly affect its overall economic performance and seriously undermine the general perception that South Africa is essentially self-sufficient. Furthermore, South Africa's manufacturing and service sectors are extremely dependent on the Frontline States. As a regional economic power, like Nigeria in West Africa or Brazil in South America, South Africa's industrial growth is determined to a large extent by its neighbors' ability to purchase its products, especially in light of international sanctions. For reasons explained

## TABLE 10
## Indicators of Economic Dependence on South Africa, 1985

| | Botswana | Lesotho | Swaziland | Malawi | Mozambique | Zimbabwe |
|---|---|---|---|---|---|---|
| Trade Main Partner Exports to South Africa | South Africa | South Africa | South Africa | South Africa | South Africa | South Africa |
| % of exports | 17 | — | 20 | 6 | 5 | 17 |
| % of imports | 88 | 95 | 90 | 36 | 14 | 22 |
| Migrant workers Number | 29,169 | 150,422 | 13,418 | 30,603 | 59,391 | 16,965 |
| % of wage in the Labor force | 23 | 86 | 15 | 8 | 20 | 2 |
| South Africa Supplies | | | | | | |
| Electricity (%) | 19 | 100 | 50 | — | 33 | 1 |
| Oil (%) | 100 | 100 | 100 | 70 | — | — |
| Overseas trade via SA (%) | 100 | 100 | 33 | — | — | 66 |

Source: Martin Holland, *The European Community and South Africa: European Political Cooperation Under Strain* (London: Pinter Publishers, 1988), p. 23.

below, Africa is the only major external market for South African manufactured goods such as plastics, rubber products, chemicals, machinery, and nonmetallic mineral products. It is estimated that South Africa enjoys approximately $2.5 billion per year trade surplus in goods and nonfactor services (transportation, insurance, and tourism) with its neighbors.[27] South Africa's ability to find alternative markets is limited by several interrelated factors. First, international economic sanctions exclude many South African products which can be obtained elsewhere from major Western markets. Second, in an attempt to circumvent the punitive effects of sanctions, South Africa decided to become self-sufficient in key industries by using high tariffs to protect its industries. This means that many manufactured goods are much more expensive than the same products made elsewhere. Third, many products have an extremely high local content, making them uncompetitive in international markets. Fourth, as in many Third World countries, South Africa's production costs have risen faster than those of its major industrial trading partners, making its manufactured products uncompetitive in international markets. Fifth, South Africa's small domestic market makes it difficult for its industries to realize economies of scale.[28] Compounding these problems is domestic instability which discourages foreign investments. Under these circumstances, African markets are essential for South Africa's economic growth. Moreover, trade with the Frontline States and other African countries (1) provides a certain amount of legitimacy for Pretoria in the West; (2) diminishes the likelihood that the West will impose comprehensive economic sanctions; (3) perpetuates dependency which can be used as leverage to prevent its neighbors from supporting ANC activities; and (4) opens up the possibility of political relations with black Africa. Consequently, Pretoria's Ministry of Foreign Affairs does not hesitate to point out South Africa's economic relations with countries such as Zaire, Cote d' Ivoire, Equatorial Guinea, Ghana, Mauritius, the Comoros, Liberia, Somalia, as well as the Frontline States. Extensive trade with Zaire, for example, paved the way for former President Botha's visit to that country in 1988,[29] despite the lack of diplomatic relations between the two countries. Economic interdependence and political cooperation with the Frontline States continue to be major objectives of Pretoria's foreign policy. Despite their efforts to become more self-sufficient, the Frontline States, especially Botswana, Lesotho, and Swaziland, find it extremely difficult, if not impossible, to extricate themselves from the web of regional interdependence.

Zimbabwe, an ardent supporter of sanctions against South Africa, clearly demonstrates the dilemmas of interdependence in southern Africa. Since independence Zimbabwe has tried to reduce its trade with South Africa, but its geographic proximity to that country, the poverty of neighboring black states, and the high cost of Zimbabwe's manufactured products combine to make the South African market attractive. Despite sharp declines in Zimbabwe's exports to South Africa, down by twelve percent in 1987, imports continued to rise. While South Africa was Zimbabwe's third largest export market in 1987, after the United Kingdom and West Germany, it was its principal foreign supplier, with 20.7 percent of the market, followed by Britain with 11.5 percent, the United Sates with 9.4 percent, and West Germany with 8.7 percent.[30] Economic ties are facilitated by the presence of a South African Trade Mission in Harare and by various commercial agreements between the two countries, even though they do not have diplomatic relations. Mutually beneficial trade, especially during periods of drought, takes precedence over political considerations. For example, in 1986 when South Africa experienced a severe drought and Zimbabwe had an extremely good maize crop, they arranged the sale of about two hundred thousand tons of grain. Similarly, the Zimbabwe-South African Preferential Trade Agreement, due to expire in March 1982, was extended to give Zimbabwe continued access to South African markets for its manufactured exports, thereby preventing the loss of roughly $60 million in exports and saving approximately seven thousand jobs.[31] While Zimbabwe's concern about employment for its citizens is not radically different from Britain's, it is generally argued that the Frontline States are appendages of South Africa and, as such, have no choice. But from Britain's perspective, deep historical ties between London and Pretoria as well as other economic factors have also reduced Britain's options. In both cases, economic factors predominate other considerations. This is particularly applicable to Zambia.

Serious economic problems in Zambia have rendered that country extremely vulnerable to pressure from Pretoria. Zambia's inability or unwillingness to make difficult economic choices that would require comprehensive changes in current economic policy as well as long term planning increases its dependence on South Africa. Furthermore, Zambia's pivotal role in sanctions against Rhodesia influenced it to import more products from South Africa. Many of these items can be purchased from Zimbabwe at a lower price, but without the credit arrangements offered by South African companies. At the heart of the problem is Zambia's extremely weak economic performance which forces it to rely on credit and to buy on short notice. Although India, Japan, and Western Europe could supply Zambia with lower-cost products, Zambia's lack of planning and its huge external debt virtually eliminate competition from outside the southern African region.[32] Even though the IMF may have inadvertently influenced Zambia to increase its trade with South Africa by requiring it to buy from the cheapest source, it is clearly Zambia's domestic economic situation which perpetuates this dependence. Moreover, waste, mismanagement, and corruption exacerbate the problem. For example, in late 1985, during the international debate on sanctions against Pretoria, the government-owned Zambia Airways imported ten automobiles from South Africa for top managers. Even more ironically, the Zambian government bought seventy-one Mercedes Benz from the same source for a ministerial conference of SADCC, an organization whose primary objective is to help the Frontline States reduce their dependence on South Africa.[33] In contrast to both Zimbabwe and Zambia, which advocate that others apply sanctions that they themselves are unable or unwilling to implement, Botswana, Lesotho, and Swaziland generally concede the economic logic of links with South Africa, partly because of their obvious vulnerability to Pretoria's sanctions and their integration into South Africa's economy through the Southern African Customs Union.

Historical ties to South Africa and British indifference combined to make Botswana, Lesotho, and Swaziland virtual economic hostages as well as partners of South Africa. The interdependence of these four countries is demonstrated by their participation in the Southern African Customs Union, established in 1910 by the Southern African Customs Union Agreement. With a total population of roughly three million, Botswana, Lesotho, and Swaziland have always been at a disadvantage in their dealings with their powerful neighbor, an experience common to regional economic arrangements in Africa and Latin America. Given the relative lack of industrialization in the three smaller countries, South Africa's highly developed industrial sector has unlimited access to their markets under provisions which allow the free movement of goods throughout the member states. Economic interaction is facilitated by the fact that even though the smaller countries have their own currencies, the rand remains legal tender in Swaziland and Lesotho, and the new currencies are informally tied to the rand. Interest rates and other monetary policies are determined by South Africa, and major commercial banks in Swaziland and Lesotho are closely linked to South African banks.[34]

In addition to free trade, the Customs Union Agreement provides for the sharing of the area's total import and excise revenues accruing from the common external tariff. Under the 1910 arrangement, South Africa received about ninety-eight percent of all revenues collected. In an attempt to achieve greater fairness in income distribution, Botswana, Lesotho, and Swaziland managed to get South Africa to implement a new formula in 1969 that provides for revenues to be divided according to the value of actual imports of each country in relation to that of the common customs area as a whole.[35] Even though South Africa operates the Customs Union in a way that protects its own industry, the smaller countries derive significant benefits from membership in the Union. Approximately half of their total government revenue came from this source in 1983. For Lesotho, which received sixty-seven percent of government revenues from Britain in 1967, the Southern African Customs Union had replaced Britain as the primary source of government expenditures in 1981, providing roughly sixty-three percent of government recurrent spending.[36] Lesotho's obvious vulnerability to Pretoria's sanctions has influenced international aid donors to allocate resources to help reduce its dependency. But given

Lesotho's complex ties to South Africa, aid is often used as a political symbol of opposition to apartheid, a fact clearly understood by Lesotho. Trade links are further cemented by extensive South African investments in the Frontline States.

Although the Frontline States condemn apartheid and have distanced themselves politically from Pretoria, South African investments in these countries continue to grow. Apart from their dependence on the companies' capital, skills, and access to international markets, many governments make a distinction between the South African government and the private sector when justifying this ongoing relationship. Although business interests do not always coincide with those of governments, this fact is often obscured by the emotive nature of the apartheid issue. But even if South Africa's neighbors did not differentiate, their precarious economic situation would continue to influence them to adopt pragmatic policies on investments, despite their opposition to apartheid. None of South Africa's neighbors have prohibited private South African investments, despite the adoption of such restrictions by many Western countries. About sixty percent of Botswana's mining sector, ninety percent of Zimbabwe's mining sector and sixty percent of its manufacturing sector, and twenty-five percent of total foreign investment in Swaziland is controlled by South African interests.[37] Anglo-American Corporation and De Beers have significant interests in mining industries in Botswana, Lesotho, Swaziland, Zimbabwe, Zambia, Tanzania, Ghana, Sierra Leone, and Mauritania. De Beers, which is principally involved in selling about eighty percent of the world's diamonds on the international market through its Central Selling Organization in London, markets diamonds from Botswana, Angola, and Tanzania. In 1969 De Beers formed a joint venture with the government of Botswana, known as Debswana, to mine and market that country's diamonds. As an equal partner in Debswana, Botswana is directly involved in the company's decision making process. Moreover, Debswana's acquisition in 1987 of a five percent share of De Beers, valued at $380 million, gives Botswana a stake in the international operations of the parent company.[38] In light of the fact that diamonds account for over eighty percent of Botswana's exports, this is not an insignificant development. In addition to their substantial role in mining throughout southern Africa, investors from South Africa are also involved in other sectors of the region's economy. Companies such as Anglo-American, Barlow Rand, Sanlam, Delta, South African Breweries, and Frasers own many of the breweries, food processing, and grain milling industries in Botswana, Lesotho, Swaziland, and Zambia. They also control and operate shopping centers and supermarkets in Swaziland and elsewhere. Constant interaction between many of the Frontline States and South Africa through labor migration virtually guarantees the further exhange of goods and services across extremely porous borders.

Regarded largely as native reserves, Botswana, Lesotho, and Swaziland were integrated into South Africa's economic life in the late nineteenth and early twentieth centuries as the discovery of gold led to rapid industrial expansion, and as agriculture demanded large numbers of laborers who could be employed for low wages. Many of the Frontline States, colonized from South Africa, were treated as sources of cheap labor. Migrant workers were not only essential to mining and agricultural industries in South Africa but also provided income for colonial governments. The 1901 agreement between South Africa and Portuguese authorities is illustrative of arrangements made to obtain laborers. Under that agreement a private organization, the Witwatersrand Native Labor Association, was given exclusive rights to recruit up to one hundred thousand workers annually from southern Mozambique. The Portuguese authorities in Mozambique received a fee for each laborer as well as part of the miners' wages. Approximately sixty percent of the miners' wages went to the government of Mozambique in the form of gold, at the official price. The gold was then sold at world market prices and returning miners were paid their remitted wages in escudos at official exchange rates.[39] By recruiting laborers from Botswana, Malawi, Mozambique, Lesotho, Zimbabwe, and Swaziland, mining companies and agricultural industries kept wages artificially low and diminished the likelihood of labor unrest or the emergence of strong labor unions. Although political developments in the region since the end of Portuguese rule in Angola and Mozambique and deteriorating economic conditions in South Africa have contributed to a decline in the number of migrant workers, their role in South Africa's economy continues to be of great interest to the private sector. The benefits derived by neighboring states from having laborers in South Africa are also substantial.

Lesotho's dependence on these resources makes it vulnerable to pressure from the South African government; the mining industry in particular has an interest in retaining experienced workers. These sometimes conflicting interests influence industry and government to take different positions on the issue of retaliation against the Frontline States. When South Africa threatened to repatriate workers from Mozambique in 1986, both the Chamber of Mines and various farmers' associations in the Transvaal publicly objected, and the government agreed to reduce the number instead of totally eliminating workers from Mozambique.[40] Increasingly, however, black South Africans are recruited to replace miners from neighboring countries, partly due to pressure from black labor unions in South Africa. Nevertheless, violence and the lack of job opportunities in Mozambique influence workers to enter South Africa illegally, a trend which is likely to continue. The large number of people crossing national boundaries on a regular basis and extensive economic links between South Africa and the Frontline States inevitably result in the development of family and cultural ties.

Until the emergence of apartheid as the legal framework of government in South Africa, the general assumption shared by Britain and the Union of South Africa was that Botswana, Lesotho, and Swaziland would become part of South Africa. Consequently, many people from these states were relatively free to settle in parts of South Africa. They shared the experiences of many black South Africans and developed strong ties to various individuals and groups working to achieve racial equality. These links are perpetuated by the daily encounters of migrant workers and shoppers with apartheid and by family members who permanently settled in South Africa. For example, the South Sotho community in South Africa is larger than the population of Lesotho itself.[41] Botswana allows its citizens to travel to South Africa and vice versa. South African entertainers work in Botswana and the two countries continue sporting contacts. Both Swaziland and Lesotho encourage South African tourists to visit and are largely integrated into the South African tourist industry. This exchange of people is facilitated by the region's interdependence in areas such as transportation, communication, electricity, and water supplies.

Colonial interests determined in the 1930s that principal railway lines would run from landlocked Zambia, Zimbabwe, and Botswana through South Africa. One of the major challenges confronting the Frontline States is to find ways to reduce their dependence on transportation routes controlled by South Africa. Although they have made significant progress by enlisting the assistance of many Western countries, and China in the case of Zambia and Tanzania, many states still rely on South African technicians, rolling stock, and steam and diesel-electric locomotives.[42] Political instability, supported in part by South Africa, impedes the construction and maintenance of alternative routes, thus rendering the neighboring states vulnerable to South African leverage. However, South Africa's need for revenues counterbalances its political objectives in the region. Similarly, South African Airways is permitted to conduct normal business with the Frontline States and countries as far away as Kenya. In the area of communications the neighboring states are becoming increasingly independent of South Africa by developing their own telecommunication systems, although this may ultimately encourage more interaction with South Africa on a more equal basis. Another manifestation of regional interdependence is South Africa's reliance on electricity generated by the hydroelectric project at Cabora Bassa in Mozambique, and Mozambique's dependence on electricity, produced in Mozambique but fed to Maputo through the South African grid. Botswana, Lesotho, and Swaziland use electricity from the Electricity Supply Commission grid in South Africa, although Botswana's coal-fired central power station makes it less susceptible to interruptions in power supply from South Africa.[43] Finally, South Africa's water shortage gives landlocked Lesotho a limited amount of leverage vis-à-vis Pretoria. In order to obtain much needed water, South Africa negotiated a treaty with Lesotho in 1986 to develop the Highlands Water Project at a cost of $1 billion. In 1987 they agreed to open trade missions in each country and to exchange trade representatives. Given Pretoria's crucial role in the overall construction and operation of the project, and the economic benefits which will accrue to Lesotho, the Highlands Water Project will consolidate economic as well as political ties between the two states. Geography, history, and internal economic and political problems sharply diminish Lesotho's maneuverability vis-à-vis Pretoria, a reality recognized by both countries. Economic relations, transportation and communication systems, and the common cultural and historical experiences of the southern African countries have conspired to foster both cooperation and conflict between South Africa and its neighbors.

## POLITICAL AND MILITARY TIES: PRETORIA'S UNWILLING PARTNERS

If political and military alliances between South Africa and black Africa in general and the Frontline States in particular are perceived by Pretoria as conferring a certain degree of legitimacy to the apartheid regime, the vast majority of African leaders view such ties as domestic as well as international political liabilities and an affront to their dignity. Yet South Africa's status as the region's economic and military superpower influences it to utilize both military and economic leverage to coerce neighboring states into compliance with its overall objective of regional dètente on Pretoria's terms. Thus agreements such as the Nkomati Accords with Mozambique and the Swazi-South African Agreement Relating to Security Matters are regarded by Pretoria as important steps toward achieving its major regional foreign policy goal. But despite their vulnerability to South Africa's sanctions, most Frontline States have eschewed any overt military or political arrangements, and Pretoria has been unable, partly because of mutual interdependency, to force the larger countries such as Zimbabwe and Zambia to emulate Mozambique or Swaziland. Only Malawi, among the southern African states, has diplomatic relations with Pretoria, although Botswana, Lesotho, and Swaziland have what essentially amounts to official ties with that regime.

Malawi's decision to establish formal political links to South Africa seems to have been motivated by purely pragmatic concerns and the idiosyncrasies of President-for-life Hastings Banda. While Malawi has remained neutral in international politics, rejecting the socialist rhetoric of Mozambique, Tanzania, and Zimbabwe and maintaining ties with black and white Africans, its establishment of relations with South Africa in 1967 was partly influenced by economic considerations. As early as 1970 John Vorster, South Africa's Prime Minister, visited Malawi, and in 1971 Banda went to Pretoria. Many South Africans had important positions in the Malawi Development Corporation, Air Malawi, and Malawi's Ministry of Information. Furthermore, South Africa provided loans totaling twenty-five million rand to finance the construction of Malawi's new capital at Lilongwe and a new railway after international funding sources rejected both proposals.[44] Although Banda accepted technical and financial assistance from South Africa, unlike the leaders of Swaziland and Lesotho, he made a deliberate effort to reduce the number of Malawians working in South Africa by emphasizing the development of labor-intensive or large-scale estate argriculture.

Growing interdependence among nations necessitates contacts among officials of countries that do not have formal diplomatic relations. Indeed it may be argued that diplomatic recognition is no longer as crucial as it used to be as far as interaction among nations is concerned. Where the fate of countries is so closely interconnected, as they are in southern Africa, it is virtually impossible for them not to cooperate politically. In the case of Botswana and South Africa, diplomatic contacts, or their equivalent, take the form of telephone conversations, exchanges of written messages, and occasional meetings of officials in Gaborone or Pretoria to address a wide range of issues and resolve conflicts as they arise.[45] In 1973 Botswana and South Africa concluded an agreement which provides for the stationing of a Botswana labor representative in Roodeport, South Africa, to be responsible for the welfare of Botswana miners on the Witwatersrand.[46] This role is tantamount to what is generally regarded under international law as a consular function. In the area of national security Botswana faces a much more difficult dilemma as far as South Africa is concerned. Pretoria's fears about ANC guerrillas using Botswana to infiltrate South Africa have led to cross border raids on Gaborone and negotiations between the two countries aimed at addressing Pretoria's security anxieties. While complying with its neighbor's demands regarding border patrols and military surveillance, Gaborone astutely avoided signing a security accord with Pretoria, as Swaziland and Mozambique have done.

Overstretched in its efforts to dominate the region militarily as well as to suppress opposition to apartheid at home, Pretoria decided to pursue a two-track policy of destabilizing its neighbors and taking advantage of their weakness by essentially coercing them into concluding security pacts. The Swazi-South African Agreement Relating to Security Matters, signed in 1982, is the kind of arrangement Pretoria would like to have with all the Frontline States. The agreement provides for the two countries to assist each other in efforts to combat terrorism, insurgency, and subversion. It pledges both parties to (1) respect each other's sovereignty; (2) refrain from the unlawful threat or use of force against the other; and (3) prevent the introduction of foreign military forces or bases inside their territories except under specific conditions.[47] A South African Trade Mission, with many of the functions associated with any embassy, was established in Swaziland in 1984, and Pretoria gave that country a loan for road improvement. A similar agreement, the Nkomati Accord, was concluded between Mozambique and South Africa in 1984, but under different circumstances.

For much of Mozambique's existence as an independent state, South Africa has been involved in a brutal and systematic attempt to undermine the Machel government through military assistance to the opposition Renamo group. As will be discussed later in this chapter, Pretoria's actions were clearly designed to overthrow what it regarded as a Marxist regime on its borders. Shortly before the agreement was signed, and during the period it was technically binding on both states, South Africa continued to resupply Renamo with military weapons and facilitated their operations inside Mozambique. By May 1984, however, the two countries signed the Nkomati Accord under which Mozambique agreed to prevent the ANC from using its territory to attack South Africa, and South Africa undertook to end its support for Renamo. Given South Africa's economic and military superiority in the region, why did it sign the Nkomati Accord? A combination of economic and military realities forced Pretoria to reassess its policy of confrontation and to emphasize regional diplomacy. The price of gold plunged from arond $850 an ounce in 1980 to $340 an ounce in 1984, causing the value of the rand to decline from eighty-five cents to fifty cents (U.S.). A severe drought in 1984 substantially reduced the maize crop from roughly fourteen million tons in 1981 to 3.5 million tons that year, forcing the country to import approximately $500 million worth of grain at a time when its currency was greatly devalued. Moreover, in battles with well-trained Cuban troops in southern Angola in 1983, the South Africans suffered severe defeats, which had a major psychological impact on them. Finally, Renamo's lack of clear political objectives and leadership problems caused many in Pretoria to question the wisdom of their destabilization policy.[48] Weakened by Renamo's ruthless attacks and plagued by economic problems and widespread starvation, Mozambique had relatively little to lose from military and political cooperation with South Africa. Indeed, it hoped to derive important benefits from the Nkomati Accord. These included an increase in the sharply reduced number of Mozambicans allowed to work in South Africa's mines; withdrawal of South African support for Renamo; an increase in rates paid by South Africa for electricity from Cabora Bassa; technical assistance for its railroads and aircraft; and funds to rehabilitate Maputo harbor, used by the Transvaal for its exports.[49] But many of these benefits were not realized, and the destabilization policy escalated to such an extent that Pretoria and Mozambique renewed the Accord in 1988. However, attributing the failure of the agreement solely to Pretoria's realpolitik overlooks serious conflicts within the South African military in particular and the government in general about cooperation with Maputo. Business interests must also be considered.

Political schisms within Afrikanerdom were reflected in Pretoria's contradictory approach to implementing the agreement generally regarded as a cornerstone of its regional policy. Although factions within the South African Defense Force clearly opposed the treaty, Pretoria made a serious attempt to honor its obligations. South Africa gave Mozambique vehicles and equipment worth about two million dollars, compared to the $1 million of nonlethal supplies provided by United States. Pretoria proposed joint patrols along the Ressano-Garcia Maputo road, offered to send reconnaissance flights over the Cabora Bassa powerline to help Maputo defend it against Renamo attacks, sharply decreased supplies to Renamo, and set up radar stations to detect low-flying aircraft.[50] These actions were clearly consistent with Pretoria's foreign policy objectives and reflected its attempts to avoid stretching its resources too thinly, especially in light of its serious economic problems and its involvement in the Angolan conflict. Like the superpowers, South Africa was painfully being made aware of the limits of military power as a foreign policy instrument. As Christopher Coker, an astute observer of military affairs in the region, observed, "the problem was that South Africa could not police Nkomati itself. Although Botha promised to consider military intervention 'on merit' after receiving representations to this effect from the U.S. and British governments, the SADF had too few troops to launch a sweep through the province of Manica as the Zimbabwean army did in the Tete."[51] The probability that Pretoria had unleashed a monster, which it could not control, and which now threatened South Africa's security by creating chaos on its borders at a time when it was suffering severe military setbacks in Angola, is supported by Pretoria's attempts to revive the Nkomati Accord in 1988.

Negotiations between Mozambique and South Africa about restoring regional stability by reactivating the Nkomati Accord received added impetus in early May 1988. Major issues discussed included the training of Mozambican troops by South Africa to defend the electric power lines against sabotage by Renamo; the provision of rationpacks, boots, vehicles, tents, uniforms, medical equipment, radios, and mine detectors; and substantial economic assistance for Mozambique. At the end of that month Niel van Heerden, director of Pretoria's Department of Foreign Affairs and a leading negotiator in the Angolan-South African peace talks, Lieutenant General Kat Liebenberg, South Africa's army chief, and representatives from the police, the National Intelligence Service, and the Trade Department met with Lieutenant General Tobias Dai, Mozambique's army commander, to renew the two countries' commitment to the original objectives of the Nkomati Accord.[52] These developments indicated that business interests, which favor regional stability, had prevailed, at least temporarily, over factions in the military who favor continued destabilization in Mozambique. With large investments in the Cabora Bassa dam as well as in other projects in Mozambique, South African businessmen clearly have interests which conflict with those of radical military elements. To underscore his support for regional cooperation, on South Africa's terms, former President Botha and President Chissano met in September 1988 to reaffirm their commitment to the Accord. South Africa's interest in stability is evidenced by its provision of about $14 million worth of military and economic assistance, and by its agreement with Portugal and Mozambique to extend a $16 million loan for restoring power lines and pylons at Cabora Bassa.[53] In light of South Africa's deteriorating economic conditions, partly due to the impact of sanctions, the allocation of substantial amounts of money to Mozambique indicates that government's shift in policy. But even as a South African Navy ship sailed north to Mozambique to deliver promised non-lethal material at the end of 1988, Mozambican officials and neutral observers were accusing South African Intelligence of surreptitiously giving aid to Renamo, in clear violation of the Accord. The Secretary on Ideology in the Mozambican government, Jorge Rebelo, stated that "the support of South Africa to the bandits not only did not end, but was increased" since Mozambique and South Africa agreed to cooperate militarily.[54] Thus, despite South Africa's pledge to prevent Renamo from operating inside Mozambique, officials in Maputo continue to rely on a military cooperation agreement signed with Zimbabwe in 1988 that provides for joint military operations against Renamo and to hope that British military training assistance will contribute to the creation of any army that is capable of restoring stability in the country. Pretoria's general policy of regional destabilization has eroded Mozambique's confidence in bilateral peace agreements.

## THE FRONTLINE STATES AND PRETORIA'S DESTABILIZATION POLICY

Although South Africa's security ultimately depends on regional stability, the government's determination to maintain white political control influenced it to attempt to eliminate all possible threats to the status quo. For ideological reasons, the Marxist regime in Mozambique became an obvious target of South Africa's strategy to counter what it called the "total onslaught" led by Moscow. But an economically and military strong Zimbabwe that could effectively compete with South Africa for markets and power in the region would also call into question many of the psychological assumptions of apartheid, reduce the region's economic dependence on, and thus vulnerability to, South Africa, and be in a position to offer assistance to the ANC. As dedicated practitioners of power politics, the Afrikaners obviously realized that strong neighbors would not have to follow the dictates of Pretoria and could effectively challenge the five principles articulated by Botha for regional co-existence. These included: (1) a ban on cross-border violence; (2) removal of foreign forces hostile to any country in the region; (3) peaceful resolution of disputes; (4) re-

gional cooperation; and (5) toleration of different socio-economic and political systems.[55] While these objectives appear to be reasonable, closer
analysis of them within the context of politics in southern Africa demonstrates their inconsistency with Africa's commitment to ending white minority rule in South Africa and the goal of the Frontline States to achieve
greater economic independence from Pretoria through the creation of
SADCC. But if South Africa's political leaders wanted to resolve both
the internal problem of apartheid and threats from neighboring states
through peaceful means, their reliance on military power not only belies
that intention but might also inadvertently shift power away from the
politicians to the generals. As is the case throughout Africa, reliance
on the military to solve political problems invariably leads to an increase
in that institution's power, a problem that is exacerbated by the concomitant erosion of political legitimacy and the subsequent increased dependence on the coercive machinery of the state to maintain power.[56] Although
this does not suggest that the National Party is seriously threatened by
the military, it partly explains the apparent inability of political authorities
to reverse the regional destabilization policy they initiated.

Due in part to the ease with which South Africa can control Botswana,
Lesotho, and Swaziland, and the presence of a large, well-trained army
in Zimbabwe, Pretoria targeted Mozambique for its sustained policy of
destabilization. Occasional raids on the smaller neighboring countries
seemed sufficient to obtain their future compliance with South Africa's
demands. Although there is evidence to support Mugabe's claim that
South Africa maintains a training camp in the Transvaal for approximately
six thousand supporters of Bishop Muzorewa and members of Rhodesia's
notorious Selous Scouts who would be used to intervene in Zimbabwe
if South Africa deems it necessary, Mozambique remained the principal
target of Pretoria's destabilization policy.[57] The major instrument of this
policy was, and continues to be, Renamo. Renamo was created in 1976
by the Rhodesian Central Intelligence Organization of Ian Smith's regime
to collect information on the liberation movements that were fighting
Smith for black majority rule and to harass the newly-independent Mozambican government which was backing Mugabe's forces, but it was
encouraged by South Africa after Zimbabwe gained its independence to
undermine Mozambique's Marxist regime.[58] South Africa evacuated Renamo personnel from Zimbabwe shortly after Mugabe had won the pre-
independence elections, taking them directly to military barracks in
Pretoria for further training. Thousands of Mozambican workers in South
Africa were recruited, often coerced, and trained at special bases such
as Phalaborwa, then taken back to Mozambique. In an attempt to establish
Renamo's political wing, the Voice of Free Africa radio station, operating
from the studios of the South African Broadcasting Corporation near
Johannesburg, supplied the appropriate propaganda.[59] But South Africa
was not the only country supporting Renamo; Malawi was also involved.

President Banda's participation in Pretoria's destabilization of his neighbor's governments seems to contradict his commitment to SADCC. His reliance on transportation routes destroyed by Renamo would appear to further militate against an alliance with South Africa. Yet there are several reasons for Banda's support for Renamo. First, Malawi's close political and economic ties to South Africa may have influenced him to disregard broader consequences. Second, Banda has long claimed part of northern Mozambique as Malawian territory and may believe that through his support for Renamo he will recover territory that would give his landlocked country direct access to the Indian Ocean. Third, Malawi is host to a large number of Portuguese investors who lost their property in Mozambique, and these individuals are supporting Renamo financially. Finally, Banda had close personal ties to Orlando Christina, Renamo's secretary-general until his death in South Africa in 1983.[60] By 1983, however, Renamo's destruction of the transportation routes upon which Malawi depended resulted in extremely high transportation costs for Malawian exports, a price that proved to be too much for Banda. Capitalizing on Banda's disillusionment with Renamo, Mozambique's former President Machel visited Malawi. The two leaders signed an agreement which provided for cooperation between the two countries on security matters and pledged that they would not permit their territory to be used as bases for support groups engaged in violent acts against the other.[61] Nevertheless, Renamo continued to operate from Malawi in 1986. Malawi deployed some of its own troops to defend the rail line against Renamo and assisted a large refugee population from Mozambique. South Africa has effectively used Renamo to demonstrate the Frontline States' vulnerability to sanctions against Pretoria, and to escalate transportation costs by forcing neighboring countries to use South African railroads. Destabilization would therefore not only impede regional efforts to reduce dependence on South Africa but would also provide significant revenues for Pretoria, at a time when economic sanctions and internal political unrest are taxing the economy.

Destabilization is extremely costly for the Frontline States. Zimbabwe, Zambia, Malawi, and Mozambique are forced to ship their goods by longer and more expensive routes through South Africa. Instead of using the four hundred mile railway to Mozambique's ports, Malawi must use trucks to ship its products 1,500 miles through South Africa, at a ninety percent increase over what it normally costs. Zimbabwe and Zambia are also paying more for transportation as well as for security to protect remaining railroads and bridges from Renamo's attacks. Mugabe estimates that between 1980 and 1985, destabilization has cost the Frontline States $20 billion.[62] Other estimates are even higher. However, it is extremely difficult to calculate the costs of this ruthless conflict. Mozambique's industries in the countryside have been destroyed, the infrastructure, schools, hospitals, shops, and farms have been devastated. But the human costs are most shocking. According to the U.S. State Department's Bureau for Refugee Programs, in 1987 there was a three hundred percent increase in the number of Mozambican refugees in southern Africa over the previous year. Malawi alone received about half a million refugees.[63] Zambia, Zimbabwe, South Africa, Tanzania, and Swaziland also experienced an influx of Mozambican refugees. Renamo's brutal methods of killing innocent civilians shocked the conscience of mankind. By 1988 Renamo had lost its credibility as a liberation movement. The State Department report weakened arguments supporting Renamo, especially by the Heritage Foundation and Senator Jesse Helms. Furthermore, the murder of Renamo's leader, Evo Fernandes, in April 1988 indicated serious internal rivalries.[64] Despite these problems, support from South Africa enabled Renamo to continue destroying Mozambique. Nevertheless, South African business interests, the Portuguese government, and some Portuguese businessmen demonstrated an interest in finding ways to restore stability and hope to Mozambique.

## THE FRONTLINE STATES' FOREIGN POLICY STRATEGIES

Domestic economic and political realities shape the foreign policies of the Frontline States toward South Africa. The constraints on their leaders' actions vis-à-vis Pretoria emanate from serious internal weaknesses as well as problems concerning their own political legitimacy. Not surprisingly, few African leaders are willing to point to their countries or governments as models for Pretoria to emulate. Consequently, their commitment to the struggle against apartheid is characterized by strong rhetoric in favor of majority rule and relatively few actions designed to accomplish this objective. Some governments hesitate to take meaningful steps or to let their citizens mobilize campaigns against apartheid, partly because they fear that any independent domestic initiative would ultimately challenge their own authority. In August 1985, for example, the Senegalese government, one of the few democracies in Africa, banned an anti-apartheid demonstration initiated by several opposition parties and used police to disperse the crowd.[65] The considerable gap between the declaratory and operational aspects of African policy toward South Africa is illustrated by the rhetoric on "liberation through violence from without" and the lack of military assistance to the Frontline States. Discussions within the OAU on a pan-African force, or an "African High Command," to which individual countries would contribute contingents, began in the early 1960s when Kwame Nkrumah was president of Ghana. The purpose of the African High Command was to play a direct role in ending white minority rule in southern Africa. But as James Polhemus put it, "the further in Africa one gets from southern Africa the more theorizing there sometimes is in this particular vein."[66] Faced with this reality, the Frontline

States have adopted foreign policy strategies that reflect their varying degrees of power and vulnerability.

Zimbabwe's policy toward South Africa is characterized by a mixture of harsh rhetoric condemning apartheid, pragmatism, especially in relation to economic matters, and caution. Although Mugabe views the abolition of apartheid as an extension of his own country's struggle against white domination, realities of economic interdependence with South Africa influenced him to carefully separate his political stance against apartheid from Zimbabwe's economic interests and to pursue a cautious policy that stressed modifications in relations with Pretoria. Thus, three months after gaining independence, Zimbabwe severed diplomatic ties with South Africa but maintained trade relations with that country. The challenge confronting Zimbabwe was to define a position of support for majority rule in South Africa without jeopardizing its economic or military security.[67] This general objective influences Mugabe to adopt contradictory policies toward his neighbor. The logic of his position leads him to accept Pretoria's two basic ground rules for regional co-existence, despite his political commitments. The first of these is that Zimbabwe cannot permit the ANC to launch military operations against the white minority regime from its territory. The second is that Zimbabwe, despite its support for sanctions in international forums, must not itself initiate punitive economic measures against South Africa.[68] When Mugabe was perceived as disregarding these ground rules in the early 1980s, by not taking action to prevent the ANC from using Zimbabwe as a springboard for infiltrating South Africa and by restricting repatriation of profits by foreign firms, many of them South African, Pretoria responded by withdrawing twenty-five locomotives on loan to Zimbabwe just at the time when it was transporting its bumper grain harvest to market. Pretoria also refused to renew the preferential trade agreement between the two countries. However, in early 1982, following a visit to South Africa by Chester Crocker, U.S. Undersecretary of State for African Affairs, Pretoria decided to renew the trade agreement as well as leases on the locomotives.[69] Cognizant of Pretoria's willingness and ability to apply military and economic sanctions against its neighbors, Mugabe continues economic relations with South Africa while simultaneously attempting to reduce them by promoting regional economic cooperation. While castigating Thatcher for refusing to impose meaningful sanctions against Pretoria, Mugabe does not follow his own advice, partly because of the belief that his case is exceptional but Britain's is not. Air Zimbabwe and South African Airways fly reciprocal routes, tourists travel between the two countries, and despite threats to stop the flow of money from Zimbabwe to former Rhodesians now resident in South Africa, Mugabe continues to pay their pensions. In the diplomatic area, official relations at the ministerial level are not permitted, but there is an arrangement for regular high-level contacts between the two countries' intelligence services.[70]

Zambia's policy toward South Africa is even more complex than Zimbabwe's. Unlike the other Frontline States which have either explicitly or implicitly agreed not to support ANC activities against South Africa, Zambia is where the ANC has its headquarters. Clearly, from Pretoria's perspective, Kaunda is instrumental in furthering efforts leading to the total communist onslaught. Moreover, Kaunda's strong advocacy of economic sanctions against South Africa sets him apart from leaders in Botswana, Swaziland, Mozambique, Malawi, and Lesotho. In fact, in 1986 Kaunda actually threatened to leave the Commonwealth because of Thatcher's refusal to comply with demands to adopt punitive measures against apartheid. But Zambia's extremely serious economic problems and Kaunda's commitment to humanism and nonviolence moderate his policy toward South Africa. Kaunda, who has consistently advocated dialogue with his neighbor, hosted a meeting between Pretoria and Swapo in 1984 and arranged the 1985 talks between the ANC and South African business leaders, academicians, and opposition leaders. Zambia's support for the ANC has not deterred the South African Foreign Ministry from maintaining contacts with Kaunda, whom they view as a moderate and an important link to the Frontline States in particular and black Africa in general.[71]

In comparison to Zambia, Zaire pursues an even more contradictory South African policy. Prior to 1988 when Zaire and South Africa made public improvements in their relationship, president Mobutu adopted a South African policy of condemning apartheid in international forums such as the United Nations, the Nonaligned Movement, and the OAU while closely cooperating with Pretoria in many different areas. Mobutu's human rights record would not suggest that he can gain the moral high ground vis-à-vis apartheid; the hypocritical nature of Zaire's stance against apartheid is amazing. For example, in 1973 Mobutu publicly agreed to terminate his participation in the International Red Locust Control Service, operated by South Africa, because of apartheid, but privately asked Pretoria to continue supplying airplanes, equipment, and experts.[72] Another example of the gap between rhetoric and actual practice was Zaire's position on South Africa's involvement in the Angolan civil war in the mid-1970s. After South African military supplies and advisers had been used by Zairian units inside Angola, Zaire actually condemned Pretoria in the United Nations for intervening in Angola.[73]

Botswana, Lesotho, and Swaziland pursue predictable foreign policies, given their close economic and cultural links to South Africa and the ease with which Pretoria could force them to comply with its demands. The foreign policy strategies of the smaller countries also reflect contradictions between their opposition to apartheid and their extreme dependence on South Africa for basic services, employment, transportation, trade, and access to the outside world. But in Lesotho's case, its vulnerability is sometimes used as an asset. Its position as an independent enclave surrounded by South Africa has been used by both its government and international aid donors as justification for providing economic assistance.[74] Swaziland is in a similar position, although it is less critical of apartheid. Botswana's relative economic strength, stable democratic traditions, and toleration and promotion of a non-racial society profoundly challenge many assumptions of apartheid, enhance its international credibility on apartheid and give it some flexibility in its relations with Pretoria. Botswana's foreign policy strategy consists of (1) observing South Africa's basic ground rules for regional cooperation; (2) developing ties with black African countries to avoid being isolated; (3) not creating any impression that it condones racial discrimination in South Africa; (4) developing contacts with international aid donors to reduce its dependence on South Africa; (5) supporting regional integration efforts designed to promote trade between the Frontline States; (6) developing its economic resources; and (7) maintaining a high international profile to prevent any diplomatic and economic isolation that might result from its proximity to South Africa.[75] The major foreign policy strategy of the Frontline States as a group is to develop their economic resources to reduce their dependence on South Africa. The main instrument used to achieve this objective is SADCC.

## SADCC: COUNTERING PRETORIA'S REGIONAL STRATEGY

Zimbabwe's independence in 1980 facilitated the creation of SADCC, a regional economic integration effort initiated by President Sir Seretse Khama of Botswana in 1979. Formally constituted in Lusaka, Zambia in April 1980, SADCC's major objective was to diminish the Frontline States' economic dependence on South Africa. In order to achieve this overall goal, the member states pledged to mobilize domestic and regional resources to carry out national, inter-state, and regional policies designed to lessen dependence and build genuine regional coordination, and to take joint action to secure international support for the SADCC strategy.[76] The Frontline States' determination to foster regional economic independence from South Africa countered Pretoria's strategy of formal political and economic cooperation aimed at preserving the status quo. As indicated earlier, rejection of Pretoria's vision for the region played a significant role in that country's decision to destabilize its neighbors. As early as 1980 the economic as well as political implications of SADCC were clear to South African officials, who watched their country's share of Malawi's imports plummet from forty-one percent in 1979 to thirty-two percent in 1981 after Malawi joined SADCC. Malawian technocrats and businessmen were convinced that South Africa was not always the cheapest source for imported goods.[77] Zimbabwe could effectively compete for a larger share of the southern African market.

Furthermore, the Frontline States were attracting technical and financial assistance from Scandinavia, Britain, West Germany, Canada, the United States, and elsewhere to rehabilitate vital railroads and develop the region's infrastructure, a clear threat to South Africa's dominance. The Tazara railway, between Zambia and Tanzania, and the Dar es Salaam Port were designated as priority projects. With funds secured from foreign sources, Tazara has been upgraded and is diverting traffic away from South Africa. The "northern corridor" project, which involves the rehabilitation of roads and harbors along the northern shores of Lake Malawi in order to transport goods to Tazara or the Tanzam highway, will significantly reduce the high cost of transporting cargo from Malawi through South Africa.[78] But South Africa's destabilization of Mozambique seriously impedes the realization of broader SADCC objectives.

There are many problems confronting regional economic integration efforts which are internal. Among the difficulties facing SADCC are the following: (1) internal political and economic problems which undermine both long-term political stability and economic growth; (2) rapid population growth in all the member-states that prevents any real economic progress; (3) the economies of the region are currently oriented toward markets outside the region; (4) as is generally the case elsewhere in Africa, the most developed countries attract investments, thereby broadening the gap between states; (5) there is little economic complementarity among member states: most produce minerals or agricultural products for exports; and (6) problems may arise because leaders might be more concerned about preserving their power than about making political compromises essential for the functioning of regional industries and various projects.[79] Despite the challenges facing SADCC, it has already attracted international support for rehabilitating railways, agricultural development, telecommunications systems, and other projects that will help reduce Pretoria's leverage against the Frontline States. Nevertheless, historical ties, internal economic weaknesses, and the inability or unwillingness of many of the region's leaders to make hard choices on political and economic reforms will undoubtedly contribute to the Frontline States' economic interaction with South Africa, albeit with somewhat diminished economic vulnerability. The reality of this ongoing interdependence is manifested by the Frontline States' position on sanctions against Pretoria as a foreign policy instrument.

## THE FRONTLINE STATES AND SANCTIONS

Like the other nonsuperpowers, the positions of the Frontline States on sanctions are shaped to a large degree by their perceptions of the resulting costs and benefits from using coercive economic measures as foreign policy instruments. Given the interdependence of southern Africa, the Frontline States are likely to be affected by sanctions against South Africa.

Although they have not imposed sanctions, they generally support international economic measures against apartheid, arguing that Pretoria's destabilization policy is affecting them to a greater degree than would sanctions designed to end apartheid. But there is no guarantee that destabilization will cease or that apartheid will be abolished if comprehensive sanctions are imposed. In fact, the opposite could occur, partly because the military, which is responsible for destabilizing the region, would inevitably gain more power as civilian authorities turn to the coercive machinery of the state to maintain power, as is the case in many African countries. In brief, it is extremely difficult to determine with any certainty if sanctions would ultimately prevent Pretoria from undermining regional stability. But in light of regional interdependence, it is inevitable that the Frontline States would also be negatively affected by sanctions against Pretoria, despite some opportunities which might be created for particular countries. A weaker South African economy would certainly have negative consequences for Lesotho and Swaziland because of their virtual integration into that country's economy. Furthermore, South Africa could resort to economic retaliation against the Frontline States. But South Africa's dependence on regional markets, transportation revenues, dividends and profits from South African companies operating in various countries, and pension remittances for ex-Rhodesians reduces Pretoria's ability to impose sanctions against its neighbors without causing additional damage to itself.[80] While South Africa would probably decrease imports from neighboring states, it is likely that its currency would be weakened, thereby making its exports cheaper for the Frontline States. But this would be contrary to basic SADCC objectives of reducing dependence on South Africa. Each country takes a position on sanctions that is consistent with its interests.

Zimbabwe's strong opposition to apartheid and its support for Commonwealth sanctions against Pretoria are in sharp contrast to its actual behavior. Even though Mugabe promised to terminate air links between the two countries and favored banning overflights of aircraft serving South Africa, flights between Zimbabwe and South Africa actually increased as countries such as Australia and Scandinavia prohibited direct flights to the latter. This contradiction between declaratory and operational policy generally characterizes Zimbabwe's position on sanctions. While economic links to South Africa are clearly an important factor influencing Zimbabwe's policy, that country's leaders are also aware that sanctions against Rhodesia stimulated its manufacturing sector, making it capable of exporting goods to its neighbors.[81] Furthermore, there are internal disagreements on applying sanctions against South Africa. Mugabe's pragmatism, which belies his rhetoric, seems to be shared by government ministers. For example, in November 1985 the Finance Minister, Dr. Bernard Chidzero, noted that, due to historical and geographic reasons, the long existing trade, investment, and financial arrangements, there was an umbilical relationship between Zimbabwe and South Africa. Consequently, disrup-

tion in trade with Pretoria would result in Zimbabwe's economy functioning at a reduced rate.[82] But if transport routes through Mozambique could
be secured, Zimbabwe would capture regional markets now dominated
by South Africa. However, it is unlikely that the Frontline States could
effectively protect railroads from being destroyed by Renamo or by South
Africa itself. Domestic realities have an even more profound effect on
Zambia's position on sanctions.

Kaunda's confrontations with Margaret Thatcher at the Commonwealth
Summits over the issue of sanctions obscure the similarities of their actual
policies. While Thatcher is unambiguously opposed to using economic
coercive measures against Pretoria, Kaunda's stance is obviously contradictory. His rhetoric is tempered by Zambia's dire economic conditions and
strong internal opposition to sanctions. Zambia's elites have established
important connections with South Africa's private sectors, partly because
many of Zambia's industries are operated by South Africans. Their general
feeling is that domestic economic recovery takes precedence over sanctions
and the liberation struggle. The Mineworkers' Union, members of Parliament, and others urge Kaunda to avoid taking measures against Pretoria
that would effectively "finish off" Zambia's economy. Instead, they advocate more trade with South Africa to ensure that Zambia's consumers
are better supplied with commodities.[83]

Countries such as Lesotho and Swaziland are more openly opposed
to sanctions. When the United States Congress was debating implementation of a new package of sanctions against Pretoria in 1988, King Moshoeshoe of Lesotho noted that his country recognized the right of the
international community to take steps designed to dismantle apartheid
and indicated that Lesotho was willing to endure sacrifice to help achieve
that goal. But he pointed out that passage of the proposed legislation
should be accompanied by relief for the unintended targets who would
nonetheless be adversely affected. Essentially, Moshoeshoe argued that
the international community should punish Pretoria, not Lesotho.[84] However, given the inextricable links between the two societies, the world
cannot punish Pretoria without inadvertently inflicting severe damage
on Lesotho.

Swaziland's opposition to sanctions has raised speculation that that
country is playing a pivotal role in South Africa's sanctions-busting strategy. There is enough evidence to suggest that South Africa has been
using Swaziland as a conduit for its exports. Part of its strategy is to
establish warehouses in Swaziland where goods manufactured in South
Africa will be stamped with "made in Swaziland" labels and then exported. For example, the Taiwanese Chia Ho group exported flannel shirts
and other clothing to the United States from South Africa before Congress
banned textile imports from that country in 1986. After 1986, Chia Ho
established a new company, Garment Industries of Swaziland, as a venue
for a false labeling operation. The parent company then sent approximately

140,000 flannel shirts made in South Africa to Garment Industries for relabeling.[85]

Like the other nonsuperpowers, the Frontline States' South African policies are strongly influenced by domestic political and economic considerations and each country's perception of its interests. Anti-apartheid rhetoric reflects strong sentiments against racial discrimination and the continuation of white rule on the continent. But historical ties, geographic proximity, and established economic relations have created webs of regional economic interdependence from which no country, including South Africa, can extricate itself without suffering serious economic losses. It is the conflict between economic realities on the one hand and a commitment to abolish white domination on the other that inevitably results in contradictions between declared and actual policy.

# 9

# CONCLUSION

*Implications for U.S. Policy*

The United States' historical struggle with questions of race and ethnicity; its ability to deal effectively with diversity and the significant progress it has made in race relations; its deeply-rooted commitment to equality and human dignity as inalienable rights; its system of government which gives citizens a major role in the formulation of foreign policy through Congress; its definition of nationhood that is inclusive of race and ethnicity; and its economic and military power in the global system make it the logical choice for leading international efforts designed to effectuate change in South Africa. The vast majority of the nonsuperpowers, with the exception of Canada, are just beginning to come to grips with ethnic and racial diversity. For many of these racially or ethnically homogeneous societies, diversity is not frequently regarded as a positive value, and countries such as Japan and West Germany perceive ethnic pluralism as undesirable. Consequently, their ability to convince the South African government to dismantle apartheid is undermined by their lack of credibility on racial and ethnic issues. The United States' success with racial integration, despite continuing problems, gives it a unique opportunity to exert influence by example. However, since U.S. policymakers are constrained by domestic factors and by the policies of the nonsuperpowers, it is imperative for those who formulate and implement American policy toward Pretoria to take into consideration the interests and strategies of other countries involved in South Africa, and to make adjustments necessary for rendering U.S. policy more effective. Because foreign policy is essentially an extension of a country's domestic politics, the nonsuperpowers have a multiplicity of interests and face varying and diverse pressures in relation to those underlying interests. A pragmatic American

policy toward South Africa must not only focus on the moral issues involved but also on the tangible economic and strategic concerns of other
countries. A comprehensive analysis of the nonsuperpowers' relations
with South Africa vividly illustrates how national interests influence countries to declare their opposition to apartheid for moral and political reasons
while continuing to protect their economic stakes in South Africa. Although these two approaches are not necessarily contradictory, they nonetheless reflect the unwillingness of countries to jeopardize what they
regard as major national interests. Furthermore, their actions are complicated by the fact that nation-states cannot always control multinational
corporations which are responsible for global economic interaction. Moreover, the vast majority of nonsuperpowers rely on international trade
and do not believe in utilizing economic instruments to achieve foreign
policy objectives. In countries such as Japan, West Germany, and Israel,
economic issues are too closely intertwined with national security concerns
for them to implement strong economic sanctions against Pretoria without
causing significant damage to themselves. Equally important, the process
by which foreign policy is formulated in many countries directly determines the extent to which anti-apartheid groups in particular and public
opinion in general can have an impact on foreign policy.

Unlike the United States, where individuals and groups can indirectly
affect policy by lobbying members of Congress as well as the Executive
branch, most of the nonsuperpowers have political systems in which
interest groups that are outside of the ruling circle are effectively prevented
from exercising influence on foreign relations. This is particularly true
in Japan, Great Britain, and West Germany where business and political
interests overlap. Because the majority in Parliament virtually controls
the foreign policy process, public opinion is relatively unimportant once
elections are over. Thus, the level of anti-apartheid activities cannot be
viewed as an accurate measure of influence on policymakers. In Britain,
for example, opposition to apartheid is widespread and deeply-rooted.
Many South African exiles live in Britain and are extremely articulate
advocates of economic sanctions against Pretoria. But the way in which
policy is made in Britain allowed Prime Minister Thatcher to essentially
ignore the opposition and to continue normal trade relations with South
Africa. In the case of Scandinavia, for example, emphasis on community
and cooperation modifies the dominant role of the various Prime Ministers, and public opinion is able to directly shape foreign policy strategies.
However, in West Germany and Japan public opinion on apartheid does
not significantly affect relations with South Africa.

Small and middle powers generally view international organizations,
law, and issues of morality as being important to their national objectives.
For Scandinavia and Canada, apartheid is anathema not only because
of their cultural values but also because it is an issue which goes to
the heart of their perceptions of their role in the international system.

These countries' interests in the United Nations, the Commonwealth, and other international organizations are directly affected by their positions on apartheid. Israel, on the other hand, is more concerned about national security, and its isolation in international forums contributes to its general disregard for international organizations. Its preoccupation with its own survival makes the South African issue relevant primarily in relation to national security. But Israel's ties to American Jews and its own history, which is intimately connected with the Holocaust, prevent it from overlooking the moral aspects of apartheid. Given the diversity of interests among the nonsuperpowers, their commitment to strategies designed to bring about a non-racial South African society varies according to their perceptions of how particular strategies will affect their own underlying economic, political, and national security interests. Thus, their actual policies on sanctions, for example, may or may not converge with American policy. Indeed, in an attempt to protect their stakes in South Africa, some countries may directly undermine U.S. strategies for effectuating change in South Africa.

## EVALUATION OF STRATEGIES

Strategies used by the nonsuperpowers may not only be inconsistent with those adopted by the United States but may also be at cross-purposes with each other. For example, economic sanctions designed to pressure the white minority regime to respect human rights could retard the process of black empowerment by reducing economic growth. Similarly, trade sanctions against South Africa that result in significant costs to the state imposing them could effectively prevent that state from being able to contribute funds for economic development and infrastructure projects in the Frontline States. Likewise, an emphasis on economic growth in South Africa as a way of empowering blacks may inadvertently assist Pretoria in the destabilization of the Frontline States and help to strengthen its control over the black population by generating revenues for the military forces. While some inconsistencies among strategies are inevitable, serious conflicts between them clearly erode their effectiveness. The impact of various approaches must ultimately be measured by their ability to change South Africa's behavior within a reasonable period of time. How one determines the length of time required before the impact of sanctions can be judged is basically arbitrary and falls more in the realm of art than of science. Nonetheless, experience can serve as a guide.

Opinions among the nonsuperpowers on the ability of economic sanctions to force Pretoria to grant democratic freedoms to black South Africans range from those of the Scandinavians and Canadians, who believe that sanctions are needed, to those of the British, West Germans, and Israelis, who generally oppose economic sanctions as foreign policy instruments.

There is no consensus on the effectiveness of sanctions even among the most ardent anti-apartheid activists. Helen Suzman, a long-time South African anti-apartheid member of Parliament and former leader of the opposition Progressive Federal Party, believes that sanctions would harm blacks, including citizens of the Frontline States, more than whites, and would exacerbate the already alarmingly high unemployment among black workers.[1] Desmond Tutu, Nobel Peace Prize winner and Anglican archbishop, also a staunch anti-apartheid activist, disagrees with Suzman on sanctions, calling for more stringent economic measures against Pretoria. Clearly, South Africa is not invulnerable to economic pressure, despite claims to the contrary by Pretoria. The structure of its economy gives the international community a substantial amount of leverage over its economic performance. But economic pressure alone may have relatively little impact on the political structures of South Africa. Indeed, a depressed South African economy may actually strengthen right-wing proponents of rigid racial segregation, and unemployment among both whites and blacks may lead to intransigence and violence which, in turn, could prolong repressive policies.[2]

Even though economic measures may actually generate pressure on political leaders to fundamentally alter the system, the assumption that comprehensive economic sanctions would end apartheid remains largely speculative. While economic growth may buttress apartheid, it does not necessarily follow that economic decline will terminate it. Apartheid as an ideology and an expression of racial domination was enacted by the Afrikaners who, compared to English-speaking white South Africans, were relatively poor. As Robert Rotberg astutely observed, the South African government's "bottom line is the maintenance of power, not the maintenance of affluence without power or the spread of prosperity in the absence of power."[3] In other words, the South African government's behavior is similar to that of governments in countries where people do not exercise enough power to rein in political leaders. This implies that the empowerment of South African citizens is an extremely important component of any effective anti-apartheid strategy. Consequently, economic sanctions as instruments of foreign policy must be accompanied by other measures in order to play a constructive role in bringing about non-violent change.

The general assumption that sanctions in and of themselves are sufficient to pressure governments ignores some basic guidelines which are essential in order for sanctions to partially achieve their intended objectives. First, sanctions and the policy changes must be perceived to be in the interest of the states imposing them. As discussed in the previous chapters, since only Scandinavia and Canada view the implementation of sanctions to be in their interest, international coordination of and support for comprehensive sanctions will be difficult to achieve. Second, sanctions can be effective only if forcefully applied over a relatively short period of time. Given the economic interdependence of states, hurting the target state in many cases inevitably leads to hardship for sending states and benefits for countries willing to take advantage of the sanctions imposed by others. The longer sanctions are applied, the greater the opportunity for evasion.[4] Third, sanctions that are specific in nature and linked to a well-defined demand for a specific policy change tend to be more effective. As Roger Fisher argues, an adversary finds it difficult to yield to an unrelated threat because it tends to look like unprincipled blackmail. Economic sanctions usually suffer from the illegitimacy which comes from being unrelated.[5] Punishing the entire country because of specific government policies is usually counterproductive and often stimulates nationalism. Sanctions that are not carefully targeted may inadvertently strengthen the South African government. Fourth, if the cost of imposing sanctions greatly exceeds the amount anticipated by the government enacting the sanctions, then it might decide to change its policy. Fifth, the conditions under which sanctions will be lifted must be thought out prior to their imposition. The target state must know precisely what is expected of it. Imposing sanctions against South Africa until it abolishes apartheid is an unrealistic approach that may actually undermine important strategies such as black empowerment, assistance to the Frontline States, and greater communication with the South African people. Furthermore, such an approach underestimates sanctions-busting activities by Pretoria and the emergence of "sanctions fatigue" among countries imposing punitive economic measures.

The nonsuperpowers generally support the concept of black social and economic empowerment as part of an overall effort to bring about peaceful change. For Britain and West Germany, for example, empowerment is seen as the most appropriate way to prepare blacks for a future non-racial South Africa, largely because this approach does not directly threaten their economic stakes in that country and is consistent with their interests in the Frontline States, countries whose economies are closely linked to South Africa's. Although black empowerment is often perceived as a way of circumventing the decision to impose sanctions, this strategy is an extremely important component of any attempt to peacefully restructure the South African society. The creation of autonomous black organizations, the emergence of self-confidence among blacks, and the increasing bargaining power of trade unions can ultimately reduce black dependence on white-controlled agencies and structures and enable blacks to challenge the state more effectively.[6] Labor strikes and boycotts of white businesses have proven to be very effective in many cities throughout South Africa. But the capital and technical expertise needed for black empowerment are to a large extent dependent on economic growth. Sanctions that force companies to disinvest often result in black unemployment as well as lost opportunities to acquire managerial and other business skills. More important, economic stagnation reduces the purchasing power of blacks and forces them into a dependent position. In some cases, local companies that acquire foreign firms may simply ignore equal employment guidelines and reintroduce some apartheid practices in the work place. When Mobil decided to leave South Africa in 1989 representatives of the Chemical Industrial Union, which represented Mobil's employees, claimed that the sale of Mobil's assets to General Mining and Union Corporation would actually strengthen apartheid.[7] This is due in part to the way in which Mobil divested. Few blacks are financially capable of buying major shares of divesting companies. However, corporations such as Ford made it possible for the black community and black employees to benefit from the transfer of assets and arranged for employees to participate in future management of the company. Twenty-four percent of Ford's equity was vested in a trust, through which employees are to own shares of the firm. The dividends of the trust are to be allocated to development projects nationwide.[8] Ford's approach clearly suggests that economic sanctions are not necessarily incompatible with black empowerment. However, this example is the exception rather than the rule.

In light of widespread poverty in southern Africa, the nonsuperpowers' emphasis on black empowerment through economic growth should be given serious consideration by U.S. policymakers. By allowing blacks to hold more responsible positions and to enhance their economic power, foreign firms can play a crucial role in bringing about a relatively peaceful transformation of South Africa's political system. Employed blacks, working as equals with their white counterparts, will eventually develop social bonds that will contribute to the erosion of the racial stereotypes that undergird the apartheid system. Considering the other alternatives, economic and social empowerment is probably the best way to give blacks the confidence that will enable them to refuse to participate in their own victimization. The strategy of black empowerment shifts the responsibility for change away from Pretoria to ordinary black and white South Africans.

The economic and political interdependence of southern African states must be taken into consideration when analyzing the foreign policies of the nonsuperpowers toward South Africa. In a region where there is already debilitating poverty and violence, the primary emphasis of countries interested in helping the area should be economic growth and stability. The almost universal consensus on the imperative of peaceful change in South Africa facilitates efforts to rebuild the infrastructure destroyed by Renamo and opens up the possibility of involving South Africa in arrangements designed to restabilize the Frontline States. There are no short-term solutions to the chronic problems of the region that will be supported by the nonsuperpowers, but the historical, economic, cultural, and family ties between the Frontline States and South Africa suggest that the problem of apartheid must be addressed within a regional context. While this comprehensive approach certainly complicates the choice of strategies to employ against Pretoria and is likely to frustrate those who prefer simple solutions, it is clear that given the realities of southern Africa a peaceful resolution of conflict in South Africa can only be achieved by addressing apartheid in the broader context. Consequently, various strategies aimed at helping to end apartheid must be fine-tuned and carefully applied, bearing in mind that developments in South Africa affect the entire region, a reality often obscured by the rhetoric on both sides of the apartheid issue. Interdependence means that the Frontline States can benefit or lose from actions against South Africa. For example, disinvestment from South Africa is often seen as a possible gain by the Frontline States. Although sanctions have made Pretoria more dependent on Zimbabwe, Swaziland, and Botswana, there is no evidence to suggest that businesses are relocating to these states. On the contrary, there is a significant degree of disinvestment in Zimbabwe, partly because of Mugabe's economic policies. Failure on the part of international aid donors to take a comprehensive approach has also contributed to the problems of the Frontline States. Their inability or unwillingness to provide enough security assistance to the Frontline States to deter Pretoria from destabilizing the region undermines the effectiveness of sanctions in eroding South Africa's self-confidence.[9] The effectiveness of the various countries' policies must be judged not only by the extent to which they satisfy domestic political demands but also by how Pretoria responds to them.

## SOUTH AFRICA'S RESPONSE TO STRATEGIES

Two prevailing myths about sanctions are that: (1) they will not work because Pretoria will find other suppliers and become more self-sufficient, and (2) sanctions will end apartheid. The reality is far more complex than both of these views suggest; sanctions have had an impact on South Africans and they are being circumvented to some extent. Even though sanctions alone cannot force Pretoria to abandon apartheid in the near future, outside pressure can be instrumental in stimulating meaningful change, as long as the interests of all South Africans are taken into consideration. The timing of outside intervention is crucial: outside pressure is more likely to be efficacious if it supplements internal forces, especially at time when the government is distracted and losing legitimacy.[10] Despite the fact that sanctions have not created a serious recession in South Africa, they undoubtedly played a role in influencing Pretoria to cease military operations in Angola, to negotiate Namibia's independence, to release Nelson Mandela and other political prisoners, to unban the ANC, to negotiate with opposition leaders, to integrate some public facilities, and to reconsider the high costs of maintaining apartheid. The expense of keeping South African troops in Angola and public sensitivity to escalating white casualties only exacerbated problems caused by sanctions. Furthermore, sanctions helped to underscore the fact that apartheid itself was already causing economic hardship for whites and was detrimental to the country's economic growth. Failure to gain access to external capital markets and a reduction in exports only made the situation worse. Pretoria has responded by becoming more self-sufficient, circumventing sanctions, restricting the outflow of funds, adopting a strategy of "inward industrialization," destabilizing its neighbors, and implementing changes that do not threaten white political power.

Since the early 1960s Pretoria has attempted to reduce its dependence on external markets while simultaneously trying to gain legitimacy in Africa and the West. In response to the 1963 U.N. arms embargo, South Africa, with the assistance of states such as Britain, Israel, West Germany, and France, developed an arms industry that has made that country essentially self-sufficient in some areas as well as an exporter of military weapons. Yet the costs of evading international sanctions to obtain needed technical know-how and spare parts have been very high. Indeed, preoccupation with security concerns clearly contributed to the country's economic problems. Efforts to achieve economic self-sufficiency have been less successful, partly because South Africa must depend on external markets for its mineral exports, its primary source of foreign exchange.

The principal strategy to counter sanctions is "inward" industrialization, which involves switching from capital-intensive to labor-intensive development in order to prevent further increases in unemployment, to save scarce capital, and to diminish the possibility of urban unrest.[11] But this approach will also help to further the objective of sanctions by stimulating the development of an internal black consumer market and the growth of the black middle class. Inward industrialization will also challenge bureaucratic structures which have been an integral component of the apartheid system and further increase white dependence on black labor, thereby strengthening both black consumers and labor unions. State-controlled corporations such as the Electricity Supply Commission, South Africa Transport Services, the Posts and Telecommunication Service, and the Iron and Steel Corporation, which employ a total of about 400,000 workers, mostly Afrikaners, were considered for privatization by former President Botha in 1988.[12] This development indicated not only a shift from Afrikaner socialist policies but also the growing influence of the Afrikaner and English-speaking business communities in a society in which apartheid is increasingly viewed as an impediment to a healthy economy. And there is a widely held belief in the business community that no strategy will succeed without a normalization of Pretoria's financial relations and the restoration of access to global capital markets. Furthermore, it is generally recognized that forced growth in an artificial environment cannot be sustained indefinitely, and isolation from technological advances will take its toll.[13] These problems are exacerbated by the net outflow of capital, failure to attract new investments, and the emigration of scientists, engineers, computer scientists, accountants, and other skilled white South Africans. To mitigate some of the effects of sanctions, Pretoria has developed a sanctions-busting strategy and is offering incentives to East Europeans, particularly East Germans, to settle in South Africa.

In 1986, during the height of the international sanctions campaign, South Africa created an anti-sanctions and counter-trade unit, which restricted the reporting of any circumvention of sanctions, and stopped publishing export and import statistics.[14] Having had three decades to prepare for sanctions, it is not surprising that South Africa has been able to circumvent many sanctions by relabeling, finding middlemen who are willing to risk the uncertain penalties of trading with South Africa, establishing trading agencies in countries such as Paraguay and Romania, obtaining loans from banks in Switzerland, and setting up "dummy" companies abroad. Furthermore, South Africa's strategic mineral resources and gold continue to be needed by importing countries, and its economic interdependence with the Frontline States provides an opportunity for it to use Swaziland, Lesotho, and other African states as conduits for its imports and exports.[15] And as countries become more concerned about their own economic position vis-à-vis their competitors, some of which actually have increased trade with South Africa since 1987, it is likely that international support for sanctions will diminish. But evading sanctions is expensive for most South Africans.

The effectiveness of the strategies employed by the nonsuperpowers must be measured by their ability to stimulate policy changes in Pretoria. South Africa made a number of significant changes between 1979 and 1990. These include: (1) The Industrial Conciliation Amendment Acts of 1979 and 1981, which extended official recognition to black trade unions and abolished job reservations in all sectors of the economy except mining; (2) the Liquor Amendment Act of 1986, allowing hotel and restaurant owners to serve all races; (3) The Group Areas Amendment Act of 1985, permitting the establishment of free trade areas and the opening of central business districts to businesses of all racial groups; (4) the repeal of the Mixed Marriages Act in 1985; (5) the decision to allow universities to admit students on the basis of academic qualifications only, regardless of race; (6) the amendment of the Black Communities Development Act in 1984, granting permission to black South Africans to acquire property in urban areas designated for blacks and to convert leasehold rights in these areas into ownership rights;[16] (7) the release of Walter Sisulu and other prisoners connected with the ANC; (8) the integration of the country's beaches and public transportation; and (9) the release of Nelson Mandela and the unbanning of the ANC and other anti-apartheid groups in 1990. To what extent have external pressures contributed to these reforms?

Even among the most ardent proponents of sanctions, there is general acceptance of the fact that the South Africans themselves must provide the impetus for change. Clearly, internal dynamics were largely responsible for creating pressures on the political system and for the resulting reforms. Nevertheless, external pressures supplemented internal pressures, thereby contributing to policy changes in South Africa. But the Afrikaners' political misuse of language to label strategies that were obviously designed to consolidate white political power weakened their claim that they were making genuine reforms. Furthermore, increased violence and police brutality made many reforms seem irrelevant to much of the black community and, hence, the international community. Consequently, despite relatively significant changes, the international community called for increased sanctions at a time when Botha was attempting to gain wider domestic conservative acceptance of his reforms. As Merle Lipton observed, "beyond a certain point, sanctions become counterproductive. Escalating sanctions increased Botha's difficulties of political management."[17] Poor timing and the failure of sanctions proponents to try to understand the problem from Botha's viewpoint inadvertently diminished the ability of coercive economic measures to effectuate change in South Africa. Despite escalating sanctions, no major domestic reforms occurred between 1986 and mid-1989. However, de Klerk was viewed as less cautious than Botha and more willing to make changes, such as integrating the beaches and releasing important political prisoners, steps he took in late 1989 and early 1990. In light of the nonsuperpowers' policies and South Africa's response to them, what should U.S. policymakers do?

## Toward a More Efficacious U.S. Policy

Since the end of World War II, American foreign policy has been characterized by an emphasis on preventing Communist expansion and promoting human rights and democratic freedoms around the world, two objectives that have often influenced American foreign policymakers to adopt conflicting policies. In an attempt to check the spread of communism, America has found itself in allliances with regimes whose human rights policies were contrary to basic American values. Failure to clearly define and prioritize American interests all too frequently has resulted in the squandering of U.S. power and credibility in areas that are largely irrelevant to American security and economic interests. The key factor determining American involvement in a particular country has been the presence or potential involvement of the Soviet Union and Cuba. Although the U.S. clearly has wanted to encourage the abolition of apartheid through peaceful means, its preoccupation with communist expansion in Africa has influenced it to regard South Africa as vital to Western security interests, thus giving Pretoria sufficient leverage to persuade Washington that major changes in the status quo would only encourage communist aggression in southern Africa. Struggles for independence in Angola and Mozambique have been misperceived as contests between East and West, with

South Africa in the Western camp. Soviet-Cuban involvement in Angola has only served to muddle this situation.

While President Reagan did not explicitly embrace the Kissinger thesis articulated in Memorandum 39—which stated that white minority regimes in southern Africa would be long-lived and therefore America should be cooperative with them—his policy of "constructive engagement" essentially endorsed the view that blacks were largely marginal to the process of change in South Africa. Violent and non-violent struggles against apartheid were often regarded within the framework of the Soviet-American rivalry. According to Reagan, "opponents of apartheid using terrorism and violence will bring not freedom and salvation, but greater suffering and more opportunities for expanded Soviet influence within South Africa and in the entire region."[18] Apart from the fact that black South Africans were more concerned about apartheid than communism, Reagan's ideological approach seduced him into an alliance with Pretoria to fight communism in Angola by supporting Jonas Savimbi's group, Unita (the Union for the Total Independence of Angola) against the ruling MPLA (Popular Movement for the Liberation of Angola), which was backed by Cuban troops and Soviet weapons. But America's cooperation with South Africa was not only inconsistent with its strong abhorrence of apartheid but also led Pretoria to conclude that its racial policies were less troublesome than communism as far as Washington was concerned. The Reagan Administration's close ties to the white minority regime, its indifference to South African blacks, its opposition to sanctions against Pretoria, and its reliance on economic growth to stimulate change influenced domestic and international anti-apartheid groups to focus on the most negative interpretation of the policy of "constructive engagement," outlined by Chester Crocker, who later became Assistant Secretary of State for African Affairs.[19] Perhaps more important, Reagan seemed to have ignored that Americans' commitment to racial equality at home was strong enough to influence them to oppose South Africa when they perceived that racial justice and human rights were at stake. Furthermore, the American black community, human rights organizations, churches, university students, and shareholders effectively mobilized public opinion against apartheid as South Africa ruthlessly repressed black demonstrators. Television pictures from South Africa were too painful a reminder of America's own civil rights struggles to be ignored. Failure to take domestic opinion into account significantly contributed to the demise of constructive engagement by 1986, shifted power to initiate policy toward South Africa away from the Executive to Congress, and led to the passage of the comprehensive Anti-Apartheid Act of 1986 over the President's veto. But America's sanctions were not fully embraced by even its closest ally, Britain. Thatcher continued to oppose economic sanctions.

The policies of the nonsuperpowers, especially those of Britain, West Germany, Japan, and Israel, have serious implications for America's policy toward South Africa. It is obvious that normal economic relations between the nonsuperpowers and South Africa will reduce the intended effect of sanctions imposed by the United States. Yet economic interests prompt many countries to take a radically different view than that of the United States on the utilization of economics as an instrument of foreign policy. Lacking huge internal markets, Western European nations and Japan must trade in order to maintain healthy economies and are therefore more adamant than the United States about separating politics from economics in their international relations. The experiences of Britain, West Germany, and Japan during the Second World War continue to directly affect their view of business, which played the leading role in the reconstruction and economic expansion of these societies. The ruling elites generally share the belief that government should not restrict business operations abroad, especially in light of the competitive nature of global economic relations. To a large extent, economic power has become a substitute for military power in a world in which the use of force by major countries against each other is ultimately suicidal. But for Israel, economic growth and military power are inseparable due to that country's national security dilemmas. In order to guarantee its survival, Israel cooperates with Pretoria in commercial and military matters. Israel's special relationship with the United States and its access to American military technology virtually guarantee Pretoria access to products that the United States itself is prohibited from exporting to South Africa under the Comprehensive Anti-Apartheid Act of 1986. Although Israel has promised not to renew existing military contracts with South Africa, there is no certainty about when those contracts will expire. These realities undoubtedly complicate U.S. policy toward South Africa. However, America can influence its allies to adopt measures that could encourage change in South Africa.

Any U.S. effort to obtain the cooperation of Japan, Britain, West Germany, and Israel will have to take into consideration the underlying interests of those countries and the domestic constraints on their foreign policy choices. This means that America must carefully choose strategies that are consistent with its own interests and objectives as well as those of its allies. While apartheid has an inescapable resonance in American politics because of the country's history, ethnic and racial diversity, its commitment to equality, and its ongoing struggle to end discrimination, not all countries regard the South African problem as a major foreign policy concern. Neither Japan nor Germany will sacrifice their economic interests; furthermore, the racial homogeneity of those societies and their attitudes toward race militate against apartheid becoming a major domestic issue. Nonetheless, both countries are sensitive to being perceived as supporters of racial domination in South Africa. If Washington and Moscow can cooperate to reduce tensions in southern Africa, West Germany and Japan will find it more difficult to hide behind the United States and to escape closer international scrutiny of their South African policies. Moreover,

Japan's willingness to play a greater role in international politics could facilitate U.S. attempts to involve it in concerted strategies designed to influence change in South Africa.

Despite America's leadership position in the Western alliance, there are several serious problems which could ultimately diminish its ability to persuade its partners to support its policy on South Africa.[20] A major obstacle to cooperation is the failure of American policymakers to resolve internal conflicts on U.S. policy. Until Congress and the President can iron out their differences and speak with one voice, Western Europeans and the Japanese will find it easy to stand behind whichever American position they prefer. Another problem that U.S. policymakers must address is the budget deficit. As long as other countries perceive American leaders as irresponsible, they will be reluctant to follow America's suggestions on South Africa. This situation is complicated by the fragmentation of a bipolar world, demonstrated by significant changes in Eastern Europe, that is likely to undermine traditional sources of American influence in Europe. It is crucial therefore for the United States to demonstrate greater political maturity in order to be an effective leader of the nonsuperpowers. Finally, trade disputes between America and its allies and the integration of European markets in 1992 can only impede U.S. endeavors to persuade its allies to implement major economic sanctions against Pretoria. Moves toward the unification of Europe are likely to have a significant impact on postwar political and economic configurations, and U.S. policy toward South Africa will be affected by these developments. In light of the South African policies of the nonsuperpowers and realities within South Africa in particular and in the Frontline States in general, American policymakers should consider the following suggestions.

*Negotiate a Unified U.S. Position.* Although conflict between Congress and the Executive is almost inevitable under the constitutional framework, serious policy differences can be worked out through negotiations between the two branches of government. President Reagan's refusal to compromise on South African issues destroyed the consensus achieved by President Carter and inadvertently encouraged ideological extremists to deprive the State Department of its legitimate role in policy formulation. Domestic polarization on major foreign policy issues not only weakens U.S. credibility but also erodes its ability to influence its allies. More important, the failure of the American government to speak with one voice sends confusing messages to Pretoria. The more conciliatory approach of the Bush administration has lessened tensions between the White House and Congress on the issue of South Africa. Congress must realize that economic sanctions are blunt instruments that are not appropriate for every situation. The president, on the other hand, will have to take a firm and unequivocal position against apartheid in order to obtain congressional and public support. Given the fact that apartheid is an emotive issue in domestic politics, one that reminds Americans of their own struggles for racial equality, sanctions against South Africa will be an important component of U.S. policy. Consultations between the two branches of government can narrow their differences and facilitate the achievement of a clear, unambiguous U.S. policy toward Pretoria. It is only when this is realized that America will have the credibility essential for persuading its allies to develop a joint position on South Africa.[21]

*Relate Strategies to Objectives.* Disunity between the Executive and Congress exacerbates the problems involved in trying to relate policy instruments to specific policy objectives. Policymakers must have clear, identifiable goals in mind when deciding to apply sanctions, and they must relate the kinds of sanctions to be used to specific changes they would like Pretoria to make. Only when this is done can policymakers determine if the measures were effective and the conditions under which they should be lifted. To simply call for more sanctions before carefully evaluating the effectiveness of those already in force is to seriously erode the utility of sanctions as instruments of foreign policy. Regular consultations between Congress and the Executive are likely to build the communication and cooperation essential for fine-tuning strategies.

*Work With the Allies.* Although it is generally assumed that comprehensive sanctions would be more effective than unilateral measures, the difficulties in achieving a coordinated response are often underestimated or overlooked. The underlying interests of different countries are not always compatible, and many governments do not view the situation in South Africa with an equal sense of urgency. Moreover, U.S. efforts to achieve consensus on South Africa must be balanced against other competing interests. As James Barber observed, "southern Africa could become a source of tension within the Western camp, and a problem of alliance management which could overspill to strain Western cooperation in other areas."[22] The American practice of generally deciding first and consulting its allies later has already created strain in its relationship with Western Europeans. U.S. pressure on its European partners to join trade boycotts and economic sanctions against the Soviet Union in 1980 after the invasion of Afghanistan, against Poland in 1981 following its declaration of martial law, and against Libya in 1983 and 1986 for its alleged involvement in terrorism was resented by the Europeans who believe that sanctions rarely succeed in achieving their stated objectives.[23] This position is buttressed by Europeans' dependence on international trade. Since they are unlikely to support sanctions that might result in unreasonable costs to them, the price of a coordinated Western response may be a policy that deemphasizes punitive measures that are inconsistent with Western European interests. The challenge for U.S. policymakers will be to determine which countries are best suited for implementing particular strategies. In other words, there might have to be a greater emphasis on the specialization of roles. Britain could provide more military assistance and training for the Frontline States, while West Germany, Scandinavia, and Canada could focus on humanitarian aid and on projects designed to contribute to black empowerment. Through consultations with its allies, the United States could reduce the probability of different countries employing strategies that work against each other.

*Involve the Soviet Union.* Soviet-American rivalry is perceived by South Africa as beneficial to its efforts to maintain the status quo at home and to dominate its neighbors. The communist threat, greatly exaggerated, is instrumental in galvanizing public support of the apartheid regime. Cooperation between the superpowers would limit Pretoria's ability to exploit their differences and would also reduce some of the legitimate fears that white South Africans have of communist expansion and support for revolution in southern Africa. Gorbachev's decision to focus on domestic problems and to encourage negotiated settlements of regional conflicts should facilitate Soviet-American cooperation on southern African issues. Although Moscow claimed that its assistance to the ANC would continue, meetings between Soviet and South African officials in Cape Town in early 1989 underscored a shift in Soviet policy away from violent change to peaceful solutions.[24] These developments provide an opportunity for the United States to encourage South Africans to seriously negotiate the country's future.

*Talk With The Opposition.* While peaceful change in South Africa is desirable, given the nature of the conflict and Pretoria's refusal to recognize the legitimate claims of the opponents of apartheid, it is unrealistic not to expect a certain amount of violence. Afrikaner domination is based on the extensive use of violence against those who challenge the status quo. To refuse to talk with the ANC and other opposition groups is to essentially encourage Pretoria to repress them. U.S. policymakers should continue efforts initiated by former Secretary of State George Shultz in 1987 to open a dialogue with the ANC. Reagan's emphasis on working primarily with white South Africans undermined American credibility among black South Africans. By working with black and white South Africans, especially those who are trying to promote peaceful change, the United States can be instrumental in focusing Pretoria's attention on the legitimate objectives of these groups. By late 1989 President Bush had clearly recognized the importance of talking with the opposition, including the ANC. In March 1990 U.S. Secretary of State James Baker met with de Klerk in South Africa and with Mandela in Namibia during that country's independence celebrations.

*Support Regional Development.* Widespread consensus among the non-superpowers on the need to help the Frontline States reduce their vulnerability to economic pressure from South Africa will augment U.S. efforts to promote regional development. The poverty of the entire region is unlikely to allow the various states to counterbalance Pretoria's economic and military power. And since the interdependence of southern Africa effectively links Pretoria's problems to those of the Frontline States, any serious attempt to bring about peaceful change in South Africa must include policies that promote economic development of the region. This clearly suggests a long-term strategy aimed at restabilizing the Frontline States by cooperating with Britain, Canada, Scandinavia, West Germany, and Japan in their attempts to rebuild the infrastructure destroyed by Renamo. However, economic development of South Africa's neighbors could be undermined by sanctions against Pretoria that would ultimately affect the Frontline States. A major U.S. commitment to specific economic projects would favor South African business interests that oppose the destabilization of the region. But given the continued South African backing of Renamo, economic assistance to the Frontline States must be accompanied by military aid and cooperation from Western countries in order to protect the region's infrastructure from sabotage. For the South Africans to be assured that military assistance to its neighbors is for defensive purposes only, the United States and its allies will have to communicate with Pretoria.

*Encourage Communication With South Africa.* Isolating a country effectively eliminates the possibility of influencing its behavior and is generally counterproductive. Canada's decision in 1988 to increase communication with South Africans and to maintain diplomatic relations with Pretoria is extremely significant, especially in light of Canada's role as a leading advocate of sanctions. What is often overlooked is that countries desiring to preserve the status quo actively seek to isolate themselves from the rest of the world. Repression generally thrives in conditions where nations as well as individuals are isolated. The Afrikaners developed their apartheid ideology partly because of their desire to be isolated from others. But technological, social, and economic progress is retarded in societies which close themselves off from others. Instead of discouraging contacts with South Africans, greater efforts must be made to expose them to the outside world through television, contacts with black universities, and international exchanges for young South Africans of all races. Isolation breeds hostility and prejudice and reinforces narrow perceptions of others. Since South Africans will have to live together in a post-apartheid society, communication that will help to build trust and mutual understanding among whites and blacks is of vital importance and therefore should be encouraged.

*Try to Understand Their Perceptions of Reality.* The general tendency to dismiss the fears of the white minority only contributes to their reluctance to focus on how a non-racial South Africa would be in their interest. Greater attention must be given to their legitimate interests and how they perceive reality. Speaking their language, using their vocabulary and rhetoric—their terms of reference—when suggesting policy changes might be far more productive than using hateful rhetoric. The Afrikaners strongly believe that adversity is God's way of testing them and are far more comfortable dealing with threats from those perceived as the enemy.

Understanding how they think is really the first step toward changing their behavior. Working with religious groups and using religion in order to communicate with Afrikaners might be helpful especially in light of the relationship between their religious beliefs and their commitment to apartheid. Similarly, greater use should be made of legal institutions because South Africans generally believe in the rule of law, albeit narrowly defined. Since apartheid is based on law, it is also possible to work through existing legal institutions to change apartheid.

*Stop Funding Unita.* Giving military assistance to Unita not only undermines American efforts to encourage peaceful change in South Africa but also inadvertently legitimizes South Africa's cooperation with Renamo. Failure to resolve the inconsistency between America's commitment to human rights on the one hand and its anti-communist impulses on the other leads to serious contradictions in U.S. foreign policy. This is clearly demonstrated by U.S. support of the extremely violent methods used by Unita in its conflict with the Cuban-backed MPLA and its condemnation of the use of violence by the ANC in its struggle against apartheid. The net result is a confused foreign policy that indirectly supports Pretoria's regional dominance and the status quo in South Africa.

*Support Black Empowerment.* Since the nonsuperpowers strongly support the concept of black empowerment, partly because it does not immediately threaten their economic interests in South Africa, the United States could encourage them to upgrade their efforts. Even though it may be argued that by providing financial and technical assistance to the black community Western countries help to buttress the apartheid system because Pretoria can use resources that would otherwise be allocated for blacks on the military, evidence strongly suggests that strengthening the victims of apartheid is a major strategy for ending oppression. The weak in most societies tend to be oppressed either by government or by other individuals. Black empowerment is essentially about building self-confidence. This can be accomplished through developing ties with black organizations, providing technical training for blacks, funding education, health care, community improvement projects, and opening up job opportunities for blacks. Countries that do not support the use of sanctions as instruments of foreign policy could be persuaded to increase their contributions to projects designed to help blacks. American universities could play a constructive role in the process of black empowerment by providing a significant number of scholarships for South Africans who want to study science, engineering, law, business, and public administration, for example. Efforts to lessen dependence on the state and encourage the emergence of a self-sufficient society are an important means of diminishing the power and credibility of a repressive regime.[25] Regardless of the color or race of those who will govern the post-apartheid society, South Africans will need to empower themselves in order to protect their fundamental freedoms.

In light of the major political changes in Europe and in the Soviet Union itself, American foreign policymakers have an opportunity to concentrate on assisting the promotion of democracy in South Africa without the distraction of the East-West rivalry. But an effective U.S. policy will require cooperation with the nonsuperpowers. For such collaboration to occur, the United States will have to take into consideration the views, traditions, interests, policy constraints, and strategies of the nonsuperpowers.

# NOTES

## 1. THE NONSUPERPOWERS' SOUTH AFRICA POLICIES

1. See Richard J. Payne, *Opportunities and Dangers of Soviet-Cuban Expansion* (Albany, New York: State University of New York Press, 1988), pp. 1–6.
2. T. B. Millar, *Australia's Foreign Policy* (Sydney: Angus and Robertson, Ltd., 1968), p. 40.
3. Alan Tonelson, "The Real National Interest," *Foreign Policy*, no. 61 (Winter 1985–86), p. 49.
4. Donal Nuechterlein, *America Overcommitted: U. S. National Interests in the 1980s* (Lexington, Kentucky: University of Kentucky Press, 1985), p. 10.
5. Ibid.
6. James N. Rosenau, "Introduction," in *The Domestic Sources of Foreign Policy*, ed. James N. Rosenau (New York: Free Press, 1967), p. 2.
7. Charles W. Kegley, Jr. and Eugene R. Wittkopf, "Introduction," in *The Domestic Sources of American Foreign Policy*, eds. Charles W. Kegley, Jr. and Eugene R. Wittkopf (New York: St. Martin's Press, 1988), p. 2.
8. J. E. Spence, "Foreign Policy: Retreat into the Laager," in *South Africa in Crisis*, ed. Jesmond Blumenfeld (London: Croom Helm, 1987), p. 155.
9. Hedley Bull, "Implications for the West," in *Conflict and Compromise in South Africa*, eds. Robert I. Rotberg and John Barratt (Lexington, Mass.: Lexington Books, 1980), p. 176.
10. Tony Koenderman, *Sanctions: The Threat to South Africa* (Johannesburg: Jonathan Ball Publishers, 1982), p. 2.
11. U.S. Department of Commerce, Office of Strategic Resources, Mineral Facts (June 11, 1985).
12. Ibid.
13. Koenderman, *Sanctions*, p. 2.
14. Joseph Hanlon and Roger Omond, *The Sanctions Handbook* (New York: Penguin Books, 1987), p. 247.
15. U.S. Bureau of Mines, U.S. Department of the Interior, *South Africa and Critical Materials, Open File Report 76–86*, July 1986, p. S-3.
16. Hanns W. Maull, "South Africa's Minerals: The Achilles' Heel of Western Economic Security?" *International Affairs* 62 (Autumn 1986), p. 626.
17. Robert M. Price, "Security versus Growth: The International Factor in South Africa's Policy," *The Annals of the American Academy of Political Social Science* 489 (January 1987), p. 113.
18. James Brooke, "Ailing Nigeria Opens Its Economy," *The New York Times*, August 15, 1988, p. D–4.
19. See "Real African Growth Slows in 1987, External Debt Burden Remains Severe," *IMF Survey*, July 11, 1988, p. 232.
20. Sir Geoffrey Howe in *Parliamentary Debates*, Commons, 6th ser., vol. 99 (9 June–20 June, 1986), p. 921.
21. Johan Jorgen Holst, "Introduction," in *Norwegian Foreign Policy in the 1980s*, ed. Johan Jorgen Holst (Oslo: Norwegian University Press, 1985), p. 11.
22. Richard J. Payne, "Canada, South Africa, and the Commonwealth," *International Perspectives* (July–August 1987), pp. 9–12.
23. Robert Hanks, *Southern Africa and Western Security* (Cambridge, Mass.: Institute for Foreign Policy Analysis, 1983), p. 68.

24. Anthony Sampson, *Black and Gold* (New York: Pantheon Books, 1987), p. 61.

25. Passage of the Comprehensive Anti-Apartheid Act in 1986 and its provision for cutting off U.S. military assistance to countries with military ties to South Africa was the catalyst for the change in Israel's policy toward Pretoria.

26. Efraim Inbar, *Outcast Countries in the World Community* (Denver, Colo.: University of Denver Press, 1985), p. 11.

27. Ibid., p. 55.

28. A. M. Johnston, "Domestic Consensus and International Pressures," in *International Pressures and Political Change in South Africa*, ed. F. Clifford-Vaughan (Cape Town: Oxford University Press, 1978), p. 20.

29. Ibid., p. 21.

30. Ross Stagner, "Foreword," in *Ethnic Conflict: International Perspectives*, eds. Jerry Boucher, Dan Landis, and Karen Arnold Clark (Beverly Hills, Calif.: Sage Publications, 1987), p. 9.

31. Teun A. van Dijk, *Communicating Racism* (Beverly Hills, Calif.: Sage Publications, 1987), p. 41.

32. Joseph de Rivera, *The Psychological Dimension of Foreign Policy* (Columbus, Ohio: Charles E. Merrill Publishing Co., 1968), p. 27.

33. Stephen A. Garrett, "Illusion and Reality in Soviet-American Relations," *International Journal on World Peace* 3 (April–June 1986), p. 28.

34. de Rivera, *Psychological Dimension,* p. 22.

35. Arthur Schlesinger, Jr., "Foreign Policy and the American Character," *Foreign Affairs* 46 (Fall 1983), p. 6.

36. Robert I. Rotberg, *Suffer the Future: Policy Choices in Southern Africa* (Cambridge, Mass.: Harvard University Press, 1980), p. 3.

37. Benjamin Sacks, *South Africa: An Imperial Dilemma* (Albuquerque: University of Mexico Press, 1967), p. 4.

38. Amry Vandenbosch, *South Africa and the World* (Lexington, Kentucky: University of Kentucky Press, 1970), p. 14.

39. Rotberg, *Suffer the Future,* p. 31.

40. Leonard Thompson, *The Political Mythology of Apartheid* (New Haven: Yale University Press, 1985), p. 28.

41. Donald G. Baker, *Race, Ethnicity and Power* (London: Routledge and Kegan Paul, 1983), p. 13.

42. Department of Foreign Affairs, *Manifesto for the Future* (Pretoria: The Government Printer, 1985), p. 10.

43. Dean Geldenhuys, *What do We Think? A Survey of White Opinion on Foreign Policy Issues* (Braamfontein: The South African Institute of International Affairs, 1984), p. 7; and Chris Maritz, "Pretoria's Reaction to the Role of Moscow and Peking in Southern Africa," *Journal of Modern African Studies* 250, no. 2 (1987), p. 330.

44. Bureau of Information, *Talking with the ANC* (Pretoria: The Government Printer, 1986), p. 15.

45. M. L. Truu, "Economics and Politics in South Africa Today," *The South African Journal of Economics* 54, no. 4 (1986), p. 357.

46. Larry Diamond, "Roots of Failure, Seeds of Hope," in *Democracy in Developing Countries: Africa*, eds. Larry Diamond, Juan J. Linz, and Seymour Martin Lipset (Boulder, Colo.: Lynne Rienner Publishers, 1988), p. 1.

47. Human Services Research Council, *The South African Society: Realities and Future Prospects* (New York: Greenwood Press, 1987), p. 66.

48. Thompson, *Political Mythology,* p. 215; and Oliver Williams, "The Religious Rationale of Racism," in *The South African Quagmire*, ed. S. Prakash (Cambridge, Mass.: Ballinger Publishing Co., 1987), p. 155.

49. T. Dunbar Moodie, *The Rise of Afrikanerdom: Power, Apartheid, and the Afrikaner Civil Religion* (Berkeley: University of California Press, 1975), p. 1.

50. Ibid., p. 12.

51. Ibid.

52. Thompson, *Political Mythology*, p. 215.

53. George M. Fredrickson, *White Supremacy: A Comparative Study in American and South African History* (New York: Oxford University Press, 1981), p. 236.

54. Ibid., pp. 237–38.

55. Lawrence Schlemmer, "Economy and Society in South Africa," in *Change, Reform and Economic Growth in South Africa*, eds. Lawrence Schlemmer and Eddie Webster (Johannesburg: Ravan Press, 1978), p. 115.

56. Donald Baker, *Race*, p. 31.

57. Schlemmer, "Economy and Society," p. 118.

58. Robert I. Rotberg, "Creating a More Harmonious South Africa," in *Conflict and Compromise in South Africa*, eds. Robert Rotberg and John Barratt (Lexington, Mass.: Lexington Books, 1980), p. 13.

59. Pauline Baker, "South Africa: The Afrikaner Angst," *Foreign Policy*, no. 69 (Winter 1987–88), p. 61.

60. Stanley B. Greenberg, "Economic Growth and Political Change: The South African Case," *The Journal of Modern African Studies* 19, no. 4 (1981), p. 696.

61. Department of Manpower Utilization, *Report of the National Manpower Commission on High-Level Manpower* (Pretoria: Republic of South Africa, 1980), p. viii; and J. C. Van Zyl, "South Africa: Business Bears Down," *Africa Report* (March–April 1986), p. 65.

62. Thompson, *Political Mythology*, p. 192.

63. Van Zyl, "Business Bears Down," p. 65.

64. Gavin Relly, "The Costs of Disinvestment," *Foreign Policy*, no. 63 (Summer 1986), pp. 132–33.

65. Press statement by Die Afrikaanse Handelsinstituut, Association of Chambers of Commerce of South Africa, Chamber of Mines of South Africa, National African Federation of Chambers of Commerce, Federated Chamber of Industries, and Steel and Engineering Industries Federation of South Africa, March 14, 1985.

66. Rotberg, *Suffer the Future*, pp. 73–75.

67. Patrick Laurence, "Breaking With Pretoria," *The Christian Science Monitor*, May 19, 1988, p. 1.

68. Michele A. Flournoy and Kurt M. Campbell, "South Africa's Bomb: A Military Option," *Orbis* 32 (Summer 1988), p. 391.

69. Craig Charney, "The National Party: A Class Alliance in Crisis," in *The State of Apartheid*, ed. Wilmot G. James (Boulder, Colo.: Lynne Rienner Publishers, 1987), p. 24.

70. Ibid.

71. Pauline Baker, "Afrikaner Angst," p. 71.

72. John Battersby, "More Whites in South Africa are Resisting the Military Draft," *The New York Times*, March 28, 1988, p. 8.

73. Ibid.

74. Pauline Baker, "Afrikaner Angst," p. 74; and William W. Pascoe, "U.S. Sanctions on South Africa: The Results Are In," *The Backgrounder*, no. 584 (June 1987), p. 4.

75. Thompson, *Political Mythology*, p. 236; and Peter Vale, "Simple-mindedness and Repression: The Establishment Responds to South Africa's Woes," *The Round Table* (July 1987), p. 313.

76. Frederick H. Hartman, *The New Age of American Foreign Policy* (New York: Macmillan Co., 1970), p. 10; Payne, *Soviet-Cuban Expansion*, p. 14; and Roger Fisher,

*Dear Israelis, Dear Arabs: A Working Approach to Peace* (New York: Harper and Row, 1972), p. 19.

77. Payne, *Soviet-Cuban Expansion,* p. 15.

78. John Day, "A Failure of Foreign Policy: The Case of Rhodesia," in *Constraints and Adjustments in British Foreign Policy,* ed. Michael Leiter (London: George Allen and Unwin, Ltd., 1976), p. 150.

79. Robert O. Keohane and Joseph S. Nye, *Power and Interdependence: World Politics in Transition* (Boston: Little, Brown and Co., 1977), p. 8.

80. Brent D. Wilson, *Disinvestment of Foreign Subsidiaries* (Ann Arbor: University of Michigan Research Press, 1980), p. 8.

81. Margaret Doxey, "International Sanctions: Trials of Strength or Weakness," *Millennium: Journal of International Studies* 12, no. 1 (Spring 1983), pp. 77–87.

82. Miroslav Nincic and Peter Wallensteen, "Economic Coercion and Foreign Policy," in *Dilemmas of Economic Coercion: Sanctions in World Politics,* eds. Miroslav Nincic and Peter Wallensteen (New York: Praeger, 1983), p. 2.

83. David F. Gordon, "The Politics of International Sanctions: A Case Study of South Africa," in *Dilemmas of Economic Coercion,* Nincic and Wallensteen, p. 185.

84. David A. Baldwin, *Economic Statecraft* (Princeton, N.J.: Princeton University Press, 1985), p. 63.

85. Harold D. Lasswell and Abraham Kaplan, *Power and Society: A Framework for Political Inquiry* (New Haven: Yale University Press, 1950), pp. xviii, 10–11.

86. Lawrence J. Brady, "The Utility of Economic Sanctions as a Policy Instrument," in *The Utility of International Economic Sanctions,* ed. David Leyton-Brown (New York: St. Martin's Press, 1987), p. 298.

87. Baldwin, *Economic Statecraft,* p. 121.

88. William Minter, "South Africa: Straight Talk on Sanctions," *Foreign Policy,* no. 65 (Winter 1986–87), p. 45.

89. Robin Renwick, *Economic Sanctions* (Cambridge, Mass.: Harvard University Press, 1981), p. 79.

90. Hanlon and Omond, *Sanctions Handbook,* p. 13.

91. Gene Sharp, *Social Power and Political Freedom* (Boston: Porter Sargeant Publishers, Inc., 1980), p. 217; and Peter Lambley, *The Psychology of Apartheid* (London: Secker and Warburg, 1980), pp. 251–52.

92. Sharp, *Social Power,* p. 177.

93. Donald G. Baker, *Race,* p. 196.

94. Ibid.

95. Sharp, *Social Power,* p. 173.

96. Michael Clough, "Southern Africa: Challenges and Choices," *Foreign Affairs* 66 (Summer 1988), p. 1082.

97. Ameen Akhalwaya, "South Africa: Interview with Tony Bloom," *Africa Report* (March–April 1988), p. 64.

98. Stanley B. Greenberg, "Economic Growth and Political Change: The South African Case," *The Journal of Modern African Studies* 19, no. 4 (1981), p. 680.

99. Christopher Coker, "Collective Bargaining as an Internal Sanction," *Journal of Modern African Studies* 19, no. 4 (1981), p. 650.

100. Merle Lipton, "Reform: Destruction or Modernization of Apartheid," in *South Africa in Crisis,* ed. Jesmond Blumenfeld (London: Croom Helm, 1987), p. 55.

101. State President, Mr. P. W. Botha, *The Road Ahead* (Pretoria: The Government Printer, January 1985), p. 2.

102. John D. Battersby, "Botha Warns Right on Resegregation, *The New York Times,* November 15, 1988, p. A-5.

## 2. Britain

1. James Barber, *The Uneasy Relationship: Britain and South Africa* (London: Heinemann, 1983), p. 8.

2. Geoffrey Berridge, *Economic Power in Anglo-South African Diplomacy* (London: Macmillan Press, Ltd., 1981), p. 3.

3. Barber, *The Uneasy Relationship,* p. 92.

4. Foreign and Commonwealth Office, *Perspectives on Africa* (New York: British Information Services, 1988), p. 14.

5. Barber, *The Uneasy Relationship,* p. 92.

6. James Barber, Jesmond Blumenfeld, and Christopher Hill, *The West and South Africa* (London: Routledge and Kegan Paul, 1982), p. 3.

7. Martin Holland, "The European Community and South Africa," *Political Studies* 33 (Fall 1985), p. 400.

8. Barber, Blumenfeld, and Hill, *Africa,* p. 1.

9. Wolfram F. Hanrieder and Graeme P. Auton, *The Foreign Policies of West Germany, France, and Britain* (Englewood Cliffs, New Jersey: Prentice-Hall, Inc., 1980), p. 274.

10. James Barber, *Who Makes British Foreign Policy?* (London: The Open University Press, 1976), p. 28.

11. Hanrieder and Auton, *Foreign Policies,* p. 273.

12. Martin Edmonds, "British Foreign Policy," *Current History* 83 (April 1984), p. 158.

13. Barber, *British Foreign Policy,* p. 39.

14. See Robert J. Lieber, "British Foreign Policy: The Limits of Maneuver," in *Foreign Policy in World Politics,* ed. Roy C. Macridis (Englewood Cliffs, New Jersey: Prentice-Hall, Inc., 1985), p. 13.

15. William Wallace, *The Foreign Policy Process in Britain* (London: The Royal Institute for International Affairs, 1977), p. 160.

16. Berridge, *Economic Power,* p. 3.

17. Ibid., p. 14.

18. Lieber, "Limits of Maneuver," p. 16.

19. Ibid., p. 17.

20. Julian Baum, "Britain's Economic Lion is Strong and Roaring," *The Christian Science Monitor,* May 17, 1988, p. 1.

21. David R. Francis, "Britain's New Economic Muscle Brings Respect," *The Christian Science Monitor,* Oct. 15, 1989, p. 12.

22. Barber, *British Foreign Policy,* p. 11.

23. Wallace, *Foreign Policy Process,* p. 88; and Hanrieder and Auton, *Foreign Policies,* p. 272.

24. Ibid., pp. 89–90.

25. Ibid., p. 107.

26. Barber, *The Uneasy Relationship,* p. 2; and Graham Leach, *South Africa: No Easy Path to Peace* (London: Routledge and Kegan Paul, 1986), p. 225.

27. *Parliamentary Debates,* Commons, 6th ser., vol. 119 (July 6–July 17, 1987), p. 211 (w).

28. Barber, *The Uneasy Relationship,* p. 56.

29. Ibid.

30. Craig R. Whitney, "Labor Movement in Britain Ousts a Major Union, *The New York Times,* Sept. 6, 1988, p. A-3.

31. Deon Geldenhuys, *Diplomacy of Isolation: South African Foreign Policy Making* (New York: St. Martin's Press, 1984), p. 114.

32. *Parliamentary Debates,* Commons, 6th ser., vol. 102 (July 7–July 18, 1986), p. 1020.

33. Barrie Axford, "United Kingdom," in *International Handbook on Race and Race Relations*, ed. Jay A. Sigler (New York: Greenwood Press, 1987), p. 371.

34. Zig Layton-Henry, *The Politics of Race in Britain* (London: George Allen and Unwin, 1984), p. 176.

35. Axford, "United Kingdom," p. 338.

36. Harm J. de Blij, *South Africa* (Evanston: Northwestern University Press, 1962), p. 28.

37. Benjamin Sacks, *South Africa: An Imperial Dilemma* (Albuquerque: University of Mexico Press, 1967), p. 4.

38. Ibid.

39. de Blij, *South Africa*, p. 44.

40. Robert I. Rotberg, *Suffer the Future: Policy Choices in Southern Africa* (Cambridge, Mass.: Harvard University Press, 1980), p. 30.

41. Jeffrey Butler, "The German Factor in Anglo-Transvaal Relations," in *Britain and Germany in Africa: Imperial Rivalry and Colonial Rule*, eds. Prosser Gifford and Roger Louis (New Haven: Yale University Press, 1967), p. 190.

42. Leonard Thompson, "Great Britain and the Afrikaner Republics," in *The Oxford History of South Africa*, vol. 2, eds. Monica Wilson and Leonard Thompson (Oxford: The Clarendon Press, 1971), pp. 312–13.

43. de Blij, *South Africa*, p. 55.

44. Thompson, "Great Britain," p. 318.

45. de Blij, *South Africa*, p. 56.

46. Rotberg, *Suffer the Future*, p. 32.

47. Ibid.

48. Francis Pym, "Strains Among Friends: Coordinating Western Policy Toward South Africa," in *Europe, America and South Africa*, ed. Gregory F. Treverton (New York: Council on Foreign Relations, 1988), p. 23.

49. Michael O'Neill, "Heads of Government Meetings," in *The Commonwealth in the 1980s: Challenges and Opportunities*, eds. A. J. R. Groom and Paul Taylor (London: Macmillan Press, Ltd., 1984), p. 190.

50. Berridge, *Economic Power*, p. 124.

51. Ibid., p. 132; and Paul Taylor, "The Continuing Commonwealth," in *The Commonwealth in the 1980s*, Groom and Taylor, p. 6.

52. Richard E. Bissell, *Apartheid and International Organizations* (Boulder, Colo.: Westview Press, 1977), p. 47.

53. O'Neill, "Government Meetings," p. 194.

54. Sir Geoffrey Howe, "Britain and the Commonwealth Today," *The Round Table*, no. 289 (January 1984), p. 8.

55. Timothy Raison, MP, "Development and the Commonwealth: New Challenges," *The Round Table*, no. 296 (October 1985), p. 313.

56. Taylor, *The Commonwealth in the 1980s*, p. 314.

57. "Commonwealth Accord on Southern Africa," adopted at Lyford Cay, October 20, 1985. Reprinted in *Africa Research Bulletin*, November 15, 1985, p. 7811.

58. Dennis Austin, *The Commonwealth and Britain* (London: Routledge and Kegan Paul, 1988), p. 75.

59. A. G. Jordan and J. J. Richardson, *Government and Pressure Groups in Britain* (Oxford: The Clarendon Press, 1987), p. 87.

60. William Minter, *King Solomon's Mines Revisited: Western Interests and the Burdened History of Southern Africa* (New York: Basic Books, Inc., 1986), p. 187.

61. Martin Holland, *The European Community and South Africa: European Political Cooperation Under Strain* (London: Pinter Publishers, 1988), p. 100.

62. John de St. Jorre, *South Africa's Non-United States Economic Links*, Africa Notes, no. 43 (Washington, D.C.: Center for Strategic and International Studies, 1985), p. 1.

63. Barber, *The Uneasy Relationship*, p. 72.

64. Barbara Rodgers and Brian Bolton, *Sanctions Against South Africa: Exploding the Myths* (Manchester: Manchester Free Press, 1981), p. 50.

65. Holland, "European Community," p. 408.

66. Commonwealth Experts Group, *Statistics on Trade with South Africa* (Ottawa: Government of Canada, 1988), p. 10. Given the secrecy surrounding commercial transaction with South Africa, one should interpret these figures with caution. A very large drop in South African imports in 1985 and 1986, caused partly by financial sanctions, was followed by an increase in 1987. The U.S. dollar's decline may also make the increase of sales to South Africa appear smaller.

67. Shipping Research Bureau, *The European Community and the Oil Embargo Against South Africa* (Amsterdam: Shipping Research Bureau, 1987), p. 9.

68. Ibid.

69. Commonwealth Expert Group, *Statistics on Trade with South Africa*, p. 10.

70. Minter, *King Solomon's Mines*, p. 216.

71. Holland, *The European Community and South Africa*, p. 100.

72. W. Geoffrey Hamilton, "Western European TNCs in South Africa," *CTC Reporter* (Spring 1987), p. 42.

73. Rogers and Bolton, *Exploding the Myths*, p. 78.

74. Oye Ogunbadejo, *The International Policy of Africa's Strategic Minerals* (Westport, Conn.: Greenwood Press, 1985), pp. 63–64.

75. The Anti-Apartheid Movement, *Sanctions Begin to Bite* (London: Anti-Apartheid Movement, 1987), p. 21.

76. Hamilton, "TNCs in South Africa," p. 41.

77. Code of Conduct for Companies from the E.C. with Subsidiaries in South Africa as Revised November 19, 1985 by the Ministers of Foreign Affairs of the Ten Countries of the European Community and Spain and Portugal.

78. Martin Holland, "The EEC Code for South Africa: A Reassessment," *The World Today* (January 1985), p. 13.

79. Olajide Aluko, "Nigeria, Namibia, and Southern Africa," in *Southern Africa in the 1980s*, eds. Olajide Aluko and Timothy M. Shaw (London: George Allen and Unwin, 1985), p. 55.

80. Barber, *The Uneasy Relationship*, p. 19.

81. Business International South Africa, *Apartheid and Business: An Analysis of the Rapidly Evolving Challenge Facing Companies with Investments in South Africa* (Pretoria: Business International South Africa, October 1980), p. 445.

82. Ibid., p. 46.

83. Barber, *The Uneasy Relationship*, p. 1.

84. Ibid., p. 4.

85. Ibid.

86. de St. Jorre, *Non-U.S. Economic Links*, p. 1.

87. The Anti-Apartheid Movement, *Sanctions Begin to Bite*, p. 21.

88. *Parliamentary Debates*, Commons, 6th ser., vol. 99 (June 9–June 20, 1986), p. 930.

89. Christopher Coker, *NATO, The Warsaw Pact and Africa* (New York: St. Martin's Press, 1985), p. 75.

90. Ibid.

91. Clarence G. Redekop, "Trudeau at Singapore: The Commonwealth and Arms Sales to South Africa," in *An Acceptance of Paradox: Essays on Canadian Diplomacy in Honour of John W. Holmes* (Toronto: Canadian Institute of International Affairs, 1982), p. 175.

92. Wallace, *Foreign Policy Process*, p. 152.

93. Coker, *NATO*, p. 77.

94. Redekop, "Trudeau," p. 176; and Coker, *NATO*, p. 78.

95. Isebill V. Gruhn, *British Arms Sales to South Africa: The Limits of African Diplomacy* (Denver, Colo.: University of Denver Press, 1972), p. 6; and Redekop, "Trudeau," p. 175.

96. Coker, *NATO,* p. 81; and Redekop, "Trudeau," p. 190.

97. *Parliamentary Debates,* Commons, 6th ser., vol. 99 (June 9–June 20, 1986), p. 471(w).

98. *Parliamentary Debates,* Commons, 6th ser., vol. 120 (July 20–Oct. 23, 1987), p. 572(w).

99. Anthony Sampson, *Black and Gold* (New York: Pantheon Books, 1987), p. 217.

100. Lynne Curry, "British Companies Find it Hard to Cut Big South African Stakes," *The Christian Science Monitor,* March 12, 1987, p. 19.

101. "Arms Smugglers Gaoled," *Africa Research Bulletin,* August 15, 1985, p. 7727.

102. *Parliamentary Debates,* Commons, 6th Ser., vol. 113 (March 23–April 3, 1987), p. 632(w).

103. Margaret P. Doxey, *International Sanctions in Contemporary Perspective* (New York: St. Martin's Press, 1987), p. 137.

104. Foreign and Commonwealth Office, *Perspectives on Africa,* p. 13; and the British Embassy, *The Case Against Economic Sanctions* (Washington, D.C.: British Embassy, 1985), p. 1.

105. *Parliamentary Debates,* Commons, 6th ser., vol. 99 (June 9–June 20, 1986), p. 921.

106. Ibid., p. 929.

107. *Parliamentary Debates,* Commons, 6th ser., vol. 102 (July 7–July 18, 1986), p. 1031.

108. Joseph Hanlon and Roger Omond, *The Sanctions Handbook* (New York: Penguin Books, 1987), pp. 136–37.

109. "More Questions After Sanctions," *The Economist,* June 21, 1986, p. 53.

110. Gary Yerkey, "Britain Thwarts Sanctions Bid by Western Europe," *The Christian Science Monitor,* June 18, 1986, p. 9.

111. "Sir Geoffrey's Mission," *Africa Research Bulletin,* July 15, 1986, p. 8135.

112. "U.K. Concedes on Sanctions," *Africa Research Bulletin,* October 15, 1986, p. 7792.

113. Martin Holland, "The European Community and South Africa: In Search of a Policy for the 1990s," *International Affairs* 64 (Summer 1988), p. 418.

114. British Embassy, *Case Against Economic Sanctions,* p. 2.

115. Ibid.

116. Francis Pym, "Strains Among Friends," p. 40.

117. Foreign and Commonwealth Office, *Perspectives on Africa,* p. 15.

118. "Meeting with ANC," *Africa Research Bulletin,* July 15, 1986, p. 8135.

119. *Parliamentary Debates,* Commons, 6th ser., vol. 99 (June 9–June 20, 1986), p. 317.

120. Foreign and Commonwealth Office, *Perspectives on Africa,* p. 15; and Christopher Patten, "Britain and Africa's Development," *The Round Table,* no. 303 (July 1987), p. 342.

121. Joseph Hanlon, *Beggar Your Neighbor: Apartheid Power in Southern Africa* (Bloomington, Indiana: Indiana University Press, 1986), p. 41.

122. *Parliamentary Debates,* Commons, 6th ser., vol. 99 (June 9–June 20, 1986), p. 493.

123. "Mozambique-U.K.: Military Training," *Africa Research Bulletin,* August 15, 1985, p. 7726.

124. Karl Maier, "Rag-tag Mozambican Army Gets Boost from British Trainers," *The Christian Science Monitor,* October 21, 1987, p. 7.

## 3. West Germany

1. Maurice Cranston, "Are There Any Human Rights?" *Daedalus* 112 (Fall 1983), p. 5.

2. Lily Gardener Feldman, *The Special Relationship Between West Germany and Israel* (Boston: George Allen and Unwin, 1984), p. 1.

3. The Federal Government, *Reply to the Interpellation of the SDP Parliamentary Group on the Government Policy in Southern Africa* (Bonn, December 20, 1983), p. 5.

4. Wolfram F. Hanrieder, *The Stable Crisis: Two Decades of German Foreign Policy* (New York: Harper and Row, 1970), p. 45.

5. Ibid., p. 1.

6. Ibid., p. 51.

7. Josef Joffee, "The Foreign Policy of the Federal Republic of Germany," in *Foreign Policy in World Politics*, ed. Roy C. Macridis (Englewood Cliffs, New Jersey: Prentice-Hall, Inc., 1985), p. 78. For a general discussion of this issue see Charles Burdick et al., *Contemporary Germany: German Politics and Culture* (Boulder, Colo.: Westview Press, 1984).

8. Hanrieder, *Stable Crisis*, p. 130.

9. Nicholas Van Praag, "European Political Cooperation and Southern Africa," in *European Political Cooperation: Towards a Foreign Policy for Western Europe*, eds. David Allen, Reinhardt Rummel, and Wolfgang Wessels (London: Butterworth Scientific, 1982), p. 134.

10. Joffee, "Foreign Policy," p. 105.

11. Ibid.; and Richard J. Payne, *Opportunities and Dangers of Soviet-Cuban Expansion* (Albany, New York: State University of New York Press, 1988), p. 64.

12. Berndt von Staden, "Perspectives of German Foreign Policy," *Aussenpolitik: German Foreign Affairs Review* 36 (1st Quarter 1985), p. 16.

13. Jochem Thies, "West German Foreign Policy: An Old Tune With New Notes," *The World Today* (June 1987), p. 105.

14. Diane Rosolowsky, *West Germany's Foreign Policy: The Impact of the Social Democrats and the Greens* (New York: Greenwood Press, 1987), p. 69.

15. Peter H. Merkl, *German Foreign Policies, West and East* (Santa Barbara, Calif.: ABC-Clio Press, 1974), p. 203.

16. Rolf Hofmeier, "West Germany and Africa," in *Africa Contemporary Record*, ed. Colin Legum (New York: Africana Publishing Co., 1987), p. A257.

17. William Minter, *King Solomon's Mines Revisited: Western Interests and the Burdened History of Southern Africa* (New York: Basic Books, Inc., 1986), p. 323.

18. Klaus Freiherr von der Ropp, "Republic of South Africa: Victory of the Counter-Revolution?" *Aussenpolitik: German Foreign Affairs Review* 39 (3rd Quarter 1988), p. 296; and Wolfgang Kunath, "Genscher and Strauss—At Cross Purposes in Africa," *The German Tribune*, Feb. 7, 1988, p. 2.

19. Thies, "An Old Tune," p. 103.

20. Hofmeier, "West Germany," p. A257.

21. Von der Ropp, "Counter-Revolution," p. 296.

22. "Kohl: No Change in Bonn's Africa Policy," *The Week in Germany*, Feb. 5, 1988, p. 1.

23. Wolfram F. Hanrieder and Graeme P. Auton, *The Foreign Policies of West Germany, France, and Britain* (Englewood Cliffs, New Jersey: Prentice-Hall, Inc., 1980), p. 295.

24. Lewis J. Edinger, *Politics in West Germany* (Boston: Little, Brown and Co., 1977), p. 65.

25. Joan Pearce and John Sutton, *Protection and Industrial Policy in Europe* (London:

Routledge and Kegan Paul, 1986), p. 77; and Christopher S. Allen, "Germany: Competing Communitarianisms," in *Ideology and National Competitiveness*, eds. George C. Lodge and Ezra Vogel (Boston: Harvard Business School Press, 1987), p. 87.

26. Ulrich Albrecht, "The Policy of the Federal Republic of Germany Towards the South," in *The Foreign Policy of West Germany*, eds. Ekkehart Krippendorff and Volker Rittberger (London: Sage Publications, 1980), p. 177.

27. Peter J. Katzenstein, *Policy and Politics in West Germany: The Growth of a Semisovereign State* (Philadelphia: Temple University Press, 1987), p. 83.

28. Albrecht, "Policy," p. 179.

29. Joachim Krause and Lothar Wilker, "Bureaucracy and Foreign Policy in the Federal Republic of Germany," in *The Foreign Policy of West Germany*, Krippendorff and Rittberger, p. 162; and Albrecht, "Policy," p. 181.

30. "Bonn Growth Slowed in 1987," *The New York Times*, March 9, 1988, p. 32; and Steven Greenhouse, "West Germany's Emphasis on Exports Irritates its Trading Partners," *The New York Times*, Sept. 19, 1988, p. D-12.

31. Gordon Craig, "Germany and the United States," in *The Federal Republic of Germany and the United States: Changing Political, Social, and Economic Relations*, eds. James A. Cooney, Gordon Craig, Hans Peter Schwarz, and Fritz Stern (Boulder, Colo.: Westview Press, 1984), p. 22.

32. Lewis J. Edinger, *West German Politics* (New York: Columbia University Press, 1986), p. 92.

33. Ibid.

34. Deon Geldenhuys, "German Views on South Africa's Future," *Aussenpolitik: German Foreign Affairs Review* 36 (1st Quarter 1985), p. 100.

35. James Barber, *The Uneasy Relationship: Britain and South Africa* (London: Heinemann, 1983), p. 107.

36. Hofmeier, "West Germany," p. A256.

37. Jurgen Moltmann, "Religion and Politics in Germany and in German-American Relations," in *The Federal Republic of Germany and the United States*, Cooney et al., p. 101.

38. Ibid.

39. Barber, *The Uneasy Relationship*, p. 107.

40. Ibid.

41. Zdenek Cervenka, "The Two Germanies and Africa," in *Africa Contemporary Record*, ed. Colin Legum (New York: Africana Publishing Co., 1982), p. A191; and Merkl, *German Foreign Policies*, p. 214.

42. Lutz Holzner, "West Germany," in *International Handbook on Race and Race Relations*, ed. Jay A. Sigler (New York: Greenwood Press, 1987), p. 426.

43. Robert J. McCartney, "Parliament Official Recalls Nazi Heyday," *The Boston Globe*, November 11, 1988, p. 3.

44. Brigitte Schulz and William Hansen, "Aid or Imperialism? West Germany in Sub-Saharan Africa," *Journal of Modern African Studies* 22 (June 1984), p. 309.

45. Holzner, "West Germany," p. 435.

46. Ibid., p. 431; and Katzenstein, *Policy and Politics*, pp. 209–10.

47. Jeffrey Butler, "The German Factor in Arab-Transvaal Relations" in *Britain and Germany in Africa: Imperial Rivalry and Colonial Rule*, eds. Prosser Gifford and Roger Louis (New Haven: Yale University Press, 1967), p. 181.

48. Ibid., p. 190.

49. Elizabeth Thompson, "Mirror of a Century of Afrikapolitik," in *West German Foreign Policy: Dilemmas and Directions*, ed. Peter H. Merkl (Chicago: The Chicago Council on Foreign Relations, 1982), p. 150.

50. Butler, "German Factor," p. 210.

51. Leonard Thompson, "Great Britain and the Afrikaner Republics," in *The Oxford History of South Africa*, vol. 2, eds. Monica Wilson and Leonard Thompson (Oxford: The Clarendon Press, 1971), p. 312.

52. Ibid., p. 313.

53. Butler, "German Factor," p. 211.

54. Thompson, "Great Britain," p. 323.

55. Robin Hallett, *Africa Since 1875* (Ann Arbor: The University of Michigan Press, 1974), p. 623.

56. Shula Marks, "Southern and Central Africa," in *The Cambridge History of Africa*, vol. 6, eds. Roland Oliver and G. N. Sanderson (Cambridge: Cambridge University Press, 1985), p. 465.

57. William Kienzie, "German-South African Trade Relations in the Nazi Era," *African Affairs* 78 (January 1979), p. 85.

58. Ibid., pp. 86–87.

59. Hanrieder and Auton, *Foreign Policies*, p. 94.

60. Minter, *King Solomon's Mines*, p. 230.

61. James Barber, *The West and South Africa* (London: Routledge and Kegan Paul, 1982), p. 42.

62. Martin Holland, *The European Community and Southern Africa* (London: Pinter Publishers, 1988), p. 54.

63. Commonwealth Experts Group, *Statistics on Trade with South Africa* (Ottawa: Government of Canada, 1988), p. 10.

64. Holland, *The European Community and Southern Africa*, p. 68.

65. Willie Schatz, "South Africa: Pulling the Plug," *Datamation* 31 (October 1985), p. 22.

66. Shipping Research Bureau, *The European Community and the Oil Embargo Against South Africa* (Amsterdam: Shipping Research Bureau, 1987), p. 7.

67. U.S. Department of State, *Report to Congress on Industrialized Democracies' Relations With and Measures Against South Africa* (Washington, D.C.: Department of State, 1987), p. 20.

68. Ibid., p. 19.

69. "Divesting from South Africa," *The CTC Reporter*, no. 23 (Spring 1987), p. 39.

70. Holland, *The European Community and Southern Africa*, p. 101.

71. "Schaffer: South Africa under Delusions," *The Week in Germany*, Feb. 26, 1988, p. 2; and Hans-Dietrich Genscher, "Principles of the Federal Government's Policy Towards Africa," *Institute for International Relations Newsletter* (Bonn), no. 1 (1987), p. 2.

72. Veronica Forrester, "West Germany and Africa: New Investment Directions Point Away from Africa," *African Business* (August 1986), p. 55; and Rolf Hofmeier, "Aid From the Federal Republic of Germany to Africa," *The Journal of Modern African Studies* 24, no. 4 (1986), p. 577.

73. Wolter von Tiesenhausen, "Weizsaker Probes Africa's Problems on the Spot," *The German Tribune*, March 27, 1988, p. 2; and The Institute for International Affairs, "German Trade with Africa in 1987," *Newsletter* (Bonn), no. 4 (1988), p. 7.

74. Minter, *King Solomon's Mines*, p. 323; and Elizabeth Thompson, "Mirror," p. 156.

75. Reinhard Hermle, "The Code of Conduct in the Context of Relations Between the Federal Republic of Germany and South Africa," in *European Business and South Africa: An Appraisal of the EC Codes*, eds. Anne Akeroyd, Franz Ansprenger et al. (Munich: Kaiser, 1981), p. 44.

76. Hofmeier, "West Germany," p. A257.

77. John de St. Jorre, *South Africa's Non-United States Economic Links*, Africa Notes,

*no. 43* (Washington, D.C.: Center for Strategic and International Studies, 1985), p. 3.

78. Holland, *The European Community and Southern Africa,* p. 101.

79. L. H. Gann and Peter Duignan, *Why South Africa Will Survive* (New York: St. Martin's Press, 1987), p. 252.

80. Zdenek Cervenka, "The Two Germanies and Africa," in *Africa Contemporary Record,* ed. Colin Legum (New York: Africana Publishing Co., 1982), p. A144.

81. Holland, *The European Community and Southern Africa,* p. 101.

82. Humphrey Asobie, "The EEC and South Africa," in *The Political Economy of African Foreign Policy,* eds. Timothy M. Shaw and Olajide Aluko (New York: St. Martin's Press, 1984), p. 182; and Cervenka and Dederichs, "The Two Germanies," p. A192.

83. Serge Schmemann, "Now, Kohl Has to Plot His Way Out of the Libya Mess," *The New York Times,* January 22, 1989, p. E-5.

84. Ronald W. Walters, *South Africa and the Bomb* (Lexington, Mass.: Lexington Books, 1987), p. 35; and Zdenek Cervenka and Barbara Rogers, *The Nuclear Axis: Secret Collaboration Between West Germany and South Africa* (London: Julian Friedmann Books, Ltd., 1978), p. 86.

85. Gary Milhollin, "Bonn's Proliferation Policy," *The New York Times,* January 4, 1989, p. A-21.

86. United Nations General Assembly, *Report of the Special Committee Against Apartheid, Official Records* (New York: United Nations, 1987), p. 25.

87. Lucy Komisar, "Germany's Failure," *The Boston Globe,* December 3, 1988, p. 23.

88. David E. Albright, "The Communist States and Southern Africa," in *International Politics in Southern Africa,* eds. Gwendolen Carter and Patrick O'Meara (Bloomington, Indiana: Indiana University Press, 1982), p. 14.

89. Ibid., p. 13.

90. Christopher Coker, *NATO, The Warsaw Pact and Africa* (New York: St. Martin's Press, 1985), p. 195.

91. Cervenka and Dederichs, "The Two Germanies," p. A146.

92. Henning Melber, *The Federal Republic of Germany and Namibia* (Bonn: Information Center on Southern Africa, 1987), p. 1.

93. Henry Ashby Turner, *The Two Germanies Since 1945* (New Haven: Yale University Press, 1987), p. 204.

94. Federal Chancellor Helmut Kohl, "Principles and Current Positions of the Federal Government's Policy Toward Southern Africa," Minutes of the Plenary Debate in the Bundestag on February 4, 1988, reprinted in the *Institute for International Relations Newsletter* (Bonn), no. 1 (1988), p. 1.

95. Hofmeier, "West Germany," p. A258.

96. Willy Brandt, "The Social Democratic Party Firmly Supports the Demands of the Black Majority in South Africa," *Institute for International Relations Newsletter* (Bonn), no. 2 (1986), p. 3; and "The SPD Presidency on the Situation in South Africa," *Institute for International Relations Newsletter* (Bonn), no. 1 (1988), p. 2.

97. "SPD: Immediate European Sanctions Against South Africa Demanded," Supplement to *Institute for International Relations Newsletter* (Bonn), no. 4 (1988), p. 2.

98. "Reply by the Federal Government to the Interpellation of the SPD Parliamentary Group," (Bonn: Government of the Federal Republic of Germany, 1987), p. 7.

99. "Apartheid and the Future of Southern Africa," *Institute for International Relations Newsletter* (Bonn), no. 8 (1986), p. 6; Richard von Weizsacker, "Pretoria Should Not Feel Safe that Additional Measures Will Never be Considered Again," Bulletin by the Federal Government, no. 43/88, reprinted in *Institute for International Relations*

*Newsletter* (Bonn), no. 3 (1988), p. 1; and "Reply by the Federal Government," pp. 7–9.

100. Hofmeier, "West Germany," p. A256; and Holland, *The European Community and Southern Africa,* pp. 36–37.

101. Hans-Dietrich Genscher, "Principles of the Federal Government's Policy Towards Africa," *Institute for International Relations Newsletter* (Bonn), no. 1 (1987), p. 3.

102. Barber, *The Uneasy Relationship,* p. 108.

103. U.S. Department of State, *Report to Congress,* p. 21; and "Reply by the Federal Government," pp. 10–11.

104. Hofmeier, "Aid From the Federal Republic," p. 594.

105. Hofmeier, "West Germany," p. A260.

106. "Genscher Meets with ANC Leader in Bonn," *The Week in Germany,* June 17, 1988, p. 3.

107. Hans-Dietrich Genscher, "Objectives of German and European Policy Towards South Africa," *Federal Government Bulletin 69/88,* reprinted in *Institute for International Relations Newsletter* (Bonn), no. 4 (1988), p. 4.

108. "Institute for International Relations. A Survey of Bilateral German Development Aid to Industrial African Countries," *Institute for International Relations Newsletter* (Bonn), no. 4 (1987), p. 5.

109. John E. Bardill and James H. Cobbe, *Lesotho: Dilemmas of Dependence in Southern Africa* (Boulder, Colo.: Westview Press, 1985), p. 178.

110. "A Survey of Bilateral German Development Aid," p. 4.

111. Hofmeier, "Aid from the Federal Republic," p. 592.

112. Ibid.

### 4. Japan

1. T. J. Pempel, "Japanese Foreign Economic Policy: The Domestic Bases for International Behavior," *International Organization* 31 (1977), pp. 754–55.

2. Donald C. Hellman, "Japanese Politics and Foreign Policy: Elitist Democracy Within an American Greenhouse," in *The Political Economy of Japan: The Changing International Context,* eds. Takashi Inoguchi and Daniel I. Okimoto (Stanford: Stanford University Press, 1988), p. 358.

3. Edwin O. Reischauer, "Foreword," in *The Foreign Policy of Modern Japan,* ed. Robert A. Scalapino (Berkeley: University of California Press, 1977), p. xvii.

4. Ibid.

5. Hellman, "Japanese Politics," pp. 357–58.

6. Reischauer, *Foreign Policy,* p. xvii.

7. Ministry of Foreign Affairs, *Diplomatic Bluebook 1986 ed.: Review of Recent Developments in Japan's Foreign Relations* (Tokyo: Foreign Press Center, 1986), p. 9.

8. Yasusuke Murakami and Yutaka Kosai, *Japan in the Global Community* (Tokyo: University of Tokyo Press, 1986), p. 36.

9. Susan Chira, "Japan and the World: Applying Assertiveness Training to a Foreign Policy," *The New York Times,* September 6, 1988, p. A8.

10. Karel G. Van Wolferen, "The Japan Problem," *Foreign Affairs* 65 (Winter 1986/87), p. 289.

11. Ibid.

12. F. Quei Quo, "The Impact of Domestic Politics on Japan's Foreign Policy," in *Japan and the World,* eds. Gail Lee Bernstein and Haruhiro Fukui (New York: St. Martin's Press, 1988), p. 178.

13. Ibid., p. 180.

14. John Burgess, "Japan: South Africa Trade is Diplomatic Embarrassment of Riches," *The Washington Post*, January 8, 1987, p. A1.

15. Robert A. Scalapino, "The Foreign Policy of Japan," in *Foreign Policy in World Poltics*, ed. Roy C. Macridis (Englewood Cliffs, New Jersey: Prentice-Hall, Inc., 1985), p. 324.

16. Bradley Richardson, "Japanese Foreign Policy," in *Business and Society in Japan*, ed. Bradley Richardson and Taizo Ueda (New York: Praeger, 1981), p. 206.

17. See Seizaburo Sato, "The Foundations of Modern Japanese Foreign Policy," in *The Foreign Policy of Modern Japan*, Scalapino, p. 367.

18. Ezra F. Vogel, "Japan: Adaptive Communitarianism," in *Ideology and National Competitiveness*, eds. George C. Lodge and Ezra F. Vogel (Boston: Harvard Business School Press, 1987), p. 156.

19. Robert A. Scalapino, "Perspectives of Modern Japanese Foreign Policy," in *The Foreign Policy of Modern Japan*, Scalapino, p. 393.

20. Minoru Yanagihashi, "The Liberal Democratic Party and Foreign Policy," in *Japan's Foreign Policy Making*, ed. Hiroshi Itoh (Albany: State University of New York Press, 1979), p. 50.

21. Scalapino, "Perspectives," p. 393.

22. Clyde Haberman, "The Presumed Uniqueness of Japan," *The New York Times Magazine*, August 28, 1988, pp. 38–43.

23. Changsoo Lee and George A. De Vas, *Koreans in Japan: Ethnic Conflict and Accommodation* (Berkeley: University of California Press, 1981), pp. 382–83.

24. Scalapino, "Perspectives," p. 393.

25. J. Hung-Hwan, "Japan," in *International Handbook on Race and Race Relations*, ed. Jay A. Sigler (New York: Greenwood Press, 1987), p. 134.

26. Lee and De Vos, *Koreans in Japan*, p. 355.

27. Ibid.

28. Murakami and Kosai, *Japan*, p. 116.

29. George A. De Vos, William O. Wetherall, and Kaye Stearman, *Japan's Minorities: Burakumin, Koreans, Ainu and Okinawans* (London: Minority Rights Group, 1983), p. 4.

30. Hong N. Kim, "The Role of Big Business in the Making of Postwar Japanese Foreign Economic Policy," in *Japan's Foreign Policy-Making*, Itoh, p. 19.

31. William E. Bryant, *Japanese Private Economic Diplomacy: An Analysis of Business-Government Linkages* (New York: Praeger, 1975), p. 4.

32. Eto Shinkichi, "Foreign Policy Formation in Japan," in *The Silent Power: Japan's Identity and World Role*, ed. Yamamoto Tadashi (Tokyo: The Simul Press, 1976), p. 126.

33. Kim, "Big Business," pp. 7–8.

34. Scalapino, "The Foreign Policy of Japan," p. 310.

35. Hellman, "Japanese Politics," p. 354.

36. Jun Morikawa, "The Myth and Reality of Japan's Relations with Colonial Africa," *Journal of African Studies* 12 (1985), p. 42. Japan's economic interests led to diplomatic relations with South Africa. Its first consulate in Africa was established at Cape Town on 14 August 1918.

37. In 1926 Japan's imports from South Africa were valued at 917,000 yen while exports amounted to 10,741,000 yen.

38. Morikawa, "Myth and Reality," p. 43.

39. Joanna Moss and John Ravenhill, *Emerging Japanese Economic Influence in Africa* (Berkeley: University of California Press, 1985), p. 62; and Jun Morikawa, "The Anatomy of Japan's South Africa Policy," *Journal of Modern African Studies* 22 (1984), p. 134. Japanese imports from and exports to South Africa are equal in monetary value.

40. Martin Spring, "Japan: African Ties Under Fire," *Far Eastern Economic Review*, 26 September 1975, pp. 37–38.

41. Moss and Ravenhill, *Emerging Japanese Economic Influence*, p. 64.

42. Susumu Awanohara, "Trade Priorities Still Dominant," *Far Eastern Economic Review*, 26 September 1975, p. 36. The Byrd Amendment allowed the United States to continue importing Rhodesian chrome.

43. John Woodruff, "Japan: Finally, Trade with South Africa Slows Down," *The Boston Globe*, November 6, 1988, p. A8.

44. Bruce Roscoe, "Japanese Firms Will Help China Mine its Uranium Reserves," *Far Eastern Economic Review*, 3 July 1986, p. 81.

45. Spring, "Japan," p. 37.

46. Bruce Roscoe, "Japan Buys South African Corn at China's and the U.S.' Expense," *Far Eastern Economic Review*, 22 January 1987, p. 52.

47. Susan Moffat, "Never Mind Apartheid While Business Pays," *Daily Yomiuri*, 15 September 1985; and Robert Whymant, "Japan to Impose Sanctions on South Africa," *The Guardian*, 10 October 1985.

48. John Ravenhill, "Japan and Africa," in *Africa Contemporary Record*, ed. Colin Legum (New York: Africana Publishing Company, 1981), p. A211.

49. The Economist Intelligence Unit, *Japanese Overseas Investment* (London: The Economist Intelligence Unit, 1983), p. 64.

50. Martin Roth, "Japan and Africa," *Africa Economic Digest*, December 10, 1982, p. 10.

51. Ibid., p. 9. These companies produced about 4,000 barrels of oil per day in 1982.

52. "Japanese Commitment to Africa," *Africa*, no. 171 (November 1985), p. 64.

53. Ravenhill, "Japan and Africa," p. A212; and Lu Miaogeng, "Tokyo Draws Closer to Africa," *Beijing Review*, no. 22 (June 1985), p. 12.

54. Ravenhill, "Japan and Africa," p. A214.

55. "Japanese Commitment to Africa," p. 63.

56. U.S. Department of State, *Report to Congress on Industrialized Democracies' Relations With and Measures Against South Africa in Implementation of Sections 401(b) and 506(a) of the Comprehensive Anti-Apartheid Act of 1986* (Washington, D.C.: Department of State, 1987), p. 32.

57. Toru Kotani, "Rising Sun Over Africa," *Africa Report* (November–December 1985), p. 68.

58. F. R. Metrowich, *South Africa's New Frontiers* (Sandton, South Africa: Valiant Publishers, 1977), p. 142. Investments for establishing commercial offices were permitted.

59. Moss and Ravenhill, *Emerging Japanese Economic Influence*, p. 62; Stuart Leavenworth, "Japan's Complicity with Apartheid," *Japanalysis* 2 (1985), p. 14; and *U.N. Centre on Transnational Corporations, Politics and Practices of Transnational Corporations Regarding their Activities in South Africa and Namibia* (New York: United Nations, 1984), p. 9.

60. Anne Collier, "Japan Rethinks Ties to South Africa," *The Christian Science Monitor*, April 5, 1988, p. 7.

61. U.S. Department of State, *Report to Congress*, p. 33.

62. Edward A. Olsen, "Building Bridges to Africa," *Africa Report* (March–April 1980), p. 55. Japan's companies with offices in South Africa are urged to follow equal and fair employment practices.

63. Ravenhill, "Japan and Africa," p. A211; and Olsen, "Building Bridges," p. 55.

64. Colin Legum, ed., *Africa Contemporary Record, 1984/85* (New York: Africana Publishing Company, 1984), p. B804.

65. "Statement by Foreign Minister Shintaro Abe on the Apartheid Policy of the Republic of South Africa," 9 October 1985.

66. Morikawa, "Anatomy of Japan's South Africa Policy," p. 133.

67. The Japanese Embassy, *The Apartheid Enforcing Agencies Designated by the Government of Japan* (Washington, D.C.: 24 October 1985), pp. 1–2.

68. Morikawa, "Anatomy of Japan's South Africa Policy," p. 135. As early as 1985 Japan barred South African delegates from attending international medical and nutrition conferences.

69. Statement by Mrs. Kurokochi, U.N. General Assembly, 38th Session, Third Commmittee, 6th meeting, 10 October 1983, p. 16; and statement by the Director-General for Public Information and Cultural Affairs, The Ministry of Foreign Affairs, Japan, 26 December 1985.

70. U.S. Deparment of State, *Report to Congress*, p. 33.

71. U.N. Center Against Apartheid, "Japanese Trade Unions Mobilize Against Apartheid," *News Digest*, March 1986, p. 7.

72. Ibid.

73. Leavenworth, "Japan's Complicity with Apartheid," p. 15; and Japan Anti-Apartheid Committee, *Report to the Strategy Session of the Special Committee Against Apartheid*, New York: United Nations, 25 November 1985, p. 5.

74. Japan Anti-Apartheid Committee, *Report*, p. 1; Moffat, "Never Mind Apartheid While Business Pays," p. 1.

75. Morikawa, "Anatomy of Japan's South Africa Policy," p. 135.

76. Ibid.

77. The Commonwealth Experts Group, *Statistics on Trade with South Africa* (Ottawa: Government of Canada, 1988), p. 4; and Anne Collier, "Japan Rethinks," p. 7.

78. "Japan's Sales to Pretoria," *The New York Times*, August 13, 1988, p. 41.

79. John Woodruff, "Japan," p. A8.

## 5. ISRAEL

1. Maurice Cranston, "Are There Any Human Rights?" *Daedalus* 112 (Fall 1983), p. 5.

2. Avner Yaniv, *Dilemmas of Security: Politics, Strategy, and the Israeli Experience in Lebanon* (New York: Oxford University Press, 1987), p. 20.

3. Ibid.

4. Zeev Schiff and Ehud Yaari, *Israel's Lebanon War* (New York: Simon and Schuster, 1984), p. 39.

5. Lily Gardener Feldman, *The Special Relationship Between West Germany and Israel* (Boston: George Allen and Unwin, 1984), p. 46.

6. Ibid., p. 47.

7. Naomi Chazan, "The Fallacies of Pragmatism: Israeli Foreign Policy Toward South Africa," *African Affairs* 82 (April 1983), p. 170.

8. Statement by Ambassador Benjamin Netanyahu at the United Nations, *The Apartheid Regime's Lifeline Begins in Persian Gulf Oil Ports* (Jerusalem: Israel Ministry of Foreign Affairs, 1986), p. 2.

9. Ibid., p. 1.

10. Ibid., p. 2.

11. Israel Ministry of Foreign Affairs, *Israel's Policy Towards South Africa* (Jerusalem, 1987), p. 3.

12. Chazan, "Fallacies," p. 199.

13. Menachem Shalver, "Officials Upset by South Africa Charge," *The Jerusalem Post*, January 30, 1988, p. 4.

14. "Excerpts from U.S. Report on Israelis and Arabs," *The New York Times*, February 8, 1989, p. A8.

15. Aaron S. Klieman, *Israel's Global Reach: Arms Sales as Diplomacy* (Washington, D.C.: Pergamon-Brassey, 1985), p. 35; and Rinn Sup Shinn, "Government and Politics," in *Israel: A Country Study*, ed. Richard F. Nyrop (Washington, D.C.: The American University Press, 1979), p. 165.

16. R. D. McLaurin, Don Peretz, and Lewis W. Snider, *Middle East Foreign Policy: Issues and Processes* (New York: Praeger, 1982), p. 140.

17. R. D. McLaurin, Mohammed Mughisuddin, and Abraham R. Wagner, *Foreign Policy Making in the Middle East* (New York: Praeger, 1977), p. 172.

18. Ibid., pp. 172–73.

19. Michael Shamir and John L. Sullivan, "Jews and Arabs in Israel," *Journal of Conflict Resolution* 29 (June 1985), p. 284.

20. Yaniv, *Dilemmas of Security*, p. 11.

21. Gideon Rafael, "Five Wars, One Peace, What Next?" *Middle East Review* 20 (Summer 1988), p. 7.

22. Don Peretz, "Israeli Policy," in *The Middle East Since Camp David*, ed. Robert O. Freedman (Boulder, Colo.: Westview Press, 1984), p. 166.

23. Naomi Chazan, "Domestic Developments in Israel," in *The Middle East: Ten Years After Camp David*, ed. William B. Quandt (Washington, D.C.: The Brookings Institution, 1988), p. 157.

24. Ibid., p. 174.

25. John Kifner, "Israelis Worry About Their Image," *The New York Times*, January 25, 1988, p. A8.

26. Ibid.

27. Abba Eban, "Israel, Hardly the Monaco of the Middle East," *The New York Times*, January 2, 1989, p. A23.

28. Ibid.

29. "Excerpts from U.S. Report on Israelis and Arabs," *New York Times*, p. A8.

30. Joel Brinkley, "Shamir Upholds Force to End Violence," *The New York Times*, February 9, 1989, p. A10.

31. Anthony Lewis, "Israel Against Itself," *The New York Times*, February 12, 1989, p. E23.

32. Robert Pear, "Lawmakers Shift Pro-Israel Policy," *The New York Times*, February 12, 1989, p. A5.

33. Nissan Liviatan and Sylvia Piterman, "Accelerating Inflation and Balance-of-Payments Crisis, 1973–1984," in *The Israeli Economy*, ed. Yoram Ben-Porath (Cambridge, Mass.: Harvard University Press, 1986), p. 325.

34. John Kifner, "How Israel's Economic Revival Ran Out of Steam," *The New York Times*, January 8, 1989, p. A2.

35. John Kifner, "Israel Puts Forth an Austerity Plan to Revive Economy," *The New York Times*, January 2, 1989, p. A1.

36. Zvi Lanir, "Introduction," in *Israeli Security Planning in the 1980s: Its Politics and Economics*, ed. Zvi Lanir (New York: Praeger, 1984), p. v.

37. Klieman, *Israel's Global Reach*, p. 57.

38. Eitan Berglas, "Defense and the Economy," in *The Israel Economy*, Ben-Porath, p. 185.

39. Klieman, *Israel's Global Reach*, p. 24.

40. Peter Grose, *A Changing Israel* (New York: Vintage Books, 1985), p. 39.

41. Sammy Smooha, "Internal Divisions in Israel at Forty," *Middle East Review* 20 (Summer 1988), p. 27.

42. Chazan, "Domestic Developments," p. 175.

43. Amos Perlmutter, "Israel's Security Option," *Foreign Affairs* 64 (Fall 1985), p. 144.

44. Ofira Seliktar, "Israel: The New Zionism," *Foreign Policy* 51 (Summer 1983), p. 121.

45. Ian S. Lustick, "Israel's Dangerous Fundamentalists," *Foreign Policy* 68 (Fall 1987), p. 120; and Chazan, "Domestic Developments," p. 180.

46. Chazan, "Domestic Developments," p. 180.

47. Ofira Seliktar, "Ethnic Stratification and Foreign Policy in Israel: The Attitudes of Oriental Jews Towards the Arabs and the Arab-Israeli Conflict," *Middle East Journal* 38 (Winter 1984), p. 35.

48. Mary Curtius, "Israeli Debate on PLO Talks Getting Sharper," *The Boston Globe*, February 4, 1989, p. A1.

49. Grose, *A Changing Israel*, p. 105.

50. Michael Brecher, *The Foreign Policy System of Israel* (New Haven: Yale University Press, 1972), p. 558.

51. Ibid., p. 559.

52. Efraim Inbar, *Outcast Countries in the World Community* (Denver, Colo: University of Denver Press, 1985), p. 55.

53. Chazan, "Domestic Developments," p. 184.

54. Seliktar, "Israel: The New Zionism," p. 132.

55. Benjamin M. Joseph, *Besieged Bedfellows: Israel and the Land of Apartheid* (New York: Greenwood Press, 1988), p. 93.

56. Yossi Melman and Dan Raviv, "Has Congress Doomed Israel's Affair with South Africa?" *The Washington Post*, February 22, 1987, p. C1.

57. Joseph, *Besieged Bedfellows*, p. 94.

58. Samuel J. Roberts, *Survival or Hegemony? The Foundations of Israeli Foreign Policy* (Baltimore: The Johns Hopkins Press, 1973), p. 119.

59. Joseph, *Besieged Bedfellows*, p. 93.

60. Chazan, "Domestic Developments," p. 184.

61. Ibid.

62. Neville Rubin, "The Impact of Zionism and Israel on the Political Orientation and Behavior of South African Jews," in *Settler Regimes in Africa and the Arab Worlds*, eds. Ibrahim Abu-Lughod and Baha Abu-Laban (Wilmette, Illinois: The Medina University Press International, 1974), p. 172.

63. Leslie Rubin, "South African Jewry and Apartheid," *Africa Report* 15 (Fall 1970), p. 22.

64. Joseph, *Besieged Bedfellows*, p. 83.

65. "U.S. Jews Weigh Israel-South Africa Arms Deals," *The Jerusalem Post*, February 20, 1987, p. 3.

66. "Anti-Semitic Incidents in 1988 Put at a Five-Year High," *The New York Times*, January 29, 1989, p. A20.

67. David K. Shipler, *Arab and Jew: Wounded Spirits in a Promised Land* (New York: Times Books, 1986), p. 274.

68. Sammy Smooha, "Internal Divisions in Israel at Forty," p. 26; and Edward W. Said, *The Question of Palestine* (New York: Times Books, 1980), p. 38.

69. Suhaila Haddad, R. D. McLaurin, and Emile A. Nakhleh, "Minorities in Containment: The Arabs in Israel," in *The Political Role of Minority Groups in the Middle East*, ed. R. D. McLaurin (New York: Praeger, 1979), p. 83; and Sammy Smooha and Don Peretz, "The Arabs in Israel," *Journal of Conflict Resolution* 26 (Sept. 1982), p. 473.

70. Bernard Reich, "State of Israel," in *The Government and Politics of the Middle East and North Africa*, eds. David E. Long and Bernard Reich (Boulder, Colo.: Westview Press, 1986), p. 247.

71. Shipler, *Arab and Jew*, p. 429.

72. Mary Curtius, "Kahane Unit Barred From Israel Voting," *The Boston Globe*, October 6, 1988, p. A3.

73. Reich, "State of Israel," p. 248.

74. Shipler, Arab and Jew, p. 433.

75. Chazan, "Fallacies," p. 172.

76. Saadia Touval, *The Peace Brokers: Mediators in the Arab-Israeli Conflict, 1948–1979* (Princeton: Princeton University Press, 1982), p. 203.

77. Arnold Rivkin, *Africa and the West* (London: Thames and Hudson, 1962), p. 71.

78. Ibid., p. 78.

79. Ethan A. Nadelmann, "Israel and Black Africa: A Rapprochement?" *Journal of Modern African Studies* 19 (June 1981), p. 212.

80. Chazan, "Fallacies," p. 172; and Jane Hunter, *Israeli Foreign Policy: South Africa and Central America* (Boston: South End Press, 1987), p. 25.

81. Oye Ogunbadejo, "Black Africa and Israel," in *Africa Contemporary Record*, ed. Colin Legum (New York: Africana Publishing Company, 1984), p. A120.

82. Hunter, *Israeli Foreign Policy*, pp. 25–26.

83. Gideon Shimoni, *Jews and Zionism: The South African Experience, 1910–1967* (Cape Town: Oxford University Press, 1980), p. 353.

84. Chazan, "Fallacies," p. 173.

85. Ibid.

86. Richard F. Nyrop, "Historical Setting," in *Israel: A Country Study*, Nyrop, p. 47.

87. Colin Legum, "The Middle East Dimension," in *International Politics in Southern Africa*, eds. Gwendolen M. Carter and Patrick O'Meara (Bloomington, Indiana: Indiana University Press, 1982), p. 119.

88. Arye Oded, *Africa and the Middle East Conflict* (Boulder, Colo: Lynne Rienner Publishers, 1987), p. 3.

89. U.S. Department of State, *Report to Congress on Industrialized Democracies' Relations with and Measures Against South Africa* (Washington, D.C.: Department of State, 1987), p. 27.

90. "Israeli Mission to South Africa," *The New York Times*, August 8, 1986, p. A4.

91. Joseph Pelzman, "The Effect of the U.S.-Israel Free Trade Area Agreement on Israeli Trade and Employment," in *Israel Faces the Future*, eds. Bernard Reich and Gershon R. Kieval (New York: Praeger, 1986), p. 140.

92. James Adams, *The Unnatural Alliance* (London: Quartet Books, Ltd., 1984), p. 26.

93. U.N. General Assembly, *Special Report of the Special Committee Against Apartheid: Recent Developments Concerning Relations Between Israel and South Africa* (October 26, 1987), p. 10.

94. See Glenn Frankel, "An Israeli Dilemma: South African Ties," *The Washington Post*, September 20, 1987, p. A31; "Israeli Arms Sanctions," *Africa Research Bulletin*, April 15, 1987, p. 8449; and Joseph, *Besieged Bedfellows*, p. 33.

95. Alfred T. Moleah, "The Special Relationship," *Africa Report* (November–December 1980), p. 16; and Hunter, *Israeli Foreign Policy*, p. 61.

96. Adams, *Unnatural Alliance*, p. 20.

97. Ibid.

98. Colin Legum, "The Middle East Dimension," p. 120; and Richard P. Stevens and Abdelwahah M. Elmessiri, *Israel and South Africa: The Progression of a Relationship* (New Brunswick, New Jersey: North American, Inc., 1977), p. 78.

99. Colin Legum, "Afro-Arab Relations in 1983," in *Africa Contemporary Record*, ed. Colin Legum (New York: Africana Publishing Co., 1985), p. A157.

100. U.S. Department of State, *Report to Congress*, p. 29.

101. Ibid., p. 28.

102. Colin Legum, "Afro-Arab Relations," p. A157.

103. Victor T. LeVine, "The African-Israeli Connection 40 years Later," *Middle East Review* 21 (Fall 1988), p. 14.

104. "Israel to Keep Status Quo with South Africa," *The Jerusalem Post*, January 28, 1987, p. 4.

105. Oded, *Middle East Conflict*, p. ix; and "Kenya, Israel Review Diplomatic Relations," *The Boston Globe*, December 25, 1988, p. 11.

106. Oded, p. 172; and Nadelman, "Rapprochement?" p. 215.

107. Nadelman, "Rapprochement?" p. 215; and LeVine, "African-Israeli Connection," p. 15.

108. Israel Ministry of Foreign Affairs, *Israel's Policy Towards South Africa* (Jerusalem, 1987), p. 1.

109. Michael D. Ward and Alex Mintz, "Dynamics of Military Spending in Israel," *Journal of Conflict Resolution* 31 (March 1987), p. 87.

110. Ibid.

111. Klieman, *Israel's Global Reach*, p. 129.

112. Joseph, *Besieged Bedfellows*, p. 48.

113. Ibid.

114. Benjamin Beit-Hallahmi, *The Israeli Connection: Who Israel Arms and Why* (New York: Pantheon Books, 1987), p. 120.

115. Ibid., p. 121.

116. Joseph, *Besieged Bedfellows*, p. 53.

117. Adams, *Unnatural Alliance*, p. 91.

118. "Israeli Arms Sanctions," *Africa Research Bulletin*, April 15, 1987, p. 8449; Adams, *Unnatural Alliance*, p. 93; and Joseph, *Besieged Bedfellows*, p. 53.

119. Christopher Coker, *South Africa's Security Dilemmas* (New York: Praeger, 1987), p. 54.

120. "Pretoria Bids for Israel's Fighter Plane Workers," *Southscan* 2 (November 13, 1987), p. 10.

121. Abraham Rabinovich, "Israel Should Talk to Everybody in South Africa," *The Jerusalem Post*, March 25, 1987, p. 4.

122. *World Armaments and Disarmaments: SIPRI Yearbook, 1982* (London: Taylor and Francis, Ltd., 1982), p. 188; Andrew J. Pierre, *The Global Politics of Arms Sales* (Princeton: Princeton University Press, 1982), p. 267; and Melman and Raviv, "Israel's Affair," p. C1.

123. Peter Pry, *Israel's Nuclear Arsenal* (Boulder, Colo.: Westview Press, 1984), pp. 41–42; Ronald Walters, *South Africa and the Bomb* (Lexington, Mass.: Lexington Books, 1987), p. 139; and Jeff Gerth, "Plan to Send Key Component to South Africa is Detailed," *The New York Times*, November 16, 1989, p. A5.

124. Chazan, "Fallacies," p. 177.

125. Ibid.

126. Shimon Peres, quoted by Michael Brecher in Brecher, *The Foreign Policy System of Israel*, p. 233.

127. Daniel J. Elazar, *Jewish Communities in Frontier Societies: Argentina, Australia, and South Africa* (New York: Holmes and Meier, 1983), p. 3.

128. Leopold Marquard, *The People and Politics of South Africa* (New York: Oxford University Press, 1969), p. 235.

129. Shimoni, *Jews and Zionism*, p. 150.

130. Chazan, "Fallacies," p. 176.

131. Beit-Hallahmi, *Israeli Connection*, p. 115; and Hunter, *Israeli Foreign Policy*, p. 26.

132. Chazan, "Fallacies," p. 176.

133. Klaus Freiherr von der Ropp, "Southern Africa: Between a New Order and

Chaos," *Aussenpolitik: German Foreign Affairs Review* 30 (2nd Quarter 1979), p. 237.

134. Hunter, *Israeli Foreign Policy,* p. 86.

135. Glenn Frankel, "Israel Pledges to Reduce Military Ties to South Africa," *The Washington Post,* March 20, 1987, p. A1.

136. Ministry of Foreign Affairs, *Israel's Policy Towards South Africa,* p. 2.

137. Ibid.

138. Glenn Frankel, "An Israeli Dilemma: South African Ties," *The Washington Post,* September 20, 1987, p. A31.

139. *United States Comprehensive Anti-Apartheid Act,* in *International Legal Materials* 26 (January 1987), p. 90.

140. Consulate General of Israel, *Israel Cabinet Decision Regarding Relations with South Africa* (Chicago, September 16, 1987), p. 1.

141. Ibid., p. 2.

142. U.S. State Department, *Report to Congress,* p. 29.

143. Peter Steinfels, "Jewish Aid in South African Blacks' Schooling," *The New York Times,* January 29, 1989, p. A28.

## 6. SCANDINAVIA

1. Swedish Mission to the United Nations, *Policies of Apartheid of the Government of South Africa* (November 5, 1986), p. 1.

2. Arne Ruth, "The Second New Nation: The Mythology of Modern Sweden," *Daedalus* 113 (Spring 1984), p. 92.

3. Paul M. Cole, "Sweden's Security Policy in the 1980s," *SAIS Review* 8 (Winter–Spring 1988), p. 223.

4. Hans-Henrik Holm, "Danish Third World Policy: The Feed-back Problem," *Cooperation and Conflict* 14, no. 2 (1979), p. 95; and Johan Jorgen Holst, "The Pattern of Nordic Security," *Daedalus* 113 (Spring 1984), p. 203.

5. Ruth, "Second New Nation," p. 66.

6. Barbara G. Haskel, *The Scandinavian Option: Opportunities and Opportunity Costs in Postwar Scandinavian Foreign Policies* (Oslo: Norwegian University Press, 1976), p. 17.

7. Cole, "Security Policy," p. 214.

8. Ibid., p. 215.

9. Ibid.

10. Johan Jorgen Holst, "Introduction," in *Norwegian Foreign Policy in the 1980s,* ed. Johan Jorgen Holst (Oslo: Norwegian University Press, 1985), p. 11.

11. Harry Eckstein, *Division and Cohesion in Democracy: A Study of Norway* (Princeton: Princeton University Press, 1966), p. 86.

12. Ibid., p. 85.

13. Matti Klinge, "Aspects of the Nordic Self," *Daedalus* 113 (Spring 1984), p. 273.

14. Ruth, "Second New Nation," p. 67.

15. L. A. Jinadu, "The Political Economy of Sweden's Development Policy in Africa," *Cooperation and Conflict* 19, no. 3 (1984), p. 179.

16. Holst, "Pattern of Nordic Security," p. 214.

17. Foreign Minister Thorvald Stoltenberg, *Statement on Foreign Policy in the Storting on June 1, 1987* (Oslo: Royal Norwegian Ministry of Foreign Affairs, 1987), p. 1.

18. Bernt Hagtvet and Erik Rudeng, "Scandinavia: Achievements, Dilemmas, and Challenges," *Daedalus* 113 (Spring 1984), p. 231.

19. Ruth, "Second New Nation," p. 68.

20. M. Donald Hancock, *Sweden: The Politics of Postindustrial Change* (Hinsdale: The Dryden Press, 1972), p. 249.

21. Kenneth E. Miller, *Government and Politics in Denmark* (Boston: Houghton Mifflin Co., 1968), p. 245.

22. Olav Fagelund Knudsen and Arild Underdal, "Patterns of Norwegian Foreign Policy Behavior," *Conflict and Cooperation* 20, no. 4 (1985), p. 235.

23. Jinadu, "Political Economy," p. 179.

24. Hugh Helco and Henrik Madsen, *Policy and Politics in Sweden: Principled Pragmatism* (Philadelphia: Temple University Press, 1987), p. 10.

25. Earl H. Fry and Gregory A. Raymond, *The Other Western Europe: A Political Analysis of the Smaller Democracies* (Santa Barbara: ABC-Clio Information Services, 1982), p. 217.

26. Ibid., p. 221.

27. Ibid., pp. 224–27.

28. Eckstein, *Division and Cohesion*, p. 92.

29. Hancock, *Sweden*, p. 242.

30. Ib Faubry, "Foreign Policy Making in Scandinavia," in *Foreign Policy Making in Western Europe: A Comparative Approach*, eds. William Wallace and W. E. Peterson (Westmead: Saxon House, 1978), p. 118.

31. Helco and Madsen, *Principled Pragmatism*, p. 16; and Haskel, *Scandinavian Option*, p. 15.

32. Helco and Madsen, *Principled Pragmatism*, p. 21.

33. Fry and Raymond, *Smaller Democracies*, p. 217.

34. Helco and Madsen, *Principled Pragmatism*, p. 12.

35. Erik Allardt, "Representative Government in a Bureaucratic Age," *Daedalus* 113 (Spring 1984), pp. 180–81.

36. Cole, "Security Policy," p. 215; and Henry Valen, "Cleavages in the Norwegian Electorate as a Constraint on Foreign Policymaking," in *Norwegian Foreign Policy*, Holst, p. 27.

37. Madi Gray, *Sweden and South Africa: The Two Faces* (Stockholm: African Groups in Sweden, 1987), p. 1.

38. Norwegian Information Service, *Norway in the United Nations: Norwegian Views on Some Basic Issues* (New York: November 1981), p. 6.

39. Miller, *Denmark*, p. 249.

40. Hagtvet and Rudeng, "Scandinavia," p. 228.

41. Haskel, *Scandinavian Option*, p. 13; and Klinge, "Nordic Self," p. 264.

42. Miller, *Denmark*, p. 268.

43. Franklin D. Scott, *Scandinavia* (Cambridge, Mass.: Harvard University Press, 1975), p. 255.

44. Niels Jorgen Haagerup and Christian Thune, "Denmark: The European Pragmatist," in *National Foreign Policies and European Political Cooperation*, ed. Christopher Hill (London: George Allen and Unwin, 1983), p. 112.

45. Hagtvet and Rudeng, "Scandinavia," p. 231.

46. Ruth, "Second New Nation," p. 92.

47. Lars Rudebeck, "Nordic Policies Toward the Third World," in *Foreign Policies of Northern Europe*, ed. Bengt Sundelius (Boulder, Colo.: Westview Press, 1982), p. 167.

48. "Alas, Poor Denmark," *The Economist*, September 12, 1987, p. 51; and "Sweden Votes for Carlsson," *The Economist*, September 24, 1988, p. 62.

49. Kurt Samuelsson, "The Swedish Model and Western Europe," *Journal of International Affairs* 41 (Summer 1988), p. 367.

50. "Nordic Worries About Refugees," *The Economist*, November 14, 1987, p. 58.

51. Ibid.; and "Alas, Poor Denmark," p. 52.

52. Jinadu, "Political Economy," p. 183.

53. U.S. Department of State, *Report to Congress on Industrialized Democracies'*

*Relations With and Measures Against South Africa* (Washington, D.C.: Department of State, 1987), p. 40.

54. "Norwegian Shipowners Oppose South Africa Ban," *News of Norway*, no. 7 (September 17, 1986), p. 1.

55. U.S. Department of State, *Report to Congress*, p. 14.

56. Ministry for Foreign Affairs, *Prohibition of Trade With South Africa and Namibia* (Stockholm, March 1987), p. 27.

57. Kristoffer Leonardsson, *Sanctions Busting* (Stockholm: The Isolate South Africa Committee, 1987), p. 10.

58. Ministry for Foreign Affairs, *Prohibition of Trade With South Africa*, p. 32.

59. See International Monetary Fund, *Direction of Trade Statistics* (January 1988); and United Nations, *Commodity Trade Statistics, Statistical Paper, Series D*, vol. 37, nos. 1–3 (1987).

60. Olaf Palme, "South Africa and the Nordic Countries," *Development Dialogue* (1987), p. 72.

61. Ministry of Foreign Affairs, *Prohibition of Trade With South Africa*, p. 21.

62. Ibid., p. 16.

63. Faubry, "Foreign Policy Making," p. 130.

64. Permanent Mission of Norway to the United Nations, *Norwegian Measures Against South Africa* (New York, July 5, 1985), p. 2.

65. Martin Holland, *The European Community and South Africa: European Political Cooperation Under Strain* (London: Pinter Publishers, 1988), p. 105.

66. Ministry of Foreign Affairs, Norway, *Norske Synspunkter Pa Utenrikspolitiske Sporsmal* (November 1979), p. 2.

67. Nordic Foreign Ministers, *Nordic Programme of Action Against South Africa* (Oslo, October 17–18, 1985), p. 1.

68. Permanent Mission of Norway to the United Nations, *Norwegian Measures Against South Africa*, p. 8.

69. Ibid., pp. 3–4.

70. Danish Mission to the United Nations, *Law on the Prohibition of New Danish Investments in South Africa and Namibia*, adopted by Parliament on May 19, 1985 (New York, 1985), pp. 1–2; and *Act Prohibiting Trade With the Republic of South Africa*, adopted by the Parliament on May 30, 1986 (Copenhagen, 1986), p. 1.

71. Ibid.

72. Ministry for Foreign Affairs, Sweden, *Prohibition of Investments in South Africa and Namibia and Other Measures Against Apartheid* (Stockholm, 1985), p. 2.

73. Ministry for Foreign Affairs, Sweden, *Prohibition of Imports of Agricultural Produce From South Africa* (Stockholm, December 1985), p. 27.

74. Gray, *Sweden and South Africa*, p. 2.

75. Statement by the Prime Minister to the Folketing at the Third, *Reading of the Bill to Prohibit Trade With the Republic of South Africa and Namibia on May 30, 1986* (Copenhagen, 1986), p. 2.

76. Per Haekkerup, "The South African Racial Crisis and the World," in *Sanctions Against South Africa*, ed. Ronald Segal (Baltimore: Penguin Books, 1964), p. 45.

77. Roger Leys, "Scandinavian Development Assistance to BLS," in *Canada, Scandinavia and Southern Africa*, eds. Douglas Anglin, Timothy Shaw, and Carl Widstrand (Uppsala: Scandinavian Institute of African Studies, 1978), p. 66; and William Minter, *King Solomon's Mines: Western Interests and the Burdened History of South Africa* (New York: Basic Books, Inc., 1986), p. 249.

78. Ministry of Foreign Affairs, *Norske Synspunter Pa Utenrikspolitske Sporsmal*, p. 1.

79. Gray, *Sweden and South Africa*, p. 4; and Stephen M. Davis, *Apartheid's Rebels: Inside South Africa's Hidden War* (New Haven: Yale University Press, 1987), p. 73.

80. Olaf Palme, "Speech at the Swedish People's Parliament Against Apartheid" at Folkets Hus on February 21, 1986, p. 1.

81. Sten Rylander, "The Nordic Initiative and SADCC," in *Another Development for SADCC* (Uppsala: Dag Hammarskjöld Foundation, 1987), p. 153.

82. Palme, "South Africa and the Nordic Countries," p. 71.

83. Swedish International Development Authority, *Sweden and Development Cooperation in Southern Africa* (Stockholm: SIDA, 1986), p. 3.

84. Ibid., p. 12.

85. Ibid., p. 7.

86. Ibid., p. 10.

87. Joseph Hanlon, *Beggar Your Neighbor: Apartheid Power in Southern Africa* (Bloomington, Indiana: Indiana University Press, 1986), p. 230.

## 7. Canada

1. Statement in the House of Commons by the Right Honorable Joe Clark, Secretary of State for External Affairs, on South Africa (Ottawa, March 2, 1988), p. 1.

2. Gita Anad, "Canada and SADCC: Self-Interest or Magnanimity?" *International Insights* (Spring 1985), p. 13.

3. Michael K. Hawes, *Principal Power, Middle Power, or Satellite: Competing Perspectives in the Study of Canadian Foreign Policy* (Toronto: York University Research Program in Strategic Studies, 1984), p. 3.

4. Robert O. Matthews, "Canada and Anglophone Africa," in *Canada and The Third World,* eds. Peyton Lyon and Tareq Ismael (Toronto: Macmillan of Canada, 1976), p. 89.

5. Harry Carter, "Responding to Domestic Groups Regarding Canadian Policy Towards Southern Africa," in *Groups and Governments in Canadian Foreign Policy,* ed. Don Munton (Toronto: Canadian Institute of International Affairs, 1985), p. 78.

6. Maureen Appel Molot and Brian W. Tomlin, "The Conservative Agenda," in *Canada Among Nations: The Conservative Agenda,* eds. Maureen Appel Molot and Brian W. Tomlin (Toronto: James Lorimer and Company, 1986), p. 5; and Adam Bromke and Kim Richard Nossal, "Tensions in Canada's Foreign Policy," *Foreign Affairs* (Winter 1983–84), p. 353.

7. R. Barry Farrell, "Canada: Argument Within Consensus," in *Canada in Transition,* ed. R. Barry Farrell (Chicago: Council on Foreign Relations, 1984), p. 76.

8. G. Bruce Doern and Richard W. Phidd, *Canadian Public Policy* (Toronto: Methuen, 1983), p. 23.

9. William Kilbourn, "The Peaceable Kingdom Still," *Daedalus* 117 (Fall 1988), p. 23.

10. Ibid., p. 24.

11. Richard J. Van Loon and Michael S. Whittington, *The Canadian Political System* (Toronto: McGraw-Hill Ryerson Ltd., 1981), p. 101.

12. "A Survey of Canada," *The Economist,* October 8, 1988, p. 4.

13. Dennis Austin, *The Commonwealth and Britain* (London: Routledge and Kegan Paul, 1988), p. 11.

14. Don Jamieson, Secretary of State for External Affairs, *Statements and Speeches* 6 (August 3, 1978), p. 3; and Annette Fox and William Fox, "Domestic Capabilities and Canadian Foreign Policy," *International Journal* 39 (Winter 1983–84), p. 32.

15. Brian D. Tennyson, *Canadian Relations With South Africa* (Washington, D.C.: University Press of America, 1982), p. 155.

16. Ibid., p. 161.

17. Matthews, "Canada," p. 83.

18. Prime Minister Brian Mulroney, *Statement to the House of Commons*, October 28, 1985, p. 2.

19. David H. Flaherty, "Who Rules Canada?" *Daedalus* 117 (Fall 1988), p. 105.

20. Linda Freeman, "Canada and South Africa, 1987," *Southern Africa Report* 3 (December 1987), p. 6.

21. Cathal J. Nolan, "The Influence of Parliament on Human Rights in Canadian Foreign Policy," *Human Rights Quarterly* 7 (August 1985), p. 374.

22. The Economist Intelligence Unit, *Canada: A Country Report*, no. 4 (October 1988), p. 3.

23. Alan Toulin, "Canada," *Euromoney* (May 1987), p. 3.

24. Michael M. Atkinson and William D. Coleman, "Is There a Crisis in Business-Government Relations?" *Canadian Journal of Administrative Sciences* 4 (December 1987), p. 336.

25. Nasir Islam and Sadrudin A. Ahmed, "Business Influence on Government: A Comparison of Public and Private Sector Perceptions," *Canadian Public Administration* 27 (Spring 1984), p. 101.

26. Abraham Rothstein, "Foreign Policy and the Canadian Business Community," *International Journal* 39 (Winter 1983–84), p. 145.

27. Alan M. Rugman and Andrew Anderson, "Business and Trade Policy: The Structure of Canada's New Private Sector Advisory System," *Canadian Journal of Administrative Sciences* 4 (December 1987), p. 372.

28. Ibid.

29. John Kirton and Michael Donnelly, "Japanese Investment—The Answer for Canada," *International Perspectives* (March/April 1986), p. 4.

30. The Economist Intelligence Unit, *Canada: A Country Report*, no. 1 (London, 1989), p. 14.

31. John Kirton and Blair Dimock, "Domestic Access to Government in the Canadian Foreign Policy Process, 1968–1982," *International Journal* 39 (Winter 1983–84), pp. 70–71.

32. J. Alex Murray and Lawrence Le Duc, "Public Opinion and Foreign Policy Options in Canada," *The Public Opinion Quarterly* 40 (Winter 1976–77), p. 489.

33. Douglas Anglin, "Canadian Responses," in *Canada and South Africa: Challenge and Response*, ed. Douglas Anglin (Ottawa: Carleton University, 1986), p. 48.

34. Robert O. Matthews, "The Churches and Foreign Policy," *International Perspectives* (January/February 1983), p. 18.

35. Anglin, "Canadian Responses," p. 45.

36. Canada, House of Commons, *Debates* June 13, 1986, p. 14412.

37. John W. Holmes, *The Shaping of Peace: Canada and the Search for World Order, 1943–1957* (Toronto: University of Toronto Press, 1982), p. 172.

38. Robert F. Harney, "So Great a Heritage as Ours: Immigration and the Survival of the Canadian Policy," *Daedalus* 117 (Fall 1988), p. 61.

39. Jeffrey G. Reitz, "The Institutional Structure of Immigration as a Determinant of Inter-Racial Competition: A Comparison of Britain and Canada," *International Migration Review* 22 (Spring 1988), p. 125.

40. Matthews, "Canada," p. 62.

41. Tennyson, *Canadian Relations*, p. 13.

42. Matthews, "Canada," p. 77.

43. Clarence G. Redekop, "Commerce Over Conscience: The Trudeau Government and South Africa, 1968–1984," *Journal of Canadian Studies* 19 (Winter 1984–85), p. 87.

44. Ibid.

45. Herbert H. Denton, "Canada's South Africa Trade Sours Despite Restrictions," *The Washington Post*, November 17, 1986, p. A15.

46. The Commonwealth Experts Group, *Statistics on Trade with South Africa* (Ottawa, 1988), p. 11.

47. Larry R. Stewart, "Canada's Role in the International Uranium Cartel," *International Organization* 35 (Autumn 1981), p. 658.

48. Ibid., p. 670.

49. International Defense and Aid Fund for Southern Africa, *Canadian Industry in South Africa: Misconduct or Code of Conduct,* (Ottawa, June 1985), p. 3.

50. "Trade With South Africa," *International Canada,* Supplement to *International Perspectives* (January/February 1988), p. 13.

51. Albert F. Hart, *Code of Conduct Concerning the Employment Practices of Canadian Companies Operating in South Africa* (Ottawa: Department of External Affairs, 1986), p. 6.

52. Redekop, "Commerce Over Conscience," p. 91.

53. Taskforce on the Churches and Corporate Responsibility, *Annual Report, 1985–86* (Toronto, 1986), p. 30.

54. International Defense and Aid Fund, *Canadian Industry,* p. 2.

55. "Code of Conduct," *International Canada,* Supplement to *International Perspectives* (September/October 1988), p. 40.

56. Hart, *Code of Conduct,* p. 17.

57. Redekop, "Commerce Over Conscience," p. 96.

58. Ibid.

59. Clarence G. Redekop, "Trudeau at Singapore: The Commonwealth and Arms Sales to South Africa," in *Acceptance of Paradox: Essays on Canadian Diplomacy in Honour of John W. Holmes,* ed. Kim Richard Nossal (Toronto: Canadian Institute of International Affairs, 1982), p. 177.

60. Taskforce on the Churches and Corporate Responsibility, *Annual Report, 1984–85* (Toronto, 1985), p. 19.

61. Taskforce on the Churches and Corporate Responsibility, *Annual Report, 1985–86* (Toronto, 1986), p. 12.

62. Redekop, "Commerce Over Conscience," p. 96.

63. "Southern Africa," *International Perspectives* (January/February 1988), p. 12; and "Sanctions," *International Perspectives* (January/February 1989), p. 41.

64. Kim Richard Nossal, "Out of Steam? Mulroney and Sanctions," *International Perspectives* (November/December 1988), p. 15.

65. Richard J. Payne, "Canada, South Africa, and the Commonwealth," *International Perspectives* (July/August 1987), pp. 9–12.

66. Statement on South Africa by the Honourable Joe Clark, Secretary of State for External Affairs, July 6, 1985, p. 2.

67. The Right Honourable Joe Clark, "Statement in the House of Commons," September 13, 1985, p. 1.

68. Payne, "Canada," p. 12.

69. Angus M. Gunn, *South Africa: A World Challenged* (Vancouver: Legacy Press, 1987), p. 91.

70. Freeman, "Canada and South Africa," p. 7; and Fred Langan, "Canada's South African Sanctions; Mild Effects, But Sweet for Cuba," *The Christian Science Monitor,* August 14, 1986, p. 19.

71. Gunn, *South Africa,* p. 91.

72. Taskforce on the Churches and Corporate Responsibility, *Widening, Tightening, and Intensifying Economic and Other Sanctions Against South Africa* (Toronto, July 20, 1988), p. 9.

73. "Sanctions," *International Canada,* Supplement to *International Perspectives* (November/December 1988), p. 41.

74. Jane Perlez, "South Africa Loan Reaction," *The New York Times,* February 9, 1989, p. D7.

75. Redekop, "Commerce Over Conscience," p. 85.

76. Senator Jean-Maurice Simard and Tom Hockin, MP, *Independence and Internationalism: Report of the Special Joint Committee of the Senate and the House of Commons on Canada's International Relations*, June 1986 (Ottawa: Canadian Government Publishing Centre, 1986), p. 100.

77. Department of External Affairs, *Canada's Role in Southern Africa: Background Notes* (Ottawa, February 1987), p. 8.

78. Ibid., p. 3.

79. Right Honourable Joe Clark, "Statement to the House of Commons on South Africa," March 2, 1988, pp. 2–3.

80. Right Honourable Joe Clark, "Statement in the House of Commons Following the First Meeting of the Commonwealth Committee of Foreign Ministers on Southern Africa," February 5, 1988, p. 3.

81. *A Strategy to Counteract South African Propaganda and Censorship* (Ottawa: Government of Canada, 1988), p. 2.

82. CIDA, "Southern African Development Coordination Conference," (Ottawa, 1985), pp. 7–8; and *Canada's Role in Southern Africa*, p. 15.

83. Charlotte Montgomery, "Cheers, Confusion Mark Reaction to Aid Proposals," *The Globe and Mail*, October 5, 1988, p. 1.

84. Redekop, "Commerce Over Conscience," p. 93.

85. *Canada's Role in Southern Africa*, p. 18.

## 8. THE FRONTLINE STATES

1. Roger Martin, "Southern Africa: A New Approach," *The Round Table* (July 1987), p. 327.

2. Klaas Woldring, "Aspects of Zambia's Foreign Policy in the Context of Southern Africa," in *Beyond Political Independence: Zambia's Development Predicament in the 1980s*, ed. Klaas Woldring (Berlin: Mouton Publishers, 1984), p. 243.

3. James H. Cobbe, "Economic Aspects of Lesotho's Relations With South Africa," *The Journal of Modern African Studies* 26, no. 1 (1988), p. 78.

4. Andrew Meldrum, "Zimbabwe: An Amnesty for Unity," *Africa Report* (July/August 1988), p. 41.

5. Ibid.; and Richard W. Hull, "Overcoming Zimbabwe's Vulnerabilities," *Current History* 87 (May 1988), p. 198.

6. John D. Holm, "Elections in Botswana: Institutionalization of a New System of Legitimacy," in *Elections in Independent Africa*, ed. Fred M. Hayward (Boulder, Colo.: Westview Press, 1987), p. 121.

7. "Results and Prospects of Africa's Economic Showing: Few Optimistic Signs," *Africa Report* (March/April 1989), p. 8; and Peter Robson, "Regional Integration and the Crisis in Sub-Saharan Africa," *The Journal of Modern African Studies* 23, no. 4 (1985), p. 9.

8. Carol B. Thompson, "Zimbabwe in Southern Africa: From Dependent Development to Dominance or Cooperation," in *The Political Economy of Zimbabwe*, ed. Michael G. Schatzberg (New York: Praeger, 1984), p. 199.

9. Hull, "Zimbabwe's Vulnerabilities," p. 199; and Lynda Schuster, "Zimbabwe: Lots of Graduates, Not Enough Jobs," *The Christian Science Monitor*, April 14, 1988, p. 11.

10. "Business Briefs: Zimbabwe," *Africa Report* (March/April 1989), p. 12.

11. Schuster, "Zimbabwe," p. 11.

12. Roger Hearing, "Zambia: When Copper Was King," *Africa Report* (September/October 1988), p. 40.

13. Kenneth Good, "Zambia and the Liberation of South Africa," *The Journal of Modern African Studies* 25, no. 3 (1987), p. 531.

14. Neva Seidman Makgetla, "Theoretical and Practical Implications of IMF Conditionality in Zambia," *The Journal of Modern African Studies* 24, no. 3 (1986), p. 396.

15. John D. Holm, "Botswana: A Paternalistic Democracy," *World Affairs* 150 (Summer 1987), p. 25; Louis A. Picard, *The Politics of Development in Botswana: A Model for Success* (Boulder, Colo.: Lynne Rienner Publishers, 1987), p. 4; and Colleen Lowe Morna, "Botswana: Ashes and Diamonds," *Africa Report* (January/February 1989), p. 22.

16. Caroline Allen, "An African Success Story," *Africa Report* (January/February 1987), p. 23.

17. The Economist Intelligence Unit, *Botswana, Lesotho, and Swaziland, 1987–1988* (London: Economist Intelligence Unit, 1987), p. 44.

18. Mary Benson, "The Former British High Commission Territories," in *Africa: A Handbook*, ed. Colin Legum (London: Anthony Blond, 1965), p. 315.

19. Jack Halpern, *South Africa's Hostages* (Baltimore: Penguin Books, 1965), p. 92.

20. Gwendolen M. Carter and Patrick O'Meara, "Botswana, Lesotho, and Swaziland: The Common Background and Links," in *Southern Africa: The Continuing Crisis*, eds. Gwendolen M. Carter and Patrick O'Meara (Bloomington, Indiana: Indiana University Press, 1982), p. 224.

21. Halpern, *Hostages*, p. 55; and Benson, "Territories," p. 317.

22. Patrick O'Meara, "Zimbabwe: The Politics of Independence," in *Southern Africa: The Continuing Crisis*, Carter and O'Meara, p. 20.

23. Clyde Sanger, "Southern Rhodesia," in *Africa: A Handbook*, Legum, p. 177.

24. Merle Lipton, "South Africa's Role in Agricultural Production and Marketing in Southern Africa," in *Poverty, Policy, and Food Security in Southern Africa*, ed. Coralie Bryant (Boulder, Colo.: Lynne Rienner Publishers, 1988), p. 192.

25. Thompson, "Zimbabwe in Southern Africa," p. 203.

26. Department of Foreign Affairs, *South Africa: Mainstay of Southern Africa* (Pretoria: The Government Printer, September 1985), pp. 5–12.

27. Stephen R. Lewis, "Southern African Interdependence," *CIS Africa Notes*, no. 56 (March 27, 1986), p. 3.

28. Ronald T. Libby, *The Politics of Economic Power in Southern Africa* (Princeton: Princeton University Press, 1987), p. 46; and Joseph Hanlon, *Beggar Your Neighbor: Apartheid Power in Southern Africa* (Bloomington, Indiana: Indiana University Press, 1986), p. 61.

29. James Brooke, "Mobutu Meets Botha, and Will Go To Pretoria," *The New York Times*, October 2, 1988, p. 3.

30. The Economist Intelligence Unit, *Zimbabwe and Malawi, No. 4* (London: Economist Intelligence Unit, 1988), p. 24.

31. Libby, *Economic Power*, p. 24.

32. Hanlon, *Beggar Your Neighbor*, p. 55.

33. Good, "Zambia," p. 534.

34. Hanlon, *Beggar Your Neighbor*, p. 89.

35. Carter and O'Meara, "Botswana, Lesotho, and Swaziland," p. 225.

36. James Cobbe, "The Changing Nature of Dependence: Economic Problems in Lesotho," *The Journal of Modern African Studies* 21, no. 2 (1983), p. 297; and Hanlon, *Beggar Your Neighbor*, p. 81.

37. Michael W. Clough, "Southern Africa: Descent Into Chaos," in *Global Security: A Review of Strategic and Economic Issues*, eds. Barry Blechman and Edward Luttwak (Boulder, Colo.: Westview Press, 1987) p. 137.

38. Colleen Lowe Morna, "Botswana: Ashes and Diamonds," *Africa Report* (January/February 1989), p. 22.

39. Kenneth W. Grundy, "Economic Patterns in the New Southern African Balance," in *Southern Africa: The Continuing Crisis,* Carter and O'Meara, p. 308.

40. Stephen R. Lewis, "Some Economic Realities in South Africa: One Hundred Million Futures," in *Poverty, Policy, and Food Security in Southern Africa,* Bryant, p. 53.

41. John E. Bardill and James H. Cobbe, *Lesotho: Dilemmas of Dependence in Southern Africa* (Boulder, Colo.: Westview Press, 1985), p. 166.

42. "Sanctions Against South Africa in Regional Perspective," *Bulletin* 25, no. 5 (1985), p. 50.

43. Lewis, "Southern African Interdependence," p. 2; and Graham Leach, *South Africa: No Easy Path to Peace* (London: Routledge and Kegan Paul, 1986), p. 183.

44. Hanlon, *Beggar Your Neighbor,* p. 237.

45. James H. Polhemus, "Botswana's Role in the Liberation of Southern Africa," in *The Evolution of Modern Botswana,* ed. Louis A. Picard (London: Rex Collings, 1985), p. 260.

46. Richard Dale, "Botswana's Foreign Policy: State and Nonstate Actors and Small Power Diplomacy," in *The Evolution of Modern Botswana,* Picard, p. 213.

47. "Text of Swazi-South African Agreement Relating to Security Matters," cited by Robert S. Jaster, *South Africa and Its Neighbors: The Dynamics of Regional Conflict* (London: International Institute for Strategic Studies, 1986), p. 16.

48. David Martin and Phyllis Johnson, "Africa: The Old and the Unexpected," *Foreign Affairs* 63, no. 3 (1985), p. 607.

49. Steve Kibble and Ray Bush, "Reform of Apartheid and Continued Destabilization in Southern Africa," *The Journal of Modern African Studies* 24, no. 2 (1986), p. 208.

50. Christopher Coker, *South Africa's Security Dilemmas* (New York: Praeger, 1987), p. 38.

51. Ibid., p. 39.

52. "Pretoria and Maputo Revive Accord," *The New York Times,* May 26, 1988, p. A6; and James Brooke, "South Africa Apparently Shifting Loyalty to Support Mozambique," *The New York Times,* May 3, 1988, p. A1.

53. John Battersby, "Two African Leaders Vow Cooperation," *The New York Times,* September 13, 1988, p. A11; and William Clairborne, "Botha, Chissano Meet in Mozambique," *The Washington Post,* September 13, 1988, p. A1.

54. Jane Perlez, "New Mozambique Violence is Blamed on South Africa," *The New York Times,* February 25, 1989, p. A5.

55. Leach, *No Easy Path,* p. 200.

56. Kenneth W. Grundy, *The Militarization of South African Politics* (Bloomington, Indiana: Indiana University Press, 1986), p. 6.

57. Colin Legum, *The Battlefronts of Southern Africa* (New York: Africana Publishing Company, 1988), p. 185.

58. Ibid., p. 247.

59. Martin and Johnson, "Africa," p. 606; and Mota Lopes, "The MNR: Opponents or Bandits," *Africa Report* (January/February 1986), p. 72.

60. Allen Isaacman, "Mozambique: The Malawi Connection," *Africa Report* (November/December 1986), p. 53.

61. Gillian Gunn, "Post-Nkomati Mozambique," in *Angola, Mozambique, and the West,* ed. Helen Kitchen (Washington, D.C.: Center for Strategic and International Studies, 1987), p. 92.

62. Robert G. Mugabe, "Struggle For Southern Africa," *Foreign Affairs* 66 (Winter 1987–88), p. 316.

63. Robert Gersony, *Summary of Mozambican Refugee Accounts of Principally Conflict-*

*Related Experience in Mozambique* (Washington, D.C.: Department of State, April 1988), p. 1.

64. Paul Musker, "The Splintering of Renamo," *Weekly Mail*, July 8–14, 1988, p. 10.

65. Ernest Harsch, "Across the Continent: The People's Sanctions," *Africa Report* (March/April 1988), p. 54.

66. Polhemus, "Botswana's Role," p. 263.

67. Larry W. Bowman, Michael Bratton, and Rukudzo Murapa, "Zimbabwe and South Africa," in *South Africa in Southern Africa*, ed. Thomas Callaghy (New York: Praeger, 1983), p. 336.

68. Roger Martin, "Zimbabwe: A Status Report," *CSIS Notes*, no. 92 (November 16, 1988), p. 5.

69. Jaster, *South Africa*, p. 12.

70. Martin, "Zimbabwe," p. 5.

71. Hanlon, *Beggar Your Neighbor*, p. 243.

72. Thomas M. Callaghy, "Absolutism and Apartheid: Relations Between Zaire and South Africa," in *South Africa in Southern Africa*, Callaghy, p. 373.

73. Ibid., p. 374.

74. Bardill and Cobbe, *Lesotho*, p. 68.

75. Jack Parson, *Botswana: Liberal Democracy and Labor Reserve in Southern Africa* (Boulder, Colo.: Westview Press, 1984), p. 104; and Nadia Kostiuk, "Botswana," in *The Political Economy of African Foreign Policy*, eds. Timothy M. Shaw and Olajide Aluko (New York: St. Martin's Press, 1984), p. 69.

76. Lewis, "Southern African Interdependence," p. 1.

77. Hanlon, *Beggar Your Neighbor*, p. 239.

78. Colleen Lowe Morna, "Tanzania: On the Right Track," *Africa Report* (May/June 1988), p. 46.

79. Chandra Hardy, "The Prospects For Growth and Structural Change in Southern Africa," *Development Dialogue*, no. 2 (1987), p. 47; and Kibble and Bush, "Reform," p. 214.

80. Max van der Stoel, "Breaking the Laager: A Two-Track Western Policy Toward South Africa," in *Europe, America, and South Africa*, ed. Gregory F. Treverton (New York: Council on Foreign Relations, 1988), p. 72.

81. Thompson, "Zimbabwe in Southern Africa," p. 199.

82. "Zimbabwe," in *Africa Contemporary Record*, ed. Colin Legum (New York: Africana Publishing Co., 1987), p. B929.

83. Good, "Zambia," pp. 537–38.

84. King Moshoeshoe, "Punish Pretoria, But Not Lesotho," *The New York Times*, July 5, 1988, p. A27.

85. Steve Askin, "The Business of Sanctions Busting," *Africa Report* (January/February 1989), p. 19; and "Kingdom of Swaziland," in *Africa Contemporary Record*, Legum, pp. B876-77.

## 9. Conclusion

1. Helen Suzman, "The Folly of Economic Sanctions," in *The South African Quagmire: In Search of a Peaceful Path to Democratic Pluralism*, ed. S. Prakash Sethi (Cambridge, Mass.: Ballinger Publishing Co., 1987), p. 191.

2. J. P. Hayes, *Economic Effects of Sanctions on South Africa* (London: Trade Policy Research Centre, 1987), p. 15.

3. Robert I. Rotberg, *Suffer the Future: Policy Choices in Southern Africa* (Cambridge, Mass.: Harvard University Press, 1980), p. 140.

4. Kent Butts and Paul Thomas, *The Geopolitics of Southern Africa: South Africa as a Regional Superpower* (Boulder, Colo.: Westview Press, 1986), p. 136.

5. Roger Fisher, *International Conflict for Beginners* (New York: Harper and Row, 1969), p. 149.

6. Michael Clough, "Southern Africa: Challenges and Choices," *Foreign Affairs* 66 (Summer 1988), p. 1081.

7. Nancy H. Kreisler, "Mobil Quitting South Africa, Blaming 'Foolish' U.S. Laws," *The New York Times*, April 29, 1989, p. A1.

8. Millard W. Arnold, "How Disinvesting Corporations Could Foster Economic Empowerment of Black South Africans," *CSIS Africa Notes* (March 28, 1988), p. 2.

9. Clough, "Southern Africa," p. 1074.

10. Rotberg, *Suffer the Future*, p. 290.

11. Hayes, *Economic Effects*, p. 28.

12. John D. Battersby, "Pretoria Signals Move on Economic Change," *The New York Times*, February 8, 1988, p. 26.

13. John D. Battersby, "Sanctions," *Africa Report* (January/February 1987), p. 6.

14. Martin Holland, *The European Community and South Africa* (London: Pinter Publishers, 1988), p. 44.

15. William H. Kaempfer, James A. Lehman, and Anton D. Lowenberg, "Divestment, Investment Sanctions, and Disinvestment: An Evaluation of Anti-apartheid Policy Instruments," *International Organization* 41 (Summer 1987), p. 465.

16. U.S. Department of State, *A U.S. Policy Toward South Africa: The Report of the Secretary of State's Advisory Committee on South Africa* (Washington, D.C.: Department of State, 1987), p. 21.

17. Merle Lipton, "Reform: Destruction or Modernization of Apartheid," in *South Africa in Crisis*, ed. Jesmond Blumenfeld (London: Croom Helm, 1987), p. 54.

18. "Text of President Reagan's Remarks on South Africa," *Department of State Bulletin* 85 (October 1985), p. 1.

19. Chester A. Crocker, "South Africa: A Strategy for Change," *Foreign Affairs* 59 (Winter 1980–81), pp. 324–48.

20. Gregory F. Treverton, "Introduction: Framing the Issues," in *Europe, America and South Africa*, ed. Gregory F. Treverton (New York: Council on Foreign Relations, 1988), p. 9.

21. Henry Bienen, "A New Policy—Selective Engagement," *Orbis* 31 (Spring 1987), p. 29.

22. James Barber, *The West and South Africa* (London: Routledge and Kegan Paul, 1982), p. 28.

23. John Palmer, *Europe Without America? The Crisis in Atlantic Relations* (New York: Oxford University Press, 1987), p. 14.

24. Christopher S. Wren, "Soviet Diplomats in South Africa After Three Decades of Hostility," *The New York Times*, April 27, 1989, p. A8.

25. Clough, "Southern Africa," p. 1084.

# BIBLIOGRAPHY

Adam, Gordon. "Behind Barclays' Pull-Out." *Africa Report* 32 (May–June 1987): 23–25.

Africa Groups in Sweden and the Swedish North-South Coalition. *Sweden and the SADCC States—A Review.* Stockholm: Africa Groups in Sweden, 1987.

Africa Groups in Sweden and Isolate South Africa Committee. *Workshop on Southern Africa and Sanctions Against South Africa and Occupied Namibia.* Stockholm: Africa Groups in Sweden, 1985.

"Africa-U.K." *Africa Research Bulletin,* 15 August 1986, 8171–72.

Akhalwaya, Ameen. "South Africa: Interview with Tony Bloom." *Africa Report* 28, no. 2 (March–April 1988): 64.

Albrecht, Ulrich. "The Policy of the Federal Republic of Germany Towards the South." In *The Foreign Policy of West Germany,* edited by Ekkehart Krippendorf and Volker Rittberger, 171–96. London: Sage Publications, 1980.

Albright, David E. "The Communist States and Southern Africa." In *International Politics in Southern Africa,* edited by Gwendolen M. Carter and Patrick O'Meara, 3–34. Bloomington, Indiana: Indiana University Press, 1982.

Allardt, Erik. "Representative Government in a Bureaucratic Age." *Daedalus* 113, no. 1 (Winter 1984): 169–98.

Allen, Caroline. "An African Success Story." *Africa Today* 34, no. 182 (January–February 1987): 22–24.

———. "Zambia: The Politics of Apathy." *Africa Report* 33, no. 3 (May–June 1988): 23–28.

Allen, Christopher S. "Germany: Competing Communitarianism." In *Ideology and National Competitiveness,* edited by George C. Lodge and Ezra F. Vogel, 79–102. Boston: Harvard Business School Press, 1987.

Aluko, Olajide. "Nigeria, Namibia, and Southern Africa." In *Southern Africa in the 1980s,* edited by Olajide Aluko and Timothy M. Shaw, 41–60. London: George Allen and Unwin, 1985.

American Friends Service Committee. *South Africa: Challenge and Hope.* New York: Hill and Wang, 1987.

An International Conference on the Effects of Sanctions on the Process of Peaceful Reform in South Africa. *Have Sanctions Worked?* Washington, D.C.: The Jefferson Educational Foundation, 1987.

Ansprenger, Franz. "Introductory Remarks." In *European Business and South Africa: An Appraisal of the E.C. Code of Conduct,* edited by Anne Akeroyd, Franz Ansprenger, Reinhard Hermy, and Christopher R. Hill, 9–12. Munich: Kaiser, 1981.

Archer, Robert, and Antoine Bouillon. *The Southern Africa Game: Sport and Racism.* London: Zed Press, 1982.

"Arms Smugglers Goaled." *Africa Research Bulletin,* 15 August 1985, 7727.

Arnold, Millard W. "How Disinvesting Corporations Could Foster Economic Empowerment of Black South Africans." *CSIS Africa Notes.* Washington, D.C.: Center for Strategic and International Studies, 1988.

"As Mrs. T. Fiddles . . . South Africa Stockpiles." *New Statesman*, 27 June 1986, 5.

Asobie, Humphrey. "The EEC and South Africa." In *Southern Africa in the 1980s*, edited by Olajide Aluko and Timothy M. Shaw, 174–93. London: George Allen and Unwin, 1985.

Ausland, John C. *Norway, Oil, and Foreign Policy*. Boulder: Westview Press, 1979.

Austin, Dennis. *Britain and South Africa*. London: Oxford University Press, 1966.

———. *The Commonwealth and Britain*. London: Routledge and Kegan Paul, 1988.

———. "A South African Policy: Six Precepts in Search of a Diplomacy." *International Affairs* 62, no. 3 (Summer 1986): 390–404.

Awanohara, Susumu. "Trade Priorities Still Dominant. *Far Eastern Economic Review* 26 (September 1979): 36.

Axford, Barrie. "United Kingdom." In *International Handbook on Race and Race Relations*, edited by Jay A. Sigler, 369–94. New York: Greenwood Press, 1987.

Bailey, Martin. "Refined Oil Evades Embargo." *New Statesman*, 1 November 1985, 7.

Baker, Donald G. *Race, Ethnicity, and Power: A Comparative Study*. London: Routledge and Kegan Paul, 1983.

Baker, Pauline. "The Myth of Middle Class Moderation: African Lessons for South Africa." *Issue* 16, no. 2 (1988): 45–48.

———. "South Africa: The Afrikaner Angst." *Foreign Policy*, no. 69 (Winter 1987–88): 61–79.

Baldwin, David A. *Economic Statecraft*. Princeton: Princeton University Press, 1985.

Baldwin, David A. "Thinking About Threats." *Journal of Conflict Resolution* 15 (March 1971): 71–78.

Barber, James. *South Africa's Foreign Policy, 1945–70*. London: Oxford University Press, 1973.

Barber, James. *The Uneasy Relationship: Britain and South Africa*. London: Heinemann, 1983.

Barber, James, Jesmond Blumenfeld, and Christopher R. Hill. *The West and South Africa*. London: Routledge and Paul Kegan, 1982.

Battersby, John D. "Sanctions." *Africa Report*, (Jan.–Feb. 1987): 4–10.

Baynham, Simon. "Political Violence and the Security Response." In *South Africa in Crisis*, edited by Jesmond Blumenfeld, 107–25. London: Croom Helm, 1987.

Baynham, Simon, and Greg Mills. "Lesotho: Between Dependence and Destabilization." *The World Today* (March 1987): 52–54.

Beit-Hallahmi, Benjamin. *The Israeli Connection: Who Israel Arms and Why*. New York: Pantheon Books, 1987.

Ben-Porath, Yoram. "Introduction." In *The Israeli Economy*, edited by Yoram Ben-Porath, 1–23. Cambridge: Harvard Univesrity Press, 1986.

Berglas, Eitan. "Defense and the Economy." In *The Israeli Economy*, edited by Yoram Ben-Porath, 173–91. Cambridge: Harvard University Press, 1986.

Berridge, Geoffrey. *Economic Power in Anglo-South African Diplomacy*. London: Macmillan Press, Ltd., 1981.

Berridge, Geoffrey. "Britain and Southern Africa." In *Southern Africa in the 1980s*, edited by Olajide Aluko and Timothy M. Shaw, 162–70. London: George Allen and Unwin, 1985.

Bienen, Henry S. "Economic Interests and Security Issues in Southern Africa." In *South Africa and Its Neighbors: Regional Security and Self-Interest*, edited by Robert I. Rotberg et al. Lexington: Lexington Books, 1985.

Bienen, Henry S. "A New Policy-Selective Engagement." *Orbis* 31, no. 1 (Spring 1987): 27–32.

"Big Business Prepares for Change." *Euromoney*, December 1985, 79–80.

Birnbaum, Karl E. "The Formation of Swedish Foreign Policy," *Cooperation and Conflict* 1, no. 1 (1965): 6–31.

Bissell, Richard E. *South Africa and the United States.* New York: Praeger, 1985.

Bissell, Richard E., and Chester A. Crocker, eds. *South Africa into the 1980s.* Boulder: Westview Press, 1979.

Bloom, Jack Brian. *Black South Africa and the Disinvestment Dilemma.* Johannesburg: Jonathan Bull Press, 1986.

Blumenfeld, Jesmond. "South Africa: Economic Responses to International Pressures." *The World Today*, Vol. 41, No. 12 December 1985, 218–221.

Bordill, John E., and James H. Cobbe, eds. *Lesotho: Dilemmas of Dependence in Southern Africa.* Boulder: Westview Press, 1985.

"Botha Threatens Reprisals." *Africa Research Bulletin*, 15 August 1985, 7718.

Botha, P. W. *Speech: The Road Ahead.* Pretoria: The Government Printer, 1985.

Bowen, David. "Surviving with Sanctions." *World Press Review*, August 1986, 47.

Bowman, Larry W., Michael Bratton, Rukudzu Murapa. "Zimbabwe and South Africa: Dependency, Destabilization, and Liberation." In *South Africa in Southern Africa: The Intensifying Vortex of Violence*, edited by Thomas M. Callaghy, 323–54. New York: Praeger, 1983.

Brady, Lawrence J. "The Utility of Economic Sanctions as a Policy Instrument." In *The Utility of International Economic Sanctions*, edited by David Leyton-Brown, 297–310. New York: St. Martin's Press, 1987.

Brandt, Willy. "The Social Democratic Party Firmly Supports the Demands of the Black Majority in South Africa." *IIR Newsletter* (Bonn), no. 2 (1986): 1–3.

Brecher, Michael. *The Foreign Policy System of Israel.* New Haven: Yale University Press, 1972.

Breyer, Karl. "Red Germans' Take-over Bid in Southern Africa." *German International*, no. 6/7 (1979): 20–24.

Brimelow, Peter. "Why South Africa Shrugs at Sanctions." *Forbes*, 9 March 1987, 101–4.

Bromke, Adam, and Kim Richard Nossal. "Tensions in Canada's Foreign Policy." *Foreign Affairs* 62, no. 2 (Winter 1983–84): 335–53.

Bryan, Coralie, ed. *Poverty, Policy and Food Security in Southern Africa.* Boulder: Lynne Rienner Publishers, 1988.

Bryant, William E. *Japanese Private Economic Diplomacy: An Analysis of Business Government Linkages.* New York: Praeger, 1975.

Bull, Hedley. "Implications for the West." In *Conflict and Compromise in South Africa*, edited by Robert I. Rotberg and John Barratt, 173–87. Lexington: Lexington Books, 1980.

Bureau for Information. *The National State of Emergency*. Pretoria: The Government Printer, 1987.

Bureau for Information. *Talking with the ANC*. Pretoria: The Government Printer, 1987.

Business International South Africa. *Apartheid and Business: An Analysis of the Rapidly Evolving Challenge Fancing Companies with Investments in South Africa*. Pretoria: Business International South Africa, 1980.

Butler, Jeffrey. "The German Factor in Anglo-Transvaal Relations." In *Britain and Germany in Africa: Imperial Rivalry and Colonial Rule*, edited by Prosser Gifford and Roger Louis. New Haven: Yale University Press, 1967.

Butts, Kent, and Paula Thomas. *The Geopolitics of Southern Africa: South Africa as Regional Superpower*. Boulder: Westview Press, 1986.

Buzan, Barry, and H. O. Nazareth. "South Africa Versus Azania: The Implications of Who Rules." *International Affairs* 62, no. 1 (Winter 1985–86): 35–40.

Callaghy, Thomas M. "Absolutism and Apartheid: Relations Between Zaire and Southern Africa." In *South Africa in Southern Africa: The Intensifying Vortex of Violence*, edited by Thomas M. Callaghy, 371–403. New York: Praeger, 1983.

Callaghy, Thomas M. "Apartheid and Socialism: South Africa's Relations with Angola and Mozambique." In *South Africa in Southern Africa: The Intensifying Vortex of Violence*, edited by Thomas M. Callaghy, 267–322. New York: Praeger, 1983.

"Can Pretoria Evade Sanctions? Let Us Count the Ways." *Business Week*, 1 September 1986, 38–39.

Canada. *A Strategy to Counteract South African Propaganda and Censorship*. Ottawa: Government of Canada, 1988.

Canada. Department of External Affairs. *Canada's Role in Southern Africa: Background Notes*, Feb. 1987.

Carnegie Leadership Program. *South Africa: Myths and Realities of Divestiture*. New York: Council on Religion and International Affairs, 1985.

Carswell, Robert. "Economic Sanctions and the Iran Experience." *Foreign Affairs* 62, no. 2 (Winter 1981–82): 247–65.

Carter, Harry. "Responding to Domestic Groups Regarding Canadian Policy towards Southern Africa." In *Groups and Governments in Canadian Foreign Policy*, edited by Don Munton. Toronto: Canadian Institute of International Affairs, 1985.

Cervenka, Zdenek, and Barbara Rogers. *The Nuclear Axis: Secret Collaboration beween West Germany and South Africa*. London: Julian Friedmann Books, Ltd., 1978.

Charney, Craig. "The National Party: A Class Alliance in Crisis." In *The State of Apartheid*, edited by Wilmot G. James, 5–36. Boulder: Lynne Rienner Publishers, 1987.

Chazan, Naomi. "The Fallacies of Pragmatism: Israel—Foreign Policy Towards South Africa." *African Affairs* 82 (April 1983): 169–99.

Chee, Choung. "Alien Registration Law of Japan and the International Covenant for Civil and Political Rights." *Korea and World Affairs* 10 (Winter 1986): 649–86.

Christiansen, Robert E., and Jonathan G. Kydd. "The Return of Malawian Labor From South Africa and Zimbabwe." *Journal of Modern African Studies* 21, no. 2 (1983): 311–26.

CIDA. "Southern African Development Coordination Conference." Ottawa: Government of Canada, 1985.

Clairborne, William. "South Africa: Playing the Mineral Card." *The Washington Post National Weekly Edition* (16–22 May 1988): 17.

Clough, Michael W. "Southern Africa: Challenges and Choices." *Foreign Affairs* 66, no. 5 (Summer 1988): 1067–90.

———. "Southern Africa: Descent Into Chaos." In *Global Security: A Review of Strategic and Economic Issues*, edited by Barry M. Blechman and Edward L. Luttwak, 136–63. Boulder: Westview Press, 1987.

Cobbe, James H. "The Changing Nature of Dependence: Economic Problems in Lesotho." *Journal of Modern African Studies* 21, no. 2 (1983): 293–310.

———. "Economic Aspects of Lesotho's Relations with South Africa." *Journal of Modern African Studies* 26, no. 1 (1988): 71–89.

Code of Conduct Concerning the Employment Practices of Canadian Companies Operationg in South Africa. *First Annual Report for the Year 1985.* Ottawa: Government of Canada, May 1986.

"Codes of conduct concerning employment practices of TNLs operating in South Africa." *The CTC Reporter,* no. 19 (Spring 1985): 29–32.

Coker, Christopher. "Collective Bargaining as an Internal Sanction: The Role of U.S. Corporations in South Africa." *Journal of Modern African Studies* 19, no. 4 (1981): 647–65.

———. *NATO: The Warsaw Pact and Africa.* New York: St. Martin's Press, 1985.

———. *South Africa's Security Dilemmas.* New York: Praeger, 1987.

Colelough, Christohper. "Collective Bargaining as an Internal Sanction: The Role of U.S. Corporations in South Africa." *Journal of Modern African Studies* 19, no. 4 (1981): 647–65.

Colelough, Christopher, and Stephen McCarthy. *The Political Economy of Botswana.* London: Oxford University Press, 1980.

"Commerce in Blinkers: East Asia Has Sizable Economic Ties with Pretoria." *Far Eastern Economic Review.* (7 August 1986): 14–16.

"Commonwealth Communique." *Africa Research Bulletin,* 15 September 1986, 8205.

Commonwealth Conference of Foreign Ministers on Southern Africa, *South Africa's Relationship with the Financial System.* London: Commonwealth Secretariat, July 1988.

Commonwealth Group of Eminent Persons. Mission to South Africa. *The Commonwealth Report: Report of the Commonwealth Group of Eminent Persons Appointed Under the Nassau Accord on Southern Africa.* London: Commonwealth Secretariat, June, 1986.

"Condemnation of Lesotho Massacre." *International Canada* (Dec. 1981–Jan. 1982): 9.

Conlon, Paul. *Analytical Compendium of Actions Taken By Governments with Respect to Sanctions on South Africa.* No. 16/86. New York: UNCAA, 1986.

Consulate General of Israel. *Israel Cabinet Decision Regarding Relations With South Africa.* Chicago: 16 September 1987.

Consulate General of Israel. *Israel Government Decision on South Africa.* Chicago: 18 March 1987.

"Continental Alignments." *Africa Research Bulletin* 22, no. 10 (November 1985): 7807–16.

Cooney, James A., Gordon A. Craig, Hans Peter Schwaz, and Fritz Stern, eds. *The Federal Republic of Germany and the United States: Changing Political and Economic Relations.* Boulder: Westview Press, 1984.

Cranston, Maurice. "Are There Any Human Rights?" *Daedalus* 112, no. 4 (Fall 1983): 1–8.

Cristophersen, Jens A. "The Making of Foreign Policy in Norway." *Cooperation and Conflict* 3, no. 1 (1968): 52–74.

Crush, Jonathan, and Paul Wellings. "The Southern African Pleasure Periphery, 1966–83." *Journal of Modern African Studies* 21, no. 4 (1983): 673–98.

Dale, Richard. "Botswana's Foreign Policy: State and Non-State Actors and Small Power Diplomacy." In *The Evolution of Modern Botswana,* edited by Louis A. Picard, 209–27. London: Rex Collings, 1985.

Davis, Jennifer, James Cason, and Gail Hovey. "Economic Disengagement and South Africa: The Effectiveness and Feasibility of Implementing Sanctions and Divestment." *Law and Policy in International Business* 15 (1983): 427–44.

Davis, Stephen M. *Apartheid's Rebels: Inside South Africa's Hidden War.* New Haven: Yale University Press, 1987.

Day, John. "A Failure of Foreign Policy: The Case of Rhodesia." In *Constraints and Adjustments in British Foreign Policy,* edited by Michael Leiter, 150–71. London: George Allen and Unwin, 1982.

deBilj, Harm J. *South Africa.* Evanston: Northwestern University Press, 1962.

Department of External Affairs, Canada. "Visit of the Honorable Duff Roblin to Southern Africa." Ottawa: Government of Canada, January 1986.

Department of Foreign Affairs. *Manifesto for the Future.* Pretoria: The Government Printer, 1985.

Department of Foreign Affairs. *South Africa: Mainstay of Southern Africa.* Pretoria: The Government Printer, 1985.

de St. Jorre, John. "South Africa's Non-U.S. Economic Links." *CSIS Africa Notes,* no. 43 (24 May 1985): 1–4.

DeVos, George A., William O. Wetherall, and Kaye Steerman. *Japan's Minorities: Burakumia, Koreans, Ainu, and Okinawans.* London: Minority Rights Group, 1983.

Diamond, Larry, Juan J. Linz, and Seymour Martin Lipset, eds. *Democracy in Developing Countries.* Boulder: Lynne Rienner Publishers, 1988.

Dobell, Peter C. *Canada's Search for New Roles: Foreign Policy in the Trudeau Era.* London: Oxford University Press, 1972.

*Does Signing the Sullivan Principles Matter?* Washington, D.C.: Investor Responsibility Research Center, 1985.

Doxey, Margaret P. *International Sanctions in Contemporary Perspective.* New York: St. Martin's Press, 1987.

———. "International Sanctions: Trial of Strength or Tests of Weakness." *Millenium* 12, no. 1 (Spring 1983): 79–87.

Dugard, John R. "Political Options for Southern Africa and Implications for the West." In *Conflict and Compromise in South Africa,* edited by Robert I. Rotberg and John Barratt, 17–29. Lexington: Lexington Books, 1980.

Economist Intelligence Unit. *Botswana, Lesotho, and Swaziland, 1987–1988.* London: Economist Intelligence Unit, 1988.

Economist Intelligence Unit. *Japanese Overseas Investment.* London: Economist Intelligence Unit, 1983.

Economist Intelligence Unit. *Zimbabwe, Malawi, No. 4.* London: Economist Intelligence Unit, 1988.

Edinger, Lewis J. *West German Politics.* New York: Columbia University Press, 1986.

Edmonds, Martin. "British Foreign Policy." *Current History* 87 (May 1988): 197–226.

"Embarrassment for Botha." *Time,* 25 June 1984, 50.

"European Community Places Economic Sanctions on South Africa." *European Community News No. 27.* Washington, D.C.: European Community Information Service, 1986.

Farrell, Barry R. "Canada: Argument Within Consensus." In *Canada in Transition,* edited by Barry R. Farrell, 5–31. Chicago: Council on Foreign Relations, 1984.

Faubry, Ib. "Foreign Policy Making in Scandinavia." In *Foreign Policy Making in Western Europe: A Comparative Approach,* edited by William Wallace and W. E. Paterson, 106–34. West Mead: Saxon House, 1978.

———. "Party System and Foreign Policy in Denmark." *Cooperation and Conflict* 14, no. 4 (1979): 159–70.

Federal Ministry for Foreign Affairs: Federal Republic of Germany. *Genscher Met with Boesak.* Bonn: Federal Ministry for Foreign Affairs, 1987.

Feldman, Lily Gardener. *The Special Relationship Between West Germany and Israel.* Boston: George Allen and Unwin, 1984.

Felton, John. "Israel, Other Countries Named As Violators of Weapons Ban." *Congressional Quarterly Weekly Report* 45 (4 April 1987): 623.

"Fence Mending: Botha Goes Calling in Europe." *Time,* 1 June 1984, 41.

Fisher, Foszia, Lawrence Schlemmer, and Eddie Webster. "Economic Growth and its Relationship to Social and Political Change." In *Change, Reform, and Economic Growth in South Africa,* edited by Lawrence Schlemmer and Eddie Webster, 9–27. Johannesburg: Ravan Press, 1978.

Fisher, Roger. *International Conflict for Beginners.* New York: Harper and Row, 1969.

———. "New Thinking on the U.S.-Soviet Relationship: What is a 'Good Relationship' and How Do We Build One?" Cambridge: Harvard Negotiation Project, 1987.

Flournoy, Michele A., and Kurt Campbell. "South Africa's Bomb: A Military Option." *Orbis* 32, no. 3 (Summer 1988): 385–402.

Forrester, Veronica. "West Germany and Africa: A Special African Business Survey." *African Business.* (August 1984): 30–40.

———. "West Germany and Africa Survey." *African Business.* (August 1986): 55–63.

Fox, Annette, and William Fox. "Domestic Capabilities and Canadian Foreign Policy." *International Journal* 39, no. 1 (Winter 1983–84): 23–46.

Franke, Lawrence G. "The European Connection: How Durable?" In *South Africa into the 1980s,* edited by Richard E. Bissell and Chester A. Crocker, 187–207. Boulder: Westview Press, 1979.

Fraser, Malcolm, and Olusegun Obasanjo. "What to do About Southern Africa." *Foreign Affairs* 65, no. 1 (Fall 1986): 154–62.

Fredrickson, George M. *White Supremacy: A Comparative Study in American and South African History.* New York: Oxford University Press, 1981.

Freeman, Linda. "Canada and Africa in the 1970s." *International Journal* 35, no. 4 (Autumn 1980): 815.

Friedland, Elaine A. "The SADCC and the West: Cooperation or Conflict?" *Journal of Modern African Studies* 23, no. 2 (June 1985): 287–314.

Galtung, Johan. "On The Effects of International Economic Sanctions: With Examples from the Case of Rhodesia." *World Politics* 19, no. 3 (April 1967): 378–416.

Gann, L. H., and Peter Duignan. *Why South Africa Will Survive.* New York: St. Martin's Press, 1981.

Geldenhuys, Deon. *The Diplomacy of Isolation: South African Foreign Policy Marketing.* New York: St. Martin's Press, 1984.

———. "German Views on South Africa's Future." *Aussenpolitik* 38, no. 1 (1985): 82–100.

———. *What Do We Think? A Survey of White Opinion of Foreign Policy Issues.* Braamfontein: The South African Institute of International Affairs, 1984.

"Genscher Meets with ANC Leader in Bonn." *The Week in Germany* (June 17, 1988): 2–3.

Genshcer, Hans-Dietrich. "Principles of the Federal Government's Policy Towards Africa." *IIR Newsletter* (Bonn) no. 1 (1987): 1–3.

Gersony, Robert. *Summary of Mozambican Refugee Accounts of Principally Conflict-Related Experience in Mozambique.* Washington, D.C.: U.S. Department of State's Bureau for Refugee Programs, April 1988.

Gjerstad, Ole. *Canadian Policy on Namibia: A Lack of Clout or a Lack of Commitment?* Ottawa: IDAFSA, 1985.

Goba, Bonganjalo. "The Role of Academics and Human Relationships in Southern Africa: A Christian Perspective." In *The Role of Academics and Human Relationships in Southern Africa,* edited by Eric Wainwright and Wilfred Halenke, 3–9. Johannesburg: Professors World Peace Academy, 1985.

Godfrey, Steve. *Self Reliance Versus Dependence in Southern Africa: The Case of SADCC.* Ottawa: IDAFSA, 1985.

Goldstein, Michael. *Minority Status and Radicalism in Japan.* Denver: University of Denver Press, 1972.

Good, Kenneth. "Zambia and the Liberation of South Africa." *Journal of Modern African Studies* 25, no. 3 (1987): 505–40.

Gordon, David F. "The Politics of International Sanctions: A Case Study of South Africa." In *Dilemmas of Economic Coercion: Sanctions in World Politics,* edited by Miroslav Nincic and Peter Wallensteen, 183–210. New York: Praeger, 1983.

Gray, Madi. *Sweden and South Africa: The Two Faces.* Stockholm: Africa Groups in Sweden, 1987.

Greenberg, Stanley B. "Economic Growth and Political Change: The South African Case." *Journal of Modern African Studies* 19, no. 4 (1981): 667–704.

———. "Resistance and Hegemony in Southern Africa." In *The State of Apartheid,* edited by Wilmot G. James, 51–74. Boulder: Lynne Rienner Publishers, 1987.

Grose, Peter. *A Changing Israel.* New York: Times Books, 1980.

"Growing Cooperation with African States." *Africa,* no. 183 (November 1986): 71–75.

Gruhn, Isebill V. *British Arms Sales to Southern Africa: The Limits of African Diplomacy.* Denver: University of Denver Press, 1972.

Grundy, Kenneth W. *The Militarization of South African Politics.* Bloomington: Indiana University Press, 1986.

———. *"We're Against Apartheid, But . . ." Dutch Policy Toward Southern Africa.* Denver: University of Denver Press, 1974.

Gunn, Angus M. *South Africa: A World Challenged.* Vancouver: Legacy Press, 1987.

Gunn, Gillian. "Mozambique After Machel." In *Angola, Mozambique, and the West,* edited by Helen Kitchen, 117–146. Washington, D.C.: Center for Strategic and International Studies, 1987.

———. "Post-Nkomati Mozambique." In *Angola, Mozambique, and the West,* edited by Helen Kitchen, 83–104. Washington, D.C.: Center for Strategic and International Studies, 1987.

Gutteridge, William F. "The Strategic Implications of Sanctions Against South Africa." In *Sanctions Against Southern Africa,* edited by Ronald Segal, 107–15. Baltimore: Penguin Books, 1964.

Haekkerup, Per. "The South African Racial Crisis and the World." In *Sanctions Against Southern Africa,* edited by Ronald Segal, 42–47. Baltimore: Penguin Books, 1964.

Hagtvet, Bernt and Erik Rudeng. "Scandinavia: Achievements, Dilemmas, and Challenges." *Daedalus* 113, no. 2 (Spring 1984): 227–56.

Hallet, Robin. *Africa Since 1875.* Ann Arbor: University of Michigan Press, 1974.

Hanks, Robert J. *Southern Africa and Western Security.* Cambridge: Institute for Foreign Policy Analysis, 1983.

Hanlon, Joseph, and Roger Omond. *The Sanctions Handbook.* New York: Penguin Books, 1987.

Hanrieder, Wolfram F., ed. *West German Foreign Policy: 1949–79.* Boulder: Westview Press, 1980.

Hanrieder, Wolfram F., and Graeme P. Auton. *The Foreign Policies of West Germany, France, and Britain.* Englewood Cliffs: Prentice-Hall, Inc., 1980.

Hardy, Chandra. "The Prospects for Growth and Structural Change in Southern Africa." *Development Dialogue,* no. 2 (1987): 33–58.

Harsch, Ernest. "Across the Continent: The People's Sanctions." *Africa Report* 33 (March–April 1988): 53–55.

Harvaky, Robert E. "The Pariah State Syndrome." *Orbis* 31, no. 3 (Fall 1977): 623–49.

Hasenbalg, Carol A. *Race Relations in Modern Brazil.* Albuquerque: University of New Mexico, 1981.

Haskel, Barbara G. *The Scandinavian Option: Opportunity Costs in Postwar Scandinavian Foreign Policies.* Oslo: Norwegian University Press, 1976.

Hauck, David. *U.S. Corporate Withdrawal from Southern Africa: The Likely Impact on Political Change.* Washington, D.C.: Investor Responsibility Research Center, 1986.

Hauck, David, Meg Norrhes, and Glenn Goldberg. *Two Decades of Debate: The Controversy over U.S. Companies in South Africa.* Washington, D.C.: Investor Responsibility Research Center.

Hawes, Michael K. *Principal Power, Middle Power, or Satellite: Competing Perspectives in the Study of Canadian Foreign Policy.* Toronto: York University Research Program in Strategic Studies, 1984.

Hayes, J. P. *Economic Effects of Sanctions on South Africa*. London: Trade Policy Research Centre, 1987.

Helco, Hugh, and Henrik Madsen. *Policy and Politics in Sweden: Principled Pragmatism*. Philadelphia: Temple University Press, 1987.

Hellman, Donald C. *Japan: Its Domestic Politics and Foreign Policy*. Washington, D.C.: American Enterprise Institute, 1973.

————. "Japanese Politics and Foreign Policy: Elitist Democracy Within an American Greenhouse." In *The Political Economy of Japan: The Changing International Context*, edited by Takashi Inoguchi and Daniel Okimoto, 345–80. Stanford: Stanford University Press, 1988.

Hill, Christopher R. "The Code of Conduct in Practice." In *European Business and South Africa: An Appraisal of the E.C. Code of Conduct*, edited by Anne Akeroyd, Franz Ansprenger, Reinhard Hermy, and Christopher R. Hill, 26–33. Munich: Kaiser, 1981.

Hirschmann, David. "Changes in Lesotho's Policy Towards Southern Africa." *African Affairs* 78, no. 311 (April 1979): 177–96.

Hofmeier, Rolf. "Aid from the Federal Republic of Germany to Africa." *The Journal of Modern African Studies* 24, no. 4 (1986): 577–601.

Holland, Martin. "The European Community and South Africa: Economic Reality or Political Rhetoric?" *Political Studies* 33 (September 1985): 379–417.

————. *The European Community and Southern Africa: European Political Cooperation Under Strain*. London: Pinter Publishers, 1988.

Holm, Hans-Henrik. "Danish Third World Policy: The Feed-Back Problem." *Cooperation and Conflict* 14, no. 2 (1979): 87–103.

Holm, John D. "Botswana: A Paternalistic Democracy." *World Affairs* 150, no. 1 (Summer 1987): 21–30.

————. "Elections in Botswana: Institutionalization of a New System of Legitimacy." In *Elections in Independent Africa*, edited by Fred M. Hayward, 121–47. Boulder: Westview Press, 1985.

Holst, Johan Jorgen. "Introduction." In *Norwegian Foreign Policy in the 1980s*, edited by Johan Jorgen Holst, 9–11. Oslo: Norwegian University Press, 1985.

————. "The Pattern of Nordic Security." *Daedalus* 113, no. 2 (Spring 1984): 195–225.

Holzner, Lutz. "West Germany." In *International Handbook on Race and Race Relations*, edited by Jay A. Sigler, 423–77. New York: Greenwood Press, 1987.

"Hong Kong: Trading East." *National Review*, 31 December 1986, 51.

Human Sciences Research Council. *The South African Society: Realities and Future Prospects*. New York: Greenwood Press, 1987.

Hunter, Jane. *Israel: Foreign Policy: South Africa and Central America*. Boston: South End Press, 1987.

IDAFSA. *Spear of Hope: The Children of South Africa*. Ottawa: Canadian Committee, August 1987.

IDAFSA. *Submission to the Special Joint Committee of Parliament on Canada's International Relations*. Ottawa: Canadian Committee, September 1985.

Institute for International Relations. "German Trade with Africa in 1987." *IIR Newsletter* (Bonn), no. 4 (1988): 6–12.

Institute for International Relations. "A Survey of Bilateral German Development Aid to Individual African Countries." *Supplement to IIR Newsletter* (Bonn), no. 4 (1987): 3–5.

Institute for International Relations. "Training Program for Experts from SWAPO in the Federal Republic of Germany." *Supplement to IIR Newsletter* (Bonn), no. 8 (1986): 1–2.

International Defense and Aid Fund for Southern Africa (Canada). *Nkomati Accord—Destabilization and the Defense of Apartheid.* Ottawa: Canadian Committee, 1985.

Isaacman, Allen. "Mozambique: The Malawi Connection." *Africa Report* 31, no. 6 (November–December 1986): 51–54.

"Israel and South Africa: Friends in Need." *The Economist,* 21 February 1987, 40–41.

"Israeli Arms Sanctions." *Africa Research Bulletin,* 15 April 1987, 8449.

Israel Ministry of Foreign Affairs. *Israel's Policy Towards South Africa.* Jerusalem: 18 March 1987.

"Israel's Apartheid Links." *Labour Research,* February 1987, 14–16.

Ivens, Michael. "The Corporate Role in Fighting Apartheid: British Style." In *The South African Quagmire: In Search of a Peaceful Path to Democratic Pluralism,* edited by S. Prakash Sethi, 319–31. Cambridge: Ballinger Publishing Co., 1987.

"Japan and South Africa: No, But We Saw The Film." *The Economist,* 2 April 1988, 31.

Japan Anti-Apartheid Committee. *A Report to the Strategy Session of The Special Committee Against Apartheid.* New York: United Nations, November 1985.

"Japanese Commitment to Africa." *Africa,* no. 171 (November 1985): 59–64.

Jaster, Robert S. *South Africa and Its Neighbors: The Dynamics of Regional Conflict.* London: International Institute for Strategic Studies, 1986.

Javetski, Bill, and Elizabeth Weiner. "A Little Consensus Will Go a Long Way against Pretoria." *Business Week,* 18 August 1986, 5.

Jenkins, Carolyn M. *The Economic Implications of Disinvestment for South Africa.* Pretoria: The South African Institute of International Affairs, 1986.

Jervis, Robert. *The Logic of Images in International Relations.* Princeton: Princeton University Press, 1970.

Jinadu, L. A. "The Political Economy of Sweden's Development Policy in Africa." *Cooperation and Conflict* 19, no. 3 (1984): 177–96.

Jo, Hung-Hwan. "Japan." In *International Handbook on Race and Race Relations,* edited by Jay A. Sigler, 129–53. New York: Greenwood Press, 1987.

Joffee, Josef. "The Foreign Policy of the Federal Republic of Germany." In *Foreign Policy in World Politics,* edited by Roy C. Macridis, 72–113. Englewood Cliffs: Prentice-Hall, 1985.

Johnson, Phyllis, and David Martin, eds. *Destructive Engagement: Southern Africa at War.* Harare: Zimbabwe Publishing House, 1986.

Johnston, A. M. "Domestic Concerns and International Pressures." In *International Pressures and Political Changes in South Africa,* edited by F. Clifford-Vaughan. Cape Town: Oxford University Press, 1978.

Jordan, A. G., and J. J. Richardson. *Government and Pressure Groups in Britain.* Oxford: Clarendon Press, 1987.

Joseph, Benjamin M. *Beseiged Bedfellows: Israel and the Land of Apartheid.* New York: Greenwood Press, 1988.

Kaan, Haider Ali, and Oscar Plaza. "Measuring and Analyzing the Economic

Effects of Trade Sanctions Against South Africa: A New Approach." *Africa Today* (2nd/3rd Quarters, 1986): 47–58.

Kaempfer, William H., James A. Lehman, and Anton D. Lowenberg. "Divestment, Investment Sanctions, and Disinvestment: An Evalutation of Anti-Apartheid Policy Instruments." *International Organization* 41, no. 3 (Summer 1987): 457–73.

Karis, Thomas G. "South African Liberation: The Communist Factor." *Foreign Affairs* 65, no. 2 (Winter 1986–87): 267–87.

Kegley, Charles W., Jr., and Eugene R. Wittkopf, eds. *The Domestic Sources of American Foreign Policy: Insights and Evidence.* New York: St. Martin's Press, 1988.

Keohane, Robert O., and Joseph S. Nye. *Power and Interdependence: World Politics in Transition.* Boston: Little, Brown, and Co., 1979.

Kibble, Steve, and Ray Bush. "Reform of Apartheid and Continued Destabilization in Southern Africa." *The Journal of Modern African Studies* 24, no. 2 (1986): 203–27.

Kienzie, William. "German-South African Trade Relations in the Nazi Era." *African Affairs* 78, no. 310 (January 1979): 81–90.

Kim, Hong N. "The Role of Big Business in the Making of Postwar Japanese Foreign Economic Policy." In *Japan's Foreign Policymaking*, edited by Hiroshi Itoh, 6–24. Albany: State University of New York Press, 1979.

Kirton, John. "The Foreign Policy Decision Process." In *Canada Among Nations: The Conservative Agenda*, edited by Maureen Appel Molot and Brian W. Tomlin, 25–45. Toronto: Macmillan of Canada, 1976.

Kitchen, Helen. *Some Guidelines for the Next President.* Washington, D.C.: The Center for Strategic and International Studies, 1988.

Klieman, Aaron S. *Israel's Global Reach: Arms Sales as Diplomacy.* Washington: Pergamon-Brussey's International Defense Publishers, 1985.

Klinge, Matti. "Aspects of the Nordic Self." *Daedalus* 113, no. 2 (Spring 1984): 257–76.

Knopff, Rainer. "The Statistical Protection of Minorities: Affirmative Action Policy in Canada." In *Minorities and the Canadian State*, edited by Neil Nevitte and Allan Koruberg, 87–106. Oakville: Mosaic Press, 1985.

Knudsen, Olau Fagelund, and Arild Underdal. "Patterns of Norwegian Foreign Policy Behavior: An Exploratory Analysis." *Cooperation and Conflict* 20, no. 4 (1985): 229–51.

Koenderman, Tony. *Sanctions: The Threat to South Africa.* Johannesburg: Jonathan Ball Publishers, 1982.

Kohl, Helmut. "No Change in Bonn's Africa Policy." *The Week in Germany* (February 26, 1988): 2.

———. "Principles and Current Positions of the Federal Government's Policy Towards Southern Africa." Minutes of the Plenary Debate in the German Bundestag on 4 February 1988. Reprinted in *Newsletter* (Bonn), no. 1 (1988).

———. "We Must Jointly Support the African States' Development." *Newsletter* (Bonn), no. 6 (1987): 2–6.

———. Interview on Federal Republic of Germany, Radio, 31 August 1986.

———. Statement to President Samora Machel and Prime Minister P. W. Botha in connection with the signing of a non-aggression treaty between Mozambique and South Africa on March 16. Frankfort: Federal Press Office, 16 March 1984.

Kolbourn, William. "The Peaceable Kingdom Still." *Daedalus* 117, no. 4 (Fall 1988): 1–30.

Kostiuk, Nadia. "Botswana." In *The Political Economy of African Foreign Policy*, edited by Timothy M. Shaw and Olajide Aluko, 60–78. New York: St. Martin's Press, 1984.

Kotani, Toru. "Rising Sun Over Africa." *Africa Report* 30, no. 6 (November–December 1985): 68–71.

Krause, Joachim, and Luther Wilker. "Bureaucracy and Foreign Policy in the Federal Republic of Germany." In *The Foreign Policy of West Germany*, edited by Ekkehart Krippendorf and Volker Rittberger, 147–70. London: Sage Publications, 1980.

Kurata, Phil. "The Outcasts Forge New Bonds." *Far Eastern Economic Review*, 7 November 1980: 40–41.

Lambley, Peter. *The Psychology of Apartheid*. London: Secker & Warburg, 1980.

Lanir, Zvi, ed. *Israeli Security Planning in the 1980s: Its Politics and Economics*. New York: Praeger, 1984.

Lasswell, Harold D., and Abraham Kaplan. *Power and Society: A Framework for Political Inquiry*. New Haven: Yale University Press, 1950.

Layton-Henry, Zig. *The Politics of Race in Britain.* London: George Allen and Unwin, 1984.

Leach, Graham. *South Africa: No Easy Path to Peace*. London: Routledge and Kegan Paul, 1986.

Lee, Changsoo, and George De Vos. *Koreans in Japan: Ethnic Conflict and Accommodation*. Berkeley: University of California Press, 1981.

Legum, Colin. *The Battlefronts of Southern Africa*. New York: Africana Publishing Co., 1988.

———. "The Middle East Dimension." In *International Politics in Southern Africa*, edited by Gwendolen M. Carter and Patrick O'Meara, 115–27. Bloomington: Indiana University Press, 1982.

Leistner, G. M. E. "Sanctions Against South Africa in Regional Perspective." *Bulletin* 25, no. 5 (1985): 49–59.

Leonardsson, Krisftoffer. *Sanctions Busting.* Stockholm: The Isolate South Africa Committee, 1987.

"Lesotho Water Project Gets Underway." *Africa Report* 33, no. 3 (May–June 1988): 10–11.

LeVine, Victor T., and Timothy W. Luke. *The Arab-African Connection: Political and Economic Realities*. Boulder: Westview Press, 1979.

Levy, Sam. "U.S.–Mozambique: Broken Promises?" *Africa Report* 31, no. 1 (January–February 1986): 77–80.

Lewis, Jr., Stephan R. "Some Economic Realities in South Africa: One Hundred Million Futures." In *Poverty, Policy, and Food Security in Southern Africa*, edited by Coralie Bryan, 39–92. Boulder: Lynne Rienner Publishers, 1988.

———. "Southern Africa Interdependence." *CSIS Africa Notes*, no. 56 (27 March 1986): 1–4.

Leyton-Brown, David. "Lessons and Policy Considerations About Economic Sanctions." In *The Utility of International Economic Sanctions*, edited by David Leyton-Brown, 303–10. New York: St. Martin's Press, 1987.

Libby, Ronald T. *The Politics of Economic Power in Southern Africa*. Princeton: Princeton University Press, 1987.

Lieber, Robert J. "British Foreign Policy." In *Foreign Policy in World Politics*, edited by Roy Macridis, 1–21. Englewood Cliffs: Prentice-Hall, 1985.

Lindsay, James N. "Trade Sanctions as Policy Instruments: A Re-examination." *International Studies Quarterly* 30, no. 3 (1986): 153–73.

Lipton, Merle. "Reform: Destruction or Modernization of Apartheid." In *South Africa in Crisis*, edited by Jesmond Blumenfeld, 34–55. London: Croom Helm, 1987.

———. "South Africa's Role in Agricultural Production and Marketing in Southern Africa." In *Poverty, Policy, and Food Security in Southern Africa*, edited by Coralie Bryan, 178–214. Boulder: Lynne Rienner Publishers, 1988.

Lipumba, Nguyuru H. "The State of the Economies of Frontline States and the Liberation Struggle in Southern Africa." In *Confrontation and Liberation in Southern Africa*, edited by Ibrahim Msabaha and Timothy M. Shaw. Boulder: Westview Press, 1987.

Liviatan, Nissan, and Sylvia Piterman. "Accelerating Inflation and Balance-of-Payments Crisis, 1973–1984." In *The Israeli Economy*, edited by Yoram Ben-Porath. Cambridge: Harvard University Press, 1988.

Lopes, Mota. "The MNR: Opponents or Bandits?" *Africa Report* 31, no. 1 (January–February 1986): 67–73.

Losman, Donald L. *International Economic Sanctions: The Cases of Cuba, Israel, and Rhodesia*. Albuquerque: University of New Mexico Press, 1979.

Love, Janice. "The Potential Impact of Economic Sanctions Against South Africa." *Journal of Modern African Studies* 26, no. 1 (1988): 91–111.

Lustic, Ian S. "Israel's Dangerous Fundamentalists." *Foreign Policy*, no. 68 (Fall 1987): 118–39.

Maasdorp, Gavin G. "Squaring Up To Economic Dominance: Regional Patterns." In *South Africa and its Neighbors: Regional Security and Self-Interest*, edited by Robert I. Rotberg et al. Lexington: Lexington Books, 1985.

Mackler, Ian. *Pattern for Profit in Southern Africa*. Lexington: Lexington Books, 1972.

Magubane, Bernard. "Botswana, Lesotho, and Swaziland: South Africa's Hostages in Revolt." In *South Africa in Southern Africa: The Intensifying Vortex of Violence*, edited by Thomas M. Callaghy, 355–69. New York: Praeger, 1983.

Makgetla, Neva, and Ann Seidmann. *Outposts of Monopoly Capitalism: Southern Africa in the Changing Global Economy*. Westport: Lawrence Hill and Company, 1980.

Makgetla, Neva, and Ann Seidman. "Theoretical and Practical Implications of IMF Conditionality in Zambia." *The Journal of Modern African Studies* 24, no. 3 (1986): 395–402.

Mandaza, Ibbor, ed. *Zimbabwe: The Political Economy of Transition, 1980–1986*. Dakar: Codesria, 1986.

Marakami, Yasusuke, and Yutaka Kosai. *Japan in the Global Community*. Tokyo: University of Tokyo Press, 1986.

Maritz, Chris. "Pretoria's Reaction to the Role of Moscow and Peking in Southern Africa." *Journal of Modern African Studies* 25, no. 2 (1987): 321–44.

Marks, Shula. "Southern and Central Africa." In *The Cambridge History of Africa*, vol. 6, edited by Roland Oliver and G. N. Sanderson, 422–92. Cambridge: Cambridge University Press, 1985.

Martin, David, and Phyllis Jackson. "Africa: The Old and the Unexpected." *Foreign Affairs* 63, no. 3 (1985): 602–30.

Martin, Paul. "South African Sport: Apartheid's Achilles' Heel?" *The World Today*, June 1984, 234–243.

Martin, Roger. "How British Policy Toward Africa is Shaped and Executed." *CSIS Africa Notes, no. 87*. Washington, D.C.: Center for Strategic and International Studies, 1988.

———. "Southern Africa: A New Approach." *The Round Table*, no. 303 (July 1987): 322–32.

*Massacre at Maseru: South African Aggression Against Lesotho*. London: International Defense and Aid Fund, 1985.

Matthews, Jacqueline. "Foreign Trade." In *South Africa and the World Economy*, edited by Jacqueline Matthews, 157–76. Johannesburg: McGraw-Hill Book Company, 1983.

Matthews, Robert O. "Canada and Anglophone Africa." In *Canada and The Third World*, edited by Peyton Lyon and Tareg Ismael, 60–132. Toronto: Macmillan of Canada, 1976.

Maull, Hans W. "South Africa's Minerals: The Achilles' Heel of Western Economic Security." *International Affairs* 62, no. 4 (Autumn 1986): 619–26.

McKensie, Hilary, and Jane O'Hara. "Britain's Assault on the Commonwealth." *Maclean's*, 26 October 1987, 24–25.

Meldrum, Andrew. "Mozambique Special Report: The Most Brutal War." *Africa Report* 33, no. 2 (May–June 1988): 23–28.

Meldrum, Andrew. "Zimbabwe: United We Stand." *Africa Report* 33, no. 2 (March/April 1988): 66–68.

Metrowich, F. R. *South Africa's New Frontiers*. Sandton, South Africa: Valiant Publishers, 1977.

Metz, Steven. "Pretoria's Total Strategy and Low Intensity Warfare in Southern Africa." *Comparative Strategy* 6, no. 4 (1987): 437–70.

Mever, Gerd. "West Germany Boosts Aid in Bid to Change Its Image." *New African* (Jan. 1978): 33–34.

Miaogeng, Lu. "Tokyo Draws Closer to Africa." *Beijing Review*, no. 22 (3 June 1985): 12–13.

Millar, T. B. *Australia's Foreign Policy*. Sidney: Angus and Robertson, Ltd., 1968.

Ministry of Foreign Affairs, Japan. *Diplomatic Bluebook, 1986 Edition: Review of Recent Developments in Japan's Foreign Relations*. Tokyo: Foreign Press Center, 1986.

Ministry for Foreign Affairs, Sweden. *Prohibition of Trade With South Africa and Namibia: An Unofficial Translation of the Swedish Government's Bill on Prohibition of Trade with South Africa and Namibia*. Stockholm: Swedish Government Printing, 1987.

Minter, William. *King Solomon's Mines Revisited: Western Interests and the Burdened History of Southern Africa*. New York: Basic Books, Inc., 1986.

———. "South Africa: Straight Talk on Sanctions." *Foreign Policy*, no. 65 (Winter 1986–87): 43–63.

Modie, Dunbar T. *The Rise of Afrikanerdom: Power, Apartheid, and the Afrikaner Civil Religion*. Berkeley: University of California Press, 1975.

Moffat, Susan. "Never Mind Apartheid While Business Pays." *Daily Yomiuri*, 15 September 1985.

Moodley, Kogil. "The Legitimation Crisis of the South African State." *The Journal of Modern African Studies* 24, no. 2 (1986): 187–201.

Moore, J. D. L. *South Africa and Nuclear Proliferation.* London: Macmillan Press, 1987.

"More Questions After Sanctions." *The Economist,* 21 June 1986, 53.

Morikawa, Jun. "The Anatomy of Japan's South Africa Policy." *Journal of Modern African Studies* 22, no. 1 (1984): 133–41.

———. "The Myth and Reality of Japan's Relations with Colonial Africa." *Journal of African Studies* 12, no. 1 (Spring 1985): 39–46.

Morna, Coleen Lowe. "Zimbabwe: Preparing for War." *Africa Report* 32, no. 1 (January–February 1987): 55–59.

Moss, Joanna, and John Ravenhill. *Emerging Japanese Economic Influence in Africa.* Berkeley: University of California Press, 1985.

"Mozambique-UK: Military Training." *Africa Research Bulletin,* 15 August 1985.

Mugabe, Robert G. "Struggle for Southern Africa." *Foreign Affairs* 66, no. 2 (Winter 1987–88): 311–27.

Myers, III, Desaix. *Labor Practices of U.S. Corporations in South Africa.* New York: Praeger, 1977.

Myers, III, Desaix, et al. *U.S. Business in South Africa: The Economic, Political, and Moral Issues.* Bloomington: Indiana University Press, 1980.

Neethling, Dirk. "Minerals and Energy." In *South Africa and the World Economy,* edited by Jacqueline Matthews, 25–57. Johannesburg: McGraw-Hill Book Company, 1983.

Netanyahu, Benjamin. *The Apartheid Regime's Lifeline Begins in Persian Gulf Oil Ports.* Jerusalem: Israel Ministry of Foreign Affairs, 1986.

Neuhaus, Richard John. *Dispensations: The Future of South Africa as South Africans See It.* Grand Rapids: William B. Gerdmans Publlshlng Co., 1986.

Nielsen, Waldemar. *The Great Powers and Africa.* New York: Praeger, 1969.

Nincic, Miroslav, and Peter Wallensteen. "Economic Coercion and Foreign Policy." In *Dilemmas of Economic Coercion: Sanctions in World Politics,* edited by Miroslav Nincic and Peter Wallensteen, 1–15. New York: Praeger, 1983.

"No Color Bar in South Africa's Trade." *U.S. News and World Report,* 10 April 1978, 31–32.

Norway Documentation. *Foreign Policy Review: Foreign Minister Thaavald Stoltenberg's Statement on Foreign Policy in the Storting on 1 June 1987.* Oslo: The Royal Norwegian Ministry of Foreign Affairs, June 1987.

Norway Ministry for Foreign Affairs. *Nordic Programme of Action Against South Africa.* Oslo: Nordic Foreign Ministers, 17–18 October 1985.

Novieki, Margaret A. "South Africa: A Conversation with Pietkoorhof." *Africa Report* 33, no. 2 (March–April 1988): 59–61.

Nsekela, Amon J., ed. *Southern Africa: Toward Economic Liberation.* London: Rex Collings, 1981.

Nweke, G. Aforka. *Harmonization of African Foreign Policies, 1955–75.* Boston: Boston University Press, 1980.

Oded, Arye. *Africa and the Middle East Conflict.* Boulder: Lynne Rienner Publishers, 1987.

Ogunbadejo, Oye. *The International Politics of Africa's Strategic Minerals.* Westport: Greenwood Press, 1985.

Olsen, Edward A. "Building Bridges to Africa." *Africa Report* 31, no. 2 (March–April 1986): 52–56.

"One Nation Pledge." *Africa Research Bulletin* 15 October 1985, 7793.

Ost, Friedheim. *European Council Foreign Ministers Agree on Sanctions Against South Africa.* Bonn: Federal Press Office, 1986.

Owoege, Jide, and Franklin Vivekanada. "Japan's Aid Diplomacy in Africa." *Scandinavian Journal of Development Alternatives* 4, nos. 3–4 (September–December 1985): 145–55.

Ozaki, Robert S., and Walter Arnold, eds. *Japan's Foreign Relations: A Global Search for Economic Security.* Boulder: Westview Press, 1985.

Palme, Olaf. "South Africa and the Nordic Countries: Speech to Swedish People's Parliament Against Apartheid, Feb. 21 1986." *Development Dialogue,* no. 1 (1987): 64–76.

———. Speech at the Swedish People's Parliament Against Apartheid at Folkets Hus. 21 February 1986.

Palmer, John. *Europe Without America? The Crisis in Atlantic Relations.* New York: Oxford University Press, 1987.

Parson, Jack. *Botswana: Liberal Democracy and the Labor Reserve in Southern Africa.* Boulder: Westview Press, 1984.

Pascoe, William W. "U.S. Sanctions on South Africa: The Results Are In." *Backgrounder,* no. 584. Washington, D.C.: The Heritage Foundation, June 5, 1987.

Patten, Christopher, MP. "Britain and Africa's Development." *The Round Table,* no. 303 (July 1987): 333–42.

Pearce, Joan, and John Sutton. *Protection and Industrial Policy in Europe.* London: Routledge and Kegan Paul, 1986.

Pempel, T. J. "Japanese Foreign Economic Policy: The Domestic Basis for International Behavior." *International Organization* 3 (1977): 754–55.

Permanent Mission of Israel to the United Nations. *Arab Oil Trade with South Africa.* New York: United Nations, 9 October 1986.

Permanent Mission of Norway to the United Nations. *Norwegian Measures Against South Africa.* Oslo: Ministry of Foreign Affairs, 5 July 1985.

Picard, Louis A. *The Politics of Development in Botswana: A Model for Success.* Boulder: Lynne Rienner Publishers, 1987.

Polhemus, James H. "Botswana's Role in the Liberation of Southern Africa." In *The Evolutoin of Modern Botswana,* edited by Louis A. Picard, 228–70. London: Rex Collings, 1985.

"Political Impasse Prompts Economic Crisis." *Africa Research Bulletin,* 15 September 1985, 7745.

Price, Robert M. "Security Versus Growth: The International Factor in South African Policy." *The Annals of the American Academy of Political and Social Science* 489 (January 1987): 103–22.

Purnell, Daniel W. "What's Next: Amplification of the Sullivan Principles." In *International Initiatives: Blueprint for Change in South Africa,* edited by The Carnegie Leadership Program, 7–11. New York: Council on Religion and International Affairs, 1986.

Pym, Francis. "Strains Among Friends Coordinating Western Policy Toward South Africa." In *Europe, America, and South Africa,* edited by Gregory F. Treverton, 28–41. New York: Council on Foreign Relations, 1988.

Quo, F. Quei. "The Impact of Domestic Politics on Japan's Foreign Policy." In *Japan and the World*, edited by Gail Lee Bernstein and Haruhiro Fukui, 176–293. New York: St. Martin's Press, 1988.

Rafael, Gideon. "Five Wars, One Peace: What Next?" *Middle East Review* 20, no. 4 (Summer 1988): 1–12.

Rateli, Anne. "Industry: 1980 and Beyond." In *South Africa in the World Economy*, edited by Jacqueline Matthews, 121–56. Johannesburg: McGraw-Hill Book Company, 1983.

Ravenhill, John. "Japan and Africa." In *Africa Contemporary Record 1981/82*, edited by Colin Legum, A210-A218. New York: Africana Publishing Company, 1981.

Razis, Vic. *The American Connection: The Influence of U.S. Business on South Africa*. London: Rowman and Allanheld Publishers, 1985.

"Real African Growth Slows in 1987, External Debt Burden Remains Severe." *IMF Survey* (June 1988): 193.

Redekop, Clarence, G. "Commerce Over Conscience: The Trudeau Government and South Africa, 1968–84." *Journal of Canadian Studies* 9, no. 4 (Winter 1984–85): 82–105.

Redekop, Clarence G. "Trudeau at Singapore: The Commonwealth and Arms Sales to Southern Africa." In *Acceptance of Paradox: Essays on Canadian Diplomacy in Honour of John W. Holmes*, edited by Kim Richard Nossal, 174–96. Toronto: Canadian Institute of International Affairs, 1982.

Reich, Bernard, and Gersham R. Kieval, eds. *Israel Faces the Future*. New York: Praeger, 1986.

Relly, Gavin. "The Costs of Disinvestment." *Foreign Policy*, no. 63 (Summer 1986): 132–42.

Renwick, Robin. *Economic Sanctions*. Cambridge: Harvard University Press, 1981.

Richardson, Bradley M. "Japanese Foreign Policy." In *Business and Society in Japan*, edited by Bradley M. Richardson and Taizo Veda, 200–207. New York: Praeger, 1981.

Riddell-Dixon, Elizabeth. *The Domestic Mosaic: Domestic Groups and Canadian Foreign Policy*. Toronto: Canadian Institute of International Affairs, 1985.

"Rights and Wrongs About Sanctions." *The Economist*, 5 November 1977, 77–87.

Rivera, Joseph de. *The Psychological Dimension of Foreign Policy*. Columbus: Charles E. Merrill Publishing Company, 1968.

Rivers, Bernard, and Martin Bailey. "How Oil Seeps Into South Africa." *Business and Society Review*, no. 39 (Fall 1981): 53–59.

Rivkin, Arnold. *Africa and the West*. London: Thames and Hudson, 1962.

Robson, Peter. "Regional Integration and the Crisis in Sub-Saharan Africa." *The Journal of Modern African Studies* 23, no. 4 (December 1985): 603–22.

Rodgers, Barbara, and Brian Bolton. *Sanctions Against South Africa: Exploding the Myths*. Manchester: Manchester Free Press, 1981.

Rodgers, Barbara. *White Wealth and Black Poverty: American Investments in Southern Africa*. Westport: Greenwood Press, 1976.

Roscoe, Bruce. "Japanese Firms Will Help China Mine Its Uranium Reserves." *Far Eastern Economic Review* (July 1986): 80–81.

Roscoe, Bruce. "More Licks at the Market." *Far East Economics Review* 135 (January 1987): 52–53.

Rosenau, James N. "Comparative Foreign Policy: Fad, Fantasy, or Field?" *International Studies Quarterly* 12 (September 1968): 296–329.

Rosenau, James N., ed. *The Domestic Sources of Foreign Policy.* New York: Free Press, 1967.

Roslowsky, Diane. *West Germany's Foreign Policy: The Impact of the Social Democrats and the Greens.* New York: Greenwood Press, 1987.

Rotberg, Robert I. "Creating a More Harmonious South Africa." In *Conflict and Compromise in South Africa,* edited by Robert I. Rotberg and John Barratt, 3–14. Lexington: Lexington Books, 1980.

———. "The Dynamics of Southern Africa and U.S. Policy." In *South Africa and Its Neighbors: Regional Security and Self-Interest,* edited by Robert I. Rotberg et al., 151–63. Lexington: Lexington Books: 1985.

———. *Suffer the Future: Policy Choices in Southern Africa.* Cambridge: Harvard University Press, 1980.

Roth, Martin. "Japan and Africa." *Africa Economist Digest,* 10 December 1982, 7–16.

Rudebeck, Lars. "Nordic Policies Toward the Third World." In *Foreign Policies of Northern Europe,* edited by Bengt Sundelius, 143–76. Boulder: Westview Press, 1982.

Rusher, William A. *A Short Course on South Africa.* New York: Communications Distribution, Inc., 1987.

Ruth, Arne. "The Second New Nation: The Mythology of Modern Sweden." *Daedalus* 113, no. 2 (Spring 1984): 53–96.

Rylander, Sten. "The Nordic Initiative and SADCC." In *Another Development for SADCC,* 151-56. Uppsala: Dag Hammerskjöld Foundation, 1987.

Sacks, Benjamin. *South Africa: An Imperial Dilemma.* Albuquerque: University of New Mexico Press, 1967.

"SADCC Summit Draws Pretoria's Ire." *African Business* (March 1987): 15–17.

Said, Edward W. *The Question of Palestine.* New York: Times Books, 1980.

Sampson, Anthony. *Black and Gold.* New York: Pantheon Books, 1987.

"Sanctions on South Africa." *The Economist,* 13 August 1985, 12–13.

"Sanctions Vote Vetoed." *Africa Research Bulletin,* 15 March 1987, 8415–16.

Sanger, Clyde. *Censorship in South Africa.* Ottawa: International Defense and Aid Fund for Southern Africa (Canada), 1988.

Saunders, Harold H. "Arabs and Israelis: A Political Strategy." *Foreign Affairs* 64, no. 2 (Winter 1985-86): 304–25.

Scalapino, Robert A., ed. *The Foreign Policy of Modern Japan.* Berkeley: University of California Press, 1977.

Schatz, Willie. "South Africa: Pulling the Plug." *Datamation* 31 (October 1, 1985): 22–25.

Schlegel, John P. "Canada, the USA, and South Africa." *The Round Table,* no. 301 (January 1987): 40–52.

Schlemmer, Lawrence. "Economy and Society in South Africa." In *Change, Reform, and Economic Growth in South Africa,* edited by Lawrence Schlemmer and Eddie Webster, 111–35. Johannesburg: Rayan Press, 1978.

"Scholarship Program." *International Canada.* (April–May 1984): 12.

Schultz, George P. "Toward a New South Africa." *Africa Report* 31, no. 5 (September–October 1986): 16–19.

Schuriak, Ronald H. "South Africa Candidate for Sophisticated Handling." *International Journal on World Peace* 5, no. 1 (January–March 1988): 13–23.

Seidman, Ann. *The Roots of Crisis in Southern Africa.* Trenton: Africa World Press, 1985.

Shafer, Michael. "Mineral Myths." *Foreign Policy* no. 46 (Summer 1982): 154–71.

Sharp, Gene. *Social Power and Political Freedom.* Boston: Sargeant Publishers, 1980.

Shinkichi, Eto. "Foreign Policy Formation in Japan." In *The Silent Power: Japan's Identity and World Role,* edited by Yamamoto Tadashi, 119–39. Tokyo: The Simul Press, Inc., 1976.

Shuman, Michael H. "Local Foreign Policies." *Foreign Policy,* no. 65 (Winter 1986–87): 157–71.

Sinek, Jeremy. "New Cars for Mercedes, BMW in South Africa." *Automotive News,* 16 June 1986.

Skidmore, Thomas E. *The Politics of Military Rule in Brazil, 1964–85.* New York: Oxford University Press, 1988.

Smith, Timothy. "The Role of Foreign Banks in South Africa." *Objective Justice* 13, no. 2 (November 1981): 24.

Smith, William E. "Going Part of the Way." *Time,* 18 August 1986, 28–29.

Smootha, Sammy. "Internal Divisions in Israel at Forty." *Middle East Review* 20, no. 4 (Summer 1988): 26–36.

"South Africa-EEC." *Africa Research Bulletin,* 15 Aug. 1986, 8168–70.

South Africa. Department of Manpower Utilization. *Report of the National Manpower Commission on High-Level Manpower.* Pretoria: Republic of Southern Africa, 1980.

"South Africa: Canada on Apartheid at U.N." *International Canada* (October–November 1984): 15.

South Africa Federated Chamber of Industries Information Services. *The Effect of Sanctions on Employment and Production in South Africa. A Quantitative Analysis.* Pretoria: FCI Information Services, 1986.

"South Africa: It Does Move When Pushed." *The Economist,* 9 January 1982, 40–41.

"South Africa: Sanctions Split Commonwealth." *Africa Research Bulletin,* 15 September 1986, 8203–4.

"South Africa: Sanctions." *International Canada,* (February–March 1987): 12–13.

"South Africa: Sanctions." *International Canada,* (October–November 1986): 9–10.

"South Africa: The Art of Delay." *The Economist,* 28 June 1986, 39.

"South African Economy." *The Economist,* 23 March 1985, 81.

"South African Sanctions: Where Thatcher is Right and Wrong." *New Statesman,* 20 June 1986, 9.

"South African Subsidiaries: Toothless Watchdog Barks Louder." *The Economist,* 27 May 1978, 103–4.

"Southern Africa: Easier Said Than Done." *The Economist,* 30 August 1986, 34–35.

Spence, J. E. "Foreign Policy: Retreat Into the Laager." In *South Africa in Crisis,* edited by Jesmond Blumenfeld, 155–75. London: Croom Helm, 1987.

Spiro, Peter J. "State and Local Anti-South African Action as an Intrusion Upon the Federal Power in Foreign Affairs." *Virginia Law Review* 72, no. 4 (May 1986): 813–50.

Spring, Martin. "Japan: African Ties Under Fire." *Far Eastern Economic Review* 26 (September 1975): 36–38.

Spring, Martin. "Letter From Johannesburg." *Far Eastern Economic Review* 90 (November 1975): 62.

Stagner, Ross. "Introduction." In *Ethnic Conflict: International Perspectives*, edited by Jerry Boucher, Dan Landis, and Karen Arnold Clark, 7–16. Beverly Hills: Sage Publications, 1987.

Stoppard, John M., and Louis Turner. *Britain and the Multinationals.* New York: John Wiley & Sons, 1985.

Strom, Gabriele Winei. *Development and Dependence in Lesotho: The Enclave of Southern Africa.* Uppsala: The Scandinavian Institute of African Studies, 1978.

Stultz, Newell M. "Foreign Pressures on Southern Africa." *American University Field Staff Reports*, no. 5 (1981): 1–11.

"Sub-Saharan African Debt Position Worsens." *IMF Survey* (June 1988): 193.

Sullivan, Reverend Leon. "Agents for Change: The Mobilization of Multinational Companies in South Africa." *Law and Policy in International Business* 15 (1983): 427–44.

Suzman, Helen. "The Folly of Economic Sanctions." In *The South African Quagmire: In Search of a Peaceful Path to Democratic Pluralism*, edited by S. Prakash Sethi, 189–95. Cambridge: Ballinger Publishing Co., 1987.

Tanzer, Andrew. "A Bridgehead in Asia." *Far Eastern Economic Review* 119, no. 9 (March 1983): 32–34.

Tarne, Gene. *Who Benefits from Sanctions?* Washington, D.C.: Human Events, Inc., 1987.

"Taxing Apartheid." *The Economist*, 13 July 1985, 70.

Tennyson, Brian D. "Canadian Policies Towards South Africa." *Canadian Journal of African Studies* 16 (1982): 518.

———. *Canadian Relations With South Africa.* Washington, D.C.: University Press of America, 1982.

The Stanley Foundation. *Strategy for Peace: Report of the Twenty-sixth Annual Strategy for Peace U.S. Foreign Policy Conference.* Muscatine: The Stanley Foundation, 1985.

Thies, Jochen. "West German Foreign Policy: An Old Tune with New Notes?" *The World Today* (June 1987): 103–105.

Thomas, Elizabeth. "Mirror of a Century of Afrika Politik." In *West German Foreign Policy: Dilemmas and Directions*, edited by Peter H. Merkl, 135–62. Chicago: Chicago Council on Foreign Relations, 1982.

Thompson, Carol B. "Zimbabwe in Southern Africa: From Dependent Development to Dominance or Cooperation." In *The Political Economy of Zimbabwe*, edited by Michael G. Schateborg, 197–217. New York: Praeger, 1984.

Thompson, Leonard. "Great Britain and the Afrikaner Republics." In *The Oxford History of South Africa*, vol. 2, edited by Monica Wilson and Leonard Thompson, 289–324. Oxford: The Clarendon Press, 1971.

"TNC's and South Africa: Public Hearings on the Activities of TNC's in South Africa and Namibia." *The CTC Reporter*, no. 19 (Spring 1985): 28.

Touval, Saadia. *The Peace Brokers: Mediators in the Arab-Israeli Conflict.* Princeton: Princeton University Press, 1982.

Truu, M. L. "Presidential Address: Economics and Politics in South Africa Today." *South African Journal of Economics* 54, no. 4 (1986): 343–61.

Turner, Henry Ashby. *The Two Germanies Since 1945.* New Haven: Yale University Press, 1987.

"UK Concedes on Sanctions." *Africa Research Bulletin,* 15 October 1985, 7792.

Ungar, Sanford J. Africa: *The People and Politics of an Emerging Continent.* New York: Simon and Schuster, 1986.

U.N. Center Against Apartheid. "Canadian Policy on Human Rights in South Africa." August 1989.

U.N. Center on Transnational Corporations. *Policies and Practices of Transnational Corporations Regarding Their Activities in South Africa and Namibia.* New York: United Nations, 1984.

U.N. General Assembly, Forty-first Session. Agenda Item 33. *Policies of Apartheid of the Government of South Africa: Concerted International Action for the Elimination of Apartheid: Report of the Secretary General Addendum.* A1415061Add.3 26 October 1986.

U.N. General Assembly. Official Records: Forty-Second Session. Supplement No. 22 (A/42/22). Report of the Special Committee Against Apartheid 1987.

U.N. General Assembly. Security Council. Report of the Intergovernmental Group to Monitor the Supply and Shipping of Petroleum Products to South Africa. A/42/45 of S/19 251 November 1987.

U.N. *Policies and Practices of Transnational Corporations Regarding Their Activities in South Africa and Namibia.* New York: United Nations, 1984.

UNCAA. *Bishop Desmond Tutu Calls Upon the International Community to Apply Punitive Sanctions Against the Apartheid Regime.* No. 7/86 April 1986.

UNCAA. *Declaration of the International Seminars on the United Nations Arms Embargo Against South Africa.* No. 11/86. August 1986.

UNCAA. *Declaration of the Seminar on Oil Embargo Against South Africa.* No. 12/86. August 1986.UNCAA. *United Nations Actions Against Apartheid.* No. 13/86. September 1986.

UNCAA. *Implementation of United Nations Resolutions on Action Against Apartheid by Member States.* No. 14/86. September 1986.

UNCAA. *News Digest.* No. 10/86. December 1986.

UNCAA. *News Digest.* No. 2/86. February 1986.

UNCAA. *News Digest.* No. 3/86. March 1986.

UNCAA. *News Digest.* No. 4/86. April 1986.

UNCAA. *News Digest.* No. 5/86. May 1986.

UNCAA. *News Digest.* No. 8/86. September 1986.

UNCAA. *News Digest: Resolutions on Apartheid Adopted by the United Nations General Assembly in November 1986.* Special Issue No. 2. November 1986.

UNCAA. *Register of Sports Contacts with South Africa 1 Jan–30 June 1985.* No. 24/86 December 1986.

UNCAA. *Register of Sports Contacts with South Africa 1 July–31 Dec. 1985.* No. 9/86. August 1986.

UNCAA. *United Nations Trust Fund for South Africa (1965–1986).* October 1986.

"Unchanging Apartheid Policy Deplored." *News of Norway,* no. 7, 25 September 1985.

United Nations. *Namibia Bulletin.* No. 6/86.

United Nations. *Namibia Bulletin.* No. 7/86.

U.S. Bureau of Mines, U.S. Dept. of Interior, *South Africa and Critical Materials.* Open File Report 76–86. July 1986.

U.S. Congress House. *To Prohibit Investments In, and Certain Other Activities With*

*Respect to South Africa and For Other Purposes.* 100th Congress 2nd Session. H.R. 1850, H. Rept. 100–642, Pt I.

U.S. Department of State. *A U.S. Policy Toward South Africa: The Report of the Secretary of State's Advisory Committee on South Africa.* Washington, D.C.: Dept. of State, 1987.

U.S. Department of State. *Report to the Congress on Industrialized Democracies. Relations With and Measures Against South Africa: In Implementation of Sections 401(b) (2) LB7 and 506(a) of the Comprehensive Anti-Apartheid Act of 1986.* Washington, D.C.: May 12, 1987.

U.S. Office of Strategic Resources. *Report of Interagency Materials and Minerals Field Study to the Republic of South Africa.* Washington, D.C.: U.S. Department of Commerce, July 1985.

Vale, Peter. "Simple-mindedness and Repressions: The Establishment Responds to South Africa's Woes." *The Round Table,* no. 303 (July 1987): 311–21.

Valen, Henry. "Cleavages in the Norwegian Electorate as a Constraint on Foreign Policymaking." In *Norwegian Foreign Policy in the 1980s,* edited by Johan Jorgen Holst, 25–53. Oslo: Norwegian University Press, 1985.

Van Dijk, Teun A. *Communicating Racism: Ethnic Prejudice in Thought and Talk.* Beverly Hills: Sage Publications, 1987.

Van Wolferen, Karel G. "The Japan Problem" *Foreign Affairs* 65, no. 2 (Winter 1986–87): 288–303.

Vandenbusch, Amry. *Southern Africa and the World: The Foreign Policy of Apartheid.* Lexington: University of Kentucky Press, 1970.

Vander Spug, H. I. J. "The Psychodynamic of Apartheid." In *The Psychology of Apartheid: A Psychological Perspective of Southern Africa,* edited by H. I. J. Vander Spug and D. A. F. Shamlej, 1–17. Washington, D.C.: University Press of America, 1978.

Vau Praug, Nicholas. "European Political Cooperation and Southern Africa." In *European Political Cooperation: Towards a Foreign Policy for Western Europe,* edited by Davil Allen, Reinhardt Ruumel, and Wolfgang Wessels, 134–46. London: Butterworth Scientific, 1982.

Vezina, Monique. "Towards Stronger Ties With Africa." *Statements and Speeches.* 1 October 1984.

Viljoen, S. P. "The Industrial Achievement of South Africa." *The South African Journal of Economics* 52, no. 1 (1984): 42–62.

Vogel, Ezra F. "Japan: Adaptive Communitarianism." In *Ideology and National Competitiveness,* 141–71. Boston: Harvard Business School Press, 1987.

Voight, Karsten. "Fighting Apartheid: Not Only Words, Action is in Demand." Protocol of the Debates of the Federal Parliament, 41st Session, Bonn, 24 November 1987. Reprinted in *IIR Newsletter* (Bonn), no. 1 (1988): 1–5.

von der Ropp, Klaus Freiherr. "Republic of South Africa: Victory of the Counter-Revolution?" *Aussenpolitik: German Foreign Affairs Review* 39, no. 3 (3rd Quarter 1988): 294–305.

———. "Southern Africa: Between a New Order and Chaos." *Aussenpolitik* 30, no. 2 (1979): 225–42.

von Staden, Berndt. "Perspectives of German Foreign Policy." *Aussenpolitik* 36, no. 1 (1st Quarter 1985): 11–24.

von Weizsacker, Richard. "Pretoria Should Not Feel Safe that Additional Mandatory Measures Will Never Be Considered Again." Reprinted in *IIR Newsletter* (Bonn), no. 3 (1988): 1.

Wallace, William. *The Foreign Policy Process in Britain.* London: The Royal Institute for International Affairs, 1977.

Walters, Ronald W. "Beyond Sanctions: A Comprehensive U.S. Policy for Southern Africa." *World Policy Journal* 4, no. 1 (Winter 1986–87): 91–113.

———. *South Africa and the Bomb.* Lexington: Lexington Books, 1987.

"We Are Pleased to See Increased Pressure on the Government of South Africa." *News of Norway* no. 1, 24 January, 1986.

Weisfelder, Richard F. "The Basotho Nation-State: What Legacy for the Future?" *Journal of Modern African Studies* 19, no. 2 (1981): 221–56.

Whitehill, Robert. "Arab Hypocrisy in South Africa: Apartheid's Oil." *The New Republic* February 1986, 10–11.

Williams, Doug. *The Militarization of South Africa.* Ottawa: IDAFSA, March 1987.

Williams, Oliver. "The Religious Rationale of Racism." In *The South African Quagmire: In Search of a Peaceful Path to Democratic Pluralism,* edited by S. Prakash Sethi, 149–60. Cambridge: Ballinger Publishing Co., 1987.

Wilson, Brent David. *Disinvestment of Foreign Subsidiaries.* Ann Arbor: University of Michigan Research Press, 1980.

Woldring, Klass. "Aspects of Zambia's Foreign Policy in the Context of Southern Africa." In *Beyond Political Independence: Zambia's Development Predicament in the 1980s,* edited by Klaas Woldring, 233–50. Berlin: Mouten Publishers, 1984.

Wright, Sanford. "Comprehensive International Sanctions Against South Africa: An Evaluation of Costs and Effectiveness." *Africa Today* (2nd/3rd Quarters, 1986): 5–24.

Yanagihashi, Minora. "The Liberal Democratic Party and Foreign Policy." In *Japan's Foreign Policymaking,* edited by Hiroshi Itoh, 48–63. Albany: State University of New York Press, 1979.

Yaniv, Avner. *Dilemmas of Security: Politics, Strategy and the Israel Experience in Israel.* New York: Oxford University Press, 1987.

# INDEX

Action standards: 103

Adenauer, Konrad: 114

Africa: 94, 98, 103, 107, 127; ethnicity conflicts, 204; failure to respect human rights, 204; foreign policy, 206; Muslims, 128; oil embargo, 129; one-party governments, 14; relations with Israel, 133

Africa, black: 99, 102, 163; Scandinavian ties with, 163

Afrikaners: anti-semitism, 124, 138; Dutch East India company, 36; Dutch Reformed Church influence, 13; ideology, 12; *Laager,* 16; nationalism, 12, 39, 211; relations with Israel, 126; social stratification, 16; support of National Party, 46

Algeria: 163

ANC: 34, 105, 106, 123, 205, 216, 224, 230, 243; Frontline states support of, 231; funds from SIDA, 169; headquarters in Zambia, 231; Israel's view of, 135; Norway's support of, 169; Soviet support of, 13

Anglo-Boer War: 33, 38, 39

Angola: 128; funds from SIDA, 170; oil production, 213; South African invasion of, 135

Anti-Apartheid Movement: 44

Arab-Israeli conflict: 113–25; effects on southern Africa, 128; occupation of West Bank and Gaza Strip, 125; war of 1967, 125

Arab-Israeli War: 115

The Arab League: 129

Arab States: 109, 111, 112, 115, 120, 130; boycotts, 118; effect on Israel's sanctions policies, 139; isolation of Israel, 137; Israeli strategies against, 136; leaders, 128; nationalism, 121; oil embargo, 129

Arafat, Yasser: 106, 116

Argentina: trade, 159

Australia: 89, 97, 98; benefits from sanctions against South Africa, 7

Banks, Tony: 34

BASF: 99

Begin, Menachem: 110, 114, 120, 123

Ben-Gurion, David: 114, 121, 129

Biko, Stephen: 17, 139

Black Communities Development Act: 245

Black empowerment: 23, 196; support, 241

Blood River: 13, 37

Bophuthatswana: Israeli investment, 133

Botha, P. W.: 9, 26, 92

Botswana: economy, 208, 232; foreign policy, 232; funds from SIDA, 170; relations with South Africa, 214, 223; Scandinavia in, 162; ties with Israel, 129

Brazil: anti-apartheid policy, 1; benefits from sanctions against South Africa, 7

Britain: aid to SADCC, 56; apartheid issue, 32, 34, 139; arms sales to South Africa, 134; colonies in Africa, 145, 212; economy, 41; foreign policy, 30, 56–58, 156, 158, 180–81; labor unions, 35; political parties, 28, 31, 49, 53; sanctions, 29, 52, 164, 180; South Africa policy, 32, 50, 52; ties with South Africa, 10, 36, 44, 46, 159; trade, 41, 43, 132

Brundtland, Gro Harlem: 143, 164

Cameroon: 112, 134

Canada: 89, 94, 98, 151; aid to ANC, 197; aid to SADCC, 198; benefits from sanctions against South Africa, 7; federal-state relations, 182; foreign policy, 172, 173–78, 180, 183–86; security interests, 174; South Africa policy, 172, 201; ties with South Africa, 190–93; trade, 175, 181, 182

Central Africa Federation: 207

Central African Foundation: 212

Chile: 159

Commonwealth: apartheid issue, 178, 239; Britain's membership, 41; expulsion of South Africa, 40, 179; foreign policy, 178; influence on British policy, 40; sanction debates, 130

Congressional Black Caucus: support of anti-apartheid legislation, 140

*Cry Freedom:* 105

Customs Union Agreement: 218

*Dagens Nyheter:* 148

de Klerk, F. W.: 26; world view of, 246

Denmark: anti-apartheid campaign, 154; foreign policy, 143, 146, 156; German occupation of, 145; membership in NATO and EC, 157; Nordic program of action, 165; political parties, 168; role in African colonization, 145; relations with Frontline States, 162; sanctions, 143; trade, 159, 160, 165, 167

Dutch East India Company: 36

EC: Code of Conduct, 45, 103, 133

Economic isolation: problems of, 55

Egypt: 96, 119, 120, 127–28

European Political Cooperation: 156

RICHARD J. PAYNE, Professor of Political Science at Illinois State University, has been a Visiting Scholar at the Center for International Affairs, Harvard University, received Fulbright-Hays and Ford Foundation fellowships, and is author of *Opportunities and Dangers of Soviet-Cuban Expansion* and numerous articles on African politics and international affairs.